Safe at First

Safe at First

A Guide to Help Sports Administrators
Reduce Their Liability

written by
Gil Ben Fried
University of New Haven

edited by
Herb Appenzeller

CAROLINA ACADEMIC PRESS
Durham, North Carolina

Library of Congress Cataloging-in-Publication Data

Fried, Gil, 1965–
    Safe at first : a guide to help sports administrators reduce their
liability / written by Gil Ben Fried ; edited by Herb Appenzeller.
        p.   cm.
    Includes bibliographical references and index.
    ISBN 0-89089-761-1
    1. Liability for sports accidents — United States — Popular works.
2. Sports personnel — Legal status, laws, etc. — United States —
Popular works. I. Appenzeller, Herb. II. Title.

KF1290.S66 F75 1999
344.73'099 — dc21   99-050365

CAROLINA ACADEMIC PRESS
700 Kent Street
Durham, North Carolina 27701
Telephone (919) 489-7486
Fax (919) 493-5668
E-mail: cap@cap-press.com
www.cap-press.com

Printed in the United States of America

Dedicated to my lovely wife Susan and great kids Gavriella and Arieh with lots of love.

Contents

Table of Cases and Statutes   ix
Foreword   xv

Section I Event Development

Chapter 1   Introduction   3
Chapter 2   Why Do We Need Risk Management   7
Chapter 3   Legal Terminology and Principles   21
Chapter 4   Risk Management Principles   55
Chapter 5   Event Directors and Committees   59
Chapter 6   What Can You Be Liable For?   73
Chapter 7   Waiver and Medical Releases   81
Chapter 8   Statutory Considerations   97
Chapter 9   Association Standards   125
Chapter 10 Insurance   133
Chapter 11 Putting the Pieces Together to Establish
            a Safety Committee   143

Section II Event Participants

Chapter 12 Baseball   147
Chapter 13 Basketball   169
Chapter 14 Contact Sports and Martial Arts   183
Chapter 15 Football   189
Chapter 16 Golf   203
Chapter 17 Gymnastics   213
Chapter 18 Hockey   225
Chapter 19 Racquet Sports   231
Chapter 20 Soccer   237
Chapter 21 Track & Field   241
Chapter 22 Water Sports   245
Chapter 23 Wheel Sports   259

Chapter 24   Winter Sports   267
Chapter 25   Referees and Officials   277
Chapter 26   First Aid   285
Chapter 27   Transportation   295

Section III Event Spectators

Chapter 28   Spectator Concerns   307
Chapter 29   Concessions   327
Chapter 30   Alcohol   331
Chapter 31   Parking   335
Chapter 32   Conclusion   339

Appendices

A   Sexual Abuse Prevention Manual   343
B   Incident Reporting Manual   431
C   Facility Rental Contract and Contract Hints   463
D   Facility Inspection Schedule   473
E   Facility and Equipment Repair Log   475
F   Job Descriptions   476
G   Employment Forms   477
H   Sexual Harassment Policy   487
I   Waivers   490
J   Football Equipment Forms   494
K   Concession Checklist   496
L   Actual Facility Audit for Martial Arts Studio   497

References   507
About the Authors   515
Index   516

Table of Cases and Statutes

CASES

Acosta v. Los Angeles Unified School District (WEC 133-767), Jury Verdicts Research, Vol. 36, No. 48, Pg. 24-25 (1992), 223

Adams v. Kline, 239 A. 2d 230 (DE, 1968), 297

Allen v. Rutgers, State University of New Jersey, 523 A. 2d 262 (NJ 1987), 333

Anderson v. Little League Baseball, Inc. 794 F. Supp. 342 (DC. Ariz 1992), 104, 333

Ardoin v. Evangeline Parish School Board, 376 So. 2d 372 (LA 1979), 151

Asmus v. Board of Education City of Chicago, 508 N.E. 298 (IL 1987), 160

Augustus v. Joseph A. Craig Elementary School, 459 S. 2d 665 (LA 1984), 64

Baroco v. Araserv, Inc. 621 F. 2d 189 (5th Cir. 1980), 98

Bedor v. Exdahl, 248 N.W. 2d 321 (MN 1976), 165

Benitez v. New York City Bd. Of Educ, (N.Y.A.D., 1988), 200

Bennet v. U.S. Cycling Federation, 239 Cal.Rptr 55 (CA 1987), 263-264

Berman by Berman v. Philadelphia Board of Education, 456 A. 2d 545 (PA 1983), 126-127

Beseke v. Garden Center, Inc., 401 N.W. 2d 428 (MN 1987), 332

Bishop v. Fair Lanes Georgia Bowling,Inc., 803 F. 2d 1548 (11th Cir. 1986), 336

Bridston v. Dover Corporation, 352 N.W.2d 194 (ND 1984), 137-138

Burgert v. Tietjens, 499 F. 2d 1 (10th Cir. 1974), 250

Bush v. Parents Without Partners 21 CR2d 178 (1993) , 68-69

Carabba v. Anacortes School District No. 103, 435 P. 2d 936 (WA 1968), 279-280

Chapman v. State, 492 P. 2d 602 (WA 1972), 35-36

Cimino v. Yale University 638 F. Supp. 952 (CT 1986), 99

Cornell v. Langland, 440 N.E. 2d 985 (IL 1982), 208

Coronel v. Chicago White Sox, Ltd., 595 N.E.2d 45 (IL, 1992), 153

Curtis v. State, 505 N.E.2d 1222 (OH 1986), 190

D.T. by M.T. v. Independent School Dist. No. 16, 894 F.2d 1176 (10th Cir. 1990), 71

Daniels v. S-CO Corp., 124 N.W. 2d 522 (IA 1963), 220, 222

Dawson v. Rhode Island Auditorium, Inc., 242 A. 2d 407 (RI 1968), 173

Doe v. British Universities North American Club, 788 F. Supp. 1286 (D. Conn. 1992), 63, 71

Domino v. Mercurio, 193 N.E. 2d 893 (NY 1963), 158, 280

Dudley Sports Co. v. Schmitt, 279 N.E. 2d 266 (IN 1972), 161

Eddy v. Syracuse University, 433 N.Y.S. 2d (NY 1980), 170-171

Edling v. Kansas City Baseball and Exhibition Co., 168 S.W. 908 (MS 1914), 315-316

Ehlinger v. Board of Education of New Hartford Central School District, 465 N.Y.S.2d 378 (NY, 1983), 117-118

Everett v. Bucky Warren, Inc., 380 N.E. 2d 653 (MA 1978), 228

Falkner v. John E. Fetzer, Inc., 317 N.W. 2d 337 (MI 1982), 313-314

Fidopiastis v. Hirtler, 41 Cal. Rptr. 2d 94, 34 Cal. App. 4th 1458 (CA 4th 1995), 236

Forkash v. City of New York, 277 N.Y.S. 2d 827 (NY, 1967), 281

Foster v. Houston General insurance Co., 407 So. 2d 759 (LA 1982), 67

Frances v. Village Green Owners Ass'n 42 C3d 490, 229 CR 456 (1986), 31

Freeman v. Hale, 94 Daily Journal D.A.R. 17643 (CA 1994), 271

Gale v. Greater Washington Softball Umpires Association, 311 A. 2d 817 (MD, 1973), 277-278

Gallagher v. Cleveland Browns Football Co., OH. Cuyahoga County C.C.P., No. 178718, Dec. 11, 1991. 35 Law Reporter 266 (September 1992), 307

Garrison v. Sea World, Fl. Orange County Cir. Ct., No. CI 87-9140 (FL 1992), Law Reporter, No. 1992, p. 35, 254

Gasa v. Woodbridge Tavern, 568 N.W. 2d 138 (Mich. App. 1997), 8

Gehling v. St. George's University School of Medicine, Ltd., 705 F. Supp. 761 (NY 1989), 242-243

Gifford v. Bogey Hills Golf and Country Club, Inc., 426 SW. 2d 98 (MO 1968), 208, 209

Gillespie v. Southern Utah State College, 669 P. 2d 861 (UT, 1983), 287

Govel v. Board of Education of Albany, 48 N.Y.S. 2d 299 (NY 1944), 215

Grames v. King and Pontiac School District, 332 N.W. 2d 615 (MI 1983), 179

Grant v. Lake Oswego School District Number 7, 515 P. 2d 947 (OR 1973), 213-214

Grbac v. Reading Fair Co., Inc., 688 F. 2d 215 (3rd Cir. 1982), 85-86

Greer v. Davis, 940 S.W. 2d. 582 (Tex Sup. Ct. 1996), 164

Haben v. Anderson, 597 N.E. 2d 655 (IL 1992), 333

Hanley v. Hornbeck, 512 N.Y.S. 2d 262 (NY 1987), 163

Hanson v. Reedley Joint Union High School Dist., 111 P.2d 415 (CA, 1941) , 207, 298

Hartzell v. U.S., 539 F. 2d 65 (10th Cir. 1976), 319

Heldman v. Uniroyal, Inc., 371 N.E. 2d 557 (OH 1977), 233

Henry v. Britt, 220 S. 2d 917 (FL 1969), 248

Isler v. Burman, 232 N.W. 2d 818 (MN 1975), 273-274

Jacquet v. Marion County School Board, Marion County Cir. Ct., No. 90-5272-CA-A, Sept. 30, 1992 (FL), 186

Johnson v. City of Boston, 490 N.E. 2d 1204 (MA 1986), 171

Johnson v. Zemel, 160 A. 2d 356 (NJ, 1932), 309

Jones v. Dressel, 623 P. 2d 370 (CO 1981), 87

Jones v. Three Rivers Management Corporation, 394 A. 2d 546 (PA 1978), 310

Kavafian v. Setalle Basbeall Club Association, 181 P. 679 (WA 1919), 314-315

Kelleher v. Big Sky of Montana, 642 F. Supp. 1128 (MT 1986), 121

Keys v. Alamo City Baseball Company, 150 S.W. 2d 368 (TX 1941), 312

Keys, 194, 222, 312-313

King v. National Spa and Pool Institute, 570 So. 2d 612 (AL 1990) and 607 So. 2d 1241 (AL, 1992), 129-130, 179

Kiser v. City of Anaheim, No. 88-6125, April 26, 1990, 9th Cir., ABA Journal (1990, August), p. 98, 323

Kleinknecht v. Gettysburg College, 989 F. 2d 1360 (3d Cir. 1993), 286

Kopera v. Moschella, 400 F. Supp. 131 (5th Cir. 1976), 121-122

Kungle v. Austin, 330 S.W. 2d 354 (MO 1964), 127

Langevin V. City of Bidderford, 481 A. 2d 495 (ME 1984), 83-84

Larson v. Independent School District No. 314 Braham, 289 N.W. 2d 112 (MN 1979), 48-49

La Valley v. Stanford, 70 N.Y.S. 2d 460 (NY 1947), 187

Leahy v. School Board of Hernando County, 450 So. 2d 883 (FL 1984), 196-197

Leake v. Santa Maria Valley YMCA, SM-85064 (1995), Verdicts & Settlements, March 24, 1995 p. 8, 231

Leger v. Stockton Unified School District, 249 Cal.Rptr. 688 (CA 1988), 185

Light v. Ohio University, 502 N.E.2d 611 (OH 1986), 33-35

Littlefield v. Schaefer, 955 S.W. 2d 272 (Tex. 1997), 86

Locilento v. John A. Coleman Catholic High, 523 N.Y.S. 2d 198 (NY 1987), 193

Lobsenz v. Rubinstein, 15 N.Y.S. 2d 848 (NY 1939), 233-234

Lofy v. Joint School Dist. #2, City of Cumberland. 166 N.W. 2d 809 (WI, 1969), 299

Loving v. Tenneco West, Inc., 18 Cal. Rptr. 2d. 504, 14 Cal. App. 4th 1272 (C.A. 5th, 1993), 98-99

Maddox v. City of New York, 496 N.Y.S. 2d 727 (NY 1985), 150

Martinez v. County of Los Angeles, EAC 61726, Jury Verdicts, Vol. 36, No. 37, 25-26, 237

Maussner V. Atlantic City Country Club, Inc., 691 A.2d 826 (NJ Sup. A.D. 1997), 209

McKeever v. Phoenix Jewish Community Center, 374 P. 2d 875 (AZ 1962), 251

Messina v. District of Columbia, 663 A.2d 535 (D.C. App. 1995), 131

Miller v. City of Dayton, 42 Ohio St. 3d 113 (OH 1989), 100

Miller v. Cloidt, No. L-7241-62, N.J. Sup.-Ct. Law Div., Morris County, October 31, 1964. (NJ, 1964), 28

Mokovich v. Independent School District (225 N.W. 292 (MN 1929), 191

Montes v. Betcher, 480 F. 2d 1128 (8th Cir. 1973), 252

Mora v. Board of Education, NY, New York County Sup Ct., No. 23257/89 (Nov. 2, 1992) in 36 Law Reporter 178 (1993, June), 224

Morrow v. Smith, 198 N.Y.S. 2d 737 (NY 1960), 234

Noble v. Los Angeles Dodgers, Inc., 168 CA 3d 912 (CA 1985), 337

Ollison v. Weinberg Racing Association, 688 P. 2d 847 (OR 1984), 331

O'Neil v. City of Newark, CA, Alameda County No. H-154451-0, Jury Verdicts and Settlement, Vol. 39, No. 5, February 3, 1995, 4, 315

Ornelas v. Randolph, 4 Cal.4th 1095 (1993), 100

Overcash v. Statesville City Board of Education, 348 S.E.2d 524 (NC 1986), 115

Panoz v. Golf & Bay Corporation, 208 So. 2d 297 (FL 1968), 205, 210

Pedersen v. Joliet Park District, 483 N.E. 2d 21 (IL 1985), 173-174

Pell v. Victor J. Andrew High School, 462 N.E. 2d 858 (IL 1984), 220-221

Perry v. Seattle School District #1, 405 P. 2d 589 (WA 1965), 318

Peterson v. Multnomah County School District No. 1, 668 P. 2d 385 (OR 1983), 128-129

Poindexter v. Willis, 256 N.E.2d 254 (OH, 1970), 21

Pomeroy v. Little League Baseball of Collingswood, 362 A. 2d 39 (NJ 1976), 62

Praetorius v. Shell Oil Co,. 207 So. 2d 872 (LA 1968), 152

Quinn v. Smith Company, 57 F. 2d 784 (5th Cir. 1932), 257

Randas v. YMCA, 17 CA4th 158, 21 CR2d 245 (1993), 86

Regan v. City of Seattle, 458 P. 2d 12 (WA 1969), 262-263

Rigden V. Springdale Park, Inc., 551 S.W. 2d 860 (MO 1977), 247

Rimkus v. Northwest Colorado Ski Corp., 706 F.2d 1060 (10th Cir. 1973), 119-120

Rockwell v. Hillcrest Country Club, 181 N.W. 2d 290 (MI 1970), 322

Rogers v. Black Hill Speedway, Inc., 217 N.W. 2d 14 (SD 1974), 320

Roventini v. Pasadena Indep. Sch. Dist, et al., 981 F. Supp. 1013 (S.D. Tex, 1997), 197

Russo v. Range, Inc., 395 N.E. 2d 10 (IL 1979), 91

Ryan v. Miller River Country Club, Inc., 510 A.2d 462 (CT 1986), 207

S & C Co. v. Horne, 235 S.E.2d 456 (VA 1977), 122, 257

Sawyer v. State, 485 N.Y.S. 2d 695 (NY 1985), 317

Scala v. City of New York, 102 N.Y.S. 2d 790 (NY, 1951), 154

Scott v. Pacific W. Mountain Resort, 834 P.2d 6 (Wash. 1992), 83

Short v. Griffiths, 255 S.E. 2d 479 (VA 1979), 149

Shurman v. Fresno Ice Rink, Inc., 205 P.2d 77 (CA 1949) , 316-317

Singer v. School District of Philadelphia, 513 A. 2d 1108 (PA 1986), 215-216

Smith v. National Football League (U.S. Dist. Ct., FL., No. 74-418 Civ. T-K), 189, 192

Smith v. University of Texas, 664 S.W. 2d 180 (TX 1984), 281-282

Southern Methodist University v. Clayton 176 S.W. 2d 749 (TX 1943), 61

Stearns v. Sugarbrush Valley Corp., 296 A. 2d 220 (VT 1972), 272

Steele v. Jekyll Island State Park Authority, 176 S.E. 2d 514 (GA 1970), 204

Stimson v. Carlson, 11 CA 4th 1201, 14 CR.2d 670 (CA 1992), 254

Stoud v. Bridges, 275 S.W. 2d 503 (TX, 1955), 309

Sunday v. Stratton Corporation, 390 A. 2d 398 (VT 1978) , 267-269

Swope v. Farrar, 66 Ga.App. 52 (GA 1941), 265

The T.J. Hooper, 60 F.2d 737 (2nd Cir. 1932), 128

Thompson v. U.S., 592 F. 2d 1104 (9th Cir. 1979), 60

Tiemann v. Independent School District #740, 331 N.W. 2d 250 (MN 1983), 218

Toms v. Delta Savings & Loan Ass'n, 124 N.E.2d 123 (1955), 167

Townsley v. Cincinnati Gardens, Inc., 314 N.E. 2d 409 (OH 1974), 32

University Prepatory School v. Huitt III, Corpus Christi Court of Appeals, No. 13-94-439-CV (TX 1996), 255

Van Dyke v. S.K.I. Ltd., 67 Cal. App.4th 1310, 79 Cal.Rptr. 2d 775 (CA, 1998), 25

Van Stry v. State, 479 N.Y.S. 2d 258 (NY 1984), 177-178

Van Tuyn v. Zurich American Insurance Co., 447 So.2d 318 (FL 1984), 90

Vargo v. Svitchen, 301 N.W. 2d 1 (MI 1980), 49

Vendrell v. School District No. 266 Malheur County, 360 P. 2d 282 (OR 1961), 199

Virginia State Fair Association v. Burton, 28 S.E. 2d 716 (VA 1944), 259

Wade v. Watson, 731 F. 2d 890 (11th Cir. 1981), 87-88

Wagonblast v. Odessa School District No. 105-157-166J, 758 P. 2d 968 (WA 1988), 85

Waxenberg v. Crystal Baths, 129 N.Y.S. 2d 71 (NY 1954), 232

Welch v. Dunsmuir Joint High School District, 326 P. 2d 633 (CA, 1958), 291

Wells v. YMCA of Bogalusa, 150 So. 2d 324 (LA 1963), 217-218

Wersinger v. Cheney, Nev. Fed.Dist.Ct. No. CV93-00362 (1994), 271

Westbourough Country Club v. Palmer, 204 F. 2d 143 (8th Cir. 1953), 206

Westlye v. Look Sports, Inc. 17 Cal. App. 4th 1715, 22 Cal. Rptr. 2d 781 (Cal. App. 3rd, 1993), 88

Wiggins v. Piver, 171 S.E. 2d. 393, 286

Wightman v. Town of Methuen, 526 N.E. 2d 1079 (MA, 1988), 290

Woodring v. Board of Education of Manhasset, 435 N.Y.S. 2d 52 (NY 1981), 176

Wright v. Mt. Mansfield Lift, Inc., 96 F. Supp. 786 (VT 1951), 267

Yarber v. Oakland Unified School District, 4 Cal.Ap. 4th 1516, 6 Cal.Rptr. 2d 437 (CA, 1992), 116, 175

YMCA of Metropolitan Atlanta v. Bailey, 130 S.E. 2d 242 (GA 1963), 256, 258

Statutes

28 CFR Section 41.31, 105

1968 Architectural Barriers Act, 102

California Civil Code, Section 1431.2(a), 45

California Government Code, Section 831.7, 116

California Health and Safety Code, Section 24100.1, 123

Colorado Revised Statutes 33-44-107(7), 119-120

Connecticut General Statute 52-557(h), 99

Equal Pay Act, 10, 80

Maryland Tort Claims Act of 1981, 41

Montana Revised Code Ann. Section 23-2-733 to 737, 121

New Jersey State Statute Ann. Section 2A:62A-6, 116

New Mexico Stat. Ann. Section 24-15-7 thru 24-15-13, 120

Protection Against Pedophiles Act, 1997 (Canada), 73

The Rehabilitation Act of 1973, 102, 113

Title VII

Title IX, 10-11, 13, 80, 101

Vermont Title 12 Section 1037, 120

Wisconsin Code Chapter 167-167.32, 118

Foreword

Mark McGwire (St. Louis Cardinals) and Sammy Sosa (Chicago Cubs) set home run records for major league baseball in 1998. On another level, Gil Fried hit a home run in the field of sports law and safety with his latest book *Safe at First: A Guide to Help Sports Administrators Reduce Liability in Sports*.

Safe at First is unique because it is sport specific covering the many areas of sport from baseball to winter sports. In addition to risk management strategies for over 15 different sports, the book contains important information not easily available in most single sources. *Safe at First* provides risk management strategies, forms, legal principles and terminology, waivers and medical releases. In addition, issues such as transportation, insurance, first aid and an explanation of what one can be liable for in the sport industry are also covered.

Safe at First is written for many different people who associate with sports. It addresses issues and problems that confront the participant, administrator, facility and event manger, teacher/coach, medical personnel (team physician, athletic trainer, EMT's), spectators and parents. The text is extremely valuable for students who want to enter the sport industry. Gil Fried uses his legal and sport administration background to inform his readers of practical problems that confront them in the sports arena. His style is based on clarity and the avoidance of tedious and often confusing legalese providing information that, while legally sound, is easy to understand and read. The author utilizes the case study method to illustrate legal principles with the hope that the reader can identify with a particular case or situation that is familiar to him/her. The author guides the reader from the earliest stages of event planning to the completion of the event with special attention to concerns that accompany event management.

As an added feature of the book, the author has included a *Sexual Abuse Risk Management Manual for Youth Sports/Activities Organizations*. The *Manual* is timely and should prove to be helpful to all who administer and work in youth sport programs. The 85-page manual could easily be a separate text and is a huge bonus for those who purchase *Safe at First*.

I wrote in the forward to *Employment Law: A Guide for Sport, Recreation, and Fitness Industries* that Gil Fried and Lori Miller had written a book that sets a very high standard for future authors of the Carolina Academic Press' sport law series. Gil Fried has, once again, achieved that goal in *Safe at First* and I congratulate and commend him for a book that represents a major contribution to the field of sport law and sport safety. *Safe at First* may well become the definitive text in sport law and safety.

Herb Appenzeller

Section I
Event Development

Chapter 1

Introduction

Imagine if you ran an event where all the participants are highly qualified, the facility is in perfect condition, every piece of equipment is in immaculate shape and the supervision is top notch. Could an accident happen under these circumstances? Could an accident ruin an event administrator financially? Could an accident bankrupt a sports facility? The answer is a simple, Yes!

Accidents are just that, accidents. By definition, accidents are unexpected and undesirable events. Thus, precautions need to be taken to minimize the damages that can result from accidents. Especially in the field of event management, risk management guidelines need to be established and implemented to help halt what is turning into the incremental elimination of sports in America (Fried, 1998).

Risk management guidelines are commonly referred to as standards. For the lack of a better, more succinct term, standards will often be utilized throughout this guide to refer to a level of conduct exercised by an event administrator that corresponds to the reasonably prudent person standard for similarly situated, educated and trained event administrators. Your conduct will be weighed against the conduct that others would have exercised under the same circumstances, and this is commonly referred to as the *reasonably prudent person standard*.

The Need For Standards

Standards are required to help event administrators reduce the possible and probable occurrence of a lawsuit in response to an accident. Doctors perform surgery using the most recently approved technology; accountants use the latest accounting standards; and attorneys also follow set standards when they are involved in legal proceedings. All attorneys, accountants, doctors, and event administrators have to act in accordance with various levels of expected competence. If they fail to live up to these "standards" in their industries, they could be found liable for malpractice. If an event administrator fails to live up to the standards for event administrators, then he/she can create an environment with both dangerous and expensive consequences.

Standards, such as the reasonably prudent person standard, are the guiding force behind analyzing the conduct of most occupations in our legal system. Court dockets have been filled by the get-rich-quick attitude permeating society and some litigants have been rewarded by multi-million dollar jackpots offered by sympathetic juries. To help alleviate some of the litigation explosion, you should try to observe any applicable standards that apply to your activity. By knowing the standards that might apply to your activity, you can more effectively take precautions to reduce your chances of being taken to court.

How Standards Are Developed

Standards have been developed through several basic means: litigation, governmental declarations, and industrial practices. Published athletic facility standards describe the type of building to construct, the materials to be used and the dimensions of the structure. Standards can specify the type of grass used for activity fields, the glass used in gym doors and the placement of safety equipment such as screens and mats. Athletic equipment has numerous standards for design or construction that are affected by technological advances or litigation. Effective event administrators also help establish and implement standards to minimize the possibility of being sued. Even if you do not know what the standards are in any given area, the local customs or practices of similarly experienced individuals can serve as the standard against which your conduct will be compared. Thus, industry standards exist even if no one intends to create standards.

In fact, many attorneys are against sport or recreation-related standards as no two situations are exactly the same and it is unfair to set one standard to apply throughout an industry. Nonetheless, many industry professionals appreciate having some standards to use as a benchmark with which to compare their conduct and to help determine what steps would be necessary to remedy "sub-standard" conditions.

This guide book was written to present various sport risk management strategies which some might call potential "standards." While the term "standards" has been used for convenience, the thoughts contained in the following pages represent simple suggestions based on various cases, laws and industry actions. It should be specifically noted that each community, region and state have different laws and the "standards" described throughout this guide might not apply to every situation in every location.

The cases, examples, manuals and checklists in this guidebook were designed to give an overview of some previous or potential legal challenges event administrators have or might have to face. References will be made throughout this guidebook to numerous cases in a wide variety of sports. When there is no case on point, examples might be developed and utilized to present a possible standard.

The term *"event administrator," "defendant,"* or the initials *"EA"* will be used in the text to represent a wide range of individuals or committees involved in producing sport events. The following individuals often produce or manage sport events:

- Coaches,
- Teachers,
- Athletic Directors,
- Sports Promoters,
- Sports Administrators,
- Camp Coordinators,
- Private Recreation Providers,
- Municipal Recreation Employees, and
- Youth League Directors.

If you are, or plan to work in one of these professions, this guidebook is for you.

The term *"plaintiff"* refers to the injured individual(s) who is either a participant or a spectator associated with the event. The term *"Defendant"* refers to the person(s), business(es) organization(s) and/or entities who somehow is/are alleged to be partially or wholly responsible for the plaintiff's injuries.

This guidebook *is not* designed to provide legal advice or to be a substitute for using an attorney. On the contrary, this guidebook is designed to persuade event administrators to utilize the counsel of a competent attorney to minimize the chance of falling below acceptable management standards.

The theme of this guidebook is to take the extra time and effort necessary to develop and implement a game plan based on the latest actual or perceived industry standards to help reduce the chances of being sued. While you are actively working to reduce the chances of being sued you will accomplish one additional benefit—fewer injuries from running a safer program or facility.

Chapter 2

Why Do We Need Risk Management?

Most people would say that certain sports such as football, hockey and boxing are dangerous sports that require greater supervision. While these sports do present specific safety concerns, there are numerous additional, and often less obvious safety concerns. For example, many parents worry about their children being injured while playing football. These same parents might not give a second thought about their child participating in soccer. However, research tends to indicate that the injury rate for youth soccer participation is greater than the injury rate for youth football.

One of the key components for any risk management program is communication. The more administrators know what risks they can encounter, the easier it becomes to take proactive measures to reduce risks. Thus, it is essential for us to begin this guide with some examples of how sports have gotten out of hand and produced significant risk management concerns, which we all need to understand.

- A coach and several players between age 12–14 are accused of attacking referees with punches, kicks and a metal chair after the referees ended a game early due to participant violence ("Sports illustrated," 1998).
- A 25-year-old woman was fined and charged with misdemeanor third-degree assault for fighting with a 12-year-old girl when a fight broke out at a Tinymight football game ("Parental guidance?," 1998).
- A father punched his son's basketball coach after he felt his son was not getting enough playing time (Dorsey, 1992).
- A soccer coach suffered a broken eye socket, cheek-bone and jaw after he was attacked by opposing players following a victory by the coach's team (Dorsey, 1992).
- In 1997, a 36-year-old tee-ball coach in Oklahoma was convicted of choking a 15-year-old umpire during a game (Dedman, 1998)

7

- In Georgia, a coach shot a father in the arm when the father complained that his son was not receiving enough pitching time (Dedman, 1998).
- While many would think that football is more dangerous than other sports such as cheerleading, a high school football player on average missed 5.6 days in 1997 due to injuries while a cheerleader during the same period lost 28.8 days due to injuries (Scorecard, 1997).
- While numerous injury categories have highlighted declines over the past several years sports injuries have been on the rise. Some observers feel that this rise can be attributed to the greater participation numbers for girls (Johnson, 1998).
- In 1987, the injury rate per 100,000 children between age 5 through 14 was 373.80 in basketball, 381.51 in baseball and 447.38 in football. By 1995, only baseball witnessed a decline of 2.63 percent to 371.47. Basketball injuries increased dramatically with injuries to girls increasing the injury rate to 553.78 per 100,000. Football only increased slightly to 468.77 in 1995 (Johnson, 1998).
- A softball player in Florida was awarded $52,000 after being hit by a softball during warm-ups ("The torts of summer", 1998).
- A collision in the splash pool of a New Jersey water park resulted in a $130,000 verdict ("The torts of summer", 1998).
- A Texan was awarded $5,000 after being hit in the head with a golf ball ("The torts of summer", 1998).
- A Floridian was awarded $41,000 after slipping on some algae in an inappropriately maintained swimming pool ("The torts of summer", 1998).
- Sports illustrated highlighted a Connecticut case wherein a 10-year-old boy was suing another 10-year-old for minor injuries received when one boy took some warm-up swings in a dugout and hit the other child in the head (Scorecard, 1998).
- In 1990, approximately 560,000 bicycle accidents sent mostly youngsters to hospital emergency rooms producing an estimated economic cost estimated at $1.2 billion. These costs can be dramatically reduced through utilizing helmets which can reduce head injuries by as much as 85% ("Good sports," 1992).
- Bicycle related deaths have declined 41 percent from 1987 through 1995. In 1987 the death rate from bicycle accidents was 0.75 per 100,000 and fell to 0.44 per 100,000 by 1995 (Johnson, 1998).

- In New Jersey, a mandatory bicycle helmet law was implemented in 1992. From 1987 through 1991, 41 children under age 13 died in bike accidents. After the law was passed, only 16 children died in the next three years (Johnson, 1998). Currently, 14 states now require children to wear bicycle helmets (Johnson, 1998).
- An estimated 170,000 kids get hurt on playground equipment each year with the highest rate of injury affecting kids between 6–8-years old ("Good sports," 1992).
- More American children under age 5 drown each year than are killed in motor vehicle accidents ("Good sports," 1992).
- Eye injuries can be devastating for a child and approximately 30% of youth eye injuries are sports related with 90% of these injuries being preventable ("Eye injury fact sheet," 1997).

The facts, cases or incidents highlighted above are just examples of the violence, negligence and just plain stupidity that has invaded sports. Since communication is one of the key steps to reduce sport related risks, it is essential for every EA to know what sports represent the greatest danger and how others have responded to these dangers.

The Consumer Product Safety Commission tracks sports related injuries and reached the following conclusion for 1992 based on total emergency room visits where the injured party indicated how they were injured:

1.	Basketball	752,798
2.	Bicycling	649,536
3.	Football	447,320
4.	Roller Skating (no in-line)	125,528
5.	Fishing	82,436
6.	Horseback Riding	73,484
7.	Track and Field	65,551
8.	Weightlifting	65,153
9.	Golf	37,556
10.	Tennis	31,042

("Sports-related ER visits," 1995)

Since this data is several years old, the CPSC has produced additional and more recent reports analyzing sports related injuries. In a study from 1992 through 1994, seven soccer fatalities were reported with five deaths being caused by goals tipping over (Rytina, 1994). The yearly injury rates for soccer range around approximately 155,000 injuries per year with 70% of all injuries occurring to individuals between ages 10-24 and less than 2% of such injuries requiring hospitalization (Rytina, 1994).

In-Line skating is rapidly becoming one of the greatest injury causing sports. In the first seven months in 1994, 10 in-line related deaths were reported across America (Rytina, 1994). The most frequent cause for such deaths (60%) involved collisions with vehicles (Rytina, 1994).

In addition to information from government entities such as the CPSC and the Center for Disease Control, numerous associations, organizations and universities produce research studies attempting to track injury concerns or risk management issues. The National Collegiate Athletic Association (NCAA) regularly publishes injury rates in many sports. Furthermore, the National Federation of State High School Associations (NFSHSA) tracks injury rates at the high school level.

Universities have also produced some very relevant research to help assist EAs in understanding and evaluating various risks. The author has conducted several major studies with the results summarized below.

In order to most effectively protect yourself and your facilities, it is imperative that you understand what lawsuits are most often encountered by others in the sport and facilities industries. In order to properly gauge the types of suits being filed in the sport, athletic and recreation industries, the editors examined 233 published sport opinions as reported by the Society for the Study of Legal Aspects of Sports and Physical Activity ("SSLASPA"). Published opinions represent cases tried in a lower court, or legal decisions rendered in a lower court that are appealed to a higher court. Only decisions from appellate courts are published in official case listings.

Of the 233 cases reported in 1995, 55 percent (129 cases) represented negligence cases. These cases examined such issues as negligent supervision, trip and fall, negligent facility construction, participant assumption of risk, liability contingent on a participant's status (invitee, licensee, trespasser), etc. Employment law cases represented 11.15 percent (26) of the published cases. The employment law cases primarily focused on wrongful termination, wrongful demotion, discrimination in employment, breach of an employment contract, Equal Pay Act cases and union-related issues such as collective bargaining agreements.

While insurance companies traditionally defend and pay damages in negligence and employment cases they rarely pay expenses or damages for intentional acts which violate a plaintiff's civil rights. Civil rights cases often involve intentional acts to deprive someone of their liberties. Civil rights cases comprised 9.8 percent (23) of the published opinions. Civil rights cases include American with Disability Acts cases, Title IX cases, students' property rights issues and discrimination cases. Cases concerning a participant's eligibility status are also traditionally not covered by insurance companies. Eligibility disputes accounted for 4.7 percent of the sports law cases in 1995.

Cases alleging breach of contract and interference with contracts represented 5.15 percent of the published cases. Lastly, cases involving professional sports and anti-trust concerns, which generated the most national publicity, only represented 3.8 percent of all published sports cases in 1995.

The study revealed that most cases are still brought following physical injuries. Issues that are typically raised in the personal injury cases often revolve around the appropriate duty owed to a sports participant/spectator, the legal distinction between willful, wanton and reckless misconduct in deciding government immunity cases and under what circumstances does a plaintiff assume certain risks.

Probably the fastest growing legal minefield involves employment law cases. While there have been few cases involving sexual harassment and outright discrimination, there are a host of additional concerns that are currently flooding courtrooms. Most cases are not brought to trial due to the desire by an employer to settle disputes prior to the media getting involved. While some sexual harassment claims have surfaced in the newspapers, there are no published opinions yet in this area (sport industry). The cases which seem to be drawing the most court exposure include:

- dismissals from women collegiate sports programs which can lead to a Title IX claim,
- equal pay disputes raised by female college coaches,
- slander suits brought by a terminated employee claiming his/her former employer slandered him/her to a prospective employer,
- wrongful termination without just cause,
- wrongful termination cases alleging termination in contravention to existing contractual requirements, and
- termination without receiving required due process consideration.

Recent significant cases have also changed the sport law battlefield. Laws which were once used to provide opportunities for competition (such as Title IX and the Americans with Disabilities Act) are now being used as tools to recover money or valuable concessions. Now that personal damages can be awarded in Title IX cases, a rush of lawsuits alleging Title IX violations are increasing rapidly at the high school level. Thus, two young ladies in Texas were able to recover damages when they brought successful Title IX claims after being sexually assaulted at their respective high schools. The inference from such cases is that a sport facility or program that receives Federal funds and that does not provide protection for women in such areas as restrooms, can face a Title IX challenge.

The recent litigation trends in the sport law field helps demonstrate the importance of keeping up with the constant legal changes and to ensure your program is following both the letter and spirit of the laws.

The author recently completed a comprehensive eight year study of award and settlement amounts in sport-related cases. The survey analyzed 281 cases throughout the United States as reported in the national publication, *From the Gym to the Jury*. The cases were reported from 1989 through 1996.

The 281 analyzed cases came from 40 different states and the District of Columbia. New York had the highest number of cases with 35 cases, followed by California and Florida, each with 28 cases.

The research highlighted 64 cases with awards over $1 million. This represents 22.77% of all analyzed cases. California had the highest number of jackpot cases with 10 cases receiving awards or settlements over $1 million. California was followed by Texas with six cases, Pennsylvania and New York each with five cases and both New Jersey and Illinois had three cases each. The 64 million dollar cases included 21 settlements and 42 jury awards. The million dollar cases were primarily concentrated in three injury categories including 21 paralysis cases, 18 wrongful death cases (eight involving children under 18-years-old) and 6 brain injury cases.

Eighteen cases had verdict or settlement amounts over $5 million. Eight of these cases entailed plaintiffs under 19-years of age. Only two of the $5 million awards were obtained through settlement while the remaining 16 awards were handed down by juries.

The most common cause of injuries that received over $1 million included swimming, diving and football. Drowning cases produced 17 million dollar awards involving 13 deaths and 4 brain injury cases. Eleven drowning cases involved minors. Diving cases represented the next major injury category with 11 cases. Only three of the 11 diving cases involved minors. The 11 dives resulted in one death and 10 paralysis victims. The last major injury category in million dollar verdicts involved tackling during football games which represents six of the seven football cases. Most football injuries occurred to youth between 13 and 16-year-olds.

While over 22% of the analyzed cases had million dollar awards, 192 (68.3%) cases involved awards equal to or less than $500,000. Furthermore, 125 cases (44.5%) had awards equal to or less than $100,000.

Activity Analysis

Swimming represented the single most frequent activity in which someone was injured. The survey results showed that 56 sports participants were injured while swimming. The next most frequent activity were 32 facility-related injuries which included trip and fall, slip and fall, and other injuries

Table 1

Activity	Number of Cases
Swimming	56
Facility	32
Football	21
Administration*	21
Baseball	14
Basketball	13
Boating	11
Skating	10
Skiing	10
Golf	9
Soccer	8
Auto	7
Exercise	6
Gymnastics	4
Bowling	3
Golf Cart	3
Hockey	3
Playground	3
Running	3
Softball	3
Track	3
Volleyball	3
Lacrosse	2

* (i.e. breach of contract, Title IX, etc...)

From the Gym to the Jury-Eight Year Analysis

that occurred while individuals were using sports-related facilities. The remaining activities with more than two cases each are highlighted in Table 1.

Incident Analysis

The most common incident which resulted in an injury involved trips, slips and falls which were reported 60 times. The remaining 15 most common incidents are highlighted in Table 2.

Table 2

Activity	Number of Cases
Falls, Slips & Trips	60
Accidents	41
Drownings	28
Collisions	26
Battery	21
Breach of Contract	19
Diving	18
Discrimination	9
Broken Equipment	7
Tackling	7
Medical Malpractice	5
Equipment	4
Heart Attacks	4
Sliding	3
Stepping	3
Foul Balls/ Pucks	3

From the Gym to the Jury-Eight Year Analysis

Injury Analysis

Various injuries are ranked in Table 3 by frequency. The average ages indicates that children are more likely to receive serious brain injuries or die while older individuals are more likely to suffer hip, ankle, leg and knee injuries consistent with trip and fall injuries. Table 3 also highlights the average judgments or settlements received for various injuries.

Award Disparities

Minors and adults were compared in relation to the injuries they suffered. Head and neck injuries represent the greatest disparity between minors and adults. However, the three adult cases which averaged approximately $12 million is significantly greater than the 14 minor cases which averaged $3,743,921. Paralysis awards highlighted in Table 4 demonstrate the

Table 3

Injury	Number	Avg. Age (in years)	Avg. Award/Sett.
Death	40	15.8	$1,264,051
Paralysis	29	25.5	$3,963,967
Various	20	14.4	$ 962,426
Leg	18	30.1	$ 286,728
Knee	15	24.5	$ 829,441
Brain	14	15.8	$4,044,655
Eye	13	27.6	$ 281,957
Cuts	12	15.0	$ 52,852
Ankle	11	30.7	$ 134,737
Emotional	11	n/a	$1,911,182
Monetary	11	n/a	$ 274,899
Arms	7	8.7	$ 132,844
Feet	7	30.7	$ 133,074
Shoulder	7	n/a	$1,823,571
Wrist	7	32.0	$ 69,285
Head	6	11.8	$ 324,750
Hand	6	11.6	$ 313,999
Jaw	5	22.0	$ 14,811
Elbow	5	n/a	$ 88,168
Hip	4	66.0	$ 114,600
Finger	4	n/a	$ 9,200
Teeth	4	n/a	$ 70,716
Neck	3	n/a	$ 531,667

From the Gym to the Jury-Eight Year Analysis

relative similarity in awards. Adult plaintiffs who suffered paralysis on average were awarded $900,000 more than minors.

In at least one comparative study (Bovbjerg, R., Sloan, F., & Blumstein, J., 1989), a relative value matrix demonstrated that awards increased gradually with age except for several slight drops at 35–50 age category and the expected drop for those 65 years-of-age or older. Thus, the relationship between age and payment for non-economic loss was an inverted "U" with lower payment in the early and later years.

The *From the Gym to the Jury* study's value matrix shows a sharp contrast to Bovbjerg, Sloan, & Blumstein's matrix as there is no bell shaped curve showing higher recoveries for those in the 36–50 age category. The sport cases show a sharp decline after adolescence with only a minor spike at the 18–35 age category. This difference can be attributable to the relative low number of sport cases involving serious injuries or deaths of in-

Table 4

Injury	Age Category	# of Cases	Avg. Award
Arm/Elbow	Minor	8	$ 112,238
	Adult	4	105,006
Death	Minor	17	1,206,121
	Adult	10	1,175,512
Eye	Minor	3	100,000
	Adult	5	223,388
Hand/Foot	Minor	4	119,243
	Adult	3	264,433
Head/Neck	Minor	3	11,971,758
	Adult	14	3,743,921
Leg/Knee	Minor	6	367,428
	Adult	19	276,430
Paralysis	Minor	6	4,150,614
	Adult	10	5,080,508

From the Gym to the Jury-Eight Year Analysis

dividuals over age 36. However, the first three age categories demonstrate a downward pattern for the verdicts or settlements. Table 5 highlights the descending awards by age category except for two variants at the 1–12 and over 57 age groups whose award averages were significantly affected by one excessively large award. The 1–12 age category average would drop to $1,157,583 if a $24 million verdict was removed from the average. Similarly, the over 57 age category average would drop to only $90,703 if a $10,254,000 verdict is removed from the average.

Table 6 compares the various defendant groups based on the number of million dollar cases, the highest awards/settlements, and average awards and

Table 5

Age	Average Award
1–12	$1,728,644 ($1,157,583)
13–19	$1,572,302
20-25	$994,931
26–35	$989,522
37–54	$587,940
57+	$1,107,033 ($90,703)

From the Gym to the Jury-Eight Year Analysis

Table 6
Defendant Comparison

Defendant Group	# Mill. Cases	Average Jury/Settl.	Average Jury	Average Settlement	Highest Jury/Settl.
Association	2	$1,109,015	$2,970,000	$ 213,951	$ 7,650,000
Company	3	976,510	1,194,435	38,500	7,000,000
Government	10	1,344,377	1,343,507	1,979,500	10,028,072
Health Clubs	0	193,135	136,361	193,484	925,000
Individual	7	586,928	856,191	193,183	5,500,000
Landowner	8	986,170	1,583,986	442,190	24,000,000
Manufacturer	11	3,212,503	4,899,705	1,243,286	11,100,000
Professional	0	144,866	136,800	190,200	500,000
Resorts	6	2,238,840	2,274,990	2,196,666	10,254,000
School	9	1,075,486	869,233	1,359,083	15,067,200
Universities	8	918,164	1,333,243	480,333	5,100,000

From the Gym to the Jury-Eight Year Analysis

settlements. The results demonstrated that sporting goods manufacturers had the highest number of million dollar cases (11) and the highest average awards and settlements. Resorts with sport amenities had the second highest average award and settlements.

If the highest seven verdicts, all over $10 million, are removed from the survey, the average award (for cases involving men and women, not business or government plaintiffs) declined from $1,159,573 to $831,002. This represents a 29% decline.

The greatest disparity evidenced by the research focused on female awards involving minors and adults. On average, a female minor's average recovery was $1,885,431. However, female adults only received a fraction of this amount-averaging only $392,789. The disparity between adult and minor males was less than $100,000.

Table 7 highlights the disparity between men and women. Girls received higher jury awards then boys, but boys had higher settlement values. In contrast, men in their working years averaged significantly higher awards and settlements.

Risk Management Plan

Besides communication's importance, another critical risk management

Table 7
Average Awards/Settlements Based on Gender

Gender	Age Group	Jury Awards	Settlements
M	1–12	$750,136 (10)	$2,097,708 (12)
F	5–12	$3,701,550 (9)	$350,318 (6)
M	13–19	$1,871,802 (26)	$1,700,264 (11)
F	14–18	$199,224 (5)	$1,090,667 (3)
M	20-25	$586,115 (8)	$2,109,333 (3)
F	20-25	$1,1385,510 (4)	$150,000 (1)
M	26–35	$1,933,409 (9)	$170,375 (4)
F	26–35	$263,049 (5)	$196,500 (2)
M	37–54	$687,358 (9)	$925,000 (1)
F	38–48	$487,000 (1)	$25,000 (1)
M	59–71	$2,156,410 (5)	$62,000 (1)
F	57–67	$63,140 (2)	$50,000 (2)

From the Gym to the Jury-Eight Year Analysis

tool involves how individuals respond to dangerous conditions. Lawyers, EAs and academicians have written numerous articles about risk management in sports. One high school athletic director in New York wrote an article highlighting his risk management program and the various steps within the program. His risk management program included:

- Policy & Procedure Guide,
- Parent/Guardian Consent Form,
- Health Status Review,
- Medical examination,
- Medical Disqualification,
- Safety Committee
- Planning,
- Recordkeeping (Edwards, 1993).

This approach represents just one of numerous potential risk management plans that an EA can implement. The key point is having a plan in place to address risk management concerns. Numerous risk management plans are in place throughout the world because EAs understand they face numerous potential safety and legal concerns. Furthermore, EAs understand that an appropriate response to all these concerns is developing a comprehensive risk management plan.

Most risk management plans focus on reducing personal injury concerns. However, a comprehensive risk management plan could cover such issues as:

- operating with a fictitious business name
- partnership agreements
- corporate formation procedures and compliance
- tax issues
- contract negotiations and compliance
- selling goods
- selling food and licensing/permits
- government regulations
- zoning issues
- nuisance from noise and other hazards
- insurance
- facility rental agreements
- sponsorship contracts
- employment issues
- employment contracts
- employer liability
- liability for the acts of volunteers
- dangerous facilities
- inadequate supervision
- negligence
- product liability
- criminal law
- real estate issues
- alcohol related concerns
- crowd management
- copyright, trademark and patent issues
- property rights
- waivers
- releases
- opponent's violence
- spectators' violence
- drug testing
- transportation concerns
- first aid and OSHA regulations
- advertising liability
- and a host of additional concerns.

Thus, as highlighted throughout this chapter, there are numerous societal and facility/program concerns that are raising liability issues for all EAs. Through researching injury related data, you can educate yourself to what concerns and dangers you might face. Furthermore, you should not try to reinvent the wheel. There are numerous risk management plans already out there which can be customized to serve your needs. There are an estimated 3 million youth sport coaches throughout the U.S. However, one of the nation's largest youth sport providers (Little League Baseball) only adopted a nationwide coaches training program in 1997 (Donnelly, 1998). While some programs are just getting started there exists several well established risk management and coaching certification programs currently in existence. Some of these programs and contact information include:

Pop Warner Football and Little Scholars, (215) 752-2691, 586 Middletown Blvd., Suite C 100, Langhorne, PA 19047

Coalition of Americans to Protects Sports (CAPS), (800) 338-8678, 200 Castlewood Dr., N. Palm Beach, FL 33408

Human Kinetics, (800) 747-4457 P.O. Box 5076, Champaign, IL 61825-5076

National Alliance of Youth Sports (NAYS) and National Youth Sports Coaches Association (NYSCA), (407) 684-1141 2050 Vista Pkwy. West Palm Beach, FL 33411

National Council of Youth Sports (NCYS), (561) 625-1197 116 First Terrace, Suite 709, Palm Beach Gardens, FL 33418

Even though several risk management programs already exist, you should never adopt another risk management plan without first determining how the plan complies with all your needs. No plan can address every issue faced by two different programs or facilities. Thus, you always need to adapt any risk management plan you obtain from colleagues. Various risk management plans will be highlighted in this text to assist you in the process of developing your risk management plan.

Conclusion

While you attempt to develop a comprehensive risk management plan you should always keep in mind the great diversity of potential legal issues that can arise when putting on any event. The list above highlighted numerous concerns, but by no means is it an exhaustive list. It would be impossible to list all the potential concerns any given event might face without going through the event and performing a comprehensive risk management audit. This guide is designed to give you some of the tools necessary to conduct such an audit and to develop the comprehensive risk management plan.

Chapter 3

Applicable Legal Terms and Principles

As highlighted in the previous chapter, some *possible* legal concerns you might face while running an event include:

- tort claims,
- contract violations,
- labor conflicts,
- anti-trust claims,
- suits alleging discrimination.

Unfortunately, it would be impossible to cover these, and many other possible issues in one guidebook. As highlighted in the research mentioned in Chapter 2, negligence claims are the most common claims faced in sport programs. Thus, this guidebook will specifically examine legal claims based on negligence. *Negligence* is a form of a legal wrong called a *tort*. A tort is defined as a "private or civil wrong or injury resulting from a breach of a legal duty that exists by virtue of society's expectations regarding interpersonal conduct." This definition of "tort" is from *Poindexter v. Willis*, which can be found in a legal case report commonly referred to as 256 N.E. 2d 254, at page 259. The 1970 case was decided in Ohio. Throughout this guidebook, cases will be given with their appropriate legal citation should the reader wish to find the complete text.

Society expects people to behave in such a way that when a Mr. X puts his health and well being into Mrs. Y's hands, Mrs. Y has to act in a manner that respects and protects Mr. X's rights. Thus, *a tort is an act or omission that breaches a duty owed and causes an injury to another person.*

Negligence is just one of the numerous types of acts categorized as a tort. Other well known torts include:

- assault,
- battery,
- nuisance,
- trespass,
- intentional infliction of emotional distress.

Negligence will be the only tort examined in this guidebook because you presumably are not intentionally trying to injure a person at your event. However, others participants or spectators might try to injure an individual attending your event. Thus, this guide will cover negligence-related liability associated with running an event or the liability associated with your or other's misconduct. You could also face liability for the acts of those you do not even know at the event, if you should have realized an uninvited person might cause harm to someone at your event.

Negligence has been defined as the failure to act in a manner of a similarly situated "reasonable" individual.(Gifis, 1984). Negligence has also been defined as the failure to observe and exercise that degree of care, precaution, and vigilance that the circumstances justly demand, to protect another person from injury (Gifis, 1984). The key to negligence analysis is whether or not you acted as a reasonable person *and* exercised care to individuals you owe a duty to protect.

This chapter will first examine the four elements that constitute negligence. Next, the type of tort committed by violating one of the four elements will be examined. Lastly, the defenses to a negligence claim will be examined.

Elements of Negligence

Each of the four negligence elements have to be present for a person to recover under a negligence claim. The four elements are:

- owing someone a duty,
- breaching that duty,
- the breach of that duty was the proximate cause of the person's injury,
- the person was actually injured (van der Smissen, 1990).

An *injury* is defined as a legal wrong that causes damage to someone. An injury does not have to be physically visible. Additional injuries can include psychological injuries, emotional distress, pain and suffering and future medical or financial requirements. Loss of consortium is another category of damages which is available to the injured party and his/her spouse (and other close family members) and is designed to compensate for lost love and affection.

Duty

A *duty* is a legally sanctioned or societally imposed obligation, which if breached, creates a potential negligent atmosphere. If you owe a duty to an event participant, your actions must be conducted in a manner to avoid exposing the participant to potential hazards that are either known or likely to occur. Examples of the types of duties that you might be held accountable for include:

- the duty to provide adequate instruction/supervision,
- the duty to provide proper equipment and/or facilities,
- the duty to provide reasonable selection or matching of participants (van der Smissen, 1990).

If you do not uphold these duties in a manner that is "adequate," "proper," or "reasonable," you would have breached your duty. Numerous duties are imposed on an EA and some of the common duties that will be explored in this guidebook include the duty to:

- inspect the facilities,
- provide safe facilities,
- supervise the event,
- properly match opponents,
- provide proper equipment,
- provide emergency services in a rapid, effective manner (Appenzeller, 1998).

A typical duty you will be held accountable for is the duty to inspect and secure all playing or competition facilities that might be used during a practice/event. You have an affirmative duty to inspect the facilities being used and to locate any discoverable defects that could possibly injure an individual at the event. An *affirmative duty* is a positive duty. This positive duty requires you to take at least a certain minimum amount of precautionary steps to protect the safety of other people. If you find a defect or are informed of a possible defect, then you have an affirmative duty to correct the defect or warn everyone about the defect. The duty to warn can be accomplished through:

- setting event policies or rules,
- posting warnings on equipment, admittance tickets or facilities,
- oral warnings,
- encouraging safe participation,

- generally making sure all participants and spectators are aware of the inherent risks associated with the activity (van der Smissen, 1990).

An *effective warning* is:

- specific,
- obvious and direct,
- unambiguous,
- easy to understand,
- simple,
- complete,
- appreciated and understood by the person warned (Van der Smissen, 1990).

Two types of warnings can be given, actual and/or constructive warnings. *Actual warnings* can be either posted or verbal. If a lifeguard yells at swimmer not to dive because they are next to the shallow-end, the lifeguard has provided an actual warning. *Constructive warnings* are implied from the fact that the individual could reasonably determine that the situation was dangerous. An example of constructive warning is a high fence around an electrical power unit. The size of the fence and the barbed wire on top of the fence serve to provide constructive notice of the potential hazards in the fenced area. Under the conditions stated above, a reasonable person would be on notice that the area enclosed by the high fence is enclosed because the area is dangerous.

While the author cannot stress enough the importance of signage that effectively communicates a risk, the sign itself should not increase risks. In a California skiing case, a warning sign actually caused the injury. A skier was trying to traverse some ground between two runs (crossover trail) when he noticed a black foam rubber object ahead. He tried to avoid the object but due to the hard packed snow, his speed and his distance from the object, he hit the object and was rendered a paraplegic. The object was a sign post for a sign that provided directions to a chair lift and admonished skiers to "Be Aware - Ski With Care." Unfortunately the black wrapping around the post blended with the shadows from the lift tower and surrounding trees. Furthermore, the plaintiff approached the sign from the side (a 90 degree angle) which was impossible to see if you did not see the sign head on or from behind. The black foam around the post was designed to be placed in circles around the sign post to absorb a skiers impact. However, the ski resort employees had placed the foam protector around the actual post, rather than spaced in a circle around the post, thus depriving the foam of its hollow center to help absorb a collision. The appellate court overturned the lower court's verdict for the defendant and held that the ski resort's actions increased the risk of participating and thus the assumption of risk defense would not apply (*Van Dyke v. S.K.I. Ltd.*, 67 Cal. App. 4th 1310, 79 Cal.Rptr.2d 775 (CA 1998).

Duty to Properly Inspect

Actually finding a defect on the premises is not required to trigger your duty. You could owe a duty to warn against unknown risks or defects that you *"should" have or "could have" discovered through reasonable inspection*. Simply stated, you have to make sure the facility and equipment are reasonably safe. If any area or equipment cannot be repaired, then you have to avoid using the dangerous area or equipment. If the facility or equipment has to be used, and repairs cannot be completed, then you have to warn everyone about the potentially harmful condition. The term "reasonably safe" will be used throughout this guide because *you have a duty to provide "reasonably safe" premises, not "perfectly safe" premises.* You are not an ensurer of safety. You are only required to provide a reasonably safe facility and/or equipment.

Is it the law of the land that someone can be held liable for a hazard that he or she does not even know about? The answer is, "Yes!" As you will find out from reading this guide, an EA can owe many duties, but ordinary citizens also owe many duties. An average citizen has a duty to drive safely, shovel snow from their sidewalks, comply with all laws, etc. If a guest at your house decided to take a bath, you would have an affirmative duty to warn them about the bathtub's slippery condition. If your guest slips in the tub and you did not inform them of the tub's slippery nature, then you could have breached your duty to protect your guest. However, if you had placed non-slip mats in the tub, then your actions would indicate that you were aware of the tub's slippery nature, and the mats were your method of constructively warning your guests about the potential hazard. If you did not know about the tub's slippery nature, you still could be liable for not inspecting a potentially dangerous item. In addition, different people using the tub should receive a warning appropriate for that person. A bathtub is not inherently dangerous, but if a frail older person is trying to get out of the tub, it could be very dangerous for him/her. The issue during a trial will always focus on whether you provided a reasonably safe bathtub based on your prior notice of potential hazards and whether injury to the tub user was reasonably foreseeable.

Several years ago the author heard a story about an older lady who won a lawsuit against a supermarket when she was injured trying to separate shopping carts that were jammed together. A shopping cart might not seem dangerous, but if the store knew older people were having a hard time separating the carts, the store would have to post some form of warning. Similarly, the recent multi-million dollar injury verdict awarded to a woman injured by hot coffee at McDonald's helps highlight negligence suits and resulting large jury awards when someone breaches a duty. While it might appear that the McDonald's case was egregious, further examination into the facts can highlight the potential reasonableness of the award. The case involved a 79 year-old female car passenger who bought a cup of coffee at a McDonald's Restaurant take-out window in Albuquerque, New Mexico. While the car was stopped, and with the cup between her legs, she pried the lid off the cup. The coffee spilled resulting in third degree burns. She sued McDonald's and recovered $160,000 in compensatory damages and $2,700,000 in punitive damages (Gross and Syverud 1996). Instantly, the case generated international headlines attacking the decision. Some headlines read as follows: "Coffee Case Burns Common Sense," "No Grounds For Hot Coffee Award," "Coffee and $2.9 Million to Go," "Some Use Crying Over Spilt Coffee," and "Ronald McDonald Better Have a Really Good Lawyer."(Gross and Syverud, 1996). However, once the smoke cleared, the case appeared to possibly be a reasonable decision. The plaintiff was hospitalized for eight days, she had to undergo several skin graft operations, McDonald's intentionally heated its coffee 15–20 degrees hotter than their competition, and McDonald's knew their coffee was too hot as they had received over 700 complaints in a five year period from people who suffered burns, including serious burns. Even with all the complaints and an industry heating standard, McDonald's refused to lower the coffee temperature (Gross and Syverud, 1996). The punitive damage award appeared justified as $2.7 million represents just two days of revenue generated by McDonald's from national coffee sales (Gross and Syverud, 1996). Possibly as a result of the damages, which were later reduced to $640,000, McDonald's lowered their coffee's temperature (Gross and Syverud, 1996). Thus, punitive damages and the legal system had their intended affect, punishing and curing potentially dangerous behavior.

These examples should encourage every EA to immediately inspect all the facilities and equipment they might use. It cannot be stressed enough that *if any defects are known or found, you should immediately remedy the situation, change the facility or equipment and, at the least, warn everyone about the potential hazard.* Remedying the situation is always the top priority. The key is, *let safety determine your policy, not money.* If you do not have money to spend on repairing something, do not use it.

Duty to Properly Supervise

The duty to adequately supervise an activity, or a group of individuals, extends to you whenever a person puts his or her well being into your hands. When a person puts his/her well being into your hands, he/she expects to be protected. The major question asked by the courts is whether or not the accident would have occurred if the event had been adequately supervised. Your duty to supervise is based on acquiring prior knowledge concerning the need for supervision. The acquisition of prior knowledge is commonly referred to as being put *"on notice."* Once you have been put on notice, proper precautions need to be taken to remedy and warn participants and spectators about dangerous conditions.

Event supervisors can help control an event's flow and the actions of event participants and spectators. The only problem is determining how many people will be needed to supervise the event and what training these supervisors might require to properly perform their assignment. Some courts have determined that there should be a ratio of roughly 40 or 50 participants per supervisor. Other courts have set varying ratios from as few as one supervisor for ten children to over 500 spectators for a supervisor or police officer (See generally van der Smissen, 1990). From these varying ratios it is obvious that there is no set standard for how many supervisors are needed to adequately supervise event participants or spectators. The level of supervision required for a "reasonable EA" depends on several factors. To determine how many supervisors should be used, the following questions should be asked:

- Is the sport an individual participant or team sport?
- What kind of equipment is being used?
- What are the participants' ages?
- What are the type and number of individuals involved?
- What is the supervisor's experience/training?
- Can the supervisor appreciate the potential harm?
- Are there enough supervisors who can observe the whole area?
- Can a supervisor prevent a potential accident?

Answers to these questions can help you establish reasonable supervision guidelines depending on the responses. While an experienced coach can effectively supervise a college tennis tournament, a children's hockey game involving two teams with large numbers of children might need additional monitoring. While an experienced supervisor can reasonably manage many events, using several young camp counselors or teacher aids to supervise the same event might be unreasonable. The golden rule is to make sure all supervisory plans are reasonable.

Remember that implementing reasonable supervision standards is not, by itself, enough. The standards have to be acted upon. Supervision plans can state that there should be no more than 30 children per supervisor, but you could be liable if these plans are not implemented. Assume a teacher has to leave his class, and the supervisorial policies state that someone should supervise the children at all times. If the teacher leaves the room to take a child to the principal's office, he/she is violating the established policies and could leave the school open for a potential suit for failing to properly supervise the class. Failing to follow existing policies would be a strike against the school, as a jury could look at the policies and conclude that the school knew of the potential dangers caused by inadequate supervision, but failed to live up to its own policies. The jury might reach a different conclusion if the teacher was faced with a sudden medical emergency and had to rush a child to the school's nurse. In this situation, the teacher should never leave the class unsupervised, but send for help. This happened in the *Miller v. Cloidt* (No. L-7241- 62 N.J. Sup.-Ct. Law Div., Morris County, Oct. 31, 1964), case in which the teacher left the area and a junior high school student was rendered quadriplegic. The duty to provide reasonable supervision can be suspended when faced with sudden, serious emergencies. It should be noted that with all exceptions such as medical emergencies, a jury will be asked to determine if the medical condition really constituted an emergency, whether there were other safer options and what would a reasonably prudent person do in the same circumstance.

In *summary*, the *duty to provide reasonable supervision* includes:

- the duty to establish minimum and maximum levels of supervision for each supervisor and activity,
- the duty to implement these standards,
- the duty to utilize competent supervisors,
- the duty to monitor supervisors' actions.

Duty to Supervise Children

In discussing supervision, this guidebook has focused on children, as adults *normally* require less supervision. Children are owed a higher duty because most children cannot appreciate the inherent risks in some activities or equipment. While most adults know how dangerous a knife can be, a child might not know the potential danger inherent in the knife. Besides not knowing all the potential dangers associated with a knife, many children are *less experienced in techniques and skills* required for safely using a knife. When working with inexperienced students, teachers are held to a higher standard because more training and practice is required before the students have developed necessary skills. For example, a gymnastics teacher has to spend a lot of time working with students on basic tumbling skills before moving up to advanced apparatus dismounts. Even though children would rather perform complex dismounts, inexperienced gymnasts should not be allowed to do complex maneuvers before mastering preliminary steps.

Children are also owed a duty to be protected from dangerous conditions they might not realize are dangerous. *Attractive nuisance* is the term used to describe a situation where a child is drawn to a dangerous condition without having the ability to appreciate the danger (Gifis, 1984). A typical attractive nuisance situation is a swimming pool on personal property. A pool needs to be fenced in to protect curious children from potential harm. If you are running a motorcross event, and there is an abandoned rock quarry on the same property, the quarry could be considered an attractive nuisance because children might wander away from the event to play there. If there exists a possibility that children might go to the quarry, you have a duty to block access to the quarry. You should also warn both the children and their parents about the potential danger.

The impression you might be getting is that children should be treated with extra loving care and you need to become as protective as a parent. Treating a child in the same manner that parents treat their own child(ren) is exactly the standard you should try to achieve. *In loco parentis* means "in the place of the parents" (Gifis, 1984). If you are running an event for children, you would have a duty to supervise the children in the same manner the children's parents would supervise them. The *in loco parentis* doctrine is frequently used in cases against schools for not acting in the same manner as a reasonable parent (Gifis, 1984). For example, consider a group of school children playing softball. A parent would make sure his or her child was behind the backstop before the pitcher throws the ball. Because a parent is normally not at school to supervise his or her child, the school has to act in the parent's place. Thus, the teacher should make sure his/her actions are similar to those of a reasonable parent.

Duty to Supervise Adults

Children are not the only participants who might require additional or closer supervision. We would all like to be top-notch athletes. However, reality dictates that not everyone is in exceptional condition. Unfortunately, too many people participate in events when they are in poor physical condition. You have a duty to warn these individuals about participating in an event in poor physical condition and/or without their physician's consent. It is generally impossible to determine the shape or condition of any participant before an event. However, a general warning on an event application or waiver; to consult a physician before attempting any strenuous activity, might help discharge your duty. The problem with such a warning is that it is not very proactive. In contrast, a sign indicating that they are participating based on the fact that they "have seen a physician" is more proactive. In addition, performing beyond the minimal duty can be accomplished through providing medical personnel at the event to check individual participants before an event. However, as the cost of any such pre-event screening is prohibitive, such conduct is not considered a typical industry practice.

A special concern exists for events with senior citizens. While there is no duty to evaluate all participants, any event with senior participants should include additional safety steps to handle possible critical emergency concerns. Seniors should be asked if they have recently seen a physician or if they suffer from any condition that could be exacerbated by participating in the event. The best means of ensuring healthy participation can be accomplished by preparing a careful participation form and/or waiver specifically addressing senior athlete issues. Further discussion concerning waivers can be found in Chapter 7.

Duty During an Event

Once an event starts, you have a duty to provide first aid to injured individuals. Unfortunately, the threat of a lawsuit has scared some EAs, coaches and teachers away from providing first aid. These reluctant individuals might not have a choice, as a court could impose a duty on them to provide timely and adequate first aid. If you could have provided first aid assistance, but failed or refused to, your actions could constitute a breach of your duty to protect someone from harm. Providing good samaritan assistance is a perfect example why it is important to research local or state laws to determine if immunity protection might apply. Most states have immunity protection for good samaritans, but an EA cannot assume he/she is covered. A reasonable EA makes the time and effort to know the laws that will affect the event.

Person's Status

As observed earlier in this section, age or ability of the person attending the event are factors to be considered in establishing an EA's duty. Most EAs are kept busy trying to supervise the individuals who are supposed to be at the event. However, an EA is also responsible to ensure the safety of participants and spectators from those who are not even affiliated with the event. This duty is established from an EA's knowledge, or failure to discover that a third party might engage in misconduct that could injure a participant or spectator. The typical circumstance in which this liability scenario arises involves criminal acts of a third party. The law is fairly clear that when a property owner/manager holds property open to the public they have a duty to take affirmative steps to prevent the wrongful acts of a third party that threatens the safety of others legitimately at the premises if the owner/manager has "reasonable cause" to anticipate the wrongful conduct (*Frances v. Village Green Owners Ass'n* (1986) 42 C3d 490, 229 CR 456). The key is determining how an EA can have "reasonable cause" to believe that someone might engage in wrongful conduct against those to whom the EA owes a duty to protect them from harm. Some commentaries hypothesize that if you know about criminal activity within several blocks of your event, then you have to take proactive steps to protects individuals in your charge from the known criminal activity (Fried, 1998). Thus, you are responsible to properly investigate the surrounding community to identify possible hazards from those individuals who might not have any involvement with your event.

Duty is also determined by the status of the individual at the event. Different degrees of care are apportioned based on the attendee's or participant's status as either an:

- invitee,
- licensee, or
- trespasser (Gifis, 1984).

An *invitee* is invited onto the premises for a specific purpose and the premises' occupier receives a benefit from the invitee's presence. A typical invitee is a ticket-holding spectator at a sporting event or someone who paid to participate in an event. The term *"occupier"* is used because both a landowner and a renter could owe a duty to an invitee (or licensee). A landlord and/or renter could be liable for dangerous conditions that injured an invitee. A *renter* could be *liable for patent defects* on the premises. *A patent defect is a defect that can be recognized with reasonable care or through ordinary inspection* (Gifis, 1984). On the other hand, a *landowner* is normally only *liable for latent defects* on the premises. *A latent defect is a hidden defect that could not be discovered even through reasonable inspection*(Gifis, 1984). A landowner can be liable for latent defects if *no* inspection of the premises is performed. If the landowner knows about the latent or hidden defect, but the renter does not, the landowner has a duty to warn the renter about the defect. Once renters knows about the defect they have a duty to warn or repair the defect.

An EA owes an invitee the duty to:

- inspect and repair any dangerous conditions at the facility,
- warn the invitee about any hidden dangers,
- maintain and supervise the premises in a reasonably safe manner (see generally van derSmissen, 1990).

You also have a duty to protect an invitee against foreseeable harmful risks caused by other invitees. Thus, if a drunk is threatening other invitees, you have a duty to protect those invitees. A typical case involving injuries inflicted by one invitee against another is the *Townsley* case, below.

Townsley v. Cincinnati Gardens, Inc.
314 N.E. 2d 409 (OH 1974)

On November 2, 1969 Harry Townsley, a minor (under the age of 18), went to the Cincinnati Gardens with a friend to watch the Harlem Globetrotters. After the third quarter, Townsley went to the restroom where he was approached by a young man asking for money. Other youths then joined the man and attacked Townsley. He received a facial laceration and lost his front teeth. Only five security guards monitored 5,000 event spectators. The security was minimal as the event was considered a family event, unlike a rowdier event such as a rock concert. The Ohio Court of Appeals concluded that the facility occupier was not liable for a business invitee being beaten up in the arena restroom because the occupier did not have any prior knowledge or experience to be put on notice that an invitee would be attacked. Since the facility had no previously reported assaults at similar family events, it could not have anticipated the assault.

If an invitee only has permission to be in a certain area, then the premises occupier has to specify which areas are off-limits to the invitee. An example of a specific location being off-limits to an invitee is a racetrack's track and pit area. Normally the track and pit areas are dangerous and only specified individuals are permitted there. While certain areas may be off limits, the invitee can roam freely through the grandstands and concession areas. Rules regarding where invitees can go have to be posted and strictly enforced. If invitees go into a restricted area, thus breaching the invitation, their status changes from an invitee to a licensee. Therefore, if someone with a grandstand ticket disregards warning signs and enters the pit area, his/her status would change from an invitee to a licensee. As a licensee, you would not owe him/her as high a duty of care.

A *licensee* is on the premises with either the premises occupier's express or implied permission (Gifis, 1984). A typical licensee with *express permission* to be on the premises is the event support staff which could include concession stand operators, first aid assistants and ushers. A typical licensee with *implied permission* to be on the premises is a police officer at the event for crowd control purposes. A licensee needs to be *warned of all known unsafe conditions. In addition, you have the duty to avoid injuring the licensee through any willful or wanton behavior* (van derSmissen, 1990).

Willful or wanton behavior occurs when the premises occupier knows the likely consequences posed by a potentially dangerous situation, but does nothing to prevent a possible injury. Willful or wanton behavior can also be defined as acting with less then reasonable care under the circumstances. The following case helps highlight the manner in which courts examine willful conduct.

Light v. Ohio University
502 N.E. 2d 611 (OH 1986)

In 1982, five-year-old Lisa Light was injured when some lockers fell on her at the Grover Center recreational facility at Ohio University. The Grover Center had been available for public use. The Grover Center contained full-length lockers that could be rented on a quarterly basis, and small coin operated lockers available for short-term rentals. Individuals using Grover Center had the choice of whether or not to use the lockers. The university was unaware of any reports claiming the lockers were unsafe or unstable. Mrs. Light (Lisa's mother) did not see the accident, but she thought Lisa was trying to put something into the locker that contained her purse.

The Ohio Supreme Court first analyzed whether the Lights were invitees or licensees. This analysis was required to determine what duty the university owed them. If the Lights were business invitees, they would be using the facility by invitation, express or implied, for a purpose beneficial to the university. If they were invitees, the university would have had to exercise ordinary care to keep the premises safe. The court concluded that the Lights were licensees because the university let the public use the facility for the public's own pleasure and benefit. Any locker rental fee was considered incidental to facility usage because locker rental was optional. A licensee accepts all perils and risks associated with being on the premises with the exception of willful or wanton conduct by the licensor (university). Because the university did not have any prior knowledge the lockers would fall, its action was not willful or wanton. Thus, the plaintiffs lost their suit.

The *Light* case highlights the importance of how to classify individuals at an event. To help ensure that individuals understand what risks they are assuming, admission tickets often state a spectator's status as either a licensee or invitee.

Trespassers are the last category of individuals to whom you owe a duty, albeit a very minimal duty. A *trespasser* is on the premises without the occupier's express consent or knowledge. As long as the premises occupier *is not aware of* the person's presence, the person is considered a trespasser. Trespassers are not owed any duties except that you cannot intentionally injure them (van der Smissen, 1990). However, if the occupier knows about a trespasser's presence, and does not expel the person from the premises, then the occupier is consenting to the trespasser's presence. Consenting to the trespasser's presence can change his/her status to that of a licensee, who is owed all the rights and duties owed a licensee (van derSmissen, 1990).

In conclusion, an EA owes a duty to an individual at the event, to provide that person with a certain level of protection. Duties can be based on such variables as age, experience level or a person's physical condition. The EA normally owes a much higher duty to an inexperienced athlete. A lower duty typically is owed to a well-trained athlete who has been competing for many years. These varying duty levels, which are often based on the EA's knowledge or experience, would be presented to a jury to help establish what duty was owed to the injured individual(s).

While a trespasser is owed a minimum amount of protection, a licensee is owed more protection and an invitee is owed the highest protection. Once a duty is established, courts analyze whether or not the EA breached that duty.

Breach of Duty

The second factor required to prove negligence is breaching a duty. Breaching a duty can provide direct evidence of negligence. Direct evidence of negligence can entail violating a statutorily imposed duty, which is called *"negligence per se."* Negligence per se imposes liability because negligence can be inferred from violating a legal requirement such as a state law (Gifis, 1984). Thus, if a state law requires ski resorts to post certain warning signs, the failure to post those signs provides actual proof that the law was violated. A Ski resort, in a state that has a law requiring signage, owes individuals the duty to warn them of potential dangers and the failure to warn the public breaches the resort's duty. If an injured person sued the resort, the lawsuit could claim that the resort was negligent for failing to have proper signage as required by state law.

Once you owe someone a duty, you have to do everything in your power to uphold that duty. If you owe a duty to warn a person about a known danger, you breach that duty by not providing the warning. Thus, *breaching a duty entails not living up to a certain standard of care.*

A major question faced when developing standards is the determination of what will be the standard required to uphold a duty. *The standard for negligence is the exercise of ordinary or reasonable care* (Gifis, 1984). The *"reasonably prudent person"* standard is the name given to the *expected* standard of care (Gifis, 1984). When you have exercised reasonable care in the maintenance and supervision of a facility, then you have acted like a reasonably prudent person.

The reasonably prudent person standard fosters a number of different questions. However, the most important question is who or what is a reasonably prudent person? A reasonably prudent person is a typical individual with traits and experiences comparable to other similarly situated individuals. The reasonably prudent person standard analyzes your conduct in light of a similar EA of the same age, education, experience, etc. (van der Smissen, 1990). Thus, the reasonably prudent person represents your clone. If an EA has been running an event for over 20 years, then the EA would be expected to act in a manner similar to other EAs who have been running the same type of event for the same time period. An EA in charge of a baseball game who has not checked the field, does not live up to the reasonably prudent person standard if similar EAs would have checked the field.

To avoid breaching a duty, you have to take reasonable steps to ensure that all possible precautions are both examined and acted upon. If you have a duty to provide a safe facility, you should inspect the facility and repair any dangerous conditions. Besides acting as a reasonably prudent EA, you have to protect a person through preventing the wanton risk enhancement. A reasonably prudent EA who discovers a large gopher hole on the premises, has a duty to warn people about the risk or repair the hole. If the EA covers the hole with a piece of cardboard, to make it look like it was fixed, then the EA has breached his/her duty by wantonly enhancing the risks faced by people using the field. The EA should know that if someone stepped on the cover, his/her weight would not be supported by the cover which could lead to an injury.

Besides your duty to avoid wanton risk enhancement, you have a duty to exercise the "last clear chance" option. If you breach a duty, but you have the last clear chance to prevent an injury, you are required to take all reasonable steps to protect someone from harm. The *Chapman* case highlights this principle.

Chapman v. State
492 P. 2d 607 (WA 1972)

The question presented by this case is whether the instructor or the plaintiff had the last clear chance to avoid the injury. In 1967, an 18-year-old university student, David Chapman, was injured when he fell off a trampoline. Chapman was an experienced trampoliner and a good athlete. He selected a gymnastics class to satisfy his physical education requirement and stayed after class to use the trampoline. University policy required four spotters on each side of the trampoline during class time. However, Chapman was using the trampoline after class and there were no set rules regarding the number of spotters required. Only one spotter was watching over him. Chapman was injured when he attempted to perform a double-forward somersault and fell off the trampoline. The class instructor was 30-40 feet away, supervising another student, when the injury occurred.

Under the last clear chance doctrine, the *defendant has to actually see plaintiff's peril and appreciate the danger, but fail to take any action.* Because the instructor was over 30 feet away, he was unable to see, or have enough time to react to the student's peril. The instructor did not have enough time to react, as Chapman was not in peril until he tried the somersault flip. In fact Chapman, himself, had the last clear chance to avoid injury as he could have stepped off the trampoline before attempting the maneuver. The instructor did not see, nor did he have time to react to the student's peril.

A frequently asked question is whether or not an event administrator is liable for someone else's breach of duty? The answer is yes. You do not have to personally breach a duty to become liable to the injured person. Liability can be imposed on you for the actions of others even if you acted reasonably.

Vicarious Liability

A special relationship between an EA and another person can create liability for another's negligent actions. Many names exist for the type of relationship that imposes a managerial duty upon an EA, including a master/servant, an employer/*employee*, and/or a *principal/agent* relationship. An employee's or volunteer's negligence is imposed upon the EA by the doctrine of *vicarious liability* or *respondeat superior* (Gifis, 1984). Both terms mean that the supervising party should be responsible for a subordinate's actions, while performing work that benefits the supervising party. To impose liability upon the supervising party, the subordinate who undertook the negligent act, has to be found guilty of negligently performing work that benefited the supervising party. An example could be a Mrs. S who coaches a private school's softball team and is negligent in performing her job. If her employer controlled Mrs. S's actions and she was doing work for the benefit, and under the supervision of her employer, the employer and/or school could be liable for Mrs. S's negligent act. If the EA is considered an employee, she could be sued for her negligent action in order to get at the "deep pockets" of the EA's employer. Thus, you have to make sure all subordinates are properly supervised. Along with proper supervision, EAs have to exercise extreme caution in hiring, engaging and/or retaining both employees and volunteers. The recent increase in sexual abuse cases provides ample evidence for proper screening and supervising all employees prior to placing them with event participants (see Chapter 6 and Appendix A). An EA owes children a duty to provide safe recreational opportunities and properly trained coaches. If a coach abuses a child, the EA would have breached his/her duty and would ultimately be liable if he/she could have prevented the abuse through diligent supervision or screening. The gambit of employment law issues is very complex and cannot be covered appropriately in this guide. However, all EAs should follow all applicable employment laws and ensure all employees and volunteers have passed a vigorous background check prior to being hired or retained. For additional assistance in employment law matters, please see, *Employment Law for the Sport, Recreation, and Fitness Industries* by Fried, Miller and Appenzeller (Carolina Academic Press, 1998).

Under several situations, vicarious liability might not be imposed on an EA. Vicarious liability does not arise when the *worker is not an employee or volunteer*. Many court battles have been fought over whether or not a person is an employee or an independent contractor (Fried, Miller and Appenzeller, 1998). An employer is normally not liable for the negligent actions of an *independent contractor* (Fried, Miller and Appenzeller, 1998). An individual's status as an independent contractor or employee can be determined by examining the working relationship. The individual will normally be considered an independent contractor if:

- the worker's actions or hours are not strictly controlled,
- the worker was not hired for a broad purpose or to fill a position,
- the worker is under a contract for a specific project,
- the worker uses his or her own tools,

- the worker can work for other potential employers,
- the worker has her or his own company which markets its service to other potential EAs, and
- the worker pays his or her own taxes (Fried, Miller and Appenzeller, 1998).

While contractual terms can sometimes take precedence, such is not the case with determining an employee's or independent contractor's legal classification. Even if the employment contract specifies that the person is an independent contractor, a court could hold otherwise if the person does not meet an independent contractor's legal definition. An EA can be liable for civil and criminal penalties if the independent contractor is really an employee and no workers' compensation insurance was in place to protect the employee. Thus, significant liability can be attached to an EA in addition to liability imposed by the negligent acts of an employee.

Strict Liability

Another basis for imposing liability, even if the EA did not act negligently, is strict liability. Thus, an EA can take every conceivable precaution, but still remain liable for an injury. *Strict liability* is imposed on an EA when the activity is so *ultra hazardous* that the *mere involvement of the EA in putting on the activity exposes people to risk* (Van der Smissen, 1990). An example of an ultra-hazardous event is hang-gliding. Hanggliding is considered so risky that an EA conducting such an event could be liable for damages even if he/she did nothing to cause the injury. Waivers represent one tactic for avoiding liability associated with ultra-hazardous events (Cotten and Cotten, 1998). With extreme sport's soaring popularity, more and more attention will be focused in the future on strict liability and whether or not it is against public policy not to hold EA's strictly liable.

We started our legal analysis by looking at a duty that you might owe to a participant or spectator at an event. From there we analyzed whether or not you may have breached that duty. Even if you did not personally breach any duty, under the vicarious liability theory, you could be held liable for other individuals who might have breached a duty. We also examined various situations under which liability may be imposed even if no duty was breached such as strict liability. We will now turn our attention to the third negligent element, which is whether a breach of your duty directly caused someone's injuries.

Proximate Cause

Proximate cause is the actual cause of someone's injury (Gifis, 1984). Proximate cause has also been defined as the *natural continuous results of an action that caused an injury* (Gifis, 1984). Let's take a gymnastics example. A gymnastics coach has a duty to make sure all the equipment being used is in reasonably safe condition. To execute this duty, the coach would have to examine the equipment and undertake any necessary repairs to make the equipment safe. If a coach notices a loose bolt, but fails to replace the bolt, the coach has breached his duty. If a gymnast slips off the equipment during an event, the court would try to establish whether it was the loose bolt that caused the injury or whether the gymnast just slipped-off. If the loose bolt caused the injury, then the failure to repair the loose bolt would be the injury's proximate cause. Proximate cause was dramatically highlighted in the *Welch* case, analyzed in the first aid chapter (Chapter 28). Welch was injured on the field, but was still able to move some body parts. After being carried from the field by several players, he was unable to move and became paralyzed. The football-related injury might have been serious, but it did not cause him to lose movement. Being moved from the field was the proximate cause of his paralysis.

An intervening act between your breach of duty and the injury's proximate cause can discharge your duty. This defense will be discussed in the defense section.

Injury/Damages

The last element of negligence is being injured and receiving monetary damages for the injury. The plaintiff has to be *actually injured and the injury has to have monetarily damaged him/her* (Gifis, 1984). Injuries can be as easy to prove as a broken arm, or very complex to prove, such as mental distress or soft tissue injuries. The plaintiff's ability to prove an injury will be assumed in this guide as most people would not bring a suit unless they have some injury. Furthermore, most attorneys would not bring a lawsuit if there were not significant injuries and medical/economic damages. Attorneys will not pursue a matter if there is no possibility of recovering some money.

The *types of damages* a person can be compensated for include:

- actual medical expenses,
- pain and suffering,
- actual lost wages,

- diminution in earning capacity,
- future medical and rehabilitation expenses,
- the loss of love and companionship (Fried, Miller and Appenzeller, 1998).

If your actions as an EA are extremely (grossly) negligent, the court could also impose *punitive damages*, which are *designed to punish*, instead of just compensating the injured party (Fried, Miller and Appenzeller, 1998).

Types of Negligence

Legalese, a term used for describing legal verbiage, is a complex collection of labels and terms which are required to ensure proper understanding of potential legal repercussions. Several new terms will now be added to your growing legal repertoire. These labels are important as they help classify your actions. A negligent act can come about through acting in an incorrect manner, which is called misfeasance or malfeasance. Nonfeasance occurs when you owe a duty, *but fail to act*. Negligence also has many degrees ranging from strict negligence through slight negligence.

Misfeasance is a type of negligence where the EA *performs a required duty in a wrongful manner* (Gifis, 1984). If you have a duty to supervise children in a swimming pool and you turn away from the pool for an extended period of time, you could be negligent through misfeasance.

Malfeasance is the *improper performance of a duty* (Gifis, 1984). However, unlike misfeasance that is tied to a duty, *malfeasance is the performance of a totally unlawful act that interrupts the performance of a duty*. If a person is injured on a football field, you would be malfeasant if the person was moved from the field without checking to make sure the moving process would not worsen the injury. You have a duty to provide quality first aid assistance, but you do not have a right to seriously injure a person through failing to adhere to reasonable first aid procedures.

Nonfeasance is the failure to act, under conditions where you owe a person the duty to act (Gifis, 1984). Nonfeasance exists if a participant should have received instructions before engaging in the activity, and you failed to provide the instructions.

These three categories of negligent conduct can be broken down into further degrees of negligence. As discussed earlier in this chapter, an EA can be strictly liable for ultra-hazardous activities. Liability without fault is called *strict negligence*. Other degrees of negligence include gross negligence, negligence per se, ordinary and simple negligence.

Gross negligence is negligence slightly lower then strict negligence. While the care you exercise is not examined in a strict negligence case, gross negligence stems from *a total lack of care*. *Gross negligence is excessive negligence similar to wanton or willful misconduct* (Gifis, 1984). The failure to use even a slight degree of care prevents using contributory negligence as a defense for gross negligence (Gifis, 1984). Let's use our previous gymnastics coach example wherein the coach noticed the loose bolt on the gymnastic equipment. If the coach knew about the loose bolt, but decided not to fix or warn anybody about it because he felt, "nobody would get hurt," his actions would demonstrate gross negligence. Even if the injured athlete helped contribute to his own injury by playing on the equipment, the coach would still be liable due to his gross negligence. *Punitive damages* are often awarded in gross negligence cases because the EA failed to provide at least a minimum level of care. Furthermore, because gross negligence is considered so egregious, employees in states that offer immunity protection can lose that protection if they engaged in gross, willful or wanton misconduct (See generally Maryland Tort Claims Act of 1981 and van der Smissen, 1990).

As previously indicated, *negligence per se* is negligence as a matter of law. The negligent act is contrary to the law or so contrary to common prudence that a reasonably prudent person would not have acted in that manner. Thus, if a law provides that swimming pools need to be fenced-in, and no fence is erected, you could be liable under the negligence *per se* theory.

The two remaining levels of negligence are ordinary negligence and slight negligence. *Ordinary negligence* is the *failure to use ordinary care* (Gifis, 1984). *Slight negligence* is the *failure to use a great degree of care* (Gifis, 1984). Ordinary negligence is the failure to exercise the care an ordinary person would provide in the same situation. Slight negligence is the failure to exercise the care or vigilance that an extraordinarily prudent person would exercise. Ordinary negligence is the most common form of negligence. If you checked and repaired all the equipment, but failed to notice a slight problem that an extremely cautious EA would have found, you could be slightly negligent. Different levels of negligence are important in determining both the value of a plaintiff's damage award and how difficult it would be to defend the negligence claim.

Defenses to Negligence Claims

Even if plaintiffs can show the four required negligence components, they might not be able to prove negligence due to various defenses that can be raised against the negligence claim. The strongest defense that can be asserted by an EA, besides not owing a duty, is that *all reasonable steps that could have been taken to protect the individuals, were taken*. The key to defending a lawsuit is *proof* of reasonable conduct and one of the best forms of proof is documentation. To prove that all appropriate steps were taken you could produce evidence such as *inspection checklists that document a regular, timely, and complete inspection of the facility, event or equipment.* These factual components help demonstrate that no duty was breached.

If a person's injury is not considered an accident, you could still receive a defense verdict if any one of the four negligence components is missing. You would have to show that either:

- no duty was owed to the plaintiff,
- no duty was breached,
- the person was not injured/damaged,
- or the breached duty was not the proximate cause of any injury.

The absence of proximate cause is one of the most frequently used defenses because sports injuries are often the result of the injured person's own actions. The plaintiff could reduce or eliminate an EA's negligence by assuming the risk, avoiding warnings or continuing their actions in the face of hazardous conditions.

Assumption of Risk

You could show that a participant was on notice concerning the dangers involved, but the individual decided to assume the risks. To *assume the risk,* the person has to:

- have actual knowledge of the risky conditions,
- know it is dangerous,
- understand how dangerous it is,
- and they voluntarily expose themselves to the risk (see generally van der Smissen, 1990).

A person assumes the risk when he or she *voluntarily assumes all obvious and foreseeable risks* and *where the EA did not owe or breach his/her duty.* Using the gymnastics example, assume the gymnastics coach discovered the loose nut and moved the equipment to a secured repair area. The coach then filed a repair order, put a warning sign on the equipment and verbally warned each athlete about the danger. If an athlete sneaks into the gym, moves the equipment from the repair area and is injured using the defective equipment, the coach would not be liable. The coach fulfilled his duty, the gymnast had knowledge of the risky conditions, knew it was dangerous, understood how dangerous it was, but decided to proceed anyway on his or her own volition. Courts often use a Latin phrase to describe assumption of risk. The term used is *volenti non fit injuria* which means, whomever consents cannot receive an injury (Gifis, 1984). By using known, dangerous equipment, plaintiffs consent to the risk. If they are injured, they have no one to blame but themselves.

Assumption of risk is a complete bar to recovery so the plaintiff would recover nothing if you can prove all the components of assumption of risk (van der Smissen, 1990). The assumption of risk doctrine has been abolished in states with comparative negligence statutes so not every EA can use this defense (see below).

Expressed or implied assumption of risk refers to the method in which the plaintiff receives information about the event's possible dangers. *Express assumption of risk* can be contained in a *written* waiver or through a person's *oral* acknowledgment indicating his/her knowledge and willingness to accept a given risk. Even though an express oral assumption of risk is admissible in court, a person could claim that he/she did not assume the specific risk that injured him/her or he/she might have misunderstood your warning. Due to this potential evidentiary concern, all warnings should be in writing. Chapter 7 will go into more detail on express waivers.

Implied assumption of risk is established when the event participant or spectator is aware of the risk, but agrees to accept the risk and proceed with the activity. For the person to assume the risk, the risk has to be *so obvious* or so integral to the sport that *a reasonable person would have realized the risk. Assumption of risk's most important component is the fact that the individual voluntarily assumed the risk and was not coerced, pressured or in any other way influenced into accepting the risk.* Because peer pressure can be such a strong force for children, peer pressure can be used as a possible defense to a claim that a person voluntarily assumed a risk. Young participants should understand that engaging in dangerous conduct is grounds for being dismissed from the event and anybody caught trying to pressure someone else into doing something dangerous will also be dismissed.

California has established a two-tier system for analyzing assumption of risk cases. Primary assumption of risk applies to inherent risks in sports and an individual injured while being legally tackled in football by another player would be barred from suing the other player based on the primary assumption of risk defense. However, the California courts also established a secondary assumption of risk which is not a complete bar. Under the secondary assumption of risk theory, when an individual would otherwise have assumed a risk, that assumption becomes invalid when the person who contributed to or caused the injury owed the injured party a duty to protect them. In those cases, primary assumption of risk is replaced with comparative negligence (see below), where a jury can apportion liability on a percentage basis. A typical example could be a high school football coach who owes his players a duty to properly supervise and train them. Even if a player is injured by a fellow teammate and voluntarily participated in football, primary assumption of risk would not apply. Comparative negligence under the secondary assumption of risk would apply if the coach breached a duty owed to the injured player (Cronin, 1998).

Contributory/Comparative Negligence

If a person assumes the activity's risk in an *unreasonable manner,* then he/she could be barred from recovery under the contributory negligence theory. As with assumption of risk, the affirmative defense of *contributory negligence* has to be *both alleged and proven by you, the EA.* The defense of contributory negligence is a strong defense because if a court finds the individual contributorily negligent then the individual would not recover any damages (van der Smissen, 1990). A typical example of contributory negligence might providing a warning not to use a piece of equipment that is locked-up, but the person ignores the warning and uses the equipment. The difference between assumption of risk and contributory negligence is that in assumption of risk the plaintiff could act in a reasonable method, but gets injured from an assumed risk. However, in contributory negligence, the plaintiff acts in an unreasonable manner, thereby breaking the causal link between your duty and the injury's proximate cause. Thus, although you could have breached your duty to a plaintiff the plaintiff's own negligent actions are the real proximate cause of the injury. The harshness of the contributory negligence defense has been overcome in most states through the adoption of comparative negligence statutes.

Comparative negligence is derived from statutes while the courts establish contributory negligence. In states that have comparative negligence statutes, a person's liability is determined on a *percentage basis* (van der Smissen, 1990). Damages are appropriated according to percentage of fault. Under some statutes, *if the plaintiff is over 50 percent at fault, he/she recovers nothing.* Other jurisdictions just reduce plaintiff's award by the appropriate percentage, even if the plaintiff was 99 percent at fault. Therefore, if an injured participant received a jury award of $100,000, but the jury found him 90 percent liable for his own injuries, he would only recover $10,000. You should examine applicable state laws to determine which negligence defense standard applies in your jurisdiction.

An additional concern associated with comparative negligence is the concept of joint and severable liability. Many states are adopting joint and severable liability to replace an inadequacy in the law. Previously, if two or more defendants were found liable, they would all owe money to the plaintiff(s). However, some of the defendants might have no money. Thus, a major corporation could be minimally at fault, but as that corporation had the deep pocket, they would be responsible for a lion share of the damages. Under new laws passed in many states, defendants in comparative negligence cases will be jointly and severally liable (they all need to raise required damages between all defendants) for economic damages such as medical bills and lost wages. However, the defendants would only be liable for their own percentage of fault when noneconomic damages are established. Putting the following concept into an example can be analyzed if three defendants each helped produce a road race in which someone suffered an injury. The injured party suffered $100,000 in economic damages and $1,000,000 in noneconomic damages such a pain and suffering. All three defendants would be responsible for $33,333 of the economic damages. Assume that the jury found one defendant 90 percent at fault for the injury. That defendant would be responsible for $900,000 in noneconomic damages and the $33,333 in economic damages (California Civil Code, Section 1431.2(a)).

Other Acts

Another possible defense to a negligence claim is the occurrence of another act that discharges your duty. Your actions are not the proximate cause of a person's injury when the injury is caused by an *intervening act*. If a person is running laps over an uneven track and the person trips over his/her own untied shoe lace, the untied shoe lace (not the uneven track) could be the intervening cause that contributed to the fall.

There are many situations outside the scope of human control that can cause an accident and they are called *Acts of God*. For example, you cannot be held responsible for a sudden and unexpected wind storm or lightning storm that causes an injury. Similar to Acts of God are *sudden emergencies*, where the situation requires you to breach a duty to one person for the benefit of another person. If you have to run to prevent a drowning, and while running you trip over another patron, the circumstance would probably protect you from a suit by the person you tripped over.

Children

You should not feel overly secure in knowing you have a defense to a negligence claim because defenses can have exceptions. As with the higher duty owed to children, children also have special defenses. Children *under the age of seven* are normally *not responsible for their own negligence* (see generally van der Smissen, 1990). Children *between the age of seven and 13* are normally not responsible for their own negligence, but *the child could be considered negligent if he/she understood that he/she was doing something wrong* (Greenwald, 1980). To determine if a child acted reasonably, his/her conduct would be compared to a child of similar age, knowledge, experience and education. If young children might not be capable of acting negligently, they also cannot be capable of contributory negligence. Thus, a child that does not follow instructions and gets injured, can possibly avoid a contributory negligence defense because the child could not comprehend the warning. In addition to children, adults with low mental abilities and intoxicated individuals also can use the defense that they could not comprehend or understand the dangers they were facing.

Immunity

Immunity is another defense from liability for an individual or organization. When someone is immune from liability, they might act incorrectly, but because our society favors reduced restrictions on certain organizations and people, they would not be liable for their misdeed(s). The immunity protection afforded the President of the United States is a perfect example demonstrating the immunity concept. The scandal surrounding sexual harassment claims against President Clinton represent a challenge to the traditional immunity protection designed to insulate the President from private claims while serving as President. The President can be sued as an individual if his/her car hit someone. However, if the President makes an executive decision that adversely affects someone else, the injured person cannot sue the President. Thus, the President is immune from suits related to his/her job as president, but can be sued for his/her personal actions outside the presidency realm. The rationale behind immunity is that public service would be impossible if every decision opened the decision-maker to potential suits. Furthermore, most non-presidential related claims are also postponed until after the presidential term has expired. This delay allows the President to concentrate on running the country, rather than fighting lawsuits.

Immunity is established through three different means: statutorial, judicial or contractual means (van der Smissen, 1990). *Statutory or sovereign immunity* protects a *governmental unit* from being sued *while performing services for taxpayers*. Sovereign immunity serves the purpose of:

- protecting public funds,
- providing for smooth governmental operations,
- assuring protection for individuals doing work benefiting the public.

The current trend is to hold governmental agencies liable for their actions. However, sovereign immunity can only be abolished through statutes. *State Tort Claim Acts* in a number of states *rescind* or *limit state governmental immunity,* or limit the amount of monetary claims (see generally van der Smissen, 1990). You should check with an attorney to determine if your association or employment with a governmental unit can provide you with immunity. For example, Alabama has a statute that specifically precludes any lawsuit against the state, no matter what claim might otherwise be available (see generally van der Smissen, 1990). However, state employees can still be sued if they violate certain rules and the violation of those rules injures someone (see generally van der Smissen, 1990). It should also be noted again that immunity normally only applies to acts of simple negligence, not willful or wanton behavior.

Some courts have extended immunity to organizations that are providing services for the community. Nonprofit organizations that provided services to the injured person were once given significant immunity protection by the courts. However, the *charitable immunity* defense has lost favor in most states. Currently, only several states still accept the charitable immunity defense as a complete or partial/limiting defense (van der Smissen, 1990).

Contractual immunity can be established through waivers or consent agreements where a person contractually agrees to hold you immune for any injuries that might occur. These waivers are analyzed using contract law principles. In order for contractual defenses to work, the contract has to be valid. Thus, courts could examine the bargaining position of the contracting parties or whether a party received something of value for giving up their right to sue (called *consideration* in legalese).

Besides organizational immunity, an individual's actions could also be protected through their status as public officials. *Official immunity* is the personal immunity accorded a public official *while performing his/her official duties.* To determine whether or not an employee is covered by official immunity, courts examine:

- the employee's job,
- the employee's function,
- the extent to which the governmental agency pursues the employee's function,
- the degree of governmental control over the employee's work,
- whether or not the negligence stems from a decision requir-

ing judgment or discretion (see generally van der Smissen, 1990).

The last component of this analysis is usually the most important element for determining individual immunity coverage. A decision that requires judgment or discretion is the decision whether or not to hold an event. Decisions that are not immune are normally based on established rules, and if you fail to follow the rules, you can lose your immunity protection.

Administrative personnel are only immune for *discretionary acts, not ministerial acts* (see generally van der Smissen, 1990). A *discretionary act* requires the exercise of *judgment and choice*. Thus, high level policy decisions at the planning level (i.e. whether or not to hold an event) are immune unless you engage in willful or wanton negligence. On the other hand, *ministerial acts* are simple, defined duties, like the checking and maintenance of equipment. For an act to be considered ministerial, the manner in which the act has to be performed has to be a well-established standard, violate state or federal laws or violate express policy statements. You are not immune from liability for negligently performing ministerial acts, *even if the acts are performed in good faith*. Supervision is one activity that is considered a ministerial function. The following complex case helps show the logic behind the immunity defense and why certain individuals do not receive immunity.

Larson v. Independent School District No. 314, Braham
289 N.W. 2d 112 (MN 1979)

On April 12, 1971 Steven Larson, was injured while performing a headspring over a rolled mat. The headspring drill was considered a "high danger drill" and a young, inexperienced instructor was incorrectly supervising the drill. Instead of straddling the rolled up mat, the instructor was standing near the mat and could not prevent the injury. The school principal was also sued on the theory of failure to reasonably administer the curriculum. The principal provided the instructor with the curriculum guide, which highlighted the physical education guidelines. The court concluded that due to the instructor's inexperience, the jury could reasonably have believed the principal should have utilized closer supervision.

In analyzing the immunity issue, the Minnesota's Supreme Court determined that under the state's immunity theory, state officials are not absolutely immune from suits, but could be liable in performance of ministerial, rather than discretionary duties. The court defined discretionary decision making as decisions made at the planning level, not the performance level. The judgment by the physical education instructor, in how to spot and teach advanced gymnastics exercise, was not decision making entitled to protection under the doctrine of discretionary immunity. Thus, the instructor was liable for his negligent spotting. The court also concluded that by avoiding his responsibility to supervise the instructor, the principal was not engaged in decision making at the planning level. Thus, the principal might not have been protected by discretionary immunity.

As seen in the *Larson* case, individuals who do the actual work are not the only ones who might not benefit from immunity protection. Another case where a school principal lost his immunity protection occurred in *Vargo v. Svitchen,* below.

Vargo v. Svitchen
301 N.W. 2d 1 (MI 1980)

In 1973, 15-year old high school student, Gregory Vargo, reported to a weight training session required for football tryouts. At the coaches' urging, Vargo pushed himself beyond his limits and was very seriously injured while lifting 250-300 pounds. The Michigan Court of Appeals analyzed Michigan's statutory immunity laws which provided in part that, "all governmental agencies shall be immune from tort liability in all cases wherein the government agency is engaged in the exercise or discharge of a governmental function." The court extended the immunity coverage to a school principal if the principal was engaged in discretionary, not ministerial, decision making. The court went on to look at the definition of the two terms. From analyzing other cases, the court concluded that a ministerial officer has a line of conduct marked out for him, and he has nothing to do but follow the instructions. Even though a principal has supervisory power, he/she has to follow certain guidelines to minimize student injuries, and by failing to follow those guidelines, the principal can lose his/her immunity. Because the principal encouraged, pressured, and intimidated Vargo to lift heavy weights without inquiring into his training or capabilities, the principal was not protected by governmental immunity.

Conclusion

If you are being sued, the most likely charge that will be faced is a charge of negligence. This charge can be avoided if you can identify the duty owed to individuals at the event, how could those duties be breached, what could be the proximate cause of breaching those duties and what injuries could occur. With these concepts in mind, you can take a proactive approach to running an event. A proactive approach is designed to eliminate any potential legal hurdles before they trip you. By carefully analyzing the duties presented in this guide, you will become more familiar with potential safety risks and take the required actions necessary to have an enjoyable, liability free, sporting event.

This section was designed to be a primer for the legal novice. No attempt has been made to make you a legal expert. The goal was to give you some terms and definitions to help make the legal language more manageable. If you feel intimidated by all the potential legalese in sports law, there is potential solace around the corner. For years legal writing has prided itself on using large words and fancy language, which is often unnecessary. Currently there is a trend to return legal writing to basic English and that is also the author's goal. However, a legal dictionary is a worthwhile investment and can help clarify any questions you might have. You should always remember that this guide is not a substitute for an attorney.

To help you appreciate the legal process and the terms contained therein, the following represents a brief narrative describing a negligence claim and the legal process pursued from the injury through the case's ultimate conclusion.

Detailed rules specify the how, when, and where questions associated with bringing a lawsuit. These rules differ in each court and are often very complex. An example provides the best method of discussing the structure and processes involved in a lawsuit. The following is a fictitious example of such a case. Sarah Jones was a high school student and interscholastic basketball star in New Haven, Connecticut. While playing in a sanctioned interscholastic event, Jones attempted to slam dunk the ball, but slipped on a water puddle. Jones tore her knee ligaments. She incurred over $10,000 in medical bills, missed the remainder of the volleyball season, lost $4,000 from not being able to work and missed her chance to possibly receive a basketball scholarship from the University of New Haven.

After Jones left the hospital, her father set up an interview with a lawyer to discuss their legal options. The lawyer was Ruth Smith, a young lawyer just out of law school. Smith asked numerous questions and discovered from Mr. Jones that he heard one coach tell a official immediately after the accident that the school had failed to mop the floor prior to the match and the roof had been leaking for over two months. Utilizing her legal prowess, Smith thought she had a great negligence case and accepted the Jones as clients.

Smith initially performed research and discovered that the likely parties that should be sued included the school, the school district, the volleyball officials, the athletic director, the coach, and the high school athletic association. Jones, who brought the suit to recover her damages, was called the *plaintiff* while all parties being sued were called *defendants*. Jones and all the defendants lived or operated in Connecticut. Because there was no federal question, or litigants from different states, Smith's only option was to bring the suit in a Connecticut state court. Based on the medical expenses and potential future damages, Smith had to bring the case in a specific court with proper jurisdiction.

Smith remembered that special rules applied whenever a governmental entity is sued. Thus, after some initial research, Smith filed a *governmental claim* against the school district. Smith filed the claim specifically to avoid a statute of limitations issue. The *statute of limitation* required the suit to be filed within a certain time period, or Jones would have been forever barred from filling suit. *Each state has their own rules concerning filing a claim against the state. These governmental claim rules are designed to provide the state with notice it might be sued. Some states require the filing of a claim while others allow a party just to name the state in a lawsuit.*

Smith prepared a *complaint* which described key facts available to Jones and provided enough information for the opposing side to know why they were being sued. The complaint specifically identified all known defendants, the reason why jurisdiction was proper and a statement setting forth what remedies Jones demanded. Smith had a specified amount of time within which she had to serve the defendants with a copy of the complaint that she had already filed with the chosen court. Smith was required to personally serve each defendant with the complaint. Some states allow a party to mail a complaint or to serve the complaint through a sheriff. A complaint indicates the title of the case, identifies all the parties, designates in which court the case is being filed and tells the story of the dispute in a specified legal form.

Within a specified time after receiving the complaint, the defendants filed an *answer* indicating why they were not liable for Jones' injuries. Along with their answer, the defendants served Jones (through her attorney) with several discovery requests. *Discovery* was used as a means to find out what Jones knew about the incident and her damages. The discovery requests included a request to produce all relevant documents in Jones' possession such as medical bills, a request to admit certain facts such as admitting she did not miss any work or she did not receive lower grades as a result of the injury ("Request for Admissions"), specific questions such as her age, her address or if she has a driver's license (called interrogatories) and a request to take Jones' deposition. Smith responded by serving similar discovery requests on all the defendants. Jones was required to attend a *deposition* where she had to answer numerous questions, under oath, asked by the defendants' attorneys. Smith had the right to request the same types of discovery from the defendants. Discovery is the process used to discover information about the opposing parties in a suit. Answers have to be given under oath or the penalty of perjury. Additional discovery tools not specifically addressed above could include: a request to inspect the gym, an independent medical examination of Jones and possibly an independent psychological evaluation if Jones was claiming severe or extreme emotional distress.

After several months of discovery, the defendants filed a *motion for summary judgment*. Summary judgment motions are brought when a party concludes that as a matter of law the undisputed facts are in their favor and they should win without having to go to trial. These motions are solely based on applicable case law and the facts uncovered through the discovery process. The judge determined that there were still issues of facts that were in dispute and as such, the judge denied defendants' summary judgment motion. The parties tried to settle the case, but when they were unable to reach a mutually acceptable settlement, they started preparing for trial. Both sides obtained witnesses on their own behalf. The court chose a trial date which was approximately two years after Jones was first injured. Summary judgment is one of several possible pre-trial motions. Other such motions include a demurrer, motion to sever, motion to strike, motion to remove for lack of subject matter jurisdiction and other motions which attack the complaint or require the production of requested discovery material. Such motions are brought when, as a matter of law, one party is or should be required to alter its case. For example, an injured high school athlete might have suffered a great injury, but due to governmental immunity bestowed to the high school principal, the principal could bring a summary judgment motion to be dismissed from the case as a matter of law.

Smith thought the facts favored her client. Her client made a good witness. Thus, Jones demands a trial by *jury*. The plaintiff in a civil case always has the choice of whether or not he/she wants a jury. The twelve member jury was required to decide who was telling the truth and ultimately what were the facts. Each side prepared trial memorandum explaining its case and provided the memorandum to the judge. After resolving some disputes concerning what evidence would be allowed at trial, the judge allowed the parties to pick a jury. Utilizing a process called *voire dire*, each side interviewed prospective jurors and had the right to dismiss all biased jurors or a limited number of jurors that they just did not want. The size and role of a jury vary in different states. Some juries only examine facts or certain components of a case while other juries are responsible for analyzing all facts and determining damages.

Smith provided an eloquent *opening statement* which Perry Mason would have envied. The defendants also had a strong opening statement on their own behalf. The trial proceeded with Smith calling Sarah as the first witness. After answering all the questions asked by Smith, Jones was *cross-examined* by defendants' attorneys who were attempting to refute Jones' testimony or highlight any inconsistencies. Jones' father was a *fact witness* because he had specific facts concerning the accident and injuries. Both sides also acquired the services of *expert witnesses* to testify about the standard of care for schools, doctors to testify about Jones' injuries and several high school volleyball coaches. The trial continued with each side presenting its witnesses and the other side having the opportunity to cross-examine each witness. Documentary evidence was also introduced by each side. Throughout the trial, each side repeatedly made *objections* to certain questions or the introduction of some evidence. The judge was forced to determine, as a matter of law, which side was correct and which questions or evidence were legally allowable. *The plaintiff always presents his/her case first in civil cases.*

Each side concluded its questioning and then made its final *closing statement*. The closing statements provided a summary of the facts and law expoused by each side during the trial. The jury was given specific instructions by the judge concerning the law and how the jury was to apply the facts to the law. Based on the evidence presented, the jury returned a verdict in Jones' favor. The jury awarded Jones $14,000 for *actual lost damages* (medical expenses) and $20,000 for *pain and suffering*. The lost scholarship was too speculative, thus, the jury was barred from awarding damages for that loss.

The defendants were not happy with the jury's conclusion. The defendants' attorneys knew they could not challenge the jury's evidentiary conclusion, but felt the judge gave the jury an incorrect instruction concerning the school's duty to Jones. The judge could have overturned the jury's decision if the judge felt it was not supported by law or the facts. However, the judge affirmed the jury's decision. Defendants filed a *notice of appeal* which is the first step in the appeals process. Each side was required to submit a "brief" that outlined its legal analysis and then argue its case in front of three appellate judges. The appellate court, after carefully reviewing the lower court's actions, determined that the lower court made a *procedural mistake* in using an incorrect jury instruction. Therefore, the appellate court *remanded* (sent back) the case to the lower court to retry the case using the correct instruction. The number of judges hearing an appeal varies in different courts. An appellate court can remand a case, uphold the lower court's decision or overturn the lower court's decision.

Before the new trial began, the sides reached a *settlement* in which the school paid Jones $18,000. By the time Jones finally settled the case, she was in college and three years had elapsed since she brought the suit. The appellate court's reasoning was published in the state's official case registry and became precedence for any future cases dealing with the appropriate jury instruction to give concerning a school's duty to its students. However, from reading the published appellate court's decision, a reader would not know that the case was settled once it was remanded to the lower court. The appellate court report only indicated that it was remanding the case to be retried. Rarely does one discover what happens to cases because most lower court decisions are not officially published (see below). Furthermore, most cases are settled and the settlement terms are often confidential. While Jones' fictitious case went to trial, it is estimated that less than five percent of all cases filed ever reach a trial (Fried, 1998). Most cases are either dismissed prior to trial, settled or defeated through summary judgment or other defensive maneuvers.

Only state appellate and state Supreme Court cases are officially published. All Federal cases are published. Cases are commonly found in the following reporters: Federal District Court cases can be found in Federal Supplement volumes (cases are cited using the initials "F. Supp."), Federal Appellate cases can be found in the Federal Reporter ("F." or "F.2d" which is the second volume of Federal Reporters), U.S. Supreme Court cases can be found in three different reporters-United States Supreme Court Reports ("U.S."), Supreme Court Reporter ("S. Ct."), and Supreme Court Reports, Lawyer's Edition ("L. Ed."). Nine different reporters exists for various state courts or regional groupings of courts. These cases are found in the following reporters: Atlantic Reporter ("A." or "A. 2d"), Northeastern Reporter ("N.E." or "N.E. 2d."), Northwestern Reporter ("N.W." or "N.W. 2d."), Pacific Reporter ("P." or "P. 2d."), Southeastern Reporter ("S.E." or "S.E. 2d."), Southern Reporter ("So." or "So. 2d."), Southwestern Reporter ("S.W." or "S.W. 2d."), New York Supplement ("N.Y.S."), or California Reporter ("Cal.Rptr.").

Chapter 4

Risk Management

The safety management process highlighted throughout this text is called risk management. Risk management means that most, if not all, hazardous conditions can be managed in such a way that the potential for harm or lawsuits is significantly reduced. Similar to the management issues faced by any business, risk management requires analyzing priorities, personnel, time constraints, financial constraints, organizational resources, government regulations, association standards, and countless other internal and external environmental constraints. However, similar to a business manager, the person responsible for risk management activities is required to balance all these variables to make the event as safe as possible and to prevent injury, but also to possibly save money, avoid litigation or comply with insurance requirements. The rationale for implementing a comprehensive risk management program is the basis behind the "front headlines test" and the "ECT" approaches advocated by the author.

The "front headlines test" is a simple process by which an individual can identify potential legal concerns and develop effective procedures or tactics to minimize or eliminate risks that the media would love to report. Ask all your associates to examine their actions prior to undertaking any activity to determine how such activity would look if it was reported on the front page of a major newspaper. While saving someone's life would look great on the front page, sexually harassing a subordinate employee or not providing reasonable accommodations to a disabled patron would help destroy an organization's image.

Another useful risk management tool is the "ECT" approach. By remembering the simple ECT approach you can conceptualize the entire risk management process. The ECT approach first requires deflECTing liability to others. Through waivers, releases, contract or indemnity clauses, liability should be moved from your shoulders to someone else's shoulders. After you deflECT liability, you have to reflECT on your risk management objective. Why do you want to implement a risk management program? Is your goal only to save some money or are you trying to save lives? ReflECT could entail preparing risk management manuals, educational materials or a pre-event safety conference. After you finish reflECTing, you have to inspECT your program and facilities. The inspECTion has to be conducted in a manner that you can detECT potential dangers. After detECTing all potential hazards, you have to once again reflECT on what has been seen and write down your observations. Write down the name of who did the inspection, when the inspection was conducted, what was found and who should be responsible for correcting the hazard. After reflECTing on what had been found, you have to make sure that someone corrECTs the hazards. CorrECTion could be accomplished by repairing the problem, posting warning signs or blocking access to the area. After the corrECTions had been performed, it is time to re-inspECT the hazard. It is not unusual for someone to claim they have corrECTed a problem when in fact they might have worsened the situation or created an all new hazard. Thus, you have to follow-up to make sure all hazards have been addressed. Lastly, you should take a photograph of facilities before and after events. A picture is worth a thousand words. If a dispute ever arises concerning facility set-up or related issues, the photograph can provide useful information in showing that a potential hazard was not there prior to the event starting or that the equipment/facility was not set-up in the manner claimed by the plaintiff.

No matter what risk management technique you use, and there are countless variations available, the key to all such plans is planning. The following represent the highlights of a plan developed by Joseph B. McCullough and published in 1995 in the URMIA Journal (University Risk Management and Insurance Association). The plan focused on a university's response to a catastrophic event such as a student death. Athletics and sports was the number one cause for catastrophic events with the leading activities being rugby, sailing, football, basketball and swimming/diving (McCullough, 1995). The first key highlighted for responding to a catastrophic event is communication. All key persons such as a university president, university counsel, public relation officials, etc. need to be immediately notified as well as all possible insurers. Some insurance policies specifically deny coverage if they are not informed about a catastrophic incident/claim within a set number of hours after the incident/claim arose. This is due to the fact that the insurance company would want to possibly send its own investigators to the site to conduct its own analysis.

A liaison has to be appointed to directly contact the injured/deceased person's family. Such a task is a very difficult task, especially if the next of kin/parents/guardians are in a different state or country. The family members should have all transportation arrangements made with their input, but the university should pay the transportation and accommodation costs. The liaison should coordinate all medical care and act on behalf of the family members. If the student is deceased, then the liaison should coordinate any disposition of the body with the family members. The liaison should not coordinate an autopsy unless specifically agreed to by the family members. Some religions prohibit the desecration of the body after death and the family members might oppose such a procedure. That is why fast and thorough communication is critical. If an autopsy was performed on someone without the family's permission, the family could then possibly bring a new claim of emotional distress associated with the unauthorized autopsy.

The communication process goes even further with the liaison being responsible for any and all communications with the family members. For example, the family should not be sent letters concerning overdue books or unpaid parking fees. The liaison could also coordinate communication with crisis counselors for students, staff and the community.

Besides the liaison, an individual needs to be responsible for securing all necessary documentation and evidence. Any signed waivers, referee notes, inspection logs, athletic equipment or whatever is available should be kept. A list of all critical information should be developed in advance to ensure you keep the right information. For example any newspaper articles about the weather should be kept. Any film footage shot by local or national television coverage, including local news teams, should be obtained.

A good risk management plan would also include a communication strategy to deal with the media. Only one designated individual should speak with the media. That individual should be trained to provide specific, objective facts rather than subjective opinions. The media will always accept an answer such as "I do not know, but I will look into that questions and hope to have an answer by tomorrow morning." Such a comment could not be attacked in the same manner that a "no comment" statement could be perceived when aired on the news.

As highlighted by some of the strategies suggested by McCullogh, the key to a successful risk management program revolves around communication and documentation. Documentation means more than writing something down. Documentation requires the utilization of all the elements in the communication process from encoding, worrying about noise, sending the message, choosing the proper channel, reception by the listener, decoding the message and any relevant feedback (Zikmund and d'Amico, 1996). Appendix B is an Incident Reporting Manual developed for the Houston Park and Recreation Department. This manual highlight some of the key communication forms and strategies that should be considered by any event facing a multitude of different risk related concerns.

In addition to the need for accurate communication, the diverse concerns that need to be covered by a risk management program are also highlighted by the need to communicate with a multitude of parties from family members to the media. The media should always play an important part in a risk management program as negative media attention can destroy an event and the people involved in producing, running and sponsoring the event.

Chapter 5

Event Director and Committee

During litigation, one key issue addressed from the very beginning is responsibility. Responsibility forms the basis for America's favorite activity—blaming. Blaming is an important part of the American business culture as individuals try to point blame at one another to avoid liability. Similarly, defendants want to point the blame at someone else to reduce or avoid liability. If an event administrator can shift event responsibility onto someone else, he/she could reduce his/her own potential liability. Therefore, the first question to ask in determining whether or not to hold a sport event, is who is going to be responsible for the event? The second question would be—what can someone be liable for when running an event. This chapter focuses on those individuals or entities that develop and execute an event. Chapter 6 will focus on what specific managerial issues can lead to liability concerns.

Events do not just "happen." It would be impossible to have a tournament, for example, with no one organizing or sponsoring the event. The four major categories of possible event organizers are:

- government agencies,
- non-profit organizations,
- businesses,
- individual citizens.

Government Agencies

Numerous government agencies conduct various sports events either to benefit the public or the agency's own employees. Government agencies can include public schools, athletic departments, park and recreation departments, government sports agencies and other government affiliates. If the event sponsor is a government agency, the sponsor and the individuals involved might be immune from tort liability (See Chapter 3). To receive governmental immunity the agency has to be acting and performing its function to benefit its constituency. You should always remember that *a government agency can lose its immunity if it makes a profit from an event* that is not reinvested back into programs to benefit the general public (see generally van der Smissen, 1990).

The public benefit nature of an agency can be altered when the agency charges a fee for the event. When a government agency charges an *incidental fee* for an event that contributes to the public health and welfare, the agency would still be performing its governmental function. Typically, incidental fees are charged when ordinary tax dollars received by the agency are insufficient to support the event, and all the money raised by the fee is utilized for running the event or other governmental functions.

However, the public benefit nature is lost, and a *proprietary function* is entered into when the event is designed to generate profit or generate other non-public benefits. By performing a traditional for-profit business function, instead of a governmental function, the agency could be liable in the same manner as a for-profit business.

Even if you are not a government employee you could still receive governmental immunity based on the status of the facility owner. Thus, immunity *might* extend to a tennis tournament director if the event is held on public land, public assistance is used to help run the event and/or the event benefits the community. A government agency can also be immune from liability for accidents on its premises even if the event is not administered by the agency. The *Thompson v. U.S.* case represent a perfect example of this concept.

Thompson v. U.S.
592 F. 2d 1104 (9th Cir. 1979)

Mr. Thompson was injured during a European-style scramble motorcycle race on federally owned land. The Bureau of Land Management granted a permit to the Sportsman Racing Association for a race on Federal land. Thompson claimed that his injuries were caused by the defective racetrack and negligent spectator control. There was a dispute as to whether Thompson had his accident in response to a spectator running across the track or his own maneuvering to pass another racer. But the issue before the court was whether or not the Federal government was immune from liability.

The court held that the U.S. Government, as the landowner, was immune from liability for the injuries where the negligence claim resulted after the event sponsor took possession of the land. The decision was based on the fact that the Bureau of Land Management did not supervise the race and the permit language clearly indicated that the sponsor was responsible for public safety and race supervision. The Federal employee was also immune, as the issuing of the permit by the employee was determined to be a discretionary act on a planning or policy level and not a ministerial act on the operational level.

In summation,whenever a government entity undertakes to produce an event, careful planning requires analyzing how much will be charged and who is in control of the premises or event in order to be properly covered by government immunity statutes.

Nonprofit Organizations

Athletic events are frequently administered by *nonprofit organizations* dedicated to promoting or providing a public service for the community's benefit. An organization's nonprofit status is not determined by the amount of money they make, rather by the characterization of their ownership and/or services. Typically, charitable organizations are characterized by their 501 (c)(3) nonprofit status and a board of director comprised of various concerned citizens. However, nonprofit organizations can also be developed by for-profit organizations. Some typical nonprofit organizations that sponsor or produce sports events include churches, private hospitals, private schools, private universities and medical research organizations.

In a limited number of states, nonprofit organizations could be immune from tort liability under the theory of *charitable immunity* (van der Smissen, 1990). The charitable immunity defense was used approximately half a century ago in the *Southern Methodist University v. Clayton* case.

Southern Methodist University v. Clayton
176 S.W. 2d 749 (TX 1943)

This case involved injuries to Mrs. Clayton when she fell from a temporary bleacher that collapsed during the 1940 Southern Methodist University and Texas A & M college football game. Clayton claimed that the University was negligent in allowing the stands to be filled beyond their normal capacity, in failing to sufficiently brace the bleachers and in constructing the bleachers with old and defective material. The court concluded that if the University was required to pay damages, money dedicated to charitable purposes would be used to pay the damages, thus depriving the University's benefits to the public. The public charities liability exception rested not on the status of the person injured (business invitee), but rather upon the public benefit provided by the University.

During the past several decades the charitable immunity defense has been severely reduced by several state court decisions or legislation. Texas no longer allows the charitable immunity defense (see generally van der Smissen, 1990). However, in a 1976 Little League case, a New Jersey court upheld the theory of charitable immunity.

Pomeroy v. Little League Baseball of Collingswood
362 A. 2d 39 (NJ 1976)

Mrs. Pomeroy was injured while watching her son play in a Little League baseball game. While watching the game, the bleachers under Pomeroy collapsed. The charter of the league stated that the goal of the league was to teach sportsmanship, loyalty, courage and other traits that benefit the community. New Jersey had a charitable immunity statute that covered the baseball league because the league was formed exclusively for educational purposes. Pomeroy was barred from recovery because at the time of the accident, she was a beneficiary of the league's charitable work.

While nonprofit immunity is hard to find, nonprofit organizations have a strong advantage over many other organizations and that benefit is image. Some people feel that nonprofit organizations do not have money, feel bad about suing an entity that promotes public good and/or some people or businesses/attorneys might not sue a nonprofit organization for fear of negative publicity. While image will not stop all potential suits, it can prevent some. A nonprofit organization should not rely upon either charitable immunity or image, they should undertake aggressive risk management education, purchasing insurance and all other appropriate risk management strategies.

Businesses and Individuals

For-profit organizations or individual EAs are subject to liability without having the ability to plead statutory or charitable immunity. The major difference between for-profit organizations and individual EAs administering an event is the extent of liability for each party.

A negligent for-profit *corporation* could be liable only to the extent that the judgment would be paid from corporate assets, and not personal assets. However, an *unincorporated EA or a business partnership* could have to satisfy a judgment with partnership assets and/or personal assets. Assume Acme Corporation sponsors a marathon where one of the participants is injured due to Acme's negligence. Acme's major stock owner, Mr. Big Bucks, is worth $100 million. However, Acme itself as a corporation, only has $1 million in assets. The injured participant could potentially receive a maximum of $1 million, the total amount of the corporate assets. This example assumes Acme does not carry liability insurance. The example also assumes that the corporation is operating as a legitimate corporation, following all appropriate corporate laws. If the corporation failed to follow all necessary laws, the corporate veil could be pierced and Mr. Bucks could then face a claim against his personal assets.

On the other hand, if Ms. Jane Doe or a partnership of Mr. Jones and Ms. Johnson sponsor an event, they do not have the protection of the "corporate shield." Without the protection of the corporate shield, they might have to satisfy a legal judgment with both their business and personal assets. If the partnership has $10,000 after an event and is sued for $20,000, the additional $10,000 in damages might have to be paid from the partner's own personal property.

A *risk/benefit analysis* is the most effective method to help decide who should sponsor an event. The benefits of a government agency sponsoring an event include the immunity defense, possible free facility use, additional government support, manpower, etc. However, possible disadvantages include having to follow strict rules, strict financial reporting requirements and bureaucratic headaches. If a choice is available, the risk/benefit analysis is the only effective way to help decide who should run the event. If no choice is available then the risk/benefit analysis is still helpful in determining whether or not to hold the event.

Once the event sponsor is determined, then you have to make sure everyone that is, or may get involved with the event knows who is running the event. The importance of letting people know who is in charge is essential for providing protection to other organizations that might be affiliated with the event. This is especially important with the huge impact sponsorship dollars are having on sporting events. For example, a big bank might be willing to pay the event managers a large sum to be the title sponsor (naming the event the "X Bank Triathlon"), but they are also interested in not exposing themselves to potential liability. If an event sponsor provides the event managers with financial, marketing or other resources, that is normally the extent to which they want to be involved with the event. The extent to which a sponsor or an EA are involved with an event should be specifically set forth in the sponsorship agreement. However, in addition to ensuring that the event sponsor knows his/her contractual responsibility, you have to make sure the sponsor executes his/her contractual obligations. In the following case a school allowed an organization to use the school grounds and assisted in some of the event preparation. However, the school failed to follow through with all the support services promised and this led to a lawsuit against the school.

Augustus v. Joseph A. Craig Elementary School
459 So. 2d 665 (LA 1984)

Six-year-old Jasmin Augustus was injured at an after-school event partially sponsored by the school. The school closed at 3:00 p.m. and all gates to the school were locked at 3:15 p.m. However, on the day in question, the Tambourine and Fan Club held a track event on the school grounds after school ended. The club had the permission of the school board and the principal to use the premises. The school teachers distributed flyers to the students informing the parents that the club, and not the school supervised the event. The flyer indicated that tight supervision would be provided. Augustus and a friend returned to the school at 3:30 p.m. to participate in the practice. When they arrived, the gates were open. Some children were playing with a tetherball set, but no supervisors were visible. While waiting for the event to start, some children turned over the tether ball set which had a rubber tire, filled with cement, as its base. While the children were rolling the cement-filled tire base on the ground, other children were jumping over the base. Unfortunately, Augustus fell while trying to jump over the base and the base rolled over his head.

The court concluded that even though the club ran the event, the fact that the school gave the club permission to use the facility and the flyer stated that there would be supervision made the school responsible for supervising the event.

If you are a school principal or a member of the school board and you allow another organization to use your premises, you should make sure the organization explicitly accepts all the duties of inspection, maintenance, supervision and assumption of all liability. Any confusion over who is involved in the event has to be settled when the event is planned to ensure that accountability is placed with the appropriate organizations or individuals. Any event co-sponsors, event sponsor, event managers and others affiliated with an event should sign a detailed written contracts stating exactly:

- who are the event managers,
- who owes what duties,

- who is responsible for what activities,
- who is liable for breaching a given duty or responsibility.

Several sample contract can be found in the Appendix C.

Event Type

Once the event sponsor is identified, you have to determine the type of event to run. There are countless events that can be run. The first question that has to be asked is whether or not the event is designed to be a highly competitive event for skilled athletes or an enjoyable, fun, intra-family competition. If the event is a highly skilled competition for world-class athletes, there could be a lower demand for supervision. Conversely, if the event is a company picnic, more supervision and management might be required to prevent harm to a wide variety of individuals. The main issue to remember is that children are owed the highest duty of care and that a different duty level applies to each participant or spectator depending on their age, maturity, experience, etc. Thus, if many different age groups are present at the event you would owe each age group a different level of protection ranging from a lower level for adults through a high level for children.

Many EAs have a fear of "overmanaging" an event and/or taking so many precautions that the event might lose some of its excitement. However, normally the only excitement that is lost is the excitement of an injury. Most spectators at a basketball game want to see the game, they are not interested in being in the middle of "excitement" during a fight between rowdy fans. By effectively managing risks at an event, the event will normally run more smoothly, and if people feel safe, they will enjoy themselves even more. If "overmanaging" an event scares you, you should remember the cliché that, "it is better to be safe than sorry." Lowering the risks does not necessarily lower the excitement, but it will benefit you in the courtroom.

Deciding on an Event

The following checklist presents some concerns you should examine in deciding what event to produce.

Participant Concerns:

1) the participant's age,
2) the participant's sex,
3) the participant's weight,

4) the participant's dexterity,
5) the participant's skills,
6) the previous competitive experience to which individuals could be exposed.

Activity Concerns:

1) the sport or activity's difficulty,
2) the number of event sites used and the distance between them,
3) the facility's adequacy for the activity,
4) the need to modify or alter the facility,
5) the facility's design,
6) the activity's inherent danger, if any,
7) the equipment required.

Management Concerns:

1) the supervision required,
2) the number of volunteers required,
3) whether trained volunteers and EAs are available,
4) whether adequate funds are available,
5) whether adequate insurance coverage is available and at what cost,
6) the event's location,
7) the facility's adequacy for spectators,
8) the security required,
9) whether adequate parking spaces, restrooms and other required amenities (i.e. locker rooms, etc.) are available.

The event facility's condition is obviously an important concern. In the specific event chapters to follow, a more complete analysis will be provided concerning proper facility usage. However, one area of event administration that is often overlooked is the use of multiple facilities and the transportation of individuals from one event area to another. This is appearing more frequently due to the popularity of multi-sport events such as triathlons, and the deterioration of older sports facilities. More complete information will be provided in the Transportation chapter (Chapter 29), but one case will be highlighted at the present time to help illustrate the point.

———————

Foster v. Houston General Insurance Co.

407 So. 2d 759 (LA 1982)

In 1977, Robert Foster was a 17-year-old mentally retarded student chosen for his school's Special Olympics basketball team. Only one assistant coach was walking with the group of students to a gymnasium three blocks away. On the way to the gym, Foster impulsively ran into the street. He saw a car coming and tried to stop, but he slipped and was hit by the car. Foster died three days later. The court concluded that the participant's mental condition required the use of additional supervisors. The head coach, who did not go with the team, was found negligent for failing to see that the group was accompanied by a sufficient number of supervisory personnel and breached a duty by failing to select the safest route to the basketball gym. The coach should have used the route that would expose the students to the fewest traffic hazards.

You have to make sure the chosen facility and any adjacent area are reasonably safe. For example, a road-running race should not be chosen if the race route would require using roads with blind curves, potholes and loose gravel. If an event is being held for senior citizens, and a lot of walking between sites is required, there is a potential risk of fatigue. The risk associated with fatigued participants should encourage EAs to change the event, provide transportation or hold events closer together.

Another example may be a parking lot that would need to be used at night. If the parking lot's lighting is inadequate, a person could claim that a reasonable EA would not have used the site for a night event, should have improved the lighting, or should have hired extra security personnel. Similarly, holding an event in a high crime area could unnecessarily expose individuals to criminal activity. These are just some of the concerns which help influence whether or not to hold an event, the type/structure of the event and the facility to be used for the event.

This guide encourages a *proactive approach to running events*. A proactive approach would include analyzing all the surrounding conditions and circumstances before deciding to run an event. All local facilities capable of hosting an event should be inspected. All possible support services have to be examined to ensure adequate volunteers, maintenance, safety support, etc. By taking a proactive approach most problems can be eliminated. Facility risk management planning is an integral component in proper event planning. If you plan an event, and then decide to find a facility, you might have to compromise some safety concerns in order to fit the facility into the event, instead of fitting the event into the facility.

Event Director and Committees

Once a commitment to hold an event has been made, one person should be chosen or appointed as the directing EA. The *directing EA* should coordinate all the individuals working to produce the event. Ultimate responsibility normally lies with the directing EA so the person chosen for this position has to thoroughly understand the event and the risk involved. If you are that person, you have to be concerned with such issues as:

- the event's size,
- the event's operational scope,
- how many event workers/volunteers would be required,
- what training and supervision is required for event workers,
- the event site,
- numerous administrative issues discussed in the next chapter.

To assist you in handling the various event components, you should recruit committees for various managerial activities. Two committees that *should* be mandatory for all events are an *event safety committee* and an *event personnel committee*.

A risk management supervisor, responsible for total event safety should manage the *event safety (or risk management) committee*. The term "event safety committee" will be utilized throughout this text as the term "safety" often is a more forceful term compared with "risk" which might lead to additional respect to the committee and its activities. An attorney is a logical person to fill this role. If an attorney is not available, someone with strong analytical skills may also be a very good candidate. The safety committee should be concerned with:

- checking, inspecting and repairing the event location,
- warning individuals about potential risks and hazards,
- monitoring to ensure proper participant and spectator supervision,
- evaluating security measures.

The following represents a typical case in which the event safety committee could have effectively prevented an injury with a little foresight.

Bush v. Parents Without Partners
(21 C.R. 2d 178 (C.A. 3rd, 1993).

The plaintiff in this case went to a dance sponsored by the defendant, Parents Without Partners. She had noticed some white flaky substance on the floor, but did not dance until after the floor had been swept once. While dancing, she slipped and fell. The substance was Ivory Snow Flakes and was used to make it easier for dancers' feet to slide on the floor. The court concluded that while the dancer assumed some risk of dancing on the slippery surface, the dance hall also had a duty to maintain the facility in a safe and usable condition. Thus, the summary judgment granted to the defendants in the lower court, based on assumption of risk being a complete bar to plaintiff's case, was overturned on appeal.

The *Bush* case shows that a simple item such as how slippery a floor should be represent the type of issues that an event safety committee should be analyzing. If the dance hall and promoter had examined other options such as polishing the floor, they could have possibly developed a safer strategy. The same thinking can go towards most decisions for an event. It is often the little decisions that create the big safety concerns. A good example of the little things that often lead to litigation involves team mascots. A number of cases were brought in the late 1990's against teams and mascots for injuries caused by mascots. Fans sued under such claims as humiliation or personal injury caused by a mascot (see generally From the Gym to the Jury, 1997–1998). In one California case, the mascot for the Rancho Cucamonga Quakes bumped a fan who turned his head and then was hit by a foul ball. Normally (as will be highlighted in Chapter 11), a baseball spectator assumes the risk of being hit by a foul ball. However, the court held that this assumption of risk might not apply because the fan was distracted by the mascot's tail ("Fans suit over mascot revived," 1997).

The event safety committee is responsible for developing *uniform policies and procedures for inspection, repair and maintenance*. However, it is not enough just to develop uniform policies and procedures. Committee members have to make sure the *policies and procedures are followed* or they have minimal value. Policies that are not followed can actually be used as a weapon against you. An injured party can use the policies as evidence that you knew about a hazard, and did not act to protect the injured party. To help ensure compliance with policies or procedures, the committee should develop and use *inspection schedules* and *repair/maintenance logs* so a complete record exists showing that both you and the committee were acting reasonably. *Inspection schedules should detail when inspections should be performed and the required status of every area, facility or piece of equipment inspected. Repair and maintenance logs explain when an item was inspected or repaired, what repairs were performed and the item's general condition.* Examples of both inspection schedules and repair/maintenance logs can be found in Appendix D and E.

The *personnel committee* is responsible for all personnel involved in the event. The major concerns for the committee include:

- developing appropriate job descriptions,
- recruiting the right people,
- screening all workers and volunteers,
- making sure all personnel are properly trained.

The committee has to develop *detailed job descriptions* that describe the duties to be performed by each worker or volunteer. The *description* should answer the *who, what, where, when and how questions for each position.* The job descriptions should also state the *minimum qualification required and any special training* or preparation that might be required to perform the job. An example of a job description for a grandstand usher might be as follows:

> The exhibition football game between University X and Y College should draw approximately 10,000 spectators into Z Field. Our usher to spectator ratio is 1:300. Thus, we need 34 ushers. Each usher should have been an usher in at least one prior Z Field football game. The ushers should be professional in appearance, confident in their abilities and able to communicate effectively to spectators. Mr. T will be in charge of all ushers and an usher review session will be held two hours before the event. All ushers have to attend this meeting. Prior to notifying Mr. T, no ushers will be allowed to leave their assigned location. In case of an emergency, the ushers should immediately contact a security official on their walkie-talkie. If a spectator violates stadium rules, the ushers are authorized to give one warning before telling the spectator to leave. If a spectator has to be removed from the stadium, security personnel should be called in to escort the spectator. Ushers are required to stand at the front of their section whenever they are not assisting spectators. Ushers are allowed to watch the game, but their concentration should be on the spectators sitting in their assigned section. If an usher violates any of these duties or performs his/her job incompetently, Mr. T can dismiss them and he/she will receive a pro rated hourly pay rate.

The usher is responsible for providing the following services:
1) seating assistance,
2) resolving disputes,
3) enforcing rules (i.e. no smoking),
4) checking tickets,
5) acting on complaints,
6) keeping aisles clear,
7) anticipating problems,
8) notifying security in the event of problems.

Specific job descriptions (see Appendix A and F), similar to the usher job description, are necessary to determine who is accountable for what activities. After reading a job description, all workers should know exactly what they are supposed to do and how/where they should perform their jobs.

The personnel committee has to recruit qualified, well trained, experienced individuals. These individuals should have strong inspection skills, be meticulous in their work ethic, follow orders well and be punctual. Each individual should be properly screened which could include a criminal history background check, contacting references and thoroughly interviewing the individual. Sample application forms, reference check forms and interview questionnaires are included in Appendix G.

If a lifeguard is needed, the person recruited for the position has to be well versed in safety techniques, CPR, first aid, water towing techniques and any other knowledge that could provide the individuals in the water with the highest level of protection. If an inexperienced lifeguard is hired and the lifeguard is not able to administer CPR, you and the committee could be liable for *negligently hiring* an unqualified lifeguard. Negligent hiring is especially critical when state or local laws require certain certifications that the job candidate does not possess or in certain states require teachers to go through background checks, but no checks are made.

For example, in *D.T. by M.T. v. Independent School Dist. No. 16* (1990), the plaintiff sued the Oklahoma School District alleging the negligent hiring of a 30-year-old male teacher-coach who sexually molested three elementary school students. Similarly, the plaintiffs in *Doe v. British Universities* (1992) argued that the defendant should be liable for negligently hiring a camp counselor who sexually assaulted a camper. Hence, the negligent hiring tort could be easy to prove if background checks should have been performed, but were not performed. ·

Documentation

Each committee should follow one key principle-document everything. Some attorneys recommend not documenting anything. "Do not leave a paper trail." This phrase is often quoted by some attorneys. This quote is accurate is you want to hide the truth or run from your responsibility. However, if you take affirmative steps to make your event safer, your documents will help highlight what steps were taken, when, by whom, etc. If you fail to document safety meetings or safety recommendations, the failure to document such information could fall below the standard of care established by the industry and can help reinforce a negligence claim. Thus, the authors of this guide recommend properly documenting objective facts in a timely manner. More specific issues associated with documentation can be found in Appendix B.

Conclusion

By determining who is going to sponsor the event, what event is going to be sponsored and who will run the event, a general framework can be established for the event. The event planning process will help determine whether or not the event will be successful. By taking the time to answer all the important questions, you can help ensure a safe and enjoyable time for everyone. The *event safety committee* develops the policies and procedures that will guide everyone's actions. The *personnel committee* recruits the right people who ensure safety policies are correctly implemented. With these two committees working together, duties will be highlighted and individuals capable of successfully implementing the duties can be secured to drastically reduce the potential for litigation. Event policies developed by the safety committee can be supplemented by using a defense strategy that warns participants and spectators while possibly eliminating potential liability concerns.

While the final event organizer and potential committees are crucial, numerous issues unrelated to the actual activity or event can also arise. The primary issues that can arise involves liability for administrative or management functions. The following chapter will discuss several major liability areas arising from manager activity ranging from hiring employees/volunteers to entering contracts and defamation claims.

Chapter 6

What Can You Be Liable For?

This chapter will highlight some of the recent cases or actions highlighted in recent years which demonstrate the breadth of administrative liability. Administrative issues can range from employment concerns to contract issues and the development, implementation and enforcement of various administrative rules. The chapter concludes with analyzing employee or volunteer conduct ranging from constitutional rights violations and civil rights (discrimination) claims to sexual abuse.

Employment Concerns

The personnel committee has one of the most difficult jobs in any event. One of its duties is the hiring or retaining of volunteers to help run the event. In years gone by, parents or a neighbor could be counted on to help coach a team or officiate an event. However, those days are long gone. Some questions that should be asked include: Are the individuals properly trained? What safety knowledge do they possess? Do they understand the concerns associated with mismatched opponents or illegal/improper equipment? Do they have a criminal history which might raise a concern for those working with children? These represent some of the sample employment-related issues that could arise in any event. While numerous events can be run by volunteers, you or the organization sponsoring the event are liable in the same light whether the person you put in charge of the event is an employee or just a volunteer (Fried, Miller and Appenzeller, 1998).

Background checks are a key concern when dealing with children. Some individuals such as pedophiles have a high rate of recidivism so why tempt fate by putting such individuals in a one-on-one supervisory relationship with a child. While individuals that have served their time should be allowed to reenter the workforce, you assume significant risks when you allow individuals that have a history of "crimes against people" to work with people. Based on this concern, the Canadian government has been proactive in this regard by requiring anyone who has a supervisory position with children to submit to a background check (Protection Against Pedophiles Act, 1997). Background checks represent a duel edged sword. If the background check uncovers problems then you could be liable if you still decide to give the person a chance. However, if you deny an opportunity based on alleged misconduct, you could be opening yourself up to a defamation claim. Lastly, if you decide not to have a background check then you could be liable if a background check could have uncovered a past history of problems.

In one case decided in 1997, a wrestling coach took the team manager home and sexually assaulted her. The student sued the school claiming it negligently hired the wrestling coach. The court concluded that a negligent hiring claim could be raised only if the school "knew or should have known" that the coach had a particular unfitness for the position which caused a danger to a third person. The school knew or should have known about the unfitness when they hired the coach and the coach's unfitness was the proximate cause of the student's injuries. However, the student was unable to prove that the school failed to exercise reasonable care in the hiring process ("Tort law," 1997).

Employment law concerns extend beyond hiring issues to unionization, workers' compensation, sexual harassment, wrongful termination and a host of other concerns. Concerns can also be raised based on your treatment of current employees. In one case, a town was forced to pay $1,000 in legal fees after its school failed to renew a football coach's contract and delayed the litigation process. The coach claimed he was facing retaliation because he complained to police after being assaulted by one of the football players (Byron, 1996). The principle raised in this case is do not do anything that you might regret-such as punishing someone for doing something right. For example in one defamation case, a female Little League coach was verbally harassed by a team member's father. The father also happened to be the Little League president. When the coach raised the concern with a league district administrator she was told that he would have the father retract the statements or be removed from his official capacity. When the abuse continued, the coach filed suit (Owens, 1996). The suit probably could have been avoided if the administrators would have done what they promised to do. Similar problems have been raised in other cases such as when a volunteer coach was dismissed after parents contended he inappropriately touched children. The coach claimed his dismissal arose after an "off-the-record" meeting which did not provide him an opportunity to respond or present contrary information. When no investigation or charges were brought, the former coach brought a slander suit demanding $40,000 from the nonprofit soccer league (Gatehouse, 1997).

Because there are too many employment related issues that could not be provided in this text. We would strongly recommend obtaining a copy of *Employment Guide for the Sport, Recreation and Fitness Industries* by

Gil Fried, Lori Miller and Herb Appenzeller available from Carolina Academic Press.

Management

Event management concerns can be as diverse as employment related issues. In one, not so uncommon, incident lawsuits were flying in Oklahoma City when two rival groups fought over public fields that were run by a non-profit organization and a for-profit organization wishing to take over the duties. The two sides were claiming misuse of funds and conspiracy to take over youth programming (Parrott, 1997).

In a different scenario, Sharon, MA school officials wanted to implement a program to allow schools to have advertisements at sporting events and other activities. However, the officials also wanted to have the right to reject any undesirable ads such as alcohol and tobacco advertisements (Wiley, 1996). While such a managerial decision would seem appropriate, especially in a school setting, the school's lawyers indicated that the schools could have an all, or nothing advertising policy. Otherwise there could be discrimination by the school officials for any message they did not feel was appropriate. Thus, the school might allow a Christian group to advertise, but not a Muslim group, which would result in discrimination based on religion or free speech. Similar concerns could be raised if event managers made a policy prohibiting "loud rap music", but allowing loud rock music. The best means to avoid such potentially discriminatory conduct is to utilize other tools available that could accomplish similar results. For example, to prevent alcohol or tobacco advertisements at the schools, the local municipality could pass an ordinance barring all such advertisements within 100 yards of a school. In the noise example, local authorities could pass a noise ordinance limiting noise production to a certain level-affecting all music.

Managerial decisions could also lead to positive results. For example, an athletic director could demand that a coach sign a buyout clause when they accept the employment contract. Thus, if the coach leaves early, the coach has to pay a penalty which can be viewed as protection for management. Such an arrangement was in place when Chris Gobrecht left Florida State to coach at the University of Southern California. Florida State settled the dispute with Gobrecht for $108,000 paid by Gobrecht to the University ("Gobrecht, Florida State settle," 1997).

The three disputes highlighted above represent just some of the managerial issues that could pose both concerns and opportunities when examining strict managerial issues. Competition, government regulations and contracts can be both positive and negative influences on an event. As with a host of additional managerial concerns, the key is to focus on details. Are you doing everything by the book? Are you examining every issues to address both risks and benefits associated with any given managerial action? Only then can you hope that your event will be as safe as possible. However, numerous issues lie outside management's prerogative including the conduct of others. However, through implementing comprehensive rules, you can hopefully reduce the occurrence of unwanted activities.

Rules and Regulations

As previously discussed, some individuals are concerned about over-managing an event. However, as highlighted by the following incidents, rules are a necessary part of any event.

Westlake High School canceled the wrestling season after allegations arose about hazing where the wrestlers assaulted other students in an offensive manner ("Hazing forces suspension," 1998). Similar hazing incidents have sparked litigation against the assailants and their schools (Kelly, 1998).

Eligibility rules represent a significant stumbling block. Many teams have seen their vision of championships fade due to a player being declared ineligible at the last minute (Salmon, 1996). However, many times the event administrators know that someone is ineligible or know about other rule violations but fail to take any corrective steps. In a handful of cases, the event administrators just do not know any better. Such ignorance represents the lowest point for any event administrators that failed to read rules which were easily available. In one case involving the New Orleans Recreation Department an eligibility dispute was raised and one of the suit's allegations was that at a preseason meeting with administrators and coaches no copies of league eligibility rules were distributed ("With suit dismissed, NORD teams play," 1997). More complex eligibility issues could be raised such as when Northwestern was faced with a suit by a basketball player who faced a serious risk of dying while playing. The University did not want the athlete to compete, but the athlete wished to assume the risk associated with his heart condition. The issue went to United States Supreme Court which refused to overturn the lower court's decision in favor of the university ("High court refuses to hear appeal," 1997).

Eligibility issues are not the only rules that can cause serious penalties. A Little League party landed one coach into hot water when a party was thrown for some Little League teams. The party violated the township's 20-year-old regulation which prohibited celebrations of Little League victories (Murray, 1997). Participation rules also need to be communicated effectively before an event or season to ensure everyone knows the rules. Besides communicating the rules, it is a good idea to have every athlete sign an entry form, application or similar document indicating that they have read/heard all the applicable rules and agree to abide by them. In a high school basketball case, a suspended player sued to regain eligibility. The athelete was suspended for smoking. The court upheld the suspension and the school was able to produce a signed copy of the school rules prohibiting smoking on or off campus (Fachet, 1996). Cases involving suspension for alcohol and smoking related rule violations are on the rise and students caught violating these rules are increasingly suing to recover possibly lost athletic scholarships (Long, 1997).

While most rules are considered reasonable if they promote the welfare of athletes, the event or a community, not every rule meets these high standards. Rules that are designed to punish someone or implemented/enforced in a discriminatory manner will typically draw judicial intervention. However, rules can also harm others in a manner that causes real economic damages. For example the National Collegiate Athletic Association (NCAA) has recently lost a suit brought by restricted earnings coaches. The NCAA adopted a rule specifying a certain level of compensation for some beginning coaches. The rule was designed to provide equality between some school that could not afford additional coaches and to give young coaches a chance to gain valuable experience. However, the rule also impermissibly limited salaries in violation of the Sherman Antitrust Act ("Court upholds ruling barring NCAA from limiting salaries," 1998).

Constitutional Rights

The previous section highlighted rules adopted by an organization that could violate a federal law, or provide the basis to effectively manage participant conduct. However, some rules, such as trying to limit potential advertisers discussed previously in this chapter, can raise constitutional concerns. One example that has arisen over the past several years involves rules or policies designed to limit communication in and around public stadiums. Several court cases were filed in Denver and Pittsburgh where the stadiums tried to block individuals from selling programs or other items in designated areas (Fried, 1997). Courts allow reasonable restriction on commercial speech as long as such rules are uniformly applied and allow reasonable time, place and manner exceptions. Thus, a complete ban against stadium hawkers on public land at all times would run afoul of constitutional protections.

Besides free speech concerns, administrators need to be concerned about freedom of religion claims. Prayers before athletic contests are not new, but can raise significant separation of church and state issues. A greater degree of concern is raised when prayers are injected into grade school and high school settings. In contrast, courts are more willing to allow prayers when the individuals being asked to pray are college students or professionals such as politicians who listen to prayers opening legislative sessions (Fried and Bradley, 1994) No matter what age or maturity level is involved, the key concern is whether the state is endorsing or favoring one religion or any religion. If the state is not involved in the process, such as student led, planned and initiated silent prayers, the courts are more willing to accept such behavior (Fried and Bradley, 1994). Courts are more willing to accept such behavior as there is no coercion on any individual to pray as no one knows what others are doing during their "quiet" time. Even though there exists ways to get around banned religious activity through moments of silence, actual prayers are still common and some coaches, in violation of the Constitution, utilize a no pray-no play rule. Out of 18 high schools surveyed in Riverside County, California in 1996, 14 schools said team prayers (Christensen, 1996). In nine of the public schools in the survey, the prayer was led by a coach or school official. Thus, potential constitutional violations abound, and most administrators are not even aware of such problems until they receive a phone call threatening litigation.

While constitutional violations might appear to be a more clear cut case, there exists a fine line between a coach's or EA's authority to manage an event and participants, versus the participant's right to participate. A coach's authority to reprimand can now lead to litigation. In one case a coach dismissed an athlete for insubordination and being disrespectful which resulted in the athlete filing suit to gain the right to compete (Reid, 1998). This case is not unusual as numerous coaching decisions are now bringing parents from the grandstands to the courts to force coaches to play their children (Fried, Miller, and Appenzeller, 1998). However, while coaches sometime lose in court, most courts are willing to uphold a coach's decision. In one recent case, the court held against a swimmer when a coach asked the swimmer to take a pregnancy test which was positive and the student gave birth four months later ("Pregnant swimmer sues over coach's treatment," 1997). In another case, a high school student-athlete wrote disparaging comments against a coach in a school publication. The coach benched the player for a playoff game and the player's parents brought suit. A judge dismissed the suit and fined the parents for filing such a frivolous case (Tedford, 1998).

While the cases above highlight some of the absurd cases that can affect an administrator for making a legitimate decision, other cases are not so simple. Discrimination cases represent one of the most difficult concerns for event administrators. The potential political, social and economic fall-out from such cases can be devastating. Even if an issue does not reach litigation, discrimination issues-even if erroneous judgments are made on both sides can split a town apart (Fried and Hiller, 1997). Discrimination cases can be very diverse ranging from racial slurs by a coach to players (Coleman, 1996), to suits against sports associations for not allowing a wheelchair using coach to coach due to a perceived injury risk to participants ("League settles lawsuit coach in wheelchair called no hazard," 1997). Numerous laws can raise discrimination concerns from disability-related laws to age, race, gender, nationality, religion and/or sexual orientation laws. While an EA can try to teach tolerance and mutual respect, the best advice to help avoid discrimination claims is to have established policies understood by all parties and enforced in a consistent manner. Similarly, all individuals should be reminded of the principle "do not do onto others what you would not want others to do to you." Sensitivity training and diversity management materials are available from many bookstores and represent an invaluable asset for working with diverse populations.

Sexual Abuse

While the stigmatism associated with a discrimination claim is significant, possibly the hardest dispute to deal with (besides a participant or spectator dying or suffering a catastrophic injury) involves sexual abuse of a minor. While it is unknown whether the incidents of sexual abuse are on the rise or if more people are reporting abuse then in the past, sexual abuse cases which formerly focused on clergy are now being focused on coaches and EAs. The following represent just a few of the sexual abuse cases reported over the past several years. By no means is this an exhaustive list and probably represents less than one percent of all sexual abuse cases (both civil and criminal) in sport.

- A baseball umpire was accused of molesting two girls ("Law and Order: Umpire Arrested in Molestation, 1997).
- A health club employee was ordered to pay a 17-year-old co-employee $1.1 million dollars after sexually assaulting her (Flynn, 1997).
- A $175,000 settlement was reached in a case where a coach used playing time as an incentive to coerce sex from a 16-year-old basketball player (Murphy, 1997).
- A gymnastics center was sued by the parents of three girls who

were videotaped while changing clothes ("Parents Sue Auburn Coach," 1997).

The cases above provide insight into the magnitude of the problems and costs associated with sexual assault. The long term emotional impact can be insurmountable for some victims which highlights why so much attention needs to be placed in protecting children. Based on the seriousness of this issue, Appendix A was added to the guide to give a complete analysis of sexual abuse in youth sports and set forth an easy to implement program to make your event a less likely target for sexual abuse.

While sexual abuse is a hot topic, sex discrimination is also a major concern. Title IX compliance is a challenge facing any athletic program where the program or its parent organization receive any federal funds. More and more schools, colleges and universities are being sued by individuals, coaches, or the Department of Education for failing to meet Title IX mandates (Cohen, 1997). Title IX compliance is outside the scope of this guide and anyone facing any Title IX challenge should seek the assistance of a qualified attorney to help analyze the current legal requirements.

Other gender based issues that need to be addressed include sexual harassment in sports which can destroy the workplace and paying men more then women for doing the same job which is a violation of the Equal Pay Act. Sexual harassment claims have been raised against many sport-related employers (Fried, Miller and Appenzeller, 1998) and numerous schools where individuals have utilized their position of power to demand sex from coworkers/subordinates or create a hostile work environment (Batsell, 1997). Similar to a sexual abuse policy highlighted in Appendix A, you should also consider adopting a sexual harassment policy which all employees and volunteers should sign. A sample sexual harassment policy can be found in Appendix H.

Chapter 7

Waiver and Medical Releases

We all have used or seen ladders. We might have used a ladder to hang Christmas lights or to prune trees. No matter what we might have used ladders for, most people understand that there are risks when working on a ladder. Gravity wins in any competition and if you do something wrong on a ladder there is a great chance you will fall and get hurt. While most individuals understand the risks inherent in ladders, others need to be warned. In one notorious case, a Pennsylvanian placed his ladder on some frozen horse manure to work on his roof. The manure melted and the ladder fell—resulting in a fall and a subsequent $330,000 judgment against the ladder manufacturer for failure to warn about the viscosity of manure (McClurg, 1997). Now, some ladders come with over 30 separate warnings informing consumers about potential ways they can be injured while using a ladder. The warnings can never cover all potential ways people will be injured as humans are an adventurous species who will always find new ways to hurt themselves. That is where waivers and medical release come to play.

Numerous individuals utilize the terms "release" and "waiver" interchangeably. However, they are two different types of contracts. A release is used after someone has already been injured. By signing a release the injured party is agreeing to release someone from any future liability, primarily based on receiving a settlement. A waiver is signed before someone undertakes an activity and is designed to forgo possibly filing suit if that person is injured while participating. The key to remembering the difference between release and waiver is that by signing a contract before an event you "waive" your right to bring a suit in the future. However, if you sign a release after an injury, you are releasing the party who injured you from any future liability. As this guide is designed to foster risk management practices, only waivers will be discussed in the following pages.

Waivers are used to provide a *warning* and to *indemnify* (to save harmless) EAs, and others, from potential liability. A waiver is designed to perform two functions; protect you from liability and provide an explicit warning concerning hazards (the type and severity of possible injuries) associated with event participation. By signing a waiver, a participant voluntarily relinquishes his/her right to sue you. A waiver first and foremost is a contract. Like all other contracts, a waiver has to conform to standard contract law. Courts scrutinize waivers very carefully because a waiver produces a conflict between contract law and tort law (see generally van der Smissen, 1990 and Cotten and Cotton, 1997). By waiving his/her right to sue you, the participant could be absolving you of liability for your negligent actions.

General waivers are written in very broad language and the enumerated dangers are normally commonly known. A commonly seen general waiver is found on the back of admission tickets for various professional sports. These waivers provide that the spectator assumes the risk of foul balls, can be expelled for violating rules, or that the facility has the right to make and distribute photos with the spectator's image. A general waiver is ineffective if:

- the participant did not assume the risk that caused the injury,
- the waiver was flawed, and/or
- both parties did not voluntarily and intentionally accept the waiver.

If a spectator does not know there is a warning on the back of a ticket, how can he/she voluntarily and intentionally accept the risks warned about on the ticket?

Because general waivers are normally very simple, they are often designed for their bark rather than their bite. Court's carefully examine and scrutinize waivers. Thus, you cannot absolve yourself of all liability by using a general waiver. However, when participants or spectators see a waiver, they often assume you cannot be sued. The truth though, is that spectators can sue, so you want to create a waiver that provides the greatest amount of protection. By knowing what courts look for in a valid waiver, you can more effectively design your waiver. In examining waivers, courts pay particular attention to the *signee's age*, the *public policy behind the waiver*, and the *waiver's wording*.

Parental Consent

Most interscholastic athletic events require a parent's signature on a consent/waiver form so his/her child can participate in an event. These forms are effective for providing a warning, but they normally cannot prevent a child's suit. When *parents sign* a waiver, they normally are *giving up their right to sue*. However, parents normally cannot give up their child's right to sue.

Scott v. Pacific W. Mountain Resort
834 P. 2d 6 (Wash. 1992).

Before participating in skiing, parents signed a waiver on behalf of their child who was a minor. The child was injured and sued. The ski resort brought a summary judgment motion claiming that the waiver barred the child's suit. The lower court granted the summary judgment motion, but the appellate court reversed. The appellate court concluded that the parents lacked the necessary authority to waive the child's future claim. Thus, the waiver was unenforceable against the child's claim.

California is one state where a parent's signature on a release can bind a minor (Cotten and Cotten, 1997). Children normally cannot initiate a lawsuit themselves until they reach majority (age 18) or find someone who will initiate the lawsuit on their behalf.

Because a child can sue many years after an accident, it is essential that all records (including waiver(s), if any) of a serious injury are retained by the event administrator for *several years after the injured child reaches the age of majority*. The following case illustrates this point.

Langevin v. City of Bidderford
481 A. 2d 495 (ME 1984)

Langevin was a 14-year-old high school freshman in 1977 when he injured himself performing a sprint drill during freshman football try-outs. The facility was too small and while trying to stop, he put his arm through the glass portion of a gym door. As a 14-year-old, Langevin suggested that his mother bring suit for him, but she refused to take any legal actions.

The court concluded that even though Langevin did not file the suit within the statute of limitations time period, he could still file the suit after reaching majority age. Langevin was able to file the suit because he was a minor when injured and he did not have an opportunity to sue until he reached majority, which was five years later.

This case helps highlight an important topic; record keeping. The school made a report about Langevin's accident, but unfortunately, they destroyed the report three years later. If Langevin was 18 when the accident occurred, this might have been a reasonable period after which they could have destroyed the records. However, since Langevin was a minor, the school should have waited at least several years (a maximum of three years depending on the state and its statute of limitation laws) after he reached majority before discarding the records. As each state has its own statute of limitations, every EA should contact a competent attorney within that jurisdiction to ensure documents are kept for the legally appropriate time period.

Children are not bound by contracts entered into before they reach majority (Cotten and Cotten, 1997). If a child under 18-years-old signs a contract, he/she could void the contract before reaching majority (Cotten and Cotten, 1997). Contracts signed by minors are voidable because it is presumed that minors do not understand their rights. Even so, signed waivers are still invaluable for providing children with necessary warnings which can serve as the basis for a possible assumption of risk and/or contributory negligence defenses. A signed waiver can also be used as evidence that the child was warned. After reaching majority, a child can affirm (accept) a waiver signed as a youth, and then become bound by the terms of the waiver (*Jones v. Dressel*, 623 P.2d 370 (Co. 1981).

Parent(s)/guardian(s) signatures should be obtained whenever possible as you can possibly prevent a suit from the injured child's parents. Similarly, you can provide parents with specific warnings about their child's participation. The assumption of risk defense can be brought against a parent's loss of consortium or any other claim a parent might have.

Equally important to developing waivers for participants and any parent(s)/guardian(s) is the need for developing a waiver that is clear, precise and follows public policy to provide individuals with significant advance warning concerning possible risks. Lastly, when a child signs a waiver it provides an implicit agreement that he/she will follow the rules, coach's requests, etc.

Public Policy

Because a conflict exists between contract and tort law, public policy plays a major role in determining whether a waiver is valid. Public policy is a major concern in determining the validity of a waiver because individuals should be responsible for their actions. Waivers for participating in sporting events are normally readily accepted by courts because individuals, as a general rule, voluntarily participate freely in sports. By voluntarily participating in a given sport, a participant is voluntarily accepting the normal risks inherent in that sport.

Grbac v. Reading Fair Co., Inc.
688 F. 2d 215 (3rd Cir. 1982)

The plaintiff in this case was the widow of Michael Grbac, who was killed while driving in a stock car race at the Reading Fairgrounds (PA). Before a driver could race at the Fairgrounds, they were required to sign a "Release and Waiver of Liability and Indemnity Agreement." The agreement provided in part that the driver released the fairgrounds:

> [f]rom all liability to the Undersigned, his personal representatives, assigns, heirs, and next of kin for all loss or damages, and any claim or demands therefore, on account of injury to person or property or resulting in death of the Undersigned, whether caused by negligence of the Releases or otherwise.

The court concluded that the release was enforceable because it did not violate public policy, was supported by adequate consideration (value given to secure a contract) and was applicable to negligent acts that occurred after the deceased signed the agreement. The court also concluded that the release was related to private affairs and not essential services. Thus, Mrs. Grbac could not allege that her husband was forced into signing a waiver for essential services, which could have invalidated the agreement as a public policy violation.

In contrast, the *Wagonblast* case held that a waiver violated public policy when the waiver was adopted to insulate the school from _all_ negligent acts.

Wagonblast v. Odessa School District No. 105-157-166J
758 P. 2d 968 (WA 1988)

Wagonblast was a consolidation of two cases involving interscholastic releases in Washington. In both cases, the school districts required parents and students to sign releases before the students could participate. The releases absolved the schools of all liability from any negligent act that could have arisen from the student's participation in athletics.

The releases contravened public policy because the school districts owed their students a duty to employ ordinary care and to anticipate reasonable dangers. However, the court concluded that the releases were basically designed to relieve the districts of their duty of care. In determining whether the waiver violated public policy, the court examined whether the activity was suitable for governmental regulation, how essential the service was and whether the services were available to the general public. Even though the release violated public policy it was still valid for providing evidence that appropriate warnings were given prior to participation.

Besides violating public policy, a waiver can be declared <u>invalid</u> if:

- there is a major discrepancy in the parties' bargaining position,
- pressure or physical threats were used to get a person to accept the waiver,
- the EA was grossly negligent or acted in a willful or wanton manner,
- or the document did not meet all the standards set forth by prevailing legal doctrines such as the Uniform Commercial Code (UCC) (*Littlefield v. Schaefer*, 955 S.W.2d 272 (Tex. 1997)).

Normally there is equal bargaining position when a person signs a release for a sporting event because the person does not have to participate (Cotten and Cotten, 1997). Having the ability to "walk-away" from an event makes the defense of unequal bargaining positions very weak.

In the absence of fraud or misrepresentation, waivers are normally *valid even if they are not read*. For example, in the *Randas v. YMCA* case the court concluded that a party cannot avoid the terms of a waiver after signing the waiver, on the grounds that he/she failed to read the waiver (*Randas v. YMCA*, 17 CA 4th 158 (1993)). The same result was reached when a bar patron was injured in a sumo wrestling event and claimed he failed to read the release (*Gara v. Woodbridge Tavern*, 568 N.W.2d 138 (Mich.App. 1997)).

Waivers also *do not have to be signed* to be valid as long as they are *understood and approved by the participant* (Cotten and Cotten, 1997). However, a waiver cannot be acquired through duress. *Duress means pressure*, so someone cannot be pressured or forced into signing a waiver. A contract that someone is forced into signing, because there are no other options, is called an adhesion contract (Gifis, 1984). An *adhesion contract* is imposed on the public, for *necessary or essential services*, on a "take-it-or-leave-it" basis. As in the *Grbac* case, the following case helps demonstrate that participation in sports is not an essential service.

Jones v. Dressel
623 P. 2d 370 (CO 1981)

On November 17, 1973, William Michael Jones, who was seventeen years old, signed a contract with the defendant Free Flight Sport Aviation, Inc. for a parachute trip. A covenant not to sue and a clause exempting Free Flight from liability were included in the contract. The contract provided in its relevant clause that:

> [T]he [plaintiff] exempts and releases the Corporation, its owners, officers...from any and all liability, claim demands, or actions or causes of action whatsoever arising out of any damage loss or injury... whether such loss, damage, or injury results from negligence...or some other cause.

Jones suffered serious injuries during a plane crash on takeoff in October 1974, ten months after he reached majority. By continuing to use Free Flight's services, he ratified (accepted) his earlier contract signed as a minor. The exculpatory agreement was valid because:

- it was not an adhesion contract (there was no discrepancy in bargaining position and the services could be obtained elsewhere),
- the agreement was not against public policy,
- parachuting is not of practical necessity,
- the wording was clear and unambiguous,
- the agreement expressly used the word negligence.

Use of the term "negligence" was important because the waiver expressly stated which rights Jones was giving up (which specifically included injuries sustained while on the aircraft).

A waiver can protect you from liability for simple or ordinary negligence, but a waiver does not protect you from your gross negligence or willful and wanton acts. The following case illustrates this point.

Wade v. Watson
731 F. 2d 890 (11th Cir. 1981)

Dennis Wade, the deceased, worked as a mechanic with a pit crew during racing event. Watson was a race car driver entered in the Grand National Race at the Atlanta International Raceway. Wade was a member of Watson's pit crew. During the race, Watson made an unsafe and unreasonably high-speed entry into the pit area and killed Wade. Wade's heirs sued Watson claiming gross negligence. To participate in the event, Wade signed a liability release. One document signed by Wade provided in part that:

> In consideration for receiving permission to enter the premises, being permitted and privileged to participate or assist others participating in said event...each of the undersigned, for himself, his heirs, next of kin, personal representatives and assigns, hereby RELEASES, REMISES AND FOREVER DISCHARGES AND AGREES TO SAVE AND HOLD HARMLESS AND INDEMNIFY NASCAR AND SANCTIONING BODY AND THE PROMOTERS PRESENTING SAID EVENT, THE OWNERS, AND LESSEES OF THE PREMISES, THE PARTICIPANTS THEREIN, THE OWNERS, SPONSORS AND MANUFACTURERS OF ALL RACING EQUIPMENT USED IN SAID EVENT AND THE OFFICERS, OFFICIALS, DIRECTORS, AGENTS, EMPLOYEES AND SERVANTS OF ALL OF THEM, OF AND FROM ALL LIABILITY CLAIMS, DEMANDS, CAUSES OF ACTION AND POSSIBLE CAUSES OF ACTION WHATSOEVER, ARISING OUT OF OR RELATED TO ANY LOSS, DAMAGE OR INJURY (INCLUDING DEATH) THAT MAY BE SUSTAINED BY OUR RESPECTIVE PERSONS OR PROPERTY, THAT MAY OTHERWISE ACCRUE TO ANY OF US OR TO OUR RESPECTIVE HEIRS, NEXT OF KIN OR PERSONAL REPRESENTATIVES WHILE IN, ON, ENROUTE TO, FROM OR OUT OF SAID PREMISES FROM ANY CLAIM WHATSOEVER INCLUDING NEGLIGENCE OF ANY OF THE FOREGOING.

The document released the promoter from liability for all claims and possible causes of action. However, the release did not bar a suit based on *gross negligence*. The release barred any claim for simple negligence, but Wade could not have assumed he was waiving his right to be free from grossly negligent conduct, thus his heir's gross negligence claim was still valid.

Another concern raised by waivers relates to strict liability and whether a waiver can be utilized by a manufacturer or merchant to avoid a strict liability claim. This question is answered in the *Westlye* case.

Westlye v. Look Sports, Inc.
17 Cal.App. 4th 1715, 22 Cal. Rptr. 2d 781 (Cal. App, 3rd, 1993)

The plaintiff fell while snow skiing and was injured. He claimed his injuries were the result of defective ski equipment rented from a ski shop, but distributed by Look Sports, Inc. Plaintiff's claim was based on strict liability.

The lower court granted the defendants' summary judgment motion as the plaintiff signed a waiver indicating the equipment was rented in "as is" condition and he expressly assumed the risk of injury. The waiver specifically provided that:

PLEASE READ & SIGN THIS AGREEMENT
IT RELEASES US FROM LIABILITY

The undersigned accepts for use as is the equipment listed on this form and accepts full responsibility for the care of this equipment while it is in his or her possession, and agrees to reimburse the Klein's Ski Shop for any loss or damage other than reasonable wear resulting from use.

It is understood the bindings furnished herewith are bindings designed to reduce the risk or degree of injuries from falling, and that despite the fact that adjustments are according to manufacturers recommendations, it is understood that the bindings will not release under ALL circumstances and are no guarantee for the user's safety.

It is understood how the binding works. Do not change any binding adjustment, come back to the rental shop for free assistance. The undersigned acknowledges that there is an inherent risk of injury in the sport of skiing, and use of any ski equipment, and expressly assumes the risk for any damages to any persons or property resulting from the use of this equipment.

It is furthermore expressly agreed that the undersigned shall hold the Klein's Ski Shop and/or it employees, the Sugar Bowl Corporation and/or its employees harmless and release them from any and all responsibility or liability for damage and injury to the equipment user or to any person or property whether resulting from the negligence (active or passive/past, present or future) or whether resulting from the selection, inspection or adjustment of this equipment (active or passive/past, present or future) by the Klein's Ski Shop and/or its employees or whether resulting from the use of this equipment by the user (at 10840).

Even though the waiver appeared to clearly preclude a case alleging negligence, the appellate court concluded that since the case was not merely a general negligence case, but rather a strict liability case, the waiver did not preclude a strict product liability claim.

Waiver's Wording

Your choice of words has to be very exact because the contract's wording is construed against the contract's author (Cotten and Cotten, 1997).

Thus, if there is any doubt about a word's meaning, the participant's/spectator's interpretation of the word is normally used.

Van Tuyn v. Zurich American Insurance Co.
447 So. 2d 318 (FL 1984)

Van Tuyn signed a release form before mounting a mechanical bull operated by a nightclub insured by Zurich American. After riding the bull for 15 minutes, the bull started moving very fast. Van Tuyn lost her balance and was injured when she fell off the bull. The release provided a warning about the bull's dangers and had explicit language indicated that the rider assumed any and all risks. The release provided in part that: "I hereby voluntarily release, waive, and discharge [defendants] from any and all claims, demands, damages and causes of action of any nature whatsoever." The court concluded that the waiver was devoid of any language manifesting any intent to either release or indemnify the club for *its negligence*. The court concluded that the waiver must *clearly state* that it releases the party from liability for its own negligence. The release's terms "voluntary release, waive and discharge" were not enough to release the club from liability for its own negligence.

Terms such as "save completely harmless", "assumes all risks" or "not liable for any injury" are not specific enough to protect an event sponsor or an EA from a potential suit resulting from their own negligence. The waiver should always explicitly state that the party signing the waiver is forgoing all right to sue the event administrator for any "negligent" acts by the EA, the facility owner, all volunteers/employees, event sponsors and any other individuals affiliated with the event. *Clear, unambiguous* and *precise* wording should be used so a participant can understand all the rights he/she is waiving. The waiver's terms should not be inconspicuous or hidden among other event-related information. On the contrary, you should make sure the *waiver's terms stand out*. The waiver should be *printed boldly*, close to where the participant is required to sign the entry form. The waiver language should be printed in larger type (larger than 12 point) than all other sections in the entry form or application document. Furthermore, a waiver could be a separate form, in addition to the entry form, which provides additional credence that the individual knew or should have known he/she was signing a waiver.

What constitutes an effective waiver? There is not one correct answer, but for any waiver to be effective the person accepting the waiver has to understand what rights they are waiving.

Russo v. Range, Inc.
395 N.E. 2d 10 (IL 1979)

Russo, an adult with normal intelligence, was injured sliding down a slide at the defendant's amusement park. The back of Russo's admittance ticket read: "the person using this ticket assumes all risk of personal injury." A sign was posted on top of the slide that warned sliders to "slide at their own risk." The court concluded that an indemnity contract is not only established by a warning on the ticket back and by the slide, but the plaintiff's understanding and appreciation of the risk also had to be examined to determine whether a contract was reached. Because Russo did not understand and appreciate the slide's potential risks, he could not indemnify the amusement park.

The waiver's wording should be very specific in regards to what rights a person is waiving by entering into the contract. Negligent acts by event personnel *before*, *during*, and *after* the event should be explicitly stated as rights that a person gives up by signing the waiver. The persons to be protected by the waiver should also be stated explicitly. The organization sponsoring the event, the facility owner, the EA, all committee members, employees, referees, volunteers, sponsors and anyone else connected with the event should be protected through the waiver.

Waivers should:

- be sport specific (each event/activity should be described),
- explain how to prevent possible injuries,
- state the activity's physical demands,
- acknowledge the inherent risks involved,
- explain the major or frequent risks inherent in the event,
- state what harm can occur,
- state how the harm can occur,
- state the harm's consequences (both physical and financial),
- describe all possible injuries from minor to major injuries,
- describe all locations where an injury can occur (from the locker room to the event area and parking lot),
- provide proof that participants were clearly warned,
- do not assume that any risk is obvious,
- explain terms such as paralysis, concussion, etc.,
- explain the types of injuries certain equipment, is and is not, designed to prevent,

- highlight the changes in risks correlated with a change in skill/competition,
- state an athletic trainer's role and make sure all participants know they are not doctors,
- explain the inability of coaches and officials to detect all rule violations.

The following is a very simple general waiver drafted by the authors that could provide you with a minimal amount of protection.

> The EA is not an insurer of a participant's safety, thus all participants participate in the event at their own risk. By entering into this event, the participant agrees to hold harmless, indemnify, and waive all current or future rights against any of the event administrators, facility owners, sponsors, volunteers, officials and any other individuals involved in the event, for any and all negligent acts connected with the event, pre-event activities and post-event activities whether occurring on or off all premises utilized by the event.

A more detailed release used by the United States Badminton Federation for their National Championship provides as follows:

Release And Covenant Not To Sue

> In consideration of my being permitted to participate in the 1991 U.S. National Badminton Championships and for good and valuable consideration, I, the person named below, hereinafter called ENTRANT, do hereby agree and covenant with, and release and discharge the United States Badminton Association, the United States Olympic Committee, the United States Olympic Training Center, sponsors, their employees, agents, officers, members, heirs, assigns, executors and administrators and any and all participants in this event as follows:
>
> Entrant does hereby promise, agree and covenant that he/she will never, at any future time, sue or bring action against the forenamed or any of them, by reason of any claim for damages, whether for property damage, physical injury or death, arising out of this event, whether such damage arises from the conduct of the tournament or conditions of the premises or from any cause whatsoever, and Entrant does hereby release, remise, and discharge the forenamed, or any of them from any and all claims, actions, suits, causes of action and demands of any nature, whether at law or in equity, arising from or alleged to arise from any accident or other occurrence during or in connection with this tournament or the condition of the premises on which this event takes place.

At this point, you are probably tired of reading the legalese contained in the cases and waivers presented in the preceding pages. Some people might feel that legalese (whereas, wherefore, therein, said, etc.) makes a document more "airtight." Some waivers are so full of legalese, they have sentences with several hundred words in them. On the contrary, the current legal trend is to write contracts in "plain English." The author encourages the "plain English" approach as courts will accept a waiver more readily if the participants could understand the contract without being an attorney himself or herself. In plain English, the above badminton waiver's last paragraph might read as follows:

> The Entrant releases and waives all rights, and will not sue or bring any legal action or claim against the Event Sponsors and the previously named individuals. By signing this waiver, the Entrant waives all claims against the Event Sponsors for any injury claim or other claim that occurred before, during, or after the event. Also waived are all claims for injuries or other damages caused by an event occurring before, during, or after the tournament; or damages caused by the facility's condition.

As you can see, plain English language is easier to understand, easier to create and can provide a maximum protection level. Appendix I contains several sample waivers that can serve as a rough draft for your possible waivers.

Specific waivers can supplement both complex and simple waivers. Specific waivers and warnings can provide you with additional protection over and above a normal waiver. A specific waiver and warning for baseball sliding, developed by the authors, could read as follows:

> participation in baseball can be a dangerous activity and the participant assumes the risk of receiving serious injuries including, but not limited to, broken bones, sprains, concussions and abrasions from sliding into a base. Participants assume full responsibility for their actions if they attempt to foil (break-up) a double play by sliding into an opponent, running outside the base path or any other activity that could cause a collision between the participant and any other participant. The participant also assumes full responsibility for facial injuries and possible eye injuries that could occur as the result of a head-first slide.

Medical Releases

Besides waivers, medical releases signed by a participant's doctor are another important instrument that can provide indemnity protection and also serve as a health warning. Medical releases are used before a participant is allowed to participate in the event. A medical release differs from a waiver in that the medical release provides the EA with evidence of a person assuming the risks of participating despite their physical condition. If a person is in poor physical condition, he/she would most likely fail his/her physical and a doctor would be unwilling to sign the release. Medical releases can help weed out high risk participants, but they do not indemnify you from lawsuits (you still should use a waiver).

Medical releases should be designed so event participants receive the greatest warning of any possible medical conditions that could be increased, worsened or developed through event participation. If medical releases are utilized, they will impose an additional duty on the event safety committee, as all the releases have to be analyzed, and all individuals not physically fit for the event should be barred from the event or required to sign specific assumption of risk forms after being thoroughly warned. These specific assumption of risk forms/waivers are currently being used for college and professional athletes with heart problems, one kidney, one eye, etc., who insist on continuing their participation. Normally, these forms are written by experienced attorneys and signed by both the athlete and all his/her relatives. Relatives are forced to sign the waivers to preclude subsequent claims that they did not know about the medical condition or they were not aware about potential risks.

Conclusion

To ensure proper waiver usage, the EA has to make sure the following questions are answered affirmatively:

- Is the waiver written in simple language?
- Does the waiver contain any evidence that consideration was given and other critical elements for a valid contract are present?
- Is the waiver written in such a way that the terms can be interpreted broadly by the signer and courts?
- Is the warning printed in large type?
- Is the waiver specific as to what rights are being waived through utilizing specific terms such as "negligence?"
- Is the written waiver reinforced with oral or other warnings?
- Does the waiver inform individuals of all the potential risks faced by participating in the event? This will be the key issue raised in an assumption of risk defense so you have to make sure the individual know the risks they will assume and that they agree to assume these risks.
- Has an attorney checked the waiver/release's wording?
- Is the participant free from pressure to sign the waiver?
- Is the waiver signed by the participant?
- If the participant is a child, has a parent signed a waiver of his/her rights?

- Is the waiver's title descriptive and accurate?
- Is the waiver's exculpatory language clear, large and near a signature line to help emphasize its importance?

Waivers were covered in this section to help demonstrate the all-important concept that a good offense needs to be supplemented by a strong defense. Offensive strategies include inspecting the facility and equipment, picking a quality site and having well-trained personnel to supervise the event. Defensive strategies can also be offensive in nature. Waivers and medical releases can be both defensive (protecting you from suits) and offensive in nature (by warning participants and helping to establish an assumption of risk defense). Even if a waiver, medical release, permission slip, application form or any other document does not act as a complete bar, the document still provides risk warnings and serves as an effective public relations tool.

Since waivers can be so complex, the authors recommend the following book to help you or your attorney understand waiver related concerns: *Legal Aspects of Waivers in Sport, Recreation and Fitness Activities* by Doyice J. Cotten and Mary B. Cotten. The book was published by PRC Publishing, Canton, OH in 1997.

Chapter 8

Statutory Considerations

Laws enacted by various governmental units (local, county, state and federal) can be used as either an offensive or defensive device. Laws that function as offensive tools can dictate what risks a participant or spectator assume while competing in an event, and can provide immunity for sponsors of non-profit events. Laws that function as defensive tools set out standards that can be used to show you acted in compliance with all governmental requirements.

This guide has already touched on comparative negligence statutes as a method by which state legislators have determined how fault should be shared between plaintiffs and defendants. The breadth of sport/athletic legislation adopted at various governmental levels is potentially infinite in scope. While running an event, you might face legislative restraints from taxes, zoning laws, traffic laws, environmental regulations and even crowd assembly laws. There are so many potentially applicable legislative requirements that this guide will only touch on the following topics: standards of care for land users, insurance requirements, immunity provisions for recreational activities providers, and governmental standards for both sport-related individuals and sport facilities.

Each state has its own set of laws and regulations that affect events within its borders. The laws listed in this chapter are highlighted as examples of statutes that can be found in some states. Local, state, and federal statutes are constantly changing, which makes it impossible to present all the applicable statutes. If possible, the event safety (risk management) committee should include an attorney who could examine all applicable laws and regulations.

At this point it is important to note that you might need to follow state laws from states other than the state where the event is held. If your event is held in State A, but it is heavily advertised and promoted in State B, there might be enough presence in State B to make the laws of that state apply to a case filed by an injured individual from State B. This scenario helps highlight how important it is to carefully examine all applicable laws and regulations wherever you are promoting or running the event.

Recreational User Statutes

Most states have statutes covering recreational premises utilized by the general public. The care owed or the immunity extended to a land occupier depends on the *facility* and *whether there is a charge to use the facility*. If a facility falls under the "recreational user statute" definition, the facility owners are normally provided with fairly broad immunity coverage. The following case highlights how courts define recreational facilities.

Baroco v. Araserv, Inc.
621 F. 2d 189 (5th Cir. 1980)

On April 10, 1973 Araserv, Inc. entered into a contract with the state of Alabama for operating a recreational facility on public land. The contract required Araserv to provide two lifeguards, some life saving equipment and to take all proper precautions to protect patrons. Araserv hired only one lifeguard and did not purchase safety equipment. On May 12, 1974, Baroco tried to save a drowning teenager. Another teenager alerted him to the swimmer's peril. Baroco sent the teenager to alert the lifeguard while he went out to save the distressed swimmer. Baroco was unable to save the teen and in the process of trying to save the teenager, he drowned.

Alabama has a statute entitled "An Act to Clarify and Codify the Common Law with Respect to the Duty of Care Owed by Landowners Towards Persons Who May Be Upon Their Premises for Hunting, Fishing, Sporting or Recreational Purposes and Not for Purposes Connected with the Landowner's Business." Under the statute, a "beach" was not considered a premises for sporting or recreational purposes. The statute providing some immunity for landowners opening their land for recreational purposes was also inapplicable in this case because Araserv charged customers using the facility. Because Araserv was unable to use the statute as a defensive shield, its actions was examined in a stricter light, with no immunity protection. Araserv owed Baroco the duty to provide him with the highest level of protection owed to an invitee.

In a similar case, a California court held that recreational user immunity protections did not apply to those attempting to rescue a recreational user. In the *Loving* case, a father was teaching his daughter how to build a campfire on some land when the fire got out of control. Loving noticed the smoke and tried to rescue them. He was injured in the process and sued the landowner claiming they failed to keep the property clear of combustible and flammable vegetation. The court concluded that the recreational user statute in California applied to those using property for recreational purposes, but did not bar any claim from a rescuer attempting to rescue recreational users (*Loving v. Tenneco West Inc.*, 18 Cal. Rptr. 2d 504, 14 Cal.App. 4th 1272 (C.A. 5th 1993).

While it is often an easy question whether or not an individual is a covered recreational user, the harder question relates to the land ownership and usage. Two major factors in most state statutes related to recreational land users revolve around the premises occupier's status and the *type of activities* for which the property is held open to the public. Recreational user statutes normally apply only to organizations opening their land for public use without a fee.

Cimino v. Yale University
638 F. Supp. 952 (CT 1986)

Margaret Cimino was a spectator at the Harvard-Yale football game held at the Yale Bowl on November 19, 1983. Cimino sued the university for damages from injuries received when the crowd tore down the goal post which struck her head. Connecticut General Statute 52-557(h) provided immunity, "for injuries suffered... where the owner of the land charges the person or persons who enter or go on the land for the recreational use thereof." The court stated that the statute was inapplicable because the statute applied to participants in recreational activities and not to spectators. The statute also only authorized recovery based on negligence, not actions in nuisance (allowing a public disturbance to occur), which was the theory behind Cimino's suit. The court also determined that the goal post was not a public nuisance because the stadium was on private property. The plaintiff was awarded $1 million in damages.

Recreational user statutes normally apply only to natural (non manmade) areas. Parks, beaches, picnic areas and other areas open to the public often receive some statutory coverage, as in the following case.

Miller v. City of Dayton
42 Ohio St. 3d 113 (OH 1989)

Robert Miller was injured sliding into second base during a softball tournament that was played on a city-owned field. The public was not charged for using the field. Miller's team, the Detroit Police Department Softball Team, paid $200 to enter the tournament, but no money went to the city. The city was neither a tournament sponsor or organizer.

Under the Ohio recreational user statute, a recreational user is defined as "a person to whom permission has been granted, without payment of fee...to enter upon premises to hunt, fish, trap, camp, hike, swim, or engage in other recreational pursuits." The court analyzed the statute by examining, "the character of the property upon which the injury occurs and the type of activity for which property is held open to the public." The main focus of the court's analysis was the nature and scope of activities for which the premises were held open to the public, not what the public used it for. The court also stated that the presence of man-made improvements alone did not remove the property from statutory protection, rather the property's use had to fit within the intent of the statute. Thus, a gymnasium would not fit under the Ohio recreational users statute, but a park was still immune even if man-made elements such as dugouts, fences and bases were added.

The controversy surrounding what constitutes recreational usage was highlighted in a recent California case. The appellate court in *Ornealas* held that an open field used for storing a piece of old farm equipment was not considered a recreational use. However, on appeal the California Supreme Court concluded that the specific language utilized by the recreational immunity statue did not differentiate between adults or children who might have a different opinion about the field. An adult might not consider playing on old farm equipment to be recreational, but a child might think otherwise. Thus, a vacant lot with farm equipment stored on it still qualified as recreational land (*Ornelas v. Randolph* (1993) 4 Cal.4th 1095).

Recreational immunity statutes require analyzing whether or not the public is charged a fee for using the facility. The rationale behind extending immunity to land occupiers not charging a fee for using the land is the public benefit theory. If someone undertakes an activity to benefit the public, he/she can often receive some statutory immunity protection. If someone received no benefit from opening their land for others to use, few individuals would be willing to assume such a risk, while opening themselves up to a potential lawsuit as well. The Ohio recreational users statute highlighted in the *Miller* case above is an excellent example of this concept.

Federal Regulations

A plethora of government regulations have been adopted by both federal and state governments. However, Federal regulations such as Title IX, Title VII and the host of other anti-discrimination laws have a potentially chilling effect on events. If an event is not able to meet one of the legal requirements, would the EA be barred from hosting that event? This question is a legitimate question and can be highlighted in the following news clippings. The Walt Disney Company agreed with the Justice Department to implement policies and procedures to aid deaf and hearing-impaired park patrons. Disney will add sign-language interpreters, audiovisual aids and captioning devises at over 100 rides, performances and attractions ("Disney to aid deaf park patrons under Justice Dept. agreement," 1997). In a separate case a professional team and ballpark owner sued their architect for malpractice for failing to meet certain ADA requirements when designing the facility. Some of the alleged deficiencies include: a lack of accessible routes from the locker room to the dugout and for wheelchairs to reach the box-seats, lack of wheelchair-companion seating, improper line of sight over standing spectators and the lack of an accessible route from the parking lot to the facility (Shackelford, 1997). These various concern highlight why the Americans with Disabilities Act might be the most important piece of legislation this century. While other federal laws such as the Civil Rights Act of 1964 (Title VII) are important, only the ADA will be specifically analyzed in this guide.

In a watershed event for millions of Americans, President Bush signed the American's with Disability Act ("ADA") into law on January 26, 1992. The new law promised millions of Americans the opportunity to receive equality in ways never before experienced by some or long forgotten by others. The ADA has been dubbed the Emancipation Proclamation and the Bill of Rights for individuals with disabilities. (Schend, 1992) Approximately 45 million individuals benefit from protections provided by the ADA. (Schend, 1992)

The Civil Rights Act of 1964 is considered a sweeping legislative enactment entitling women and minorities the equality they need to be gainfully employed. The ADA is even more sweeping because while it is unusual for someone to change their sex, nationality, race or religion; it is not uncommon for a health individual to be suddenly stricken by heart disease, diabetes, arthritis or a variety of other maladies. These unwanted maladies become the basis for potential discrimination or exclusion. The ADA was designed to remedy ravages that can occur when an individual is struck with an illness or injury which will forever bar their ability to function "normally" in today's society.

Nowhere can the ADA's affect be seen more prominently then in facilities. Sport and recreational facilities are especially prominent in ADA coverage due to the publicity generated by such facilities and the number of individuals who attend events or engage in activities at such facilities. Sport facilities have become the target for organizations such as Paralyzed Veterans of America who have engaged in concerted effort on behalf of their 17,000 members to challenge new sport facilities which do not meet ADA requirements. The group filed claims against five arenas claiming that while spaces are available at each site for wheelchairs, most seats do not offer a clear view of the action when surrounding fans stand up. Regulations under the ADA require all wheelchairs seats to be designed so that the wheelchair using patron is not isolated, has the choice of various seats and ticket prices and in places where fans are expected to stand, facilities must provide a line of sight "comparable" to the view from seats provided to other spectators.

Specific ADA rules are being proposed for various sports facilities. The United States Architectural and Transportation Barriers Compliance Board has put forth proposed ADA recommendations for sports facilities. Recommendations were developed for sports facilities, places of amusement, play settings, golf, recreational boating and fishing facilities and outdoor development areas. The sports facility recommendations are set forth in over 200 pages describing the layout of baseball dugouts, entrance turnstiles and other sports facility components.

The ADA does not operate in a vacuum with reference to sports facilities. Other laws work with the ADA to create a complete compendium of laws covering all sports facilities. The 1968 Architectural Barriers Act and the Rehabilitation Act of 1973 provide an extensive regulatory framework for sports facilities. State and local laws can also affect facility design, construction and renovations. Building codes determine such specific issues as how many steps can be built without needing a handrail, the number of inches required per person, per seat, in bleacher seating (usually 17–20 inches allocated for each seat) and the number and size of exits based on the number of individuals expected to possibly use each exit.

These laws are all coming into play in a variety of sports facilities ranging from stadiums and arenas to schools and bowling alleys. The scope and applicability of ADA facility requirements are best understood when analyzed in light of the express purpose of the ADA.

1) Purpose Behind ADA

The underlying principles of the ADA entail the equal opportunity to participate, and benefit from program and facilities in the most integrated setting possible. In other words, the goal of the ADA is mainstreaming; allowing individuals with disabilities the opportunity to mainstream into American society. To help bring about mainstreaming, facilities and the programs must: integrate the disabled individual to the maximum extent possible, provide separate programs when required to ensure equal opportunity and must not exclude individuals with disabilities from regular programs (unless there is a significant injury risk).

2) ADA Requirements for Sports Facilities

Title III of the ADA covers places of public accommodations and commercial facilities. For a facility to be considered a place of public accommodation, the facility's operation has to affect interstate commerce. Public facilities which meet this test include, but are not limited to, any establishment serving food and drinks, entertainment facilities (movie theaters, concert halls, etc.), public gathering places (auditoriums, convention centers, stadiums, arenas, etc.), public transportation centers, places of recreation (parks, zoos, bowling alleys, etc.), places of education (private schools), and places of exercise or recreation (gymnasium, golf courses, etc.). The only exception from Title III coverage are private clubs and religious organizations.

Under the ADA a place of public accommodation is required to remove all architectural barriers to access if such removal is "readily achievable." When an architectural barrier cannot be removed, the facility must provide alternative services. However, any new construction or facility alteration must comply with all ADA accessibility standards. New construction projects are required to be readily accessible and usable unless the facility would be structurally impracticable.

Commercial facilities are facilities not intended for residential use and whose operations affect interstate commerce. Examples of commercial facilities include factories, warehouses and office buildings. Existing commercial facilities are not required to remove architectural barriers even if the removal is readily achievable. Commercial facilities also do not need to provide alternative services as do places of public accommodation. Only newly constructed commercial facilities and alterations to existing commercial facilities need to meet ADA requirements.

The primary focus in analyzing sports facilities revolves around the public accommodation requirements. Public accommodations may not discriminate against individuals with disabilities. Disabled individuals cannot be denied full and equal enjoyment of the "goods, services, facilities, privileges, advantages or accommodations" offered by all covered facility. The ADA applies to covered facilities no matter whether they are owned by the private, non-profit or government sectors.

Full and equal enjoyment covers more than just facilities. It also covers programs held within the facilities. The landmark cases setting forth

ADA requirements for sports programs under Title III is *Anderson v. Little League Baseball, Inc.*. Little League Baseball adopted a policy in 1991 that prohibited wheelchair using coaches due to the potential collisions that could occur between a player and coach. Anderson, a wheelchair user who also was an on-field coach, contended that the policy change was instituted to prevent him from coaching during a 1991 season-end tournament. The local Little League office refused to enforce the rule and Anderson's team was eliminated early in the tournament. The issue arose again in 1992 when Anderson coached an all-star team.

The court examined whether Anderson posed a risk to other participants. The court also examined whether Little League's claimed "direct threat" (to others) was based on generalizations or stereotypes about the effects of a particular disability. The court held that each coach had to be individually assessed. There was no evidence that Little League Baseball, Inc. undertook any type of inquiry to ascertain the nature, duration and severity of risk, the probability that injury could actually occur or whether reasonable modifications of policies, practices or procedures could reduce the risk. Thus, any rule developed by an organization (that utilizes places of public accommodation) must provide the opportunity to evaluate each program participant on their own merits. Any policy that results in an absolute ban on any handicapped individual(s) will always be struck down if there is at least one person who does not pose a "direct threat" or can prove they do not epitomize a generalization or stereotype.

The unfair and indiscriminate application of stereotypes has resulted in several successful suits against sports facilities. A California ski resort violated the ADA with its policy that prohibited persons in wheelchairs from riding cable cars to the resort's recreational facilities. The court concluded that the resort's policy responds not to an actual risk, but to "speculation, stereotypes, and generalizations." The resort was forced to modify its policies (Fried, 1998). A Philadelphia gym facing significant legal challenges agreed to pay $35,000, adopt a non-discrimination policy and provide mandatory staff AIDS/HIV education to settle an ADA (Title III) lawsuit. The suit was brought by an AIDS victim who claimed the gym owner publicly humiliated him, threw him out and told him never to return to the gym because he had AIDS (Fried, 1998).

3) What Handicaps Are Covered by ADA?

The ADA employment provisions clarify what constitutes a disability under the ADA. Individuals covered by the ADA include those with *significant physical or mental impairments*, a *record of an impairment* and those *regarded as having an impairment*. A person with a record of disability is protected even though they might not currently suffer any impairment.

Thus a cancer patient in remission is still covered by the ADA. The United States Supreme Court will analyze this issue in 1999 when it hears a case about a former mechanic with high blood pressure who was terminated. However, when he went to trial his blood pressure was under control and the court concluded he no longer had a disability that significantly affected his life (Savage, 1999). Furthermore, those regarded as having an impairment are protected even if they never had any impairment. A person has a disability if she has a condition that *substantially limits at least one "major life activities."* Major life activities is defined by the Department of Justice's regulation to include "functions such as caring for one's self, performing manual tasks, walking, seeing, hearing, speaking, breathing, learning and working." (28 CFR Section 41.31)

Not all physical or mental impairments constitute a disability. The impairment has to be *significant.* To help determine significance, the following factors are examined: the length of time the condition has existed, the number and types of life activities affected, the extent to which the disability limits opportunities and whether the condition is medically diagnosable.

Common examples of protected disabilities include: paralysis, diabetes, arthritis, cancer, epilepsy, asthma, vision impairments, hearing impairments, speech impairments, learning disabilities, muscular dystrophy, heart disease, and manic depressive disorder. Conditions commonly regarded as impairments include dwarfism, albinoism, cosmetic deformities, controlled diabetes and visible burn injuries. The ADA specifically excludes homosexuals, bisexuals, transvestites, transsexuals, pyromaniacs, kleptomaniacs and compulsive gamblers. Other conditions that are not covered by the ADA include: colds, broken bones, appendicitis, hair color, hair type or left-handedness.

Disabled individuals are not the only ones protected by the ADA. The ADA prohibits discrimination against any individual or entity because they have a known relationship or association with a person(s) who is disabled. Thus, the roommate of a disabled participant cannot be excluded from attending. This does not mean the roommate can get into a stadium for free. If the roommate and the disabled patron both have tickets, they should be allowed to sit together. Furthermore, individuals who exercise their rights under the ADA or assist others in exercising their rights are protected from retaliation.

The above enumerated physical attributes and conditions presents a complicated list of potentially disabled individuals. Unfortunately, most of the disabilities covered under the ADA are not readily visible. Thus, the notion that you can see when a disabled person uses your facility is a fallacy. Therefore, you have to prepare your facility for any and all potential users. The hallmark for proper preparation entails providing reasonable accommodation.

4) What Constitutes a Reasonable Accommodation?

Reasonable accommodation refers to correcting both architectural and program related barriers. An architectural barrier represents a building's physical element that impedes access for disabled individuals. Examples of architectural barriers include: steps and curbs rather than ramps, unpaved parking areas, conventional doors rather than automatic doors, office layouts that do not allow a wheelchair to move through an office, deep pile carpeting which is difficult for wheelchairs to traverse, or mirrors, paper towel dispensers and sinks that are positioned too high on a bathroom wall.

All covered facilities must reasonably modify their policies, practices and procedures to avoid a discrimination. Modifications do not need to be undertaken if they would fundamentally alter the nature of the goods, services, facilities, privileges, advantages or accommodations. A perfect example of this rule was seen at the inaugural Disney World Marathon. One disabled participant sued claiming the race organizers were not reasonably accommodating his needs. The race organizers replied that by having the disabled individual compete, the race would be fundamentally altered. The court agreed with the race organizers. The judge concluded that the race organizers were providing reasonable accommodation to disabled individuals through the running of a wheelchair user division in the race (Fried 1998). However, the disabled prospective participant who filed the claim was no ordinary wheelchair user. He used a motorized wheelchair. The court thought that the use of a motorized wheelchair would significantly alter the nature of the event. By allowing a motorized wheelchair the court would have opened the door for a disabled person to claim the next year that they wished to participate while driving in a customized van. The court was unwilling to let the law go so far as to alter the vary nature of the event (Fried 1998).

There is no need to provide individual prescription devises such as glasses, wheelchairs or hearing aides. Neither is there a requirement to provide individualized assistance such as eating, dressing and toileting assistance. Thus, while it is fairly easy to determine what accommodations do not need to be provided, it is much more difficult to determine the appropriate level for achieving reasonable accommodation.

5) Do I Have to Prepare for Every and All Potential Handicaps?

Most facility operators when faced with possible access barriers often have to struggle with a prioritization process. Which repairs should be completed first? What repairs or changes can be implemented over time? In order to provide guidance, the Department of Justice has established priority suggestions for removing barriers. The primary concern and priority is the removal of any and all barriers that would prevent a disabled individual from entering the facility. The next priority is to provide access to areas where goods and services are made available to the general public. The third priority is to provide access to restrooms. The fourth priority entails removing all barriers to using the facility. Such repairs can include adding floor level indicators in elevators, lowering telephones and lowering paper towel dispensers in bathrooms. These repairs relate only to areas that are not exclusively used by employees as work areas.

Reasonable accommodation for ensuring equal communication can include a multitude of auxiliary communication aids such as: qualified interpreters, transcription services, audio recordings, speech synthesizers, telecommunication devices for the deaf (TDD's), telephone handset amplifiers, video text displays, written material (including large print), note takers, assistive listening devices, closed caption decoders and/or brailled materials. Besides purchasing needed equipment, any and all equipment must be kept in accessible location and in working condition. Most auxiliary aids are relatively inexpensive, such as amplifiers for telephones. However, purchasing and maintaining a significant amount of auxiliary equipment can become costly for smaller businesses.

6) How Much Will It Cost Me?

Public accommodations are only required to remove barriers when such removal is "readily achievable."(ADA Section 302(b)(2)(A)(iv)) "Readily achievable" means that the repairs or modifications can be made without significant difficulty or expense. (ADA Section 301(9))

Several factors influence the costs associated with barrier removal. These factors include the nature and cost of needed remedial action, the financial strength of the facility or organization required to provide the accommodation and the relationship of the facility in the overall financial picture of the parent company. Companies with significant capital will be held responsible for undertaking more repairs than a financially strapped business. ADA related costs are generally not that significant. A 1995 survey concluded that 15% of all ADA compliance requirements in the employment area did not cost anything and 50% cost less than $500 (Fried, Miller and Appenzeller, 1998).

Cost is only one factor to be considered when attempting to make a facility barrier free. However, cost is not a factor to be considered when facility alterations are being undertaken. An alteration is defined as any physical change that affects facility usability. Such changes can include remodeling, renovations, rearranging walls and other activities that affect's a facility's use. Any alterations begun after January 26, 1992 must be useable by disabled individuals to the maximum extent feasible. An example of an unfeasible alteration can be demonstrated through analyzing a renovation project for a facility entrance. While performing renovations, the facility manager is told that the only way to increase the doorway size to accommodate a wheelchair would affect the building's structure. Thus, it would be technically unfeasible to widen the entrance. Only that portion of the accommodation plan can be avoided. All other ADA alteration requirements still have to be followed.

Traditionally, landlords are responsible for facility repairs and modifications. Thus, landlords are typically responsible for financing required renovations or repairs. Lease agreements can provide the tenant with a right to modify a facility. If a lease agreement specifically allows a tenant to renovate a facility, it will be the tenants responsibility to pay for ADA required modifications. If a lease is silent concerning responsibility for required repairs, the Department of Justice could force both the landlord and tenant to pay.

While some accommodations might seem impossible for a company to afford, tax benefits can make such improvements attainable. Internal Revenue Service ("IRS") Code, Section 190, specifies that up to $15,000 of allowable expenditures for ADA required compliance can be deducted rather than capitalized. All expenditures over $15,000 constitute capital expenditures. Furthermore, under IRS Code Section 44, eligible small business with sales less than $1 million and less than 30 employees can receive a credit equal to 50 percent of the accommodation's cost for costs that exceed $250, but do not exceed $10,250 in any tax year. This credit applies to expenditures that are both reasonable and necessary. These tax benefits are best discussed through an example.

Sam Jones is the owner of Health-T, fitness facility. Mr. Jones employs 15 employees and has sales of $400,000 per year. After hiring an ADA compliance consulting company, Jones discovered he needed to modify the facility's front entrance so a wheelchair could enter through the front door. The company also concluded that a ramp had to be built to provide access between the aerobic area and a soon to be built tennis playing area. In year one, Jones spent $18,000 to modify the front entrance. Jones takes a $15,000 tax deduction and capitalized the remaining $3,000 expense. In year two, Jones spent $12,000 on the required ramp. The amount by which $12,000 exceeds $250, but not $10,250 is $10,000. Fifty percent of $10,000 is $5,000. Thus Jones was eligible for a $5,000 tax credit on his next tax return.

7) What Will Happen If I Just Do Nothing?

The ADA is enforced through several means. Private citizens can file their own ADA claim. Such a claim can be filed in Federal court. Private claims are only entitled to injunctive relief and attorney fees. Thus, if a bowling alley does not provide any reasonable accommodation, a patron can sue to force the alley to build a ramp so a wheelchair user could reach the lanes.

A private citizen can also file a claim with the attorney general. After receiving a complaint, the attorney general can then sue the facility owner and seek injunctive relief. The attorney general can also recover monetary damages and civil penalties.

8) Practical and Inexpensive ADA Solutions for Sports Facilities

The purpose of this chapter is not to scare facility administrators. However, it should be specifically noted that the Justice Department has clearly indicated that the days of ADA education are now over and the Department is now in a phase of ADA enforcement (Fried, 1998).

There are numerous ADA solutions that can be implemented at little or no costs. While facility renovation costs and repairs are hard to reduce, it is much easier to implement program-wide attitude changes which can significantly reduce the chance of incurring an ADA complaint and provide evidence that ADA compliance is being developed and fostered throughout the organizational staff.

For extensive repairs or renovations, facility operators can hire an ADA consulting firm to determine what repairs are needed. Another option involves performing a complete facility review and program review to discover first-hand what potential problems exist. The first step necessary when undertaking your own ADA review is to designate one individual within your organization as the ADA expert. This "expert" will have to review literature in the field, become familiar with ADA regulations and specifications and listen to the needs of employees and customers.

The second step involves undertaking a comprehensive facility audit. All facility components should be analyzed and evaluated for accessibility. A written evaluation should be prepared to track needed repairs, facility evaluation dates, repair dates, repair costs, priorities and similar concerns. Such documentation is critical when facing an ADA investigation.

A convenient approach to conducting a facility audits entails working from outside to inside a facility; following the same travel path a disabled person might use. The following represent specific concerns that should be examined. This is not an exhaustive list, rather a framework for further analysis.

Parking Area

Does your facility have ample parking spaces for individuals with special parking needs?

Are international symbols for the disabled used to identify parking spaces?

Is there adequate spacing between a disabled individual's potential parking space and other spaces so a wheelchair could easily be moved around a car's/van's side?

Are there directional signs indicating the facilities entrance?

Sidewalks/Ramps

Are sidewalks at least 68 inches wide to allow two wheelchairs to simultaneously move past one another on the sidewalk?

Are ramps clearly set apart with colored paint and the international handicapped symbol?

Can the ramp or curb be reached easily by someone parking in the handicapped parking space?

Entrance Ways

Are entrance doors/paths unlocked and accessible?

Is there a minimum of 60 x 60 inches of level space in front of the entrance door to allow maneuvering?

Are doors easy to open? (push or pull doors need to be opened with less than 8.5 pounds of pressure. Sliding doors and interior doors require less than 5 pounds pressure. Fire doors require at least 15 pounds pressure.)

Are doormats at the most one-half inch high and in the proper place as not to obstruct access?

Can doors be grasped with one hand without the need for a tight grip or wrist turning?

Are automatic doors set to open only when someone is less than two feet away from the doors? (This could cause an individual in a wheelchair to be hit by the doors)

Are there accessible doors next to revolving doors?

Is there any metal or wood plating on the very bottom 7 1/2 inches of a glass door?

Is the door threshold flush with the floor or entrance surface?

Are interior floors covered with a non-slip surface?

Is high-plush carpeting used in transit areas?

Stairs

Are treads no less than 11 inches and covered with non-slip paint?
Are the stair's risers and run a uniform height?
Are the stair nosing abrupt and do they extend past the lip over 1 1/2 inches?
Do the handrails extend at least 12 inches past the top and bottom stair?
Is the handrail's height between 34 and 38 inches above the stair treads?
Is the handrail grab bar less than 1 1/2 inch in diameter and easy to grip?
Are their tactile designations at the top and bottom of the stair run?

Public Restrooms

Is an accessible restroom available for each sex?
Are restrooms and appropriate stalls clearly marked with international symbols?
Are restrooms identified with Braille or raised/incised lettering on the door or by the door frame?
Are mirrors and paper dispensers mounted within 40 inches from the floor?
Is the toilet appropriately placed at the right height and distance from any hot plumbing fixtures?
Is there an area of at least 30 x 48 inches provided in front of the toilet for a wheelchair to move around?
How are faucets activated (levers, handles or motion detectors)?
Does the handicapped stall have a door that swings out and provides at least 32 inches of clearance?
Are handrails appropriately placed in stall?
Are toilet paper and seat covers within easy reach of a person on the toilet?
Are flush controls mounted lower than 40 inches from the floor and easy to grasp?
Is there unobstructed access to the bathroom?

Telephones

Are the telephone dials and coin slots no more than 48 inches above the ground?
Is the receiver cord at least 30 inches in length?
Are phone directories usable at a wheelchair level?
Is the handset equipped with an amplification mechanism?
Are usage and payment instructions available in Braille?

Water Fountains

Is the fountain at least 27 inches high and 17–19 inches deep?
Are there easy to control buttons, levers or motion detectors?
Is some signage available showing how to operate the fountain?
Are drinking cups available for fountains that are too high?

Elevators

Is an elevator required for accessibility to all facility levels?
Is an audible and visual signal provided to identify the elevator's
    travel direction?
Are elevator call buttons located 42 inches above the ground with-
    out any obstructions such as ash trays?
Are Braille or raised/indented floor level designation buttons within
    the elevator?
Do the elevator doors open at least 32 inches and provide ample
    wheelchair accessibility within the elevator?
Does the elevator stop flush or within 1/2 inch at each floor level?
Is the elevator equipped with automatic bumper or other safety
    closing mechanism?
Does the elevator have handrails mounted 34 to 36 inches above
    the elevator's floor?
Is the control panel located no more than 48 inches above the el-
    evator's floor?
If an elevator's automatic doors are not functioning correctly is a
    maintenance plan in place to make immediate repairs?

The third step involves evaluating policies, procedures and facility practices. All policies, procedures or practices that may affect individuals with
disabilities need to be addressed. These practices can be modified with little cost or effort. For example, a receptionist could be asked to answer all
phones in louder voice and clearly enunciating the company's name. Wait-
ers could be instructed to ask each party being served how he can accommodate any special needs that any patron might have. The key to any such
effort is co-opting all employees into the process with the view that they
should not be afraid to ask how they can help or what they can do. For example, a sporting good's store normal practice might be to require a driver's license when accepting a personal check. If someone does not have a
license, the sales clerk should not automatically reject the check. The sales
clerk should ask for other pieces of identification, or ask why the customer
cannot produce a driver's license. Some disabled individuals do not have
driver's licenses.

A fourth step involves acquiring and maintaining, in readily usable fash-
ion, any necessary auxiliary aids such as interpreters, taped text, Braille

text and assistive listening devises to name a few. There is no requirement that the most expensive method of accommodation needs to be pursued. Any method of accommodation or auxiliary aid needs to be effective for their intended purpose.

The fifth step involves following-up to make sure your plans are acted upon. In one case handled by the author, a handicapped individual defecated on herself in a restaurant even though the restaurant had accessible restrooms. The individual sued the restaurant for violating the ADA. While the restroom did indeed meet the ADA requirements, a food shipment had been received earlier in the day and the only place the employees thought about putting the boxes was in the hallway to the restrooms. While there was a wide enough path for a person to fit through, there was no room for a wheelchair to fit through. Constant vigilance is required to ensure that changing circumstances do not render a facility inaccessible.

Lastly, facility owners should always check with their accountant to determine if they can receive a tax break.

Numerous solutions exist to solving ADA related compliance problems. Only technology and ingenuity limit the development of solutions that create accessibility. Assistive listening system and devices presents a perfect example of methods that can be used to provide accessibility.

9) Hear This!

Under the ADA, integral components of an event or facility need to be accessible. Of special concern for sports facilities are sound related issues. If sound, music or other auditory components of a program constitute an integral component of an activity, then the facility needs to provide assistive listening devises. An example of an auditory component comprising an integral element of a sport activity is music for an aerobics class. Auditory related issues are also a key concern under the Architectural Barriers Act and Title V of the Rehabilitation Act of 1973 as the United States has over four million hearing-aid users and fifteen million others who have hearing losses that require some additional hearing assistance (Fried, 1998).

There are four different assistive listening services (ALS) that utilize input from existing public address (PA) systems to distribute sound. An FM system uses sound form a PA system fed into an FM transmitter to transmit sound to individual FM receivers. An FM system produces excellent sound quality, is highly reliable, allows the listener to choose their seating location and installation and operating costs are also fairly low. A typical system costs about $1,500. However, the FM system transmits through walls affecting listeners in other rooms and access is restricted to those with FM receivers. Similar to the FM system is the AM system which can be received even with a small AM portable radio. However, AM systems often have poor sound quality and the sound is poor in steel reinforced buildings. AM transmitters costs from $350 to $1,000.

Sound can also be distributed through an induction loop. This system involves a wire loop around a room that receives input from a PA system and retransmits the sound through a magnetic field within the loop. The receiver is equipped with an amplifier so the sound level can be controlled by the listener. Individuals with hearing-aids can use their aids without any additional devices. These systems are also easily installed, inexpensive and portable. Loop receivers cost about $75 each and a typical complete systems costs about $1,000. Their major disadvantage is that amplification only occurs when someone sits within the loop. Additional sound quality is often uneven and fluorescent lights can interfere with sound transmission.

Infrared systems use invisible, harmless, infrared light beams to carry information from the transmitter to a special portable receiver worn by the listener. The system is easy to operate, not subject to electrical interference and provides the best system for transmitting confidential information. A typical infrared system costs about $2,000. The major drawback with an infrared system is that the listener has to be within the transmitter's sight-line to receive the transmission.

10) Complying with the ADA

The Department of Justice is past the stage of ADA education and is now aggressively pursuing ADA violators. Sport facility administrators have to develop a mind-set, and co-opt other employees into accepting the mind-set, of providing all potential facility and program users with reasonable assistance. The key to ADA compliance was recently highlighted in a youth baseball case in Hemet, California. The national governing body for the baseball league backed the youth league in not allowing the athlete to play in order to, in part, prevent the player from "embarrassing himself." The choice of whether or not a person might be embarrassed is solely up to that person-not others. Facility administrators and program coordinators cannot exclude anyone just because someone might be embarrassed. Participants should be provided the opportunity to determine if they in fact will be embarrassed. This is the mandate of reasonable accommodation.

Insurance Requirements

Insurance coverage is often very expensive and most EAs would rather avoid insurance hurdles, if they could. In some states EAs are required to purchase insurance coverage for their events. Various levels of insurance protection or coverage can be required in different states. Required insurance coverage could include: *blanket disability, health, catastrophic injury, worker's compensation, casualty and/or group blanket insurance policies.*

Some state statutes waive government immunity if the governmental unit purchases liability insurance (see generally van der Smissen, 1990). The theory behind such a statute is that normally governmental units are immune from liability, but they can waive their immunity protection as long as they have insurance coverage. This waiver usually only applies to the insurance coverage. If an injured person wins a jury award of $2 million, but the city only has a $1 million insurance policy, then the person recovers the insurance policy amount with the remaining million being lost to government immunity. The following case analyzed government immunity coverage when an insurance policy was present.

Overcash v. Statesville City Board of Education
348 S.E. 2d 524 (NC 1986)

In 1983, Martin Overcash was a member of the Mooresville Senior High School baseball team. In a game against Statesville High, on Statesville's home field, Overcash was walked by a Statesville pitcher. As Overcash was jogging to first base, he fell over a metal spike embedded in the base path under some dirt. Overcash sued for negligent field maintenance and sought to recoup medical expenses for his broken leg.

Under North Carolina General Statute 115C-42, any local board of education could waive their governmental immunity by securing liability insurance. Governmental immunity could be waived *only* to the extent the board was indemnified by the insurance company for the board's negligence. The court concluded that the waiver of immunity extends only to injuries that were specifically covered by the insurance policy. Because the board's liability policy contained an exclusion for injuries arising out of participation in athletic contests sponsored by the board, the board did not waive its immunity protection for athletic events.

Using insurance policies for your protection will be covered in greater detail in Chapter 10.

Save Harmless Statutes/
Government Immunity

Before highlighting various legislative enactments that can protect EAs and employees/volunteers, it is important to once again highlight a concept raised in Chapter 3. Government immunity is one of the best techniques to protect an event associated with a government entity. Government immunity can stem from various laws which might provide an outright ban to suits against the state to allowing suits only if a school waives its immunity protection through purchasing insurance. Government immunity should always be examined to determine what duty of care you might owe and protection might be afforded to you if someone was injured at your event. For example, California has a Government Code Section (831.7) which provides that the government is not liable when someone is injured while participating in hazardous recreational activity. While skydiving and bunje-jumping might seem to be hazardous, one suit was barred when the appellate court concluded that basketball was also a hazardous recreational activity that could bar a suit against a government (school district) gym (*Yarber v. Oakland Unified School District*, 4 Cal.App.4th 1516 (March 1992).

Numerous states and the federal government have adopted "save harmless legislation" which extends immunity to volunteers involved in promoting or managing sports for the public benefit (Fried, 1998). The main focus of these statutes is to limit the civil liability of managers, officials, referees, umpires, coaches or other volunteers involved in non-profit teams, leagues, educational institutions and/or municipal recreation departments. One of the most extensive save harmless laws is the New Jersey Volunteer Athletic Coaches and Officials Civil Immunity From Liability Law (N.J. STAT. ANN. Section 2A:62A-6). The New Jersey law provides immunity for negligent acts by event personnel, but does not provide immunity for willful, wanton or grossly negligent actions. Event promoters employed by a *private or public educational institution's athletic program* are also barred from receiving immunity under the law. The law's protection *takes effect only after the coach, manager or official has participated in a safety orientation and training program.* The law covers volunteers as well as compensated sports officials for acts or omissions made under their supervision.

New Jersey and the federal government are not alone, save harmless and immunity statutes are being adopted with new laws limiting damages or personal liability. A host of tort reform bills have passed in various states that limit punitive damages or only specific damages in certain cases (Fried, 1998). By analyzing whether or not any of these statutes will apply to your event, you can adapt the event to fit under the statute's require-ments, thus, potentially developing additional safeguards against poten-tial claims.

Somewhat akin to save harmless statutes are "good samaritan" statutes that provide immunity protection for individuals providing emergency medical assistance (van derSmissen, 1990). Good samaritan statutes ap-plicable to "anyone" are available in 39 states and the District of Colum-bia (van der Smissen, 1990). However, just having these statutes might not be enough. Many individuals would rather not intervene in a road-side rescue for fear that even if they might have immunity, that does not prevent someone from suing and possibly ruining your life. No matter if a good samaritan law exists, once you start providing assistance you have a legal obligation to provide the best assistance you can under the cir-cumstance and to not discontinue the assistance until emergency medical assistance or other competent replacements are present.

Governmental Guidelines

Numerous government units have established their own conduct guide-lines/standards that might need to be followed when running an event. Standards can be established by either specific legal requirements or reg-ulations for performing governmental activities. Governmental standards are established for the public benefit. Thus, breaching a governmental stan-dard normally violates a duty established to protect the general public. The *Ehlinger* case demonstrates the importance of following established gov-ernmental standards.

Ehlinger v. Board of Education of New Hartford Central School District
465 N.Y.S. 2d 378 (NY 1983)

The state of New York distributes a "screening test manual" for phys-ical fitness testing. The manual advises as follows, "to insure maximum safety and performance, the following steps are recommended:...2. Leave at least 14 feet of unobstructed space beyond the start and finish lines so pupils will be able to run at top speed past the finish line."

Carol Ehlinger, a 14-year-old student, dislocated her elbow when she struck the gymnasium wall while running the speed test portion of the New York State physical fitness test. The issue presented to the court was whether or not the school was negligent in having only eight feet of unobstructed space after the finish line, instead of the recommended 14 feet. The court denied the defendant's summary judgment motion. Ehlinger was given the opportunity to prove to the jury that the school was negligent in designing the course and that the test manual showed the standard the school should have followed.

Government units can also establish standards for states, counties, cities or even specific facilities. For example, the state of Wisconsin enacted a law that sets forth the safety standard for sporting events. (Wis. Code Chp.167-167.32). The law prohibits spectators from: pushing or pulling each other while on any arena or stadium stairs, and prohibits purchasing or consuming alcohol, unless drinking is permitted by the facility manager. Standards can be established for various activities including:

- zoning,
- permits and other regulations for running an event on public property, and
- the different activities on which a government unit can spend public funds.

One sample standard or policy developed in Texas prohibits smoking on school campuses. The head football coach and athletic director in Dayton, Texas resigned in 1995 when he was under fire for smoking on campus (Horswell, 1995).

Due to the breadth of different standards that can be established by numerous governmental units, it is recommended that an attorney assist you in determining all the applicable laws. If legal assistance is not available, whenever you ask for guidance from a government official make sure you:

- write down the government official's name and title,
- write down what the official says,
- get written copies of all referenced forms or statutes,
- send a confirming letter to the official indicating the procedures you will be taking based on the official's advice.

Government Occupational Guidelines

Governmental units often establish guidelines/standards for individuals engaged in certain professions. Some guidelines for individuals associated with an event include lifeguard guidelines, fitness trainers and rules for boxing/wrestling officials (see generally Herbert, 1998). These individuals might have to pass a minimum proficiency test and/or minimum experience requirements. If you hire a lifeguard who should be certified, and he/she is not certified, you could face a negligent hiring charge (a reasonable EA would have made sure the lifeguard was certified). Furthermore, if someone was injured based on your failure to hire a certified lifeguard you could face a negligence per se claim.

Athletic trainers are one of the most regulated professions. Some states set out guidelines for athletic trainers that require the trainers to be certified by the National Athletic Trainers Association (NATA) or meet the qualifications for athletic trainer certification (van der Smissen, 1990). Some states have set up their own Athletic Trainers Boards to establish specific policies and rules for athletic trainers. If athletic trainers are hired for an event and they do not have proper certification or training, you could once again face a negligent hiring charge. You could also face fines or other penalties for violating state law.

Specific Sport Statutes

Statutes can also control specific sports issues such as equipment standards or required protective gear. Skiing is one of the most highly regulated sports. The scope of state ski statutes is very diverse with several different approaches for determining a party's duties. Some statutes are geared towards protecting skiers while other statutes are designed to protect ski resort operators. Most state statutes have established several duties for a ski resort operator that require operators to:

- mark trails,
- mark trail grooming vehicles and snow making hydrants,
- post trail boards that indicate open trails and their difficulty,
- post the skier's obligations and duties.

The following examples of ski statutes help layout the differences in statutes and are organized starting from the pro skier-oriented Colorado statute through the pro ski-operator statutes of Montana. While these statutes highlight skiing, similar statutes also cover other sports and have to be researched on a state-by-state basis.

One duty a ski operator would have in Colorado is the statutory duty to mark man-made obstacles on slopes so they are *clearly visible in conditions of ordinary visibility* (Colo. Rev. Stat. 33-44-107(7) (1973)). This statute was raised in the *Rimkus* case.

Rimkus v. Northwest Colorado Ski Corp.
706 F.2d 1060 (10th Cir. 1973)

On January 15, 1980, Mr. Rimkus was injured while skiing down an advanced ski slope. Rimkus was injured when he fell onto a pile of rock. Rimkus tried to prove that the ski operator was negligent by showing that after the accident, the defendant put out some crossed bamboo poles at the site. Rimkus argued that marking the rocks after his accident was implied negligence. The court concluded that remedial measures taken after an accident are not admissible to prove negligence. However, Rimkus was able to prove the defendant was 80% at fault and he was only 20% at fault. Thus, he was able to recover for the ski operator's negligence.

The defendant, Northwest, tried to use the Colorado Ski Safety and Liability Act (Colo. Rev. Stat. 33-44-107(7) (1973)) as a defensive tool to show it had no duty to mark the rocks. The Act requires ski areas to mark man-made obstacles on slopes that are not clearly visible. Northwest argued that the law did not apply as the ski resort only had a duty to mark man-made obstacles, not natural obstacles. The court did not accept Northwest's argument.

The New Mexico skiing statutes (N.M. STAT. ANN. Sect. 24-15-7 thru 24-15-13) questions whether the skier's injury is proximately caused by the ski operator breaching one of the statute's enumerated duties. Under the statute a *ski operator* has to:

- mark all snow machines,
- mark each trail's starting point,
- provide proper trail maps,
- tell skiers which trails are closed,
- provide a ski patrol unit.

Under the New Mexico statute, the *skier* also has a duty to determine his/her own ability and to assume the terrain's risks. If a New Mexico ski operator failed to perform an enumerated duty, and the failure to perform that duty proximately caused the skier's injury, the skier then could recover damages from the ski operator.

The Vermont statute (VT. Title 12 Sec. 1037) does not differentiate between which risks are inherent in skiing (such as rocks, trees, etc.) as long as they are *obvious* and *necessary*. If the risk is obvious and necessary (everyone can see the risk and the risky condition serves a necessary purpose-such as a ski lift tower in an open trail), then the skier assumes such risk.

A pro ski-operator oriented statute applies in Montana. The statute (Revised Code ANN. Sect. 23-2-733 to 737) defines the risk inherent in skiing and bars recovery if the skier's injury was due to one of those specific risks. The statute is designed to preclude recovery for injuries due to the *inherent risks* involved in skiing as seen in the following case.

Kelleher v. Big Sky of Montana
642 F. Supp. 1128 (MT 1986)

David Kelleher was caught in an avalanche on December 7, 1982, while skiing at Big Sky's premises. Among Big Sky's affirmative defenses was its contention that Kelleher assumed those risks inherent in the sport of skiing (including an avalanche) pursuant to Montana's "Skier Statute."

The statute provided in relevant parts:

> A skier assumes the risk and all legal responsibilities for injury to himself or loss of property that results from participating in the sport of skiing by virtue of his participation. The assumption of risk and responsibility includes but is not limited to injury or loss caused by the following: variations in terrain, surface or subsurface snow or ice conditions, bare spots, rocks, trees, other forms of forest growth or debris, lift towers and components thereof, pole lines, and plainly marked or visible snow making equipment.

Kelleher argued that the statute acted as a complete bar to legal recovery and thus, he was denied his right to access the courts. The court concluded otherwise, stating that the skier statute was an attempt to define what risks are inherent in the sport of skiing. The court concluded that since natural conditions are highly variable and difficult to manage, the statute was designed to help individuals recognize that there are certain risks inherent in skiing, which neither the skier nor the ski area operator can reasonably control. If the ski area operator was negligent and caused a risk the skier could not assume, then the ski area operator could be liable.

Numerous laws, regulations and standards have been established for operating swimming facilities. Similar to the potentially dangerous conditions constantly present on the ski slopes, a swimming pool can be a constant accident hazard. Under Mississippi law a swimming pool owner or operator owes a duty to use ordinary care or reasonable care for patron safety. This law was tested in the *Kopera* case.

Kopera v. Moschella
400 F. Supp. 131 (5th Cir. 1976)

On January 20, 1973, six-year-old Ronnette Kopera drowned in an apartment building's swimming pool. The pool was full when the child drowned. The pool had no life-saving or resuscitating equipment for the recovery of bodies, such as poles or hooks. The pool was not fenced, covered or drained during the winter months. Even though the apartment management knew children played by and swam in the pool, at no time did the defendant employ a lifeguard.

Mississippi law recognized that a swimming pool owner owes the duty to use reasonable care for the safety of invitees and/or patrons or to guard against injury to them. Owners also have to provide a reasonably safe place and to maintain the premises in reasonably good condition. Due to the poor conditions, the pool owner was found negligent for failing to: have a lifeguard on duty, fence and secure the pool with gates, cover the pool when it is not in use, have rescue equipment nearby and failing to drain the pool during times when weather was not conducive to pool use. All these negligent acts violated state law.

Additionally, swimming facility operators have to follow local or city codes that can require special provisions ranging from the pool fence's height to the number of lifeguards required at a certain location.

S & C Co. v. Horne
235 S.E. 2d 456 (VA 1977)

On August 29, 1975, Robert Lovett, aged 14, went swimming at a pool and was watched for 10–15 minutes by the pool attendant to make sure he could swim. Two hours later Lovett's body was found at the bottom of the pool's deep end. The pool attendant was sitting with a group of people on the deck near the shallow end, eating ice cream. When Lovett's body was brought to the surface by another patron, the pool attendant tried to administer artificial respiration.

During the trial, the pool attendant was asked whether or not he could have seen Lovett if he had been sitting in the portable lifeguard chair. The pool attendant indicated that he would not have seen Lovett because the sun would have been in his eyes. The pool attendant was unable to answer why he did not move the chair so the sun would be at his back. The lifeguard chair was not situated by the water's edge and the water condition was "cloudy."

The pool's owners were liable as they failed to live up to the city code which required:

- a reliable and confident lifeguard to be on duty for the sole purpose of observing and protecting bathers,
- an elevated lifeguard chair at the edge of the pool's deep-end, and
- to maintain water clarity to the point where a person at a distance of 30 feet could observe a black and white disc, six inches in diameter, placed at the bottom of the pool's deep-end.

State law can also set out guidelines for hiring personnel associated with the facility. Under California law (Cal. Health & Safety Code section 24100.1), a pool owner or operator is required to hire adequately trained personnel. Under the statute, lifeguards need to meet certain minimal qualifications, which include a current Red Cross advanced lifesaving certificate, a senior Y.M.C.A. lifesaving certificate or equivalent qualifications and first aid knowledge (including C.P.R.).

Conclusion

All the various "laws of the land" help shape which event will be run and how the event should be run. Laws and regulations have to be closely researched and followed because breaching safety related laws which result in an injury is *negligence per se*. You are expected to know your statutorily imposed duties and if you fail to determine those duties, you are al-

Chapter 9

Association Guidelines

Event policies set out by Event Safety and Personnel Committees and government standards are supplemented by association standards. Association standards are standards established by cooperating sports organizations or other groups/associations. These standards can encompass sports rules, guides to running an event or recommended safety steps. Most sports associations have established standards from years spent modernizing their sport. However, some sports associations, especially smaller or newer ones, might not have established any standards.

Different associations that might have appropriate standards include: international, national, state, regional and local sports associations. Additionally, local schools and facilities normally have established standards for maintaining or operating their facilities. Local promoters, current EAs and past EAs of similar events can also become a source for applicable standards. For example, if you are running a fitness marathon you might have to determine if any of the following entities have adopted any standards which might need to be followed:

American College of Sports Medicine (ACSM)
American Society for Testing and Materials(ASTM)
IDEA, The Health and Fitness Source
International Health, Racquet & Sportsclub Association (IHRSA)
National Fitness Therapy Association (NFTA)
American Council on Exercise (ACE)
American Running & Fitness Association (ARFA)
Local, regional and national YMCAs
Local colleges, universities, or schools

You might be required to do some legwork to determine the potentially applicable standards that associations or groups might have developed. However, it is better to search for information before the event then before going to court.

Associations might have established standards regarding:

- the equipment to be used,
- the training required by workers or officials,
- facility set-up requirements,

- age, weight and height requirements for participants.

High school sport associations, specifically state athletic activities associations have numerous rules or regulations that affect events under their charge. In Colorado, a 20-year-old student with Down Syndrome was initially barred from playing as a back-up football player because he was too old according to the state rules. The rule was loosened after nationwide protest erupted over the association's preliminary decision ("Man granted right to play on school's football team," 1996). Besides rules at the state level, local rules can also raise concerns. In a 1996 suit, parents sued the Plano, Texas school district over a 20-year-old rule that prohibited underclassmen (freshmen and sophomores) from playing on varsity teams. Due to the litigation, the school district changed the policy (Louey, 1996).

Some associations are established or designed specifically to disseminate standards to interested individuals. One such organization is the National Operating Committee on Standards for Athletic Equipment ("NOCSAE") whose safety seals can be found on approved football and baseball helmets (van der Smissen, 1990). Several national health associations also have established sports safety standards. One association that produces authoritative position papers on various sports health standards is the American College of Sports Medicine (ACSM). ACSM published the second edition of their Health/Fitness Facility Standards and Guidelines in 1997.

Several associations have developed participation rules after experiencing numerous accidents. One such association is the National Federation of State High School Associations ("NFSHSA"). NFSHSA promulgated rules banning cheerleaders from performing some stunts including: pyramids, free-fall flips, catapulting from platforms and backwards toe pitching at all high schools that are members of the association.

If standards are already established, make sure you have reviewed the latest versions. You would appear to exercise poor judgment if you follow standards that had been discarded years ago. The event safety committee should help research and then determine all appropriate association standards when developing event safety policies and then make certain the standards are acted upon. The following case highlights how important it is to know and follow appropriate standards, but even then you might still be liable.

Berman by Berman v. Philadelphia Board of Education
456 A. 2d 545 (PA 1983)

Brad Berman was an eleven-year-old, fifth grade student in 1976. Brad joined an after-school hockey league in response to a flyer distributed to each classroom announcing the league. Daniel Caputo, the school's physical education instructor, instructed the players each session that slapshots, checking, raising hockey sticks above the waist and foul language was prohibited. Players were equipped with wooden shafted (plastic blade) sticks. However, no helmets, facemasks, mouth guards, shin guards or gloves were provided.

During a game, an opposing player made a backhand shot and his follow through motion caused the stick blade to hit Berman's mouth. Brad lost five teeth in the accident.

The previous season, Caputo requested safety equipment for the afterschool league from the Philadelphia Board of Education. However, the board did not provide funds for helmets, shin guards, gloves, facemasks or mouth guards until 1977.

Based on expert witness testimony by a member of the Safety and Protective Equipment Committee of the Amateur Hockey Association of the United States, no regulations existed prior to the accident which required any kind of mouth guards for participants in amateur ice or floor hockey. The school board tried to show that they followed the association standards and no standard of care was established upon which negligence could be established. The court determined that the school employees were held to a higher standard even though they were following established association standards. Thus, even though association standards were followed, the court concluded that the association's standards were inadequate and an instructor should have realized that additional protection was required to protect the players.

Kungle v. Austin
330 S.W. 2d 354 (MO 1964)

Sandra Kungle was thirteen-years-old when she was injured on June 9, 1960. She fell at "Tumblin Town" trampoline center. Each trampoline was suspended by 16 springs evenly spaced at each end of the mat with 32 springs on each side. On top of the entire length of the trampoline frame was a foam rubber mat covered with Naugahyde and fastened in position over the frame with brass eyelets. The mat extended over the wood frame, but did not extend to the metal frame or flange to which the springs were attached. Kungle was jumping on the trampoline and slipped. She reached out with her hands towards the foam mat, but slipped and her mouth hit the metal frame.

The lower court's verdict for Austin, the trampoline center owner, was overturned by the appellate court even though the verdict was supported by the fact that Austin followed the standard of care followed by other trampoline center operators. The proper test for the trampoline center's conduct was whether or not the operator exercised the care that a *reasonable operator* would have exercised under similar circumstances. Austin's conduct conformed to the established practices and customs of the trampoline industry, but the court determined that Austin failed to show that the other operators, with whom he compared his conduct, were "careful and prudent" operators.

Standards are constantly being adopted or changed to adapt to new information. Once a standard is developed by an EA, or by an association, their work is far from over. When new information is received about newer, safer equipment or devices that can reduce injuries, the old standards must be revised/updated. This concept makes a lot of sense, but in practice, it is very risky to follow. The "damned if you do, damned if you don't" analogy applies here. If the old standards are followed, you could be sued for not adopting new-supposedly safer standards (*The T.J. Hooper*, 60 F. 2d 737 (2nd Cir. 1932)). However, if you adopt a new standard, implement a new approach or start using new equipment, you could be sued for not sticking with the previous, tested standards. With no current solution in sight to this dilemma, the only protection you might have could come from making an event as safe as possible with proper supervision, inspection, waivers and insurance.

Sports associations, if they have not done so, should adopt information dissemination practices to assist EAs in running safer events. An association could be added to a lawsuit or a counter suit by an EA if the association does not develop or communicate appropriate standards. If the association's charter or practice indicates its responsibility for developing or promoting standards, someone could charge the association with being negligent for failing to promote an increased knowledge of possible safety problems. An injured person could also claim that the association did not live up to the "reasonable" association standard by not providing EAs with appropriate standards and guidelines. An association's liability could be established if EAs have to pay for event sanctioning or if the association's by-laws require the association to educate EAs. The following case addresses this issue.

Peterson v. Multnomah County School District No. 1
668 P. 2d 385 (OR 1983)

Peterson was a fifteen-year-old sophomore when he suffered a neck injury during football practice on the second day of pre-season football practice. A contact scrimmage was being conducted notwithstanding an advisory recommendation from the school district against such contact during the first week of practice. Peterson suffered his injuries when he tackled another player, using his helmet at the contact point. Evidence was presented that Peterson used the same technique on previous plays and had been praised by the coaches. However, prior to practice, the coaches had admonished players against using the head-contact tackling method.

The Oregon School Activity Association ("OSAA") was also named in the suit for failing to adopt the pre-season football contact scrimmage recommendations promoted by the NFSHSA and the American Medical Association (AMA). In 1965 a joint NFSHSA and AMA committee set forth recommendations concluding that "[P]ractice games or game condition scrimmages should therefore be prohibited until after a minimum of two weeks practice." OSAA was a NFSSHA member, but it did not adopt the recommendations, and did not publish or otherwise distribute the recommendations to OSAA members. OSAA functioned as a regulatory body for athletic competition between member schools, but OSAA did not undertake to regulate activities connected to player safety.

The court concluded that even though OSAA was not in the safety and injury prevention business, and initially did not have a duty to make safety regulations, since it voluntarily undertook to regulate pre-season practices, it could be found negligent in failing to promulgate enough rules for pre-season practices. There was ample evidence to show that if OSAA had promulgated safety rules, coaches and the school district would have complied with the regulations.

King v. National Spa and Pool Institute, Inc.
570 So. 2d 612, (AL, 1990) and 607 So. 2d 1241 (AL, 1992).

The plaintiff's decedents brought suit after their family member dove into a pool and was rendered quadriplegic and died shortly thereafter. The pool was manufactured in accordance with the defendant's association's minimum standards for pools. The defendant was charged with negligence in developing the construction standard. The lower court ruled in the defendant's favor, but the Alabama Supreme Court concluded that the association was possibly liable and remanded the case. The decision was based on the Second Restatement of Torts which provides that: "[o]ne who undertakes to perform a duty he is not otherwise required to perform is thereafter charged with the duty of acting with due care." Thus, even though there was no direct tie with the pool user, if the association developed standards which the manufacturer relied upon, the standards would have to be developed with due care.

While the *King* case held the association to a duty to develop standards with due care, other courts have held that associations do not owe a duty to members of the general public who utilize a product or service made by an association's member (Herbert, 1991).

Searching for, and analyzing, both government and association standards can be a time consuming process with very little enjoyment or glamour. To make the process easier you should:

- appoint or hire an attorney to help analyze all the potentially applicable standards,
- review state laws to find applicable standards under such headings as health, public safety, sports, alcohol and any other specific concerns related to your event,
- obtain pertinent regulatory information from the local police and fire departments,
- obtain pertinent regulatory information from all local and regional government agencies that might have an ordinance or law that affects the event (i.e. health inspector, zoning, parade permits, etc.),
- obtain pertinent regulatory information from all local, regional and national sports organizations that might have applicable standards for safety or event management,
- obtain pertinent regulatory information from, and secure help from individuals involved in local parks, recreation departments, schools and/or sport programs,
- make sure all the standards used are documented for evidentiary purposes.

Your most important task in acquiring standards is simply just asking for information. Most people are more than willing to provide some assistance or refer you to someone who can help. There exists numerous individuals with exceptional knowledge in certain events. However, these individuals might not be the most appropriate persons to help guide you in successfully complying with potential standards.

Whenever a case entails issues that involve any special knowledge, the jury, judge, attorneys and possibly insurance companies need to rely upon the testimony of expert witnesses to provide objective case evaluation. To qualify as an expert witness the witness must have skill, education or experience in the matter they are called to testify upon. The threshold issue in determining whether expert testimony may be used is whether the information or experience of the expert witness will help the jury and judge understand issues in the case which are normally not understood by non-specialists. In the sport facility context, experts could be used in a multitude of cases including faulty construction, crowd management practices, ticket allocation procedures, typical facility financing techniques or the dimensions for a baseball stadium's behind-the-plate screen.

Whether expert testimony is necessary to establish the appropriate standard of care required in a negligence claim depends on the incident in question. For example, an expert would not be required to testify as to what caused a traffic accident in a stadium's parking lot if the police had cited one driver for failing to yield and speeding. However, experts could be used in the same case to help prove damages. A doctor could testify as to the extent of injuries and any future medical needs. An economist could testify as to lost wages and the present value of all current and future damages.

The primary point of analysis in negligence cases is the existence of a duty and a breach of that duty. In most cases, expert testimony will be required to show that the facility manager breached a duty owed to a spectator or participant. Likewise, the facility manager's attorney would need to utilize an expert to show that either no duty was owed, or that the duty was not breached. In either case, the focal point is determining whether or not a duty is assumed by the circumstances or imposed by industry standards. Experts witnesses are utilized to clarify what is the industry standard based on their many years of working in or studying the industry. A recent case helps highlight how important a qualified expert witnesses can be and the need to understand if a facility is meeting appropriate industry standards. In addition, the case below highlights why it is important to solicit advice only from qualified individuals who can back their claims concerning industry knowledge.

In *Messina v. District of Columbia* (663 A.2d 535 (D.C.App. 1995)) a father sued the District of Columbia for injuries his daughter received after falling at a playground. The trial court concluded, as a matter of law, that Messina's expert witness failed to establish the standard of care owed by the District to the young girl. Thus, Messina failed to present a case of negligence. The case's pertinent facts are as follows. Mr. Messina's daughter was a fourth grader when she fell to the ground from some monkey bars and broke her arm. The dirt underneath the monkey bars was described as hard packed mud, dirt with some wood chips on top. Messina presented at trail an expert witness who built and designed playgrounds. The expert testified that the standard of care in the industry required the school to supply some form of resilient cushioning material such as mulch, wood chips or chopped tires under the monkey bars. The expert referenced several different publications, including one by the Consumer Products Safety Commission ("CPSC"), as the basis for the claimed industry standards. The expert claimed that these sources helped create the industry standard even though the standards were not mandated by law nor enacted by Congress.

The court allowed the expert witness' testimony but also indicated that such testimony would not be used if it consisted merely of the expert's opinion as to what he would do under similar circumstances. Rather, the court required the expert to articulate and reference a standard of care by which the District's actions could be measured.

The publications by the CPSC specifically indicated that the guidelines were not considered as CPSC standards and were not mandatory. The expert was also unable to prove that any of his research had been adopted by any government agency. These facts combined to convince the appellate court that the lower court's decision was correct and the plaintiff had failed to establish that there was a national standard of care which the District should have followed.

This case produces several important considerations for any EA. First, any expert should be questioned about and be asked to prove the existence of industry standard applicable to the particular issue in dispute. Second, industry organizations such as the Stadium Managers Association or the International Association of Auditorium Managers should try to refrain from adopting any industry "standards." Rather, such organizations should only recommend non-mandatory "suggestions."

Suggestions are especially appropriate in light of the fact that every facility is different and it is impossible to develop one standard that could cover every facility. Every facility faces a multitude of different circumstances such as a team's won-loss record, facility design, weather conditions, alcohol serving policies, whether students are attending an event, whether general seating is used, how many police officers are working the event, etc. Furthermore, there are already numerous standards promulgated by various government agencies such as building, architectural, health and permit departments.

There are already numerous standards that apply to sport facilities. By following these established standards and being vigilant in uncovering new standards, you can fulfill your duty to spectators and participants. By utilizing a competent and qualified sport industry expert, you can counter-attack any claim that you failed to meet any alleged industry standards, especially if such alleged standards are not laws nor adopted by government agencies.

Conclusion

Combining applicable government and association standards with policies developed by the event committees helps establish the event safety policies. Through following all applicable standards and utilizing waivers, you will have established a strong defense shield. However, you still might feel the need for a safety net to protect you from any slip-ups. An insurance policy can provide that protection.

Chapter 10

Insurance

Even if all known standards are implemented and followed, you might not feel completely secure. Liability deflection represents the next step. Liability can be deflected through various means, with contractual and insurance means being the most popular. Through contracts (See Appendix C) you can require another party such as a facility user, event sponsor or any other party to agree to pay any damages that might arise. Indemnity clauses can be constructed in such a manner that you can protect yourself from anything the other party(ies) will agree to accept. This could include government fines, lawsuits, canceled events, lost income and/or attorneys' fees to name just some of the items that could be covered. The only limits to what you can contractually deflect is your imagination and what the other side is willing to accept.

Additional security can be obtained by implementing an insurance management program. Insurance coverage is widely used to spread potential risks over a broad base. Even though an event can operate smoothly without insurance, not having insurance coverage could mean that anyone involved in the event might have to pay a jury award from his/her own pocket. The demand for insurance coverage has increased over the years due to various factors, including:

1. Due to events being larger, more money is required and the financial stakes are much larger.
2. The threat of litigation might be decreasing in total lawsuits filed, but the damages award are still very high (Fried, 1999).
3. "Second-Hand" exposure from security personnel to any other individuals associated with the event forces an EA to aggressively pursue insurance coverage to protect against unforeseen acts by other parties (Hazel, 1993).

The litigation explosion over the past thirty years has had its greatest impact on individuals interested in purchasing liability insurance. In the 1980s, insurance rates escalated while the coverage decreased. Some events could not even obtain insurance, no matter how much they were willing to pay (Fried, 1999). This condition has left a bad taste in some EAs' mouths and they would rather not deal with insurance salespeople and complicated forms. However, it is well worth investigating possible insurance programs that can provide you with the protection *you* desire as the sport, recreation and fitness insurance industry has many participants and is now in a "soft market" stage where insurance coverage is very reasonably priced (Fried, 1999).

You can purchase various insurance policies, but you should make sure you receive the coverage you want, not what the salesperson wants to sell you. For example, you can customize insurance policies or purchase pre-packaged policies covering all imaginable losses.

We all have had those days where nothing seems to go right. What if you planned a big sidewalk sale and it rained. Would you proceed anyway? Would you reschedule? Would you move as much of the sale as possible indoors? These represent some option. However, another option might be to call your insurance broker to see if your business interruption insurance covers your lost income. The breadth of potential insurance coverage is increasing on a regular basis as new risks are identified and specialty policies are written to help prevent additional losses.

Recent policies have been written to protect against such losses as natural disasters which previously might not have been covered losses. For example, a recent nationally published article highlighted the advent of snow related insurance policies that protected businesses if snow storms made a businesses inaccessible for more than a set number of days (Yarborough, 1998). In 1995–96, Logan International Airport purchased snow-removal insurance which was written to activate after 44 inches of snow fell. The policies provided $50,000 payment to the airport for every inch over 44 inches until 84 inches were reached. Over 100 inches fell that winter and the administrators at Logan were considered geniuses as their $400,000 investment in the snow-removal insurance brought a $2 million return from the insurer. Insurance was necessary to help cover the costs associated with snow removal, lost parking and lost concession revenue from fewer passengers. Such narrowly focused policies can be crafted to address what lost business will be covered, during which dates, whether snow removal was covered versus just lost business income and which days would be specifically addressed as key business loss dates. For example, a football stadium might want snow-removal insurance only for Sundays when home games were played against opponents with a won-loss record over 70%. Similarly, a parking garage might want coverage for lost revenue if snow closed the garage on key business days such as Thanksgiving weekend or the week before Christmas.

While specially crafted insurance policies can provide well needed protection, they also present some significant concerns. The primary concern that needs to be addressed with any insurance is the financial strength of the insurer. Specialty insurance coverage is often available only through internationally based and/or smaller insurance companies. While not all smaller insurers are facing financial hardship, you should not trust your insurance investment to an unknown company. Before purchasing any insurance you need to check on the insurer to examine any industry ratings, better business bureau complaints, adequacy of reserves and related variables affecting the insurer's solvency. While most insurers are in fairly strong financial shape, just having adequate reserves does not guarantee adequate service. This concern is especially true when dealing with international based insurers. Some insurers might repay a claim within a week or a month while others might make payments at a snail's pace. Such conduct might not harm some businesses, but if a smaller company lost significant business and did not receive a reimbursement for two-three months, they might have to terminate employees or close. While some international insurers might take a longer time to pay, others might have local or regional claims processors who can investigate and settle claims with significant authority from the insurer.

Thus, while insurance can be purchased to cover almost any conceivable loss, consumers have to practice responsible consumer decision making. *Caveat Emptor*. The key point is to ask critical questions. If you are dealing with a smaller insurer or agency, ask for references from other customers that have had claims, banks or their accountants. You should also not be shy to ask for any of their statements to be verified in writing. If an insurer is willing to make an oral representation about their strength or services offered, make sure all such information is contained in the final insurance contract.

While purchasing insurance is an important facet for effective risk management, insurance follow-up is also a critical concern. Risk managers in the insurance industry are experts in analyzing policies, insurance markets and coverage limits that enable them to maximize their insurance investment. Such insurance management techniques and claims management practices can help reduce insurance costs and maximize coverage benefits.

Catastrophic insurance plans are commonly found in athletics. These plans normally cover personal injuries over $10,000 through several million dollars and often provide for installment payments, sometimes for the injured person's life. Such policies typically are no fault policies. No fault policies provide coverage no matter who was at fault for the injury. Workers' compensation insurance policies also are a type of no fault insurance as the injured employee is able to recover regardless of whether or not the injured person, employer or a third party was responsible for the injury.

Numerous associations and organizations have insurance plans available for their members and many of these policies can provide coverage for catastrophic injuries. The National Sports Underwriters, Inc. and American Specialty Insurance Services, Inc. are just two of the companies that provide insurance protection for schools belonging to such organizations as the National Collegiate Athletic Association (NCAA), National Junior College Athletic Association (NJCAA) and the National Association of Intercollegiate Athletics (NAIA). A typical catastrophic injury plan can be made automatically available to member institutions of the associations, but member schools can also purchase additional coverage for injuries generating medical expenses under the policy threshold amount (typically $25,000). Insurance protection may also be purchased for athletic staff members. National sports governing bodies also typically carry insurance policies for sanctioned events or member athletes.

These catastrophic injury policies might be appropriate for some programs, but inappropriate for others. If an event already has secondary insurance (to take effect after a primary insurance has elapsed), catastrophic injury insurance might not be a cost effective purchase. Purchasing appropriate insurance coverage requires thoroughly understanding the various insurance policies that can be purchased.

Error and *omission insurance* provides coverage for your negligent actions. *Premises* or *business insurance* provides coverage for accidents occurring on property in your control or for your actions if you are in the event management business. *Spectator insurance* provides coverage for injuries received by spectators at the event. *Service interruption or cancellation* insurance coverage insures the EA, if the event has to be canceled, so the EA may recover any money lost due to the cancellation. A *blanket insurance* or *comprehensive general liability* (CGL) policy provides complete event or business coverage. The various policies can often cover a building, the building's contents, grounds, programs and program supervisors.

An example of the wide variety of insurance plans available in the sport industry is a *stadium protection plan*. Several major insurance companies provide stadium protection insurance for events ranging from concerts and circuses to the Super Bowl. Pricing for such plans vary based on such criteria as:

- the event's location,
- the average spectator's income,
- the expected number of fans,
- past problems at the event or facility,
- the sport involved.

Some insurance companies go to great lengths to ensure safety. In fact, some companies go as far as paying for a risk management audit for an event to sending loss control people to an event to help in crowd and crisis management situations.

Insurance contracts can always be tailored for the special event needs or for any specific coverage you would like to purchase. The only limitation is how much you are willing or able to pay for your insurance protection. Most insurance companies have agreements whereby they represent you and pay your legal fees for any suits resulting from your activities. Other insurance carriers might provide you with a maximum amount they will pay after you litigate the case. Most insurance contracts provide for *subrogation,* which means that the insurance company takes your financial position in a civil suit (Gifis, 1984). Thus, if you are sued, you still are a defendant, but your legal obligations and associated attorneys' fees and costs are paid by the insurance company. While insurance policies can cover a broad range of losses, many EAs can be covered by currently existing policies.

Insurance riders represent agreements for additional insurance coverage that are attached to existing insurance policies. Riders normally offer inexpensive insurance coverage you can receive because you are working with an insurance company that already insures you and understands your insurance needs. A recreation program might have an insurance policy covering the day-to-day programs, but special events might not be covered under the primary policy. A rider could be attached to the existing policy, providing coverage for a special event. Insurance is often obtained by being added to an existing policy as an *additional insured.* Special care should be taken when you add someone to your policy or if you are added to an existing policy. If you are added as an "additionally named insured" you would be covered by all the same provisions as the original purchaser of the insurance policy. However, if you are just an "additional insured" you would not have as comprehensive protection (Hazel, 1993). Thus, it is critical to understand insurance language to determine what you really are purchasing or what you are requesting from others to properly protect you.

Example of Insurance Coverage

Insurance is a major concern for individuals renting or leasing a facility. The rental agreement between the landowner and the individuals renting the facility might require purchasing insurance to *indemnify* (i.e. save harmless, protect from potential loss) the landowner. The following case analyzed the issue associated with insurance indemnity.

Case: Bridston v. Dover Corporation
352 N.W. 2d 194 (ND 1984)

On November 9, 1977, the University of North Dakota leased the Chester Fritz Auditorium to Judy Smith, a YMCA employee, for a dance performance. During a rehearsal, Rebecca Bridston was injured when a university employee negligently raised the hydraulic stage lift. The university commenced a third party action against the YMCA, alleging that the university should be indemnified by reason of a contractual agreement.

The lease agreement was conditioned on the YMCA purchasing insurance. The lease stated in pertinent parts:

> [P]ermittee agrees to conduct its activities upon the premises so as not to endanger any person lawfully thereon; and to indemnify the University against any and all claims... The Permittee shall be required to furnish satisfactory evidence of liability insurance, including a copy of the endorsement adding the University as an additional insured.

The court concluded that the language was clear on its face and the lease obliged the YMCA to indemnify the university against the consequences of the university's own negligence. The YMCA was required to purchase liability insurance and the university could not be sued for the YMCA's failure to purchase the insurance. Thus, the university was not liable for any damages.

Besides ensuring adequate insurance coverage, you might be responsible for making sure insurance companies pay any claim. In a 1997 case, a wrestler was injured during a wrestling practice and became paralyzed. The injured athlete was denied insurance coverage by the insurance company that claimed the policy only covered athletic practices and competition not gym classes. The insurance company attempted to characterize the practice session as a gym class rather than a training session the wrestling team members. A six-person jury concluded otherwise and held that the insurance company must pay medical and disability benefits which under the policy could be up to $500,000 in disability and $2 million in medical expenses (Weaver, 1997). While the insurance company was liable for this amount and could be sued for failing to provide coverage (under an insurance bad faith claim) the school was not liable. However, the failure to aggressively argue on the student's behalf or to purchase the right policy or delineate school activities could help foster a negligence suit against the school when the injured party might have otherwise settled for the insurance coverage.

How To Purchase Insurance

The event safety committee should be responsible for developing an insurance "plan of action." The "plan of action" should establish the framework for acquiring insurance and determining policy provisions. A sport or recreation insurance specialty provider can provide valuable assistance with understanding the insurance market and what types of policies are available. Several major sport insurance providers and carriers exist that have pre-packaged plans available through national organizations. For example, the Sportsplex Operators and Developers Association (SODA) has developed a national insurance program for those running amateur sports tournaments. Policies are available for individual teams or leagues. As more organizations utilize this insurance program, a cheaper price can be arraigned and more comprehensive/specific coverage is made available for those who do not have the clout to negotiate similar policies.

The event safety committee should work with an insurance agent and not an insurance broker. An *insurance agent* should be used because the insurance agent's statements can bind the insurance company. An insurance broker's statement might not bind a particular insurance company. Similar to all other contractual concerns, any discussion or claimed coverage should appear in the final policy contract.

The first concern for the safety committee is determining what insurance protection is needed. The following represent critical insurance concerns that need to be explored and prioritized:

- coverage for medical expenses,
- coverage for personal injuries,
- coverage for criminal activities on/off the premises,
- coverage for criminal misconduct of employees/volunteers,
- coverage for crowd related concerns,
- workers' compensation coverage,
- business interruption/loss coverage,
- automotive coverage,
- coverage for all other matters associated with facilities, personnel and event related concerns.

Another major concern for the safety committee is determining how much money should be spent on insurance and what level of protection should be purchased. Tradeoffs will have to be made; the trick is minimizing the risks while providing adequate protection. The final cost for a policy will be called the insurance policy premium, which might need to be paid completely in advance or in installments. By working with an insurance company, potential premiums may be lowered if the event safety committee can show the insurance company complete event safety plans designed to minimize potential injuries. If an insurance company can foresee a well-run event featuring a strong risk management program, it may be willing to reduce the policy premiums.

If insurance coverage is too expensive, the safety committee might recommend cooperative or self-insurance. *Self-insurance* entails gathering several organizations or teams into a group that contributes funds to form an insurance pool (van der Smissen, 1990). The insurance pool is used to help pay claims against pool members. If an insurance pool cannot be established, several event administrators could band together to purchase combined insurance coverage for all their events. By presenting several events to an insurance carrier, the per event insurance cost could be considerably reduced.

No matter what the final cost or who is purchasing the insurance, several major questions need to be asked when developing the insurance "plan of action" including:

- who is covered,
- how much coverage is received,
- what actions/harms are covered,
- under what circumstances will the coverage apply,
- for how long will the coverage apply (are pre- and post-event actions covered?),
- which locations/facilities are covered,
- what activities at that location are covered,
- what is the deductible,
- is the deductible handled on a per claim or per occurrence basis,
- what are the premiums,
- who covers the legal expenses and chooses the counsel,
- what is excluded by the coverage,
- is there subrogation?

Conclusion

The premiums for insurance coverage have declined in recent years. While insurance costs are going down the awards from sympathetic juries have increased. In addition numerous claims are now available which were not raised as frequently when the hard insurance market drove premium prices through the roof. Judgments have increased as the cost for health care and rehabilitation services have rapidly increased over the past two decades (Fried 1998). Thus, the potentially disastrous effect from a huge financial judgment highlights why insurance coverage and contract deflection techniques are so important. As discussed previously, if a person or a partnership loses a suit, they could lose both business and personal property. A corporation, on the other hand, might have to sell all of its assets. Insurance policies in today's litigious society are a necessity and should be looked upon as such, instead of being examined as a low priority option if some money is available.

An additional amount of protection, over and above insurance policies, can be achieved by structuring all warnings, waivers and supervision around the insurance policy. Thus, if a certain item is not covered by an insurance policy, a warning and waiver could specifically state that any person involved with the event voluntarily assumes the risks associated with the excluded harm.

If at all possible, the safety committee should have at least one person with an insurance background assisting the event by providing relevant insight. If the safety committee does not have access to an insurance professional, the safety committee should retain an insurance professional to work on their behalf. The insurance professional will owe the event a fiduciary obligation to act on their behalf and the possible savings that can be realized from comparative shopping are well worth the cost. In the same vein, you should not try to reinvent the wheel. Numerous insurance policies have already been written for similar events. Through thorough research and careful reading you should be able to find the most appropriate coverage available and ask the insureds under those policies if they were satisfied. You can also ask an insurance agent or broker for references that might be able to provide you with this additional insight.

Chapter 11

Putting the Pieces Together to Establish a Safety Committee

Establishing guidelines for operating an event is the first step in developing a risk management strategy that will most effectively reduce possible injuries and resulting suit. Event policies and guidelines have to be established immediately after:

- determining the event sponsor,
- determining the event to be held,
- appointing the event administrator(s),
- establishing the event safety and personnel committees.

The importance of an event *safety committee* cannot be stressed enough. The terms "safety committee" was consciously chosen by the authors over "risk management committee" as the term safety implies more grave results for some people if safety procedures are not implemented. The safety committee *has to* ensure that:

- all safety measures are evaluated,
- all guidelines for facility inspection and maintenance are established and implemented,
- appropriate warnings are developed and distributed effectively,
- a waiver is developed and reviewed by an attorney,
- an insurance policy covering the event's needs is purchased,
- first-aid guidelines and procedures are developed and implemented,
- transportation guidelines are established and implemented, and
- security is appropriately planned and implemented.

Only through examining all the potential duties and/or standards utilized by national, state and local governing bodies can you develop appropriate event guidelines and policies. After policies and guidelines are established, lines of defense such as waivers and insurance policies, have to be established. However, the most important defense is to make sure that all the *adopted polices or guidelines are followed* by all individuals involved with the event.

143

The first ten chapters in this guide concentrated on general event guidelines, not sport-specific guidelines. By analyzing specific event circumstances you can adapt the general event guidelines into *event-specific guidelines*. The next two sections highlight various sport events and the problems that can be encountered while managing those events. By understanding what others have done wrong or where unusual accidents have occurred, you can develop an appreciation for potential hazards you might face and develop methods to help eliminate potential hazards.

Numerous general principles transcend various possible events. For example, if a cheerleading event is going to be held in a gymnasium, and the locker rooms will be used, then the sections on locker rooms discussed in the basketball and football chapters should be analyzed while developing the event-specific guidelines. Therefore, it might be useful to browse through all the sections as different issues are discussed under various headings.

Section II
Event Participants

Chapter 12

Baseball

The national pastime has captivated the hearts of the young and old for over a century, but good "sportspersonship" often ends when a participant is injured on the field. Numerous risks exists in baseball. Some of these risks include:

- protrusions around the diamond,
- poor design and layout resulting in fields overlapping,
- inadequate facilities with poor screens, bleachers and barriers between the field and vehicle traffic,
- poor playing surfaces,
- apparatus from other sports left on the field, and
- inadequate fences, bases and related amenities (Nygaard, 1989).

The major baseball litigation concerns addressed in this chapter involve the playing field, equipment concerns, opponent violence and proper supervision.

Playing Field

A baseball playing field can have several visible and hidden defects to search for before a game. Participants in a baseball game should feel confident in assuming that the field is free from potentially hazardous conditions. You should always remember that you do not have to provide a *perfectly* safe playing field, rather a *reasonably safe* field. Some potentially hazardous conditions that should be examined include:

- protrusions or holes concealed by grass,
- the type of dirt used in the infield,
- the bases used (break-away bases-see below),
- the backstop's condition,
- what fencing is used,
- what batting cage is used,
- how bright are the infield and outfield lights,
- where spectator seating is located.

Outfield/Infield Grass

Due to its very nature, infield and outfield grass can hide many objects that a player might not be able to spot until it is too late. To ensure adequate field inspection, you should make sure the grass is very well trimmed. Good playing field grass does not have to be higher then two inches in height (Horman, 1993). However, each grass surface has to be evaluated on an individual basis. Some grass surface needs to be higher or shorter depending on the grass type, soil, density, climate, drainage, slope and competition level. A competent professional with significant experience in turf management and possible affiliation with the a nationally recognized industry leader such as the Sports Turf Managers Association or the Sportsplex Operators and Developers Association should be consulted to determine the appropriate height for the conditions present in your program.

The major concerns associated with playing field grass are potentially dangerous areas hidden by the grass. The event safety committee has to make sure a qualified person closely examines the entire field using an established method such as the ECT approach. Examination of the field can be accomplished by walking in a looping motion back-and-forth across the entire field area. When a player is chasing a fly ball in the outfield, he or she is not looking at the ground, but looking up at the ball. Thus, it is unlikely they will see an obstacle on the ground. By thoroughly examining the playing area, you can assure yourself that reasonable steps have been taken to protect participants from field hazards.

The list of potentially dangerous items hiding in the grass is limitless, but a playing field inspector should be on the lookout for such hazards as:

- tossed bats,
- baseballs or softballs (which, when worn are very difficult to see),
- rakes or shovels for the pitcher's mound or batters' box,
- bottles, cans or other disposed containers,
- broken glass,
- sprinkler heads,
- irrigation stand pipes,
- loose or missing drainage hole covers,
- permanent receptacles for benches or bleachers.

The following case highlights why it is important to examine a field, even for broken glass.

Short v. Griffiths

255 S.E. 2d 479 (VA 1979)

Short, a high school student, was injured when he fell on some broken glass while running laps on the school's outdoor track. Short sued the baseball coach, athletic director, school board and building/grounds supervisor claiming they:

- had a duty to establish procedures for maintaining the track,
- failed to ensure that the premises were maintained in a safe condition,
- breached their duty by not inspecting the premises,
- failed to discover the broken glass,
- failed to warn him about the glass.

These theories combined to form a charge of both simple and gross negligence. The trial court ruled for the school under the theory of sovereign immunity. However, the appellate court concluded that the lower court should not have dismissed the case based on sovereign immunity for the athletic director, baseball coach and building and grounds supervisor. The school board was immune, but under a Virginia statute, state employees were not immune for acts of simple negligence. The failure to detect the broken glass could have been considered simple negligence.

Besides being very unsightly, a field with *gopher or ground hog holes* can be very dangerous. Special care has to be taken to make sure all holes are filled in or eliminated. You have an affirmative duty to warn participants about such holes and to correct the hazards created by the holes.

Field maintenance personnel should pay special attention to the field watering mechanism. The most ideal watering system is a recessed watering system with the spigots installed and recessed to be even with the ground. If a watering hose or an above ground piping system is used, you should make sure all the equipment is properly stored away after watering the field to avoid a tripping hazard.

Should you be concerned about grass quality? The answer is yes. If the field is parched or there is not enough grass, a player that slips, trips, slides or dives for a ball, could claim that if healthy grass was present, the injury would not have been as severe. On the other hand, you also have to make sure the grass is not too thick or slick.

Maddox v. City of New York
496 N.Y.S. 2d 727 (NY 1985)

New York Yankees outfielder, Elliot Maddox, was injured on June 13, 1975, when he slipped and fell during a night game against the Chicago White Sox. Maddox was playing center field and was fielding a fly ball when his left foot slid while his right foot stuck in a mud hole. His right knee buckled, requiring several operations, and which ultimately led to his premature retirement.

Maddox was aware of the field's slippery and muddy condition on the night in question and he had informed field's groundskeepers about the puddle. Maddox continued participating in the game even though he thought the field was dangerous. Maddox alleged that the drainage system was negligently designed, constructed and maintained. The court concluded that by continuing his participation, with the knowledge and appreciation of the risk which he assumed, Maddox had assumed the risk as a matter of law. Maddox also lost his suit because, as a professional baseball player, he should have had higher knowledge about risks faced while playing on wet grass. Thus, a novice player could possibly succeed in a similar suit.

Infield Dirt

Infield dirt has to be maintained in a manner that minimizes participants' risks.

The biggest potential problem with infield dirt is the presence of rocks or hardened dirt/mud clumps. If a playing surface has irregular or hard-packed dirt, no sliding or fielding of ground/fly balls should be undertaken until the hazard is reduced or fixed. Only batting practice and throwing drills should be undertaken.

The infield dirt should be fine enough that rocks are easy to spot, but the dirt also has to be packed in such a manner that players do not sink into the sand. Before each contest the surface should be raked to loosen the dirt, eliminate any rough areas, help spot potential hazards or uneven spots and expose any protrusions that could injure a participant. Hidden dangers in base paths have resulted in numerous injuries and suits.

Ardoin v. Evangeline Parish School Board
376 So. 2d 372 (LA 1979)

David Ardoin was injured when he tripped over a piece of concrete while running the bases in a softball game. The concrete piece, estimated at 12" to 30" in diameter and about eight inches thick, was embedded in the ground directly on the path between two bases.

Based on the inherent danger of the cement slab, the school should have known about the slab. Because the danger was so serious, the court concluded that the school had constructive knowledge of the defect. The court held that the slab constituted a hazardous condition and that the school breached its required standard of care by allowing the danger to exist.

Infield dirt has to be examined carefully after a rain storm to evaluate whether the ground is too soft or muddy. Many baseball coaches and field maintenance workers water down the infield dirt before a game to avoid dust. This practice is necessary to protect participants from dust blowing in their eyes. However, the dirt should only be covered with a light coating of water, and care should be taken to avoid creating any puddles. Furthermore, a significant amount of clay contained in your infield surface mixture can make running almost impossible if the field is to wet or not dried enough (either naturally or chemically) before a game. Remember. you cannot reduce one hazard by increasing another.

It is customary to mark the first and third base lines with chalk, paint or slaked lime so the base path and foul lines are visible. This custom has gone through some changes although chalk and paint are still used. *Unslaked lime* should never be used for marking lines. A participant could be blinded by unslaked lime if they slide into a base head-first. The author has seen numerous hazardous conditions, but he was really shocked when he found the outfield lines at a Little League baseball field in California marked with half inch through one-inch size white rocks. A baseball player could trip or slip on these rocks or land on the rocks, which makes them more dangerous then not having any marking.

Two areas in the infield that constantly require special attention are the *batter's box* and *pitcher's mound*. The dirt around the batter's box is constantly dug-up and moved around by batters to improve their batting position. Participants could possibly trip over these depressions and mounds.

Praetorius v. Shell Oil Co.
207 So. 2d 872 (LA 1968)

John Praetorius, a catcher in the Eastbank Softball League, was injured while playing on the Shell Oil Company baseball field. Praetorius fell and fractured his right leg after he tripped while running to first base. The field was well kept and no holes existed between home plate and first base except for the small holes or depressions around the batter's box.

Shell Oil lost the lower court case. However, on appeal, the appellate court found that the defendant was not responsible for permitting small holes or depressions to exist because the dirt in the batter's box area was dug-up by each player. Praetorius knew about the holes around the batter's box. In fact, he had dug some of the holes himself to obtain more leverage while at bat. Thus, his award from a lower court was reversed.

The only way to prevent depressions from occurring around the batters' boxes would be to rake the area after each batter. This is an almost impossible task. The pitcher's mound suffers the same fate as each pitcher normally likes to pitch or land their follow-through from a different location. Even though you might not be able to prevent a participant from moving infield dirt, you can inform everyone that there is a rake available in each dugout and they can fix the batter's box or the pitcher's mound according to their own needs. When the participants are provided with notice, they will assume the risk of either changing the dirt or not changing the dirt because they have the option to fix the condition. However, if the pitcher's mound or batter's box areas need significant repair, play should be suspended until adequate repairs are completed.

Bases

According to the Institute for Preventative Sports Medicine, there are 1.7 million base running injuries each year in softball and baseball ("Dangerous game," 1995). Of these injuries, 75 percent come from sliding into bases. Several different bases are available for use. There are *conventional anchored bases, rubber-unanchored base (impact bases), and Break-Away bases.* The authors have heard positive reports from people using Break-Away bases, which is a manufactured brand, however every type of bases poses certain risks and all bases should be considered when examining your final choice. You can ask various base manufacturers for any safety data they might have about their products. A "break-away" base is anchored similar to a conventional base, with either a quick release mechanism or with magnets. Under pressure from someone sliding directly into the base, the Break-Away Base will become unanchored. Thus, the base absorbs some shock from the participant's leg. Care has to be taken to ensure the base is correctly installed according to the printed instructions so the base will perform correctly.

Impact bases are starting to appear more frequently as word about these bases spreads. Impact bases are designed with a flexible rubber base to compress and absorb energy on impact, rather than break away. Hollywood Bases in Marysville, CA manufacture the Hollywood Impact Base. Based on their rigidity, conventional bases provide the least flexibility when someone slides into a base. There is no one best base as each base type presents different strengths and weaknesses based on the specific activity or age group involved. A reasonably prudent EA would check with their official sanctioning body to determine what base type is recommended for that competitive level.

Backstop

The backstop/screen is an area where participants or spectators should be free from potential hazards. Individuals utilize backstops specifically for protection. Thus, the backstop has to provide that protection. If there is a hole in the backstop, and a ball goes through the hole, you could be negligent for failing to provide reasonably safe premises. You also have to be concerned about balls hitting the top of loose netting on the backstop and the hitting fans. You are required by law to provide screening or netting for the most dangerous part of the field (behind the plate and up the first and third base lines) and to provide enough screen-protected seats for those who might want such protection (*Coronel v. Chicago White Sox, Ltd.*, 1992). There is no exact percentage as to how many seats need to be covered by a screen. One court concluded that screening 15% of the stadium's seats was inadequate(*Coronel v. Chicago White Sox, Ltd.*, 1992). In addition to vertical screening for the most dangerous areas, horizontal screening is also appropriate. The area right behind home plate should have a canopy screen to protect against foul balls that fly straight back and could hit an unsuspecting fan. Such canopy screen should be at least two feet wide. Screening should also be made available underneath a press box. Foul balls can hit press box windows or siding and then fall on an unsuspecting fan below.

Before each game the *wood planks, metal brackets, screen and/or net should be examined for any wear, holes, tears, fraying or splintering.* If the problem cannot be fixed immediately, the area should either be marked as hazardous or blocked off to participants and spectators.

The same concerns about backstops also apply to *dugouts*. Most school

The same concerns about backstops also apply to *dugouts*. Most school or Little League dugouts are fenced in to protect the participants. These fences have to be examined before each game. Dugouts in college and professional fields might not be fenced in, but players at the advanced levels are held to a higher level of knowledge regarding the potential risks associated with baseball played at advanced levels.

To provide the greatest participant protection, you should make sure that both the on-deck circles and the dugouts are recessed a sufficient distance from the playing field. They should either be behind a fence, behind the backstop or in the authors' opinion at least 40 feet from home plate to provide enough reaction time to move away from a foul ball. Proper protective distances and protective equipment are not always available. The *Scala* case demonstrates the dangers associated with using facilities that are not designed for their intended purpose, such as using an out-of-season ice rink for baseball.

Scala v. City of New York
102 N.Y.S. 2d 790 (NY, 1951)

On April 20, 1947, Jerry Scala, seriously injured his leg while playing softball on a public playground in Brooklyn, New York. The playground was used for, among other purposes, ice skating and softball games. The playground had a cement floor and there was a two-inch high curb around the field. Near the curb, concrete benches were placed at irregular intervals.

The field was not specifically designed for baseball, but the players improvised and created their own diamond. The city of New York did not furnish the players with any equipment. During the game, Scala ran after a high fly-ball and tripped over the curb, causing a severe leg injury. Scala had played on the field many times prior to the accident. The court concluded that a softball player assumed the risk because he was aware of the curb and benches and voluntarily assumed the risk of playing.

This case helps demonstrate potential problems that may occur when a multi-use facility is designed to accommodate sports requiring different facility needs. If the two-inch curb was constructed of wood and only installed during the winter months, the facility would have been more adequately designed for dual-purpose use. To help prevent injuries in multiuse facilities, all potentially dangerous conditions *should be set apart from the playing area, painted a bright color and users should be explicitly warned about the potential danger.*

Multi-use facilities can raise another concern. While you can warn participants about some concerns, other concerns which seem minimal can arise resulting in litigation. For example, if a ballfield has a low fence to accommodate other usages, a baseball player could possibly throw a ball over the fence while warming up and injure other users. This minor accident occurs on a regular basis. However, in one extreme circumstance, the injured woman sued the nine-year-old baseball player ("Fair play for volunteers," 1996). While the court dismissed the case, all participants and spectators at adjoining field should either be warned or be provided with some type of protective screening.

Fences

An outfield fence is designed as a barricade to prevent a player from chasing after a fly ball and to prevent ground balls from rolling past the playing field. Fences have the potential to be very dangerous. A player chasing a high fly ball might not notice the fence and run into it. Various materials are used to construct fences. Most fences are constructed of brick, cement, wood or chain-link. Brick or cement walls are constructed with durability and strength in mind. Thus, they are potentially the most dangerous fences when a collision occurs. Chain-link or wire fences can be hazardous as clothing or skin could become entangled, ripped or torn by sharp edges. In contrast, in 1991 a film clip appeared on many sports newscasts showing an outfielder running with full force through a wood fence. The player was able to walk away from the accident even though he ran through the fence.

Currently numerous programs, especially Little League and high school programs, have adopted a new "standard" by using *flexible plastic fences* that collapse during a collision. These fences are designed so both the fence and the posts flex upon impact. As these fences are widely available and can prevent many injuries, they should be considered the ideal fence or industry standard for competition at or below the high school level. Impact reduction devices such as hanging cushions are also effective in reducing the possible damage caused by a collision with a fence.

Many fences, especially for Little League or high school fields, are only about three feet high. Shorter fences are especially dangerous because a participant could get injured by falling, rolling or trying to jump over them. If you use a chain-link or wire fence, any portion of the chain-link running over the upper stabilizing bar/pipe should be bent over the bar/pipe to prevent a participant's clothing or skin from being cut/entangled.

A warning track, starting four feet or more prior to the fence, should be an effective warning for the upcoming fence. Most school fields below the college or professional ranks do not have a warning track, so participants have to be warned in other ways. If the field does not have a warning track, you might want to consider painting the fence a bright or florescent color to help warn participants. In addition to possible financial returns, the use of bright advertisements can also make a fence more visible.

A representative of the Center for Sport Law and Risk Management based in Dallas, Texas, suggest that in lieu of a warning track, those in charge of the field should have the grass cut very low at least seven or eight feet from the fence and a line be marked to warn the players of the fence. Many school that utilize this strategy report that it serves as an adequate warning for players and avoids crashes into fences or barriers.

Batting Cages

The major concerns associated with batting cages involve *securing the nets or walls and protecting a pitcher*. Most batting cages are constructed with netting to help reduce the speed of the batted balls while keeping the balls in the cage. If nets are used, you should make sure there are no holes in the netting, nor any gaps between nets to prevent balls from leaving the cage. If the cage is constructed of sheet metal, aluminum siding, chain-link fencing or other materials, the walls should be covered with loose netting that flexes upon impact. By hitting the net before hitting the wall, the potential for deflected balls is greatly reduced. Tightly strung nets are currently being used at indoor softball fields based on the concept that a tight net will deflect the ball back into the playing area, and thus make the game more exciting. However, the netting in batting cages has to be loose enough to catch and break the balls flight without ricocheting the ball at the participants.

In practice sessions, if a pitcher is pitching to the batter, the pitcher should only pitch from behind a chain-link pitching screen so the screen blocks balls hit straight to the pitcher. A pitching screen is a 3/4 screen shaped like an "L" lying on its side. The pitcher should also consider wearing a colored shirt as a ball is harder to see when pitched from a white long-sleeved shirt. Besides protecting pitchers, all participants should use *orange or red baseballs* as they are easier to spot by the batter and pitcher. Even though batting practice is "practice," all participants should utilize batting helmets.

Lights

The days of baseball being considered a daytime activity are in the past. Numerous fields are lit for night games and you have to make sure the lights are *turned on at the right time.* You might save a little money by turning on the lights at the very last second, but lights should be turned on immediately when the shadows around the field start to get longer. There is no set time for when the lights should be turned on, but an hour before dusk could be considered a reasonable time.

You have to make sure the light intensity is appropriate and the lights adequate for their intended use. If the lights are not bright enough, an unseen ball could injure a participant. If the lights are too bright, losing the ball in the lights could injure the participant. It is recommended that light for school baseball teams should produce about 50 footcandles of light ("Sports lighting," 1997). Lights for a school softball field should produce around 30 footcandles of light. Standard baseball lights produce 1500 watts of power, but light levels on the field should be measured with a light meter. Reflectors should be utilized with the lights to help focus the light energy to the required location. Reflectors can also help decrease glare by redirecting off-field spill ligt. By focusing the lights, the chance of a ball getting lost in the glare is reduced. The following graph highlight the various footcandle needs of various sports and fields/gymnasiums.

Field Type	Maintained Light Level (in footcandles)
Baseball/Softball	
Recreational	30 baseball /20 softball
School	50/30
College	70/50
Basketball	
Recreational	30
School (high school)	75
College	100
Football	
School/Amateur	30
College	50
Soccer	
School/Amateur	30
College	50
Tennis	
Recreational	30
School	40
College	60

("Sports lighting," 1997).

One quick note should be added concerning light safety issues. Light poles can present an attractive nuisance for children. Furthermore, light poles can present other concerns such as falling over from wood rot or animals (woodpeckers) through toxic chemicals used to preserve the wood.

Spectators

In addition to possible injuries from structural hazards, spectators could also injure participants. Sometimes where spectators are located can unduly expose a participant to risk, as illustrated in the following case.

Domino v. Mercurio
193 N.E. 2d 893 (NY 1963)

Joseph Domino was injured in a softball game when he tripped over a bench close to the third base line. A fence that provided 27 feet of space beyond the third base line protected the playground. Two metal benches were stationed by the fence for player/spectator use. At the game in question, over 100 spectators were congregated on the third base line. The crowd filled the benches and overflowed onto the ground in front of the benches.

A foul ball was hit into the air between third base and home plate. While chasing after the foul ball, Domino tripped over a spectator sitting on the bench and fell over the bench breaking his leg. Evidence showed the bench had been moved to halfway between the fence and the third base line.

The Board of Education approved the softball league, provided equipment for the game and provided supervisors. The defendant was one of the umpires charged with controlling the field. Ropes and standards were available to restrain the crowd, but co-defendant, Walter, who supervised the third base line, did not feel they were needed. However, on two occasions during the game, Walter halted play and asked the fans to move back to the fence. The spectators slowly drifted forward again and were not asked to back-up.

The court held the school board liable for its employees' (the supervisors) negligence because they allowed the spectators to congregate too close to the third base line.

Equipment

Most baseball players use their own equipment, but some items are traditionally furnished by a coach or EA. Catching equipment should be required for both baseball and softball catchers. Baseball catchers should wear at least: a cup, facemask/helmet assembly, chest protector, and shin guards. Softball catchers should wear at least a protective cup, and a facemask depending on the league. Most catchers in high ark leagues do not wear facemasks, even though a cautious catcher should probably wear a mask. All catchers should have appropriate gloving to catch either baseballs or softballs. Catcher gloves should be adequately padded around the thumb and palm area.

Baseball bats should be checked to ensure they are not cracked or splintered in any way. Each bat should have a knob at the end and the knob should not be worn down. Bat handles should be taped or roughened to make sure the bats do not slip from the participant's grip. Taping a bat handle can also reduce the risk of splinters or wood slivers injuring a participant after a bat breaks or cracks.

Baseball players should only use baseball bats and softball players should only use approved softball bats. Bats for the two sports should be kept separately to avoid any confusion or misuse. Furthermore, you should make sure the type of bat used is appropriate for the given category. A large debate erupted over the past several years concerning baseballs coming off aluminum bats very quickly and causing more injuries then traditional wood bats. Balls coming off aluminum bats can come off the bat eight to twelve percent faster than off wood bats ("Danger at the plate," 1998). National publicity was generated by this debate which eventually led to the NCAA prohibiting certain bats (Farmer, 1999). The NCAA approved certain bats tested by an independent testing group, and schools/universities had to adopt the new "standard" even though they might have already purchased bats for the following season which might not have been approved (Farmer, 1999). Thus, the standard was adopted without providing any grandfather type provision, often seen in other regulations, which would have allowed teams to keep using bats already purchased before the regulations were approved.

You should also make sure the bats are properly sized for the batters that will be using them. The following case highlights this concern.

Asmus v. Board of Education City of Chicago
508 N.E. 298 (IL 1987)

Plaintiff, Michael Asmus was injured when Tammy, a third-grade class-mate swung a bat which hit Asmus in the face. Asmus was catching be-hind home plate when the accident occurred.

The plaintiff alleged that the school board breached its duty to exercise reasonable care in providing the students with safe equipment by,

> negligently furnishing them (players) with a regulation size and weight wooden bat for use by adults which was too heavy to be safely held and swung by children of the age of plaintiff and his classmates, many of whom, including Tammy, had no previous experience in swinging any type of baseball bat and who were unable because of their size and lack of experience to properly hold or swing a baseball bat of the type furnished.

The plaintiff also alleged that the school board failed to provide less dangerous equipment (such as plastic, lighter wooden or aluminum bats), a safety helmet or face mask and a backstop to separate the catcher from the batter.

The School Board's immunity protection did not bar a negligence claim alleging failure to provide effective equipment. Thus, the lower court's dismissal of the case on immunity grounds was reversed by the appellate court.

Different sized batting helmets should be provided to allow a participant the option of picking a helmet that provides the best fit and most visibility while batting and running. Some programs have gone so far as to buy helmets that fit each player. Helmets used for batting and base running should have NOCSAE safety seals. *Full coverage helmets*, which cover the ear and the jaw, should be provided to give participants the greatest amount of head protection. Newer helmets often allow the owners to attach plastic chin, jaw and/or eye socket guards, which can provide additional protection. While batters need a face guard to protect them from a potentially errant pitch or foul tip, the need for face guards also extends to the field and fielders are at a greater risk of being injured in the face. The results in one national study concluded that 11 percent of facial injuries in baseball occurred at home plate. In contrast, infielders suffered 49 percent of facial injuries (Conklin, 1998). Due to the concern about over regulating baseball, no league has required face guards for infielders and only one league (Tennessee Dixie Baseball League) requires face guards for batters (Conklin, 1998). While face guards are beneficial, care should be taken when adding anything to a helmet that might jeopardize the helmet's integrity/structure or might make the helmet too heavy. Some anecdotal evidence points to the fact that heavier helmets transfer a certain amount of pressure to the spine (Conklin, 1998). If any components of the helmet are repaired/modified, the repairs should only be performed by a person specifically trained to work on that particular helmet (see also the football helmet section for additional precautions).

Face guards are not the only safety feature that might need further analysis. Should fielders be forced to wear chest protectors? In a study from 1973 through 1995 the Consumer Products Safety Commission analyzed 88 Little Leaguers who died while playing. The largest number of these cases, 68, involved ball-impact injuries with 38 of those injuries being balls hitting a fielder's chest (Conklin, 1998).

Special care has to be exercised when children are using baseball equipment. In addition to oversized baseball bats, children should not be allowed to use metal cleats. If possible, children should also be provided with Reduced Injury Factor balls that are not as hard as standard baseballs.

A *pitching machine* can be one of the most dangerous apparatus associated with baseball training. With machines shooting balls at batters at speeds up to 100 miles per hour, a *higher standard of care* has to be exercised by individuals using such machines. This higher standard can be met through appropriate training and constant supervision during the machine's use. An additional higher level of care is required for machines with swinging arms, as an arm can become coiled for a pitch and even after a machine is shut-off, an arm could accidentally uncoil. Such an accident occurred in the *Dudley* case.

Dudley Sports Co. v. Schmitt
279 N.E. 2d 266 (IN 1972)

Danville High School purchased an automatic baseball pitching machine from Dudley Sports Co. in 1965. The machine consisted of a frame and an open-extended throwing arm. There was no protective shield covering the throwing arm. The arm required coiling a spring to generate the momentum needed for the arm's hurling action. Thus, if the coil was wound, the machine would still be able to deliver a powerful blow even if the machine was unplugged. Any slight vibration or a change in the atmospheric conditions could trigger the arm's spring. The only warning with the machine read as follows:

Warning!
Safety First.Read Instructions before rotating machine either electrically
or manually...Stay clear of throwing arm at all times!

The day after the machine was purchased, Lawrence Schmitt (a student) was sweeping in the locker room, where the machine was stored, when the arm swung and hit him in the face, causing extensive facial injuries. Schmitt did not sue the school, but sued the machine's distributor. Schmitt won $35,000 from Dudley because the machine's ability to swing the pitching arm as a result of slight vibration, even when unplugged, was a latent danger. The court concluded that this latent danger could only be discovered through examining of the machine and knowing the machines engineering, which a 16-year-old student would not ordinarily possess.

If Danville High School knew about the latent defect and purchased the machine anyway or did not warn potential users, then the high school could also have been liable in the case. Thus, anyone using a pitching machine should provide all students or potential equipment users with extensive directions and explicit warnings.

Opponent Violence

Twenty years ago, dugout-clearing brawls were normally not expected in a baseball game. That is no longer the case. In one case a Little League coach was assaulted by a coach, team manager and a 16-year-old player during a tournament. The Little League division that hosted the tournament was sued for failing to prevent a foreseeable attack and failing to stop the attack once aggression was spotted. An Illinois jury awarded the plaintiff and his wife (she had a loss of consortium claim) $757,710 ("$757.710 awarded to little league coach for assault at athletic field," 1998).

While violence is often foreseen through on-the-field agitation, in a 1993 California incident a player was beaten to death by an opponent even with adult supervision at the event. The incident reputably stemmed from the all to familiar "trash talking" and the players hurling insult at each other (Corcoran, 1993). Different disputes can also arise from non-player related activities such as officiating. In 1993 a teenage umpire was shot by an assistant coach in East St. Louis over what the coach thought was an incorrect call (Corcoran, 1993).

Based on these cases, it is clear that under certain conditions, you could have a duty to protect participants from violent conflicts. How can you predict when violence is foreseeable? If the teams have a long-standing history of bitter athletic rivalry, you can be put on notice that tempers might be higher than other games. You can also be put on notice if members of one team or both teams were involved in a fight during prior games. If one team has a strategy of intimidating players through *brush-back pitches or hitting batters,* and if you know this strategy has been used in the past, then you would be put on notice. However, no matter how much knowledge you have, a fight can occur and conclude within a second, and if you have taken all possible supervisorial precautions you should not be liable for such an altercation.

Hanley v. Hornbeck
512 N.Y.S. 2d 262 (1987)

George Hanley, an eighth-grade student, was participating in a game of wiffle ball with Hornbeck, the defendant, when the two youths became involved in an altercation. Hanley was preparing to play the catchers position, when Hornbeck, from the opposing team, also wanted to play catcher. When the school teacher tried to separate the two, Hornbeck hit Hanley in the face. The school was also named as a defendant for failing to provide proper supervision.

The trial court ruled in Hanley's favor, but the appellate court concluded that the verdict against the school should be overruled because closer supervision could not have prevented the fight. The teacher intervened right when the two players started pushing each other and in the process of separating the two, a punch was thrown. The fact that Hornbeck was involved in fights four years earlier did not put the school on notice that he would get into other fights.

Appropriate measures to take in curtailing potential violence could include:

- hiring trained security personnel,
- warning players, coaches, parents and program directors about the potential for violence and the repercussions to anyone initiating or participating in an altercation,
- instituting stricter officiating,
- excluding certain participants, spectators or teams,
- restricting attendance,
- moving the event to a neutral site,
- canceling an event which has the potential for violence.

When the tempers in a game start to flare, you have an affirmative duty to intervene and institute a cool-off period. The *cool-off period* could be supplemented with *ejecting player(s), disbursing a hostile crowd or canceling the game.*

In addition, you have to continuously warn individuals that they are engaged in a physical activity that can be rough and they have to accept some of that roughness by participating. For example, a base runner can slide into home plate and violently tackle a catcher. Would such an incident be considered outside the rules or just part of the game? This scenarios has resulted in several suits, including a suit that reached the Texas Supreme Court involving two players who were playing on competing church backed softball teams (Pinkerton, 1995). The issue was whether or not the baserunner was trying to injure the catcher. The court concluded that a material issue of fact existed concerning whether the base runner's conduct was intentional or reckless. Furthermore, the court held that the assumption of risk defense did not bar the claim (Greer v. Davis, 940 S.W.2d 582 (1996, Tex Sup. Ct)).

Supervision

One of your duties as an EA is the adoption of rules that will ensure participant safety. Two rules that should be adopted to assist in insuring reasonable supervision include a rule *preventing attacking slides* at players after a put-out, and a requirement that catchers or batters in the on-deck circle *pick up a tossed bat* after the previous batter has hit the ball. These represent just two rules that can be implemented to assist you in running a smoother event.

Supervision concerns can be very diverse depending on the situation and individuals involved. One suit was raised by a softball player hit in the head by a line-drive her coach hit while the players were engaged in a ground-ball drill (Henderson, 1996). Another case involved a youth baseball league sued by an irate father after his son was cut from a team for what might have been discriminatory motives ("Father sues after son cut from team," 1997). In yet another case a college softball player sued after she claimed her coach forced her to keep pitching when she was hurt (Hoskinson, 1996). All three cases deal with personal judgment or conduct in a manner that can be considered inconsistent with a reasonable person standard. Cutting someone from a team for the wrong reasons, doing the wrong drill or forcing someone to do something against their will all represent ineffective supervision. Similar to the *in loco parentis doctrine,* children and young athletes often look to coaches and EAs for proper conduct and when that conduct does not conform to a reasonable person standard a negligence case can be raised, traditionally on the ground of improper supervision/management.

Proper supervision relates to more than just player/administrator conduct, but also includes items which players might be wearing. *No metal spikes* should be allowed for competition below the collegiate level as rubber cleats perform very well with a much lower injury potential to opposing players. Players should be prohibited from wearing watches or jewelry that could possibly injury someone.

Special care has to be taken with children. As the saying goes, "boys will be boys," and children have a way of getting into trouble. Young participants should not be left unsupervised, and there has to be a *mature and capable supervisor* for each activity. Special care has to be exercised when a ball is hit or thrown outside of the playing area and a child is sent to retrieve the ball.

Bedor v. Ekdahl
248 N.W. 2d 321 (MN 1976)

Thirteen-year-old Paul Bedor was injured while retrieving a baseball from a highway adjacent to the playing field. The car that struck Bedor was driven by Ekdahl, who the jury found innocent. The jury concluded that the coach supervising Bedor was negligent, but Bedor was also negligent, and Bedor's negligence was the proximate cause of his injuries.

The *Bedor* result would have been different if the coach could or should have foreseen the danger associated with playing ball next to a highway. If the *Bedor* case occurred in the 1990s the result might be different as risk management knowledge has increased marketably since the early 1970s and most coaches know how dangerous it is to play by heavy traffic or parking areas.

If young children are involved in drills, each drill supervisor should be specifically trained and knowledgeable in the potential injuries inherent in that drill. For example, a high fly drill is a drill where a coach hits a high fly into the outfield and the outfielder designated to catch the ball relays the ball to a cut-off person. The coach has to inform all the players that any fly-balls hit over the cut-off person's head should be handled by the outfielders, to avoid a possible collision between an outfielder and the cut-off person. Players should also be instructed to line up in an orderly manner for catching the high-flies. Additionally, no player should throw a ball until the cut-off person is ready to catch the throw. Before undertaking any drill, a coach should spend a couple minutes going over the rules for the specific drill. Some people might challenge this step as wasting valuable practice time, but it accomplishes two important objectives. It provides the opportunity to teach the players the proper way to execute the drill (which will make the drill more effective) and it will instill a safety mind-set among the players.

In reference to competition involving children, a rule should be adopted prohibiting parents from the dugouts. Parents are known to push a child into doing more than the child can physically accomplish. If the child tries to do more than he or she can, the child can often face injury. If an injury does occur, the parents could claim that the coach should have known the child's limitations and should have taken steps to prevent such an accident. By excluding parents from the dugouts, the potential for such pressure is reduced and a coach could be free to make decisions without someone five feet away scrutinizing each decision.

Children should not be allowed to use equipment designed for adults unless they are strong enough to correctly use the equipment. This concern is most prevalent when children use heavy baseball bats (which should be replaced with lighter bats) or use helmets which are too large.

Adult softball players can sometimes require more supervision than children, due to the emotional nature inherent in frustrated weekend warriors. The emotional pressure on some players, coupled with several beers, may impair some participants and you should recognize the potential dangers such a player can face or create. A player might tell you he or she is in a reasonable condition to play, but if they are injured, they could claim that they did not know their own condition and the EA should have recognized the participant's reduced capabilities. The most effective means to help reduce alcohol related incidents is to prohibit all drinking. While this approach can be effective, it does not address the issue of other individuals who might drink "off-site" and then compete at the event.

Conclusion

The following list details some of the important steps you should undertake to help reduce the chances of a suit associated with a baseball event and, at the same time, prevent injuries. This list represents only some concerns and is not intended as a complete list setting forth all baseball-related risks. Questions you should ask yourself include have you:

- mowed the outfield/infield grass,
- checked the playing field for balls, bats, glass, etc.,

- inspected and raked the infield dirt, pitcher's mound and batter's box,
- examined the bases for wear, poor anchors, etc.,
- inspected and repaired any holes or gaps in the backstop or dugout fencing,
- inspected the on-deck circle, the dugout and the spectator seating areas to ensure they are adequately recessed from the playing field,
- inspected the outfield and sideline fences for dangerous conditions,
- inspected the batting cage for any potential safety hazards,
- adjusted the lights so they are of the proper wattage and turned on at proper time,
- inspected the participants to make sure they are using proper equipment (i.e. no broken bats, no metal spikes, etc.),
- provided adequate supervision based on the activity's demands.

While the list above is fairly detailed, you should utilize a comprehensive risk management planning approach such as the ECT method to discover all possible concerns that need to be addressed. For example, who might be liable if someone decides to sponsor a team through buying uniforms? This issue arose in a case where a company sponsored a team by providing uniforms and equipment. The court concluded that just providing uniforms and equipment did not convert the team members into employee to whom worker's compensation coverage would apply or for whom the company could be liable for their negligence through an agency relationship (*Toms v. Delta Savings & Loan Ass'n*, 124 N.E. 2d 123 (1955)).

Chapter 13

Basketball

Basketball is a game characterized by rapid bursts of speeds in a small-enclosed area. There is normally very little room around a court, thus, your concerns normally revolve around areas in the gymnasium that could pose a danger to a participant or spectator. Cases have highlighted concerns associated with contiguous courts, walls too close to the endlines, inadequate padding on basket poles, improper glass in gym doors, slippery floors and other problems associated with multiple use facilities (Nygaard, 1989). Additional concerns addressed in this chapter include locker rooms, opponent violence and other participant related concerns.

Gymnasium

A gymnasium is easier to inspect than a playing field, as most potentially dangerous conditions can be spotted relatively quickly, while a playing field can have defects concealed by dirt or grass. A gymnasium should have adequate space around the court, the floors should not be slippery, the baskets should be protected and the bleachers should be safe. While this list is relatively small, ensuring compliance with these concerns can be very difficult.

Adequate Space

Any event that is held in the gymnasium is limited by the gymnasium's size. You should always examine the room available for any activities to be conducted in the gym. Running races or sprint drills are often held inside gyms. Unfortunately, many older gyms were not constructed with a location for hanging protective padding. Protective padding is required to protect a sprinter, basketball player or any other athlete who does not have enough space or time to slow down after a quick sprint. If a participant is injured in a gymnasium running race, the participant could argue that you were negligent in using a gym for an activity contrary to the gym's intended use. Basketball courts require room for a participant to finish a lay-up or a fast break. If there is not enough room available for the par-

169

ticipant to slow down they could run into a wall. This potential problem is often seen at individual homes where baskets are hung by the garage and even an easy lay-up can carry the player right into the garage door. Based on this potential hazard you should provide adequate protective padding behind baskets, and possibly running the entire length of the court if there exists little or no room between the baseline and the wall. There is no set standard for padding depth in gymnasiums. However, the authors suggest that padding should be approximately one and one-half inch thick and the exterior cleaned on a regular basis. The padding should be hung approximately eight inches above the floor to a height of at least six feet, depending on how much room exists from the baseline to the wall.

When only a limited amount of space is available, or if the gym is too small, a coach should limit the types of drills or games played. The number of athletes in each drill should be reduced based on the available space. A coach should usually conduct: a *walk-through of the team's offensive plays, shooting and rebounding drills, two-on-two and three-on-three drills, and half court games. When space is limited, full court drills or games should not be started.*

Even areas that are designed for basketball might not be safe. A park with a fenced in basketball court might have a fence only a few feet behind the basket pole. To ensure adequate room for playing basketball the authors suggest that walls or fences should be *at least six to eight feet* from the court endlines. When there are two courts adjacent to one another you should try to ensure at least *three feet between the courts* as participants could collide with each other or with a loose basketball from the adjacent court.

There have been several cases in which gymnasiums were designed with glass doors or glass windows located around the basketball courts. Players need to have room for their forward progress, and if there is no room, a player could run into the door or window.

Eddy v. Syracuse University
433 N.Y.S. 2d 923 (NY 1980)

Mr. Eddy sustained injuries when he ran through a glass door at one end of Syracuse University's gymnasium. Eddy was a student from Harpur College who was playing a game of "Ultimate Frisbee" against a Syracuse University team. A janitor possibly let the teams into the gymnasium.

The students created an Ultimate Frisbee playing field where the west goal line was located approximately five to eight feet from the gymnasium's west wall, which was of masonry construction with glass doors in the center. Eddy was running towards the west wall when he was unable to stop, and ran into the doors. He had just enough time to stick his hand out in an attempt to protect himself. His body struck the door's handlebar, but because the door was locked, it did not open. Eddy knew about the wall and doors when he was participating in the game.

The university argued that:

- it did not authorize the gym's use,
- did not know Eddy would use the gym,
- could not foresee the manner in which the gym would be used and
- the gymnasium was not defective in its design or construction.

In upholding the plaintiff's award, the appellate court concluded that:

- it was validly submitted to the jury whether or not the glass doors constituted a dangerous condition,
- the university should have foreseen that students might use the gymnasium for the playing games other than basketball, and
- the risk presented by the glass doors could have been eliminated without imposing an undue burden upon the university.

In order to protect participants from shattered glass, several courts have recommended various solutions. Some proposed solutions include changing the window or glass door from ordinary glass or double thick window sheet glass to an all wood or all metal door, installing safety glass or covering the window with a screen or protective guard. In some jurisdictions you might have an affirmative or statutory duty to replace glass in a gym door. The following case analyzed such a state statute.

Johnson v. City of Boston
490 N.E. 2d 1204 (MA 1986)

Johnson obtained a jury verdict of $58,500 for injuries to his hand. The injuries occurred while he was running towards a music class held in the school's auditorium. In an effort to be one of the first students there, Johnson ran towards the auditorium and pushed on the swinging auditorium doors. In so doing, he put his hand through the door's glass panel.

In 1971, a state statute was enacted requiring the installation of shatterproof glazing material in entrance doors made after 1973. If the school had lived up to the new glass standard, then the city would not have been liable. However, the glass used in the auditorium doors was ordinary glass. Since 1971, it was the school department's policy to replace broken windows with wired glass or with an acrylic panel.

The court stated that the standard developed since the 1960s involved the use of annealed glass (cooled in slow controlled process so the material is less brittle). Laminated glass, wired glass, tempered glass, and putting hardware cloth or Mylar Film on annealed glass were additional methods suggested by the court for reducing risks associated with glass doors and windows. Because the school failed to install a safer glass panel, Johnson won the case.

Any *electrical, light or backboard fixture* control panels/switches along the walls should be recessed into the wall. For example, light switches should be recessed inside a box set into the wall so the cover is flush with the wall. Protruding fixtures should be replaced or painted a bright color to help warn the participants. Locking mechanism should be installed over all switches to allow you to lock the switches in a set direction. This can prevent people from turning on lights when the gym is closed. All *floor plates* (for inserting badminton or volleyball standards) should also be flush with the floor to prevent a participant from tripping on an uneven or raised surface. If a *scorers' table* is set up next to the court, the table's front and ends should be padded to minimize the shock on a player running into the table. The authors recommend that scorers' table and any press tables should be at least four feet from the out-of-bounds lines. Likewise, photographers, band members and cheerleaders should also stand at least four feet from the out-of-bounds lines. Photographers and others that are within four feet of the endlines should sign waivers and be warned about all potential risks. Individuals that are four feet away should be specifically warned about possible player collisions.

The gym should be equipped with an efficient ventilation system to provide adequate air circulation. If the temperature and humidity levels are too high and the gym does not have adequate air circulation, the gym should be closed to prevent heat stroke or heat exhaustion.

Gym Floor

The gym floor may be your biggest concern. Basketball's fast-paced flow, coupled with numerous start-stop movements and a slick finished surface, puts you on notice that a slippery or rough floor could lead to a serious injury. A gym floor can become slippery through various liquids being spilled and/or dust bunnies, as demonstrated in the following case.

Dawson v. Rhode Island Auditorium, Inc.
242 A. 2d 407 (RI 1968)

Dawson was a professional basketball player for the Harlem Magicians when they appeared for a game at the Rhode Island Auditorium on March 12, 1962. He was injured when he slipped on a water puddle, on the gym floor. He claimed the defendant (Rhode Island Auditorium, Inc.) failed to furnish a reasonably safe surface upon which to play. He also alleged that:

- they allowed water to accumulate on the surface,
- failed to warn the plaintiff about the hazardous condition,
- maintained a roof that was prone to leak, and
- had actual or constructive notice of the hazard.

The plaintiff established that the gym's roof contained scores of leaks and the leaky condition existed when the injury occurred. The court concluded that the defendant owed the plaintiff, a business invitee, the duty to use reasonable care in keeping the premises in a safe condition for the purpose which the business invitee was using the facility. The defendant had two ways to discharge his/her duty, either through eliminating the leaks by fixing the roof or advising invitees about the facility's conditions and the risks associated with those conditions. The defendant tried unsuccessfully to patch the roof, so his/her duty was to warn each participant about the floor's condition and the possible slipping hazard. Because the defendants (including additional defendants such as the basketball team) did not warn the plaintiff, they had no defense for breaching their duty.

Dust can also be very slippery, so you should make sure the gym is swept before a game, during half time, and after every game to ensure sweat, water or dust are not accumulated on the floor. The following case highlights this concern.

Pedersen v. Joliet Park District
483 N.E. 2d 21 (IL 1985)

The plaintiff, Glenn Pedersen, was playing a school basketball game on March 13, 1982 when he fell while trying to catch a pass. Mr. Pedersen suffered a torn knee ligament. Pedersen alleged that he was injured by the defendant's failure to properly and adequately maintain and clean the gym floor. Pedersen claimed the gym floor's tile surface was dusty and slippery. His expert witness stated that a tile surface was an unacceptable floor surface for basketball, that waxing increased the hazards and the school's tile floor created a dangerous condition. However, Pedersen lost the case because he was unable to show that any alleged slippery condition or dust on the floor was the proximate cause of his injuries.

A final concern about slippery surfaces is newly varnished, sealed, or finished floors. While refinishing normally increases the quality of older floors, they should still be thoroughly inspected after refinishing to make sure there are no slick or especially slippery areas. You should also be concerned with a floor that is wearing out and/or losing its finish. Special attention has to be paid to spots that have lost their layers of finish. These spots can become locations where participants could twist a knee or ankle. Rough spots are dangerous because participants cannot rotate their feet in the same manner they could on a regularly finished area. Besides safety related concerns, uneven finishes could also be a sign that some boards are warped and replacing such boards are both a safety and a cost management issue.

Constructing gym floors can also lead to injuries. Gym floors built over cement bases provide less absorption so there is a greater likelihood for users developing shin splints, knee or back problems. An ideal gym floor would be a wooden spring-loaded floor or similarly designed floor that provides a higher shock absorption level. If the industry standard is to use a high absorption style floor, then you should try to meet that standard either at your own facility or find an existing acceptable facility. American College of Sports Medicine's Health/Fitness Facility Standards and Guidelines (Hereafter "ACSM Guidelines") highlight some specific standards for gymnasiums including:

- all tile walls needs to be padded,
- all spectator areas need to be cleaned on a weekly basis,
- there should be at least five feet (10 feet is recommended) of unobstructed space around each basketball court,
- at least three feet of space should be provided for each spectator,
- the gym temperature should be between 68 to 72 degrees Fahrenheit with less than 60 percent humidity and the air being circulated at an exchange rate of eight to 12 exchanges per hour (Sol and Foster, 1992).

Padding

Padding *needs* to be placed at both ends of a basketball court, behind each basket. The padding should be hung in a manner that provides the greatest area of protection and the pad should be at least 1 1/2 inches thick. Pads should be placed high enough to prevent someone from hitting their head against a wall. Likewise the pad should not be too high or too narrow. The pad should provide the largest possible protective area. All indoor or outdoor baskets supported by metal poles should have pole padding. Currently several companies sell padding for volleyball and basketball poles which provide an acceptable protection level. Due to cost concerns, it is often unfeasible to pad every outdoor pole. Thus, all poles that are not padded should be painted a bright color, which might provide some warning to players. Padding should also be used around the bottom portion of the backboard to protect a participant's head from hitting the bottom of the backboard. Backboard padding is recommended at the college and professional level. However, just because backboard padding is not required at lower competitive levels does not mean that such padding would not be a reasonable safety precaution.

Yarber v. Oakland Unified School District
6 Cal. Rptr. 2d. 437 (CA 1992)

Anthony Yarber was injured while playing in an adult, after-school, basketball game, at an Oakland junior high school. Yarber and other players rented the gymnasium for $30. Yarber had played in the gymnasium on several previous occasions. The basketball games were not sanctioned and no referees controlled the games.

During the act of shooting, Yarber was hit by another participant and the impact of the blow propelled Yarber into the unpadded concrete wall, four feet beyond the out-of-bounds line. Yarber sustained a concussion, a head injury, and a temporary cervical spine injury.

Under California law, a school is normally liable for injuries caused by the dangerous condition on its property. However, the state statute provides immunity from liability where a plaintiff is injured while engaging in certain hazardous sports activities on school grounds. The statute applied because basketball, as played competitively by adults, can be a sport with substantial physical contact. Thus, the court concluded that basketball fell under the hazardous recreational activity statute and the school was immune from any suits brought by a participant in hazardous recreational activities.

Basketball Hoop Rim

The rim of a basketball hoop *has to* be examined to ensure there are *no metal slivers or cracks in the rim* that could cut a player's hand. The same inspection concerns are required when the rim has a chain net instead of a rope net. The rim should be checked to make sure there are no signs of any *stress damage* that could weaken the rim or cause the rim to collapse from a slam-dunk. The nuts and bolts attaching the rim to the backboard, as well as the bolts attaching the backboard to its support assembly have to be examined and tightened if they are loose. The rim should be a snap-back or breakaway rim that allows a participant to dunk the ball while minimizing the potential for breaking or shattering the backboard.

Bleachers

Gym bleachers or grandstands are often used by participants as a climbing apparatus or for cooling-off after a tough game or practice. The bleachers should be inspected to make sure there are:

- no splinters,
- no cracked benches,
- clearly marked passageways,
- nonskid footing tape or paint on steps,
- no exposed or jagged protrusions,
- no debris cluttering travel paths,
- no broken passage ways, and
- no loose nuts and bolts.

The following case demonstrates why it is so important to check the seating and viewing areas.

Woodring v. Board of Education of Manhasset
435 N.Y.S. 2d 52 (N.Y. 1981)

A wrongful death action was brought against the school district after a student died while trying to climb onto a platform. The testimony showed that the platform's railing gave way when the decedent grabbed the railing while attempting to climb up from a stepladder.

New nuts and bolts had been purchased for the railing around the gym's platform, but they were not installed and the school had no preventive maintenance or facility inspection program. In addition, the railing had not been constructed in accordance with proper construction practices. The school was found negligent because it was foreseeable that students who climbed on the railing could get injured if the railing was not properly secured.

When sliding bleachers are not in use, they should be closed and locked to prevent any unauthorized use. When stored, the bleachers should fold to a flush position, thus preventing participants from running into the bleachers. If mobile bleachers are not being used, they should be turned on their backs (so the benches themselves are in a perpendicular position) and stored in a secure area, inaccessible by children. Bleachers should be cleaned on regular basis and special effort has to be made to ensure aisles are kept clear. The guide's spectator section (Chapter 30) will discuss more thoroughly issues associated with spectator seating and safety concerns.

Locker Rooms

Most gyms are connected to or near a locker room area. Locker rooms can be very dangerous locations. Many injuries occur in residential bathrooms. By multiplying the number of locker room users and facilities, it is easy to see the great injury potential inherent in locker rooms. The most common injury associated with locker rooms is slipping on a wet, slick surface. There have been numerous cases where plaintiffs have been able to recover damages when they slipped on a water puddle on a locker room floor as highlighted by the case below.

Van Stry v. State
479 N.Y.S. 2d 258 (NY 1984)

John Van Stry was a student at the State University of New York at Farmingdale when he was injured in the school's locker room. Van Stry changed into his badminton class clothes and then went looking for a locker to store his street clothes. While walking past an aisle, Van Stry's right foot slipped and he fell at the edge of a water puddle which was:

- clear

- roughly circular
- approximately 1/8 of an inch deep
- four to five feet in diameter, and
- 20 to 30 feet from the shower.

Van Stry testified that he often saw puddles in the locker room. He had slipped, but not fallen on prior occasions, and he had informed his badminton instructor about the puddles.

The State had been put on notice through both visual inspections by its employees and complaints from locker room users to instructors. The State had a duty to eliminate the risk, but the State did not use reasonable care to eliminate the risk. The State could have eliminated the risk by: using anti-slip or sand paint, placing mats or other non-slip devices on the floor or posting warning signs. The court held that the persistent water accumulation on the locker room floor created a foreseeable risk that the State knew about (notice), thus they could be and were found to have acted negligently.

Other potential locker room problems can be avoided by:

- making sure swinging doors open out to show where puddles are,
- installing more and brighter lights,
- maintaining the existing drainage system or expanding the drainage system,
- providing adequate exhaust fans to minimize moisture accumulation,
- developing the locker room with wide traffic patterns,
- initiating a regular schedule for inspecting and draining any water accumulated on the floor.

A squeegee should always be present to push accumulated water towards the drains. Additional safeguards, besides checking for water accumulation, include checking for:

- dripping soap dispensers in the shower,
- over flowing sinks/toilets,
- electrical outlets or electrical devices used near water,
- grounded plugs,
- ground-fault interrupters on appliances used near water,
- eliminating any rusty appliances or lockers,
- locking all saunas and hot tubs that are not in use.

Locker room supervision is also a very difficult and tricky task. Since locker rooms are constructed with separated areas for dressing, showering, and lavatory use, it is impossible to see the entire locker room from one location. Privacy concerns also affect the nature and amount of supervision. When individuals are showering, they often dislike being under the watchful, albeit necessary, supervisor's eye. Individuals can always be approached in advance regarding any privacy concerns. This is especially important for children that might have been abused, sexually molested or come from cultures that emphasize modesty.

Most individuals know about the traditional towel snapping around the locker room. While some people might find this practice humorous, such conduct can also cause severe injuries. Thus, it is essential to have a locker room supervisor who controls user's conduct and rigorously enforces all the rules (*while being sensitive to privacy concerns*).

Opponent Violence

Basketball is a physically demanding sport and some teams are well known for their aggressive, physical play. However, the constant pushing and shoving in a physical game can lead to bench-clearing brawls. Referees are responsible for controlling the game tempo, but everyone involved in the event shares some responsibility. Fouls should be called early and consistently. Furthermore, rules should be implemented and enforced to punish players who fight. Special concern has to be exercised when the rivalry between two teams is especially heated. One way to defuse the tension between the teams is to separate the teams both on and off the court. *Player separation* on the court can be accomplished with the referees' and coaches' assistance. This co-operative effort between referees and coaches should continue both on and off the court. When locker rooms are adjacent to each other the teams should be sent in on a staggered basis and under strict supervision.

Grames v. King and Pontiac School District
332 N.W. 2d 615 (MI 1983)

Tamara Grames was allegedly injured when she was assaulted in the Pontiac Northern High School locker room following a basketball game between Pontiac and Walled Lake High School. Players from the Pontiac team allegedly attacked Grames, who played for Walled Lake. She alleged that the defendants failed to properly supervise activities conducted within the building.

Due to government immunity, the defendant was immune from liability. If the defendant did not have government immunity, and if there was inadequate supervision or a failure to separate contestants, the plaintiff might have won.

A staggered arrival to the gym (and departure time) is also very beneficial for emotional games. Coaches and school/league officials should also talk with their players and fans in an effort to control their actions.

Supervision

Supervision related concerns can run the gamut from simple lack of coaching skill to a coach assaulting a player. In one 1995 incident, a coach was upset with his high school aged player and allegedly swore at him. The coach then allegedly struck the player in his head with an open hand. The boy and his parents filed suit against the school and the coach after the son was cut from the team allegedly due to the parents' complaint (Chen, 1996). In a college case a former player sued the athletic director/coach for permanent injuries allegedly suffered when the injured athlete was pressured into playing while hurt which led to permanent injuries ("Court revives lawsuit by ex-St. Joe's hoop player," 1997). These are just two examples of improper supervision that led injured athletes to the court room.

One of the major concerns with supervising basketball games is watching out for size disparities that could lead to a participant getting hurt. Size disparity is an inherent factor in basketball games. With participants leaping for rebounds or trying to block a shot, contact normally occurs and all fouls cannot be eliminated. Remember that you are not an absolute ensurer of a participant's safety. However, a grossly excessive height differential between players can lead to excessive fouls and injuries that could have been prevented. High school kids should not take the same court with veteran professional basketball players unless they are the same size, weight and maturity, otherwise if a kid is injured you could be sued for allowing a small person to play against much stronger individuals. Size disparity problems can be somewhat curtailed if moving picks and offensive fouls are consistently called, but such rules can only minimize some contact.

Basketball is a game that can be played with men and women competing against each other. You should encourage this type of competition, but the game has to be closely supervised if there is a significant size disparity or one team is more physically aggressive than the other team.

Conclusion

Basketball involves a variety of risks that can pose unique concerns for an EA. However, these risks can normally be identified and corrected in fairly quick time frame. While major repairs such as structural problems might take months to correct, sweeping or mopping floors or eliminating puddles might take several minutes In contrast, trying to rid a baseball field of too much moisture might take several hours. Even though basketball presents some easier to handle concerns compared with numerous other events, the following rules can help reduce unique basketball injuries include:

- *prohibiting shooting baskets at a free basket while the action of a full-court game is taking place on the opposite side of the gym,*
- prohibiting dunking,
- preventing players from wearing jewelry,
- requiring participants to wear appropriate basketball shoes (not running shoes) to help reduce the risk of sprained ankles.

You should not forget that whenever a rule or policy is adopted, you must ensure the rule is enforced, and enforced in a fair and consistent manner.

To help ensure safety, you should take the following steps:

- check for water or liquid hazards,
- inspect the facility fixtures and bleachers and make sure they are flush against the wall and completely closed,
- inspect the facility to ensure adequate spacing around the playing area,
- allow only limited drills if space is minimal,
- replace all the glass doors and windows with safety materials,
- inspect and repair any broken planks, loose tiles, slick spots, rough spots or other flooring problems,
- provide adequate padding around the basket, walls and poles,
- check the basket rim for any damage,
- inspect the locker room for signs of water accumulation,
- supervise locker room use,
- supervise and control rough play by participants,
- provide supervision to the full extent required by the situation.

Chapter 14

Contact Sports and Martial Arts

Contact sports such as boxing, wrestling, judo and karate are designed to bring out an individual's aggressive nature in a tightly controlled environment. Should we as a society allow or condone possible barbaric sports? Some individuals and politicians think contact sports should be heavily regulated. Many states have banned "ultimate fighting" or "extreme fighting" due to the violent nature of the sport (Minzesheimer, 1997). The federal government started getting involved by proposing legislation in 1996 that would force each state to recognize the suspension of a fighter issued by a different state's boxing commission. The same law would have required pre-fight physicals, a physican at ringside for all fights and health insurance for fighters ("Boxed in," 1996). Such laws typically spring forward when someone dies in the ring or a public outcry is raised against a sport for being considered to violent. While not all sports are lumped into the same mold, it is not that far of a stretch to see other contact sports micromanaged by the public when individuals are hurt. Therefor, strict precautions need to be taken to help ensure contact is kept exclusively inside the ring or designated space (such as floor mats).

Competitive Area

Contact sports normally take place inside the "squared circle," thus you have to check to make sure the competitive area is in reasonably safe condition.

Boxing and "Big Time" Wrestling

Boxing and wrestling rings are normally elevated to improve spectator viewing. The complete structure has to be examined to ensure that it is safe for competitive use. This concern is much more pervasive when you know that several individuals weighing more then 200 pounds each will be running around and jumping in the ring. The *support brackets* for a raised ring should not be *loose, cracked, weak or in any state of disrepair*. If the platform is a permanent structure, a qualified safety engineer or inspector should inspect the platform every year for distress or other hazards.

The *boxing or wrestling mat* has to be *securely fastened* to avoid sliding underneath the fighters' feet. If two wrestling mats need to be joined together, they should be taped together on both sides of the mat (top and bottom) or securely attached with Velcro on the bottom. The one major concern with Velcro is the small seam which would be visible where the mats join. Thus, it is recommended that even with a Velcro fastening system that the mats should be taped where they are joined. The same concern applies to grego-roman wrestling and all martial arts activities conducted on mats.

The ropes surrounding the ring have to be securely attached to withstand the weight of a fighter against the ropes. Perspiration drops or spilled drinking water in the corner have to be wiped up after every round to prevent any slipping while a fighter is in that corner. The corner cushions have to be securely attached to the corner posts to protect a fighter from potential contact with the post. The authors recommend clearing all floor surfaces every other month with bacteria killing cleanser.

Greco-Roman Wrestling, Judo and Karate

All events have to be held on wrestling mats or approved padded surfaces. Care should be taken to inspect the mat before competition and to thoroughly clean the mat after each competition or match is completed. There is no steadfast rule as to when or how often mats need to be cleaned, but you should inspect the mat after each match is completed. Beside the risk of a participant slipping on sweat or spilled water, there is a concern for other participants health which could be put at risk by health-related issues (blood, infections, etc.).

Spectator Violence

The emotional charge of loyal boxing or wrestling fans can often lead to spectator violence against participants or officials. During the 1988 Seoul Olympics, a fight erupted after a decision against a Korean fighter. In protest the Korean fighter's corner workers and his fans started throwing both punches and chairs at officials, the other boxer and his corner crew. In 1989, the mother of an English boxer was so distraught over a boxing match that she attacked her son's opponent with a high-heel shoe ("Action outside the ring must have been better," 1990). These incidents could possibly have been prevented through the use of additional and/or more visible security personnel. Furthermore, barricades or short fences can also provide added safety.

To protect participants, the event guidelines should prohibit possessing and/or selling drinks in metal cans or glass bottles. Security personnel should check every bag brought into the arena for drink containers, fruits and/or any other hard object that could be thrown at the ring or participants. Ushers should ask spectators if it is all right to inspect their bag or container. If permission is granted, then a check can proceed. If permission is denied, the spectator should be told the reason why the search is necessary. If the spectator still refuses an inspection, you can offer him/her a ticket refund. While you have a duty to provide security, you cannot violate someone's privacy rights to help ensure safety. Thus, you should not perform any body searches without justifiable cause and the person's consent. These and related spectator management issues are discussed in Chapter 30

Security procedures also have to be developed and implemented to prevent spectators from entering the ring after a fight. Security officials should encircle the ring after a fight and only authorized individuals should be allowed into the ring. Authorized individuals should be given bright tags/badges so security personnel can immediately determine whether or not a person is authorized to be in the ring. The security personnel should escort the fighters to and from their dressing rooms and guard their doors after all fights, especially after an emotionally charged fight. The need to supervise spectators as well as opposing boxers and wrestlers can be seen in the following case.

Leger v. Stockton Unified School District
249 Cal. Rptr. 688 (CA 1988)

Plaintiff, Jamie Leger, was a student at Franklin High School when he was attacked in a school restroom where he was changing clothes for wrestling practice. The attacker was a non-student. Leger alleged that the school failed to provide a safe school and negligently failed to supervise him or the location where he was changing. Leger did not have to prove that prior attacks occurred in the same restroom. Rather, he only had to show that injuries to student members of the wrestling team assaulted by a non-student in unsupervised restroom was reasonably foreseeable in the absence of supervision or warning.

Because a genuine issue existed as to whether or not the school was negligent in not supervising the restroom, the court of appeals reversed the lower court's summary judgment decision and allowed the case to proceed.

"Big Time" or "Superstar" wrestlers have many diehard fans and enemies interested in approaching them. These wrestlers are on notice (assumption of risk) that fans might try to come in contact with them, but the wrestlers still should be provided with substantial security protection. Wrestlers should be specifically warned about the potential risk that they can expect when they join a team, club or sign a participation contract or waiver.

Supervision

Supervision is essential while a participant is learning a contact sport. Similar to all other sports, a reasonable EA or coach would emphasize the importance of warming-up and stretching before engaging in any strenuous activity. Furthermore, any punching or sparring drills should first be conducted in slow motion until both parties are sufficiently warmed-up.

One of the biggest concerns you can face are *mismatches* created through differences in *strength, size, reach, skill, experience and the participant's maturity level.* This concern was highlighted in the *Jacuet v. Marion County School Board* case.

Jacquet v. Marion County School Board
Marion County Cir. Ct., No. 90-5272-CA-A (Sept. 30, 1992).

Jacquet weighted 170 pounds, but was partnered with a 270 pound adult volunteer in a high school wrestling practice. During a move the volunteer fell on the plaintiff's knee tearing the knee ligaments. The injury resulted in decreased range of motion, continued knee pain and $11,800 in medical damages.

Jacquet sued under the negligent supervision theory claiming that the mismatched paring violated recognized high school wrestling safety rules that prohibit competition between mismatched weight-class opponents. The school board raised the assumption of risk and comparative negligence defenses. The jury sided with the plaintiff and awarded $231,000 which was reduced 30 percent based on the comparative negligence finding resulting in a $161,700 award.

Since boxing is an ultra-hazardous activity, *participants assume the known risk* inherent in the sport. To help ensure that boxers assume the risk of participating, they should sign a waiver or release and be formally warned about the dangers. The waiver should state that the fighter acknowledges that they are participating in an ultra-hazardous activity with known dangers and they agree to accept all inherent risks. An exception to the assumption of risk defense is when the participant does not know anything about the sport. Thus, it is incumbent on the EA to instruct each participant about the risks associated with boxing so the participant is thoroughly versed on the sport's risks.

La Valley v. Stanford
70 N.Y.S. 2d 460 (NY 1947)

Hector La Valley was a student in a required physical education boxing class. The boxers were instructed to box for three rounds. While the inexperienced students were boxing, the instructor sat in the bleachers and watched. La Valley was hit in the temple area and became dizzy. He stumbled, had a headache, then became unconscious. La Valley recovered from his injury and sued the teacher for failing to warn students about the risks inherent in boxing.

The court concluded that a teacher has a duty to exercise reasonable care to prevent injuries. The instructor should have warned the pupils and should have taught defense principles instead of permitting a slugging match. Because the teacher failed to warn or instruct the students, he was found to have been negligent.

Some supervision concerns are addressed by government agencies. State Boxing Commissions set standards for fighters and fights within the state and these standards help establish the duty you might owe. Some State Boxing Commissions set out age and health requirements that forbid a fighter from fighting without receiving a medical examination. Thus, one of your duties as a boxing or wrestling event administrator is to determine what state laws might affect your event.

Another major area of concern entails proper discipline by coaches. In one 1996 case some angry parents sued a high school wrestling coach for allegedly using excessive force while using an illegal choke hold on a student. The complaint alleged that the coach had used violence and excessive force in the past and the school had been on notice about these acts ("Eldorado wrestling coach faces lawsuit by student," 1996).

Discipline is not the only potential problem involving inappropriate coaching decisions. Numerous articles have been written over the past several years concerning weight loss techniques for wrestlers. Several wrestlers died in 1998 from different weight loss techniques utilized to help the wrestler make a certain weight (See generally From the Gym to the Jury, 1998). One disturbing case arose in 1996 when a coach and assistant coach locked three students voluntarily into a room to make them lose weight before a regional tournament. The boys had been locked into the room for several hours with only a bottle to urinate in and screwdriver to take off the door hinges in case of an emergency ("Extreme measure," 1996).

Conclusion

An EA can help prevent injuries in the ring or mats by implementing the following steps:

- the ring or mats should be supported by a strong stable base,
- the mat(s), corner cushions and ropes should be securely attached,
- spectators should be kept away from the boxers/wrestlers and the ring at all times,
- spectators should be prohibited from bringing glass bottles, metal cans and/or any other throwable objects into the facility,
- you should provide adequate supervision to ensure appropriate participant matching.

Chapter 15

Football

The most popular television show on a yearly basis is the National Football League's (NFL) Super Bowl. Enormous men hitting one another for the potential gain of a few yards of grass characterize football. Crashing helmets can be an invigorating experience for a football player, but potential high-speed collisions between competitors can also lead to tragic injuries. Over the past several NFL seasons, two professional athletes have left the playing field paralyzed. Besides injuries during competition, participant and spectator enthusiasm can also cause numerous supervision problems.

Field

Most of the major concerns associated with a baseball playing field are also associated with a football field. Before a field can be effectively inspected, all large debris should be removed and the grass portions of the field should be mowed. Because football equipment is larger than baseball equipment, more emphasis has to be given to broken glass and discarded baseball equipment rather than football equipment. While marking the field with chalk or paint you can inspect the field in easy-to-document ten-yard segments. Besides inspecting just the grass, you should also regularly inspect the entire support system which for a grass field could include a plastic liner on the dirt followed by drain tubes in the sand, followed by peat and finally topped off with the grass. The entire grass substructure needs to be properly maintained for player safety and long-life of the field.

Inspecting an *artificial turf* field might be easier than a natural grass field due to the turf's even height. However, artificial turf fields have some concerns that cannot be examined through a normal above ground inspection (i.e. problems with the base, drainage system, unmatched seams, incorrectly joined pieces, incorrectly crushed stone base under the asphalt, deterioration of the shock pad, etc.). You have a duty to make sure the artificial turf is in reasonably good condition and there are no exposed seams. The presence of an exposed seam in the Astrodome turf led to the cancellation of a pre-season NFL game in 1996.

189

In addition to inspecting outdoor areas, you should inspect indoor facilities used by football players. You should make sure that an indoor facility is appropriate for its intended use. Some schools have indoor practice areas that are large enough to provide room for a sprinting player to stop after an all-out sprint. However, most indoor facilities lack the space to perform most football drills. *Full-speed drills should not be performed in smaller indoor facilities.* The authors have worked on several cases where a football player was running a route or defending a receiver and ran into a wall. Thus, all drills should be tailored to the facility to ensure the safest conditions.

Curtis v. State
505 N.E. 2d 1222 (OH 1986)

Clarence W. Curtis, Jr. was a member of the Ohio State University football team in 1983 when he was training with the team in an indoor athletic facility at the university. Curtis was performing a "liner" drill whereby he was sprinting in a north-south direction along yard lines on the artificial turf. The turf was located inside the field house. While performing one of these drills, Curtis struck a wire-reinforced glass door with his foot, which caused serious injuries.

The court held that the university was not liable for the football player's injuries from running into the glass door. The court did not examine whether or not the school should have used safety glass instead of wire reinforced glass, but determined that the university was in accord with standard codes and regulations.

The court also concluded that even if the field house had a high window breakage rate, in the absence of proof on what caused the window breakage (i.e. vandalism, golf balls, baseballs, sports equipment, etc..) it would be impossible to say the university was on notice that the windows were dangerous. Likewise, the university was not put on notice about the danger of the windows when only one accident involved the windows in the previous thirty years.

Presumably, the injury in the *Curtis* case could have been prevented if the athletes were explicitly told not to run drills at full speed, to slow down near the walls and/or to avoid kicking-off the walls/doors with their feet. While warning people about obvious risks might seem like wasted breath, you should read warning labels on household products to help solidify the need to warn individuals about the most obvious concerns. For example, the top rung on a ladder now has a warning indicating it is not a step. Companies put such warnings on products after someone who might have used the product in an obviously incorrect manner sues them. Thus, you have to warn people not to run at full speed into a wall. You have to make sure a facility has enough room for your activity, and if the activity cannot be performed safely in that area, then the activity has to be stopped immediately. Numerous coaches might feel that a location is safe until someone gets injured. This attitude is dangerous since luck is bound to run-out sooner or later.

Unslaked Lime

As discussed previously in the baseball section, unslaked lime could lead to eye problems for someone sliding into a base. The same concerns apply to football players who could be tackled near or over the marked lines.

Mokovich v. Independent School District
225 N.W. 292 (MN 1929)

Mokovich was injured in a football game conducted by the school district. Mokovich charged that a school's agents negligently used unslaked lime to mark the football field lines, and thereby create the nuisance. During the game, Mokovich, was thrown to the ground, and his head and face forced into the lime. This resulted in the lime getting into his eyes and destroying the sight of one eye and seriously impairing the sight in the other eye.

Due to governmental immunity, the school district was immune from liability for acts of negligence. The plaintiff tried to characterize the actions of the school's agent as a nuisance rather than a negligent act. However, the court concluded that nuisance and negligence causes of actions are the same for immunity protection. Thus, the school district prevailed.

As in baseball, chalk, white paint or slaked lime should be used instead of unslaked lime to ensure the marking compound does not injure a participant. There are several companies that produce various field marking equipment and applications. These companies can serve as great resource for industry standards.

Equipment

There are several major equipment concerns unique to football that can easily create or cause an injury. Through the 1960's, football fields had their goal posts in front of the end zone. Currently, *goal posts* are located at the back of the end zone to prevent the serious injuries possible from participants colliding with a goal post. Relocating the goal posts is a perfect example of how repeated injuries have led to rule changes to benefit the participants. Padding should be secured around the center or side posts of the goal posts to lower the risk of serious injury from colliding with a post.

Sideline markers are not considered inherently dangerous equipment, but a player can be injured by coming in contact with a marker as highlighted by the following case.

Smith v. National Football League
U.S. Dist. Ct., FL., No. 74-418 Civ. T-K

Bubba Smith, a former All-Pro player and an "NFL lineman of the year," sued for injuries he received when he was tackled and his momentum carried him into an aluminum down marker that was still stuck in the ground. The collision with the marker caused a serious injury to his knee and concluded his career.

Smith claimed that the defendants knew or should have known that the markers were improper and dangerous. However, a jury concluded that the NFL was not negligent.

Even though Mr. Smith lost, the case demonstrates that even an item that does not seem to be dangerous can cause a severe injury and lead to a lawsuit.

Sideline markers should be *padded* unless they are made of *narrow gauge aluminum or thin plastic*. Markers should have *flat bottoms* instead of spiked bottoms to prevent an unintentional stabbing. A marker with a flat bottom also rests flat on the ground instead of being stuck into the ground, similar to the marker in the *Smith* case.

For the most part, football players receive their equipment from their school or team. Ideally, borrowing equipment should be avoided. Unfortunately this option is not available to 99 percent of the football program administrators. On their own, most players do not have the resources to

purchase equipment. In addition, because children are constantly changing in size, it is highly impractical for parents or players to purchase their
own equipment. For most football programs there are no other options
available. Therefore, you have to make sure all the borrowed equipment
fits each participant. The failure to properly equip a football player can
impose significant liability. To discharge your duty you have to *make sure
all loaned equipment is adjusted to fit each player, and adjusted by an individual specifically trained in equipment adjustment.*

Locilento v. John A. Coleman Catholic High
523 N.Y.S. 2d 198 (NY 1987)

Richard Locilento, a 17-year-old senior, sustained a dislocated shoulder
during an intramural tackle football game. The game was officiated by
two high school instructors. No protective equipment was provided. Locilento was injured when he tried to tackle another player.

An expert witness testified that shoulder pads serve to decrease the potential for shoulder injuries. The testimony was sufficient for the jury to conclude that the failure to equip the plaintiff with shoulder pads was a proximate cause of his injuries.

The court also concluded that there was no express assumption of risk.
Rather, plaintiff's voluntary participation indicated an implied assumption of risk, which was simply a factor relevant in the assessment of negligent conduct.

Most equipment problems involve *football helmets and pads*. The litigation explosion coupled with the high cost of insurance for helmet
manufacturers has lowered the number of United States helmet manufacturers to three, from a 1970 high of 18 (Barnes, 1989). Most suits
against helmet manufactures entail the helmet failing to provide adequate protection or improperly fitting a player. The National Operating
Committee on Standards for Athletic Equipment (*NOCSAE) seal* on the
back of football helmets must be present on all helmets you purchase,
whether new or used/reconditioned. Another reputable seal from an organization capable of evaluating football helmets could also be affixed
to the helmet. Besides obtaining safety related seals, equipment manufactures are looking towards modern technology to make helmets safer.
Manufacturers are adding new devises such as high technology materials and paint to inflation devises such as air bags to deploy upon a head-
on collision.

A recognized safety seal does not mean the helmet is and/or will remain in good shape. You should make sure each user understands how to care for his helmet. *Helmets* should not be thrown because that could lead to cracks, loosened pads or broken screws. Helmets should also be used only for protecting a person's head and should not be used as makeshift chairs for players on the sidelines or used as supports for leaning players. Misuse of helmets can also lead to:

- cracks or dents in the shell,
- missing, loose, cracked or broken inner pads,
- leaks in the air bladder (if air bladders are used),
- missing, loose, bent or corroded hardware,
- missing, loose, bent or corroded chin straps,
- cracked, bent, broken or missing face guards,
- missing or illegible warning labels.

Athletes should not be allowed to make additions, alterations or use different replacement parts on their helmets. Only a reputable helmet *reconditioning* company should be used to repair helmets. Only manufacturers-recommended cleaners should be used to clean helmets. Every helmet should be reconditioned every other year and a helmet should only be used for five to six years ("Sports injury risk management and the keys to safety," 1991). If a helmet is broken it should be destroyed!

You should make sure that whenever helmets are provided, they are fitted to each participant's head. You should make sure an inflation device (such as an air pump or a tank of compressed air) is easily accessible during games and practice to refill any air bladders that have deflated.

Each wearer should be warned that a football helmet can only provide protection for the head; not the neck. If an athlete wants protection for the neck, he could be fitted with neck support pads. Pads also have to be fitted to each player, and no player should be allowed to participate without you, or some other qualified person, checking the helmets and pads for a proper fit. The Ouchita Parish School Board in Louisiana was forced to pay $220,000 to a former football player who injured his neck in a game. In a subsequent game the coaches attached a neck roll. However, the neck roll was torn off, but the coaches let him keep playing. He was subsequently injured and the neck roll would presumably have provided protection to lesson his injury ("School board to pay for football injuries," 1996).

Every football helmet, along with football pads, should have a serial number engraved into the equipment's body or attached through adhesive tags. You should determine the exact date the item was purchased, when the equipment was manufactured and when the equipment was either reconditioned, inspected or destroyed. This information should be kept in a football equipment log. The log should also specify which athletes used the equipment in the past, who the equipment is currently being issued to and whether or not there are any problems with the equipment. Sample forms are included in Appendix J.

Other equipment concerns, in addition to football helmets, include shin guards, athletic supporters and making sure each participant is using a mouth guard every play. Any equipment that is integrally involved in any accident should be isolated from all other equipment and marked with permanent ink as equipment that should not be utilized. If you fail to secure the equipment and it is lost or altered, you could be liable for the independent claim of evidence spoliation. This refers to the fact that you should have known the equipment would have been necessary for litigation, but failed to keep the equipment in good condition.

Violence

Violence between participants is normally due to rule violations or a continuing feud between two opposing players or teams. As with baseball and basketball games, known rivalries can erupt into large-scale fights, so additional supervision and security is required for such games. Rules regarding suspension for fighting should be adopted and umpires and referees should control the flow of the game by carefully calling penalties. Referees should limit using offsetting penalties for personal fouls. If small fights or pushing matches occur several times during a game, instead of calling just offsetting penalties, officials should throw offending players out as a sign that such future conduct by others will not be tolerated.

However violence has extended past opponent violence to include team member violence against other teammates. Such violence can be due to a lack of supervision, but can also be the result of horseplay or hazing. Hazing related cases are gaining in popularity as some individuals are being seriously injured by their teammates. A New Orleans saints rookie was asking for $650,000 in damages after being injured in a hazing incident. The rookie claimed he was forced to run down a hall way while being hit, kicked and pounded with bags of coin. While trying to avoid the assault, the player broke a dormitory window and required stitches to his arm and hand ("Danish asks $650,000 over hazing incident," 1998). In a more disturbing hazing incident, several football players in Utah seized naked teammates in the locker room bound them with trainer's tape, tied them to locker room fixtures and then subjected them to humiliation. The school board expelled the students who tried utilizing the legal system to attack their expulsions made under the school districts "zero tolerance" anti-hazing policy (McDonough, 1996).

Supervision

Similar to all other contact oriented sports, significant attention has to be given to supervising football players. The duty to supervise extends to the day the players sign-up to join the team and equipment is issued.

Leahy v. School Board of Hernando County
450 So. 2d 883 (FL 1984)

On May 1, 1979, William J. Leahy was present at the first day of football practice when football equipment was being issued. Leahy, along with other freshmen, did not receive a helmet as the school did not have a sufficient number of the correct sized helmets. Players were instructed to participate in an agility drill that involved coming into contact with other players. No special precautionary instructions were given to the players who did not have helmets or mouth guards. Ten or twelve players with helmets were instructed to get on their hands and knees and position themselves in a row. The remaining players formed a line and were instructed to go after each lineman by hitting him on the shoulders with both hands, fall and roll on the ground, and then get up as fast as possible to perform the same maneuver with the next lineman. The helmeted linemen started getting rowdy and hitting harder when Leahy's turn came. When he started down to hit the lineman's shoulder pads, the lineman straightened his arm or raised his head which caused Leahy's face to come in contact with the lineman's helmet.

The appellate court reversed the lower court's verdict for the defendant and concluded that there was reasonable evidence for a jury to conclude that the defendant negligently failed to provide proper supervision, instruction and equipment. The defendant's potential liability stemmed from permitting a football player to participate in football drills without a football helmet or mouth guard. The defendant was also potentially liable for failing to give cautionary instructions regarding contact drills and failing to limit the increased intensity of the drills involving a participant without a helmet.

The appellate court established a duty owed to a participant. The duty takes the form of: "giving adequate instruction in the activity, supplying proper equipment, making a reasonable selection or matching of participants, providing non-negligent supervision of the particular contest, and taking proper post-injury procedures to protect against aggravation of the injury."

If you follow these duties to the best of your ability, you will have a very good defense against any breach of duty claim. By this point you probably realize that under the circumstances in the *Leahy* case an injury is very foreseeable and a lawsuit could be just around the corner if you act as unprofessionally as those defendants.

Supervision concerns run rampant throughout pre-season training. One of the biggest concerns involves trying to get players into shape. Some coaches feel that they should be similar to army sergeants and work their recruits till they drop. While such a technique is not technically illegal, if the temperature is too hot or players are not allowed to drink water, serious injuries will occur and you will be held liable for supervising the athletes in such a strict manner. This concern is well known, but as evidenced by the following newspaper clippings, is still a major problem with disastrous consequences.

- Parents in Texas sued their son's football coaches after his death claiming they violated regulations for hot-weather practice and medical emergencies (Tedford, 1996). The parents sued and were able to recover under an unconventional theory-constitutional rights. The parents claimed that under 42 USC Section 1983 their son had the right "to life, liberty, health, safety, and bodily integrity in a safe environment protecting him from violations of his rights by state actors." The court concluded that if children have a right to be protected from physical abuse they also have the right to be protected from being "run to death" by a coach (*Roventini v. Pasadena Independent School Dist., et al.*, 981 F. Supp. 1013 (SD Tex. 1997)).
- Six high school football players died in 1997 from on-field injuries while eight died from other causes. Of those "other cause" deaths, seven were heart related and one was heatstroke ("Study cites high school football deaths," 1998).
- A 13-year-old eighth-grader died in 1995 after the first day of summer football practice. He died from heat-related injuries ("Parents of heat stroke victim sound warning," 1996).
- Former Oklahoma University football coach Howard Schnellenberger and the university were sued by a player who suffered a heat stroke in 1995 ("Player sues OU, coach for heat stroke," 1997)

Supervision concerns can also apply to a host of additional concerns as highlighted from the following news stories.

- The Arkansas Supreme Court reinstated a lawsuit by a former football player's family against the University of Arkansas's athletic director for his suicide which was allegedly related in some manner to the AD ("Academe today's daily report," 1998).
- Tulane University conducted a study on tackling which uncovered the facts that 29% of surveyed high school football players thought it was legal to tackle with their head and a higher percentage thought it was legal to head butt an opposing player. The coaches were held to be the major problem in the study as only two of 16 surveyed coaches had shown a "free" safety video to their players ("Illegal tackling suspected in head injuries," 1997).
- In a case highlighting numerous levels of improper supervision, a 14-year-old student was left brain-damaged after being injured in a flag football game. While tackling was not allowed, the child was knocked down by opponents and hit his head on the ground. He complained about a headache, but got dressed and went to his next class. His head continued to hurt him and he asked his teacher to allow him to go to the office. His request was denied. He went on his own and was not provided with immediate assistance and was also left alone. Approximately 10 minutes later he was found stumbling in the gym and rolled off the stage further injuring himself. The gym teacher left the gym to get the principal. By the time the principal arrived the child could not walk and was beginning to lose consciousness. The parents sued claiming a lack of supervision for the football game and the failure to provide proper care after the injury (Shipley, 1997).
- A lawsuit was brought in Florida after ten high school football players were injured when the team was practicing on the field during a storm and were hit by lightning. The students claimed the coaches waited to long to send them to the gymnasium once the lighting started and if they would have been sent earlier the injuries would not have occurred ("Players sue school board," 1996).
- Supervision concerns can also apply to the medical screening of the athletes. The mother of a former Vanderbilt University football player sued after her son's death claiming the doctors at the university's medical center cleared her son and failed to diagnose his cardiac condition (Logins, 1996).

Medical screening can be a major concern if you recommend that players should use a specific doctor. That doctor might show bias or might let some questionable players through in order to continue receiving patients. Thus, while you might think you are doing your players a favor, you could be opening yourself to liability. The best strategy to avoid this type of problem is to provide a list of several "potential" doctors for individuals who request the name of a physician to perform a pre-season physical. Then the ultimate choice of physicians is still left to the patient.

Another significant football concern is playing *mismatched teams* against one another.

Vendrell v. School District No. 266 Malheur County
360 P. 2d 282 (OR 1961)

Louis Vendrell was a fifteen-year-old football player when two members of an opposing high school's team tackled him. Among other injuries, he suffered a broken neck that resulted in paraplegia.

Vendrell claimed that his injuries were directly and proximately caused by the school district negligently permitting an inexperienced football team to play an experienced football team. The court concluded that two football teams could be so disparate in size and ability that those responsible for supervising the athletic program would violate their duty in permitting the teams to play. The court concluded that allowing Vendrell to participate in a varsity football game without proper or sufficient instruction constituted sufficient facts to state a cause of action against the school district.

However, Vendrell's complaint did not state a cause of action against the members of the school board, the superintendent and the principal. These defendants did not have a duty to determine whether each member of the football team received adequate coaching or instruction, even though the injured player was uncoordinated, inexperienced, weighed only 140 pounds and was competing against a bigger stronger team. Most freshmen, the court reasoned, were uncoordinated and inexperienced players, but the school board, school superintendent and principal did not have a duty to determine whether each student was adequately trained.

Even though Vendrell could state a cause of action against the school district, immunity shielded the school district, except to the extent the immunity was lifted by an insurance liability policy.

In a 1988 New York case, an appellate court held that a school district unreasonably enhanced the risk of injury to a student engaged in an interscholastic varsity football game by playing the student in a game between mismatched teams for virtually the entire game, while he was tired. The athlete was playing because there were no adequate substitutes for him (*Benitez v. New York City Bd. Of Educ*, (N.Y.A.D., 1988).

Thus, even though you *might not* have a duty to examine the ability of each participant, individuals who notice a tired, unskilled or overmatched athlete would have a higher duty. You also could be liable for an individual's injuries if you have a duty to observe the athlete's condition, but fails to notice fatigue or related health concerns.

To avoid any potential mismatching problems, some football teams are starting to pass on certain games when the opponents have more players or are physically superior. This advice was followed by Madison College (Wisconsin) which fielded its first football team in 1998. The team lost lopsided games in the first three outings and were outscored 167–6. The college's president decided to cut his losses by canceling its game with football powerhouse Wisconsin-Whitewater. Bob Berezowitz, the Whitewater coach admitted that the Madison team would have been extremely mismatched. He commented that, "we could have lined up and played, but it probably wasn't the best idea for the safety of the student-athletes." (USA Today, 1998).

Proper supervision can also entail properly training individuals on tackling technique and not encouraging any reckless behavior. Some coaches reward players for a bone-jarring hit which might encourage inappropriate tackling. In one 1997 incident a mother heard team members encouraging a child to aggressively tackle her son. The team members were yelling "kill him, Kenny." Kenny Simmons rammed the child's leg with his football helmet breaking the other child's leg. Proper supervision would have included stopping players from making such assertions and teaching player how to avoid injuring others during practice and game situation (Bryant, 1999).

Additional supervision concerns include:

- proper instruction and coaching,
- proper practice and game management,
- preventing altercations between your own players and players from opposing teams, and
- proper supervision of all medical trainers and doctors. (See the first aid chapter for more details).

Conclusion

Football will always have some degree of risk due to the physical nature of the game. The only way to avoid such dangers is to not play. Even though many parents think football is very dangerous and do not want their children playing the game, other sports have a higher injury rate. While football injury numbers might not be as high as some other sports, the potential injuries from football are often much more severe with several paraplegia cases appearing each year. You can reduce your football field liability risk if you:

- mow the grass before the event,
- inspect the field for any glass or similar tripping hazards,
- mark field lines with slaked lime, paint or chalk,
- securely fasten padding to the goal posts,
- make sure the sideline markers are safe,
- assign each player appropriate, fitted, equipment,
- only allow a qualified person to adjust and fit the equipment to each player,
- only allow a qualified company to refurbish your helmets,
- inspect each players' equipment before play,
- make sure helmets contain the NOCSAE or other appropriate seal(s),
- make sure helmets are not repaired by unqualified individuals,
- keep track of all your football equipment purchases and repairs,
- supervise the participants to make sure they are properly trained,
- supervise the participants to make sure they follow all safety rules,
- supervise the event to prevent violence, and
- supervise the reasonable selection and matching of opponents.

Chapter 16

Golf

Golf is one of the world's most prestigious sports. From the fairways in Scotland to the greens at Augusta, and everywhere in between, individuals hit a little white ball with a club and hope the ball goes where they intended it to go. Unfortunately, the ball often winds up in an area the golfer was trying to avoid. Because the little white ball can do so many unpredictable things, the chances of another person being injured by a stray golf ball are fairly good. Injuries can also be attributed to numerous sources including the golf course's design, the equipment used, alcohol-related injuries and poor supervision.

Golfing represents a host of concerns, but one key issue that should be noted involves the golfers themselves. Numerous golfers are professionals (doctors, lawyers, etc.) who have large incomes or are worth a significant amount. This produces the prospect of higher damage awards in golf due to higher potential lost wages. Imagine if a lawyer is injured on a golf course. You have someone who more than likely will utilize his/her skill and knowledge to exact a large sum to compensate him/her for potential losses. This scenario occurred in a 1998 case. Of all the luck in the world, a golf course had a tractor operating on the course when the tractor hit an attorney and the attorney sustained head injuries and also claimed brain damage. The attorney was awarded $3,625,000 by the jury ("Bulldozer strikes golfer," 1998).

Course

Significant artistic ability and golfing knowledge are required to design a golf course that is both challenging and visually appealing. However, sometimes the concern for beauty and difficulty can lead to developing an unsafe golf course. A golf course has to be reasonably safe for an invitee. Some of the ways to make a golf course safer, besides traditional turf safety concerns include making lakes or ditches off-limits, marking and changing the tee area and general design changes.

Lakes and Ditches

Too many golfers try to follow their balls at all costs, but some areas are just too dangerous for golfers to go exploring for lost balls. Common sense would seem to indicate that if you lose a $1.50 golf ball, you should just use another ball. However, some individuals use extension arm devises or other devises to retrieve balls situated in precarious positions. Lakes and ditches should be roped or chained off-limits to prevent access and warning signs should be placed all around these secured areas at frequent intervals. The *Steele* case helps demonstrate the mentality and possible injury that could be faced by an eager golfers.

Steele v. Jekyll Island State Park Authority
176 S.E. 2d 514 (GA 1970)

W.T. Steele appealed a lower court's summary judgment decision after he slipped at the Park Authority's golf course. Steele hit his ball into a concrete drainage ditch. He had a choice of either crossing over a bridge and accepting the stipulated penalty or going into the ditch to recover the ball. He chose the latter course. The ditch had no water, but had some sand and some slick substance on the sand. While trying to retrieve his ball, Steele's foot slipped and he injured himself.

The court held that the defendant was not liable for a golfer slipping on some algae at the waterless bottom of a concrete ditch. The golf course did not have either a duty to warn about, or remove, the accumulated algae.

The defendant was not liable because the failure to remove algae under the sand is not actionable negligence. Even though the defendants prevailed, the failure to post appropriate signage and prevent access to the ditch possibly contributed to a legal bill that could have been avoided. It should be noted that even if you win a suit, it could still cost you over $70,000 to defend yourself in court, especially if the issue goes to trial and then an appeal.

Thus, if algae or other growths are at the bottom of a ditch or ravine, they should be washed away when the water level recedes. When drainage ditches are present, a chain link fence, over nine feet tall, should be placed around the ditch to prevent unauthorized access to the ditch. Smaller fences or warnings should be used for ditches in the middle of a golf course.

A *lake* could be surrounded with an attractive large chain fence two feet above the ground. This strategy will not prevent someone from entering the area, but the chain could look very attractive while serving the purpose of notifying a golfer that the lake is restricted. A sign can also be posted by the lake and on the scorecard informing participants that the area is off-limits. The chain accompanied by the warnings should be enough notice to foreclose a golfer's claim they did not know the area was off-limits.

Tee Areas

Warning signs should be posted when an area is especially slippery or muddy (normally around the tee area) because golfers could get their cleats or shoes stuck in the mud or they could slip. Golfers should be warned, preferably on the scorecard, that they should stand back several feet from the tee area to reduce the chance of being hit by another golfer.

The tee area, similar to all other areas, should be regularly inspected to uncover any hidden dangers such as glass bottles, stray balls, gopher holes, sprinklers or other items left in the fairway or rough. When someone reports a hazardous condition you have an affirmative duty to investigate and correct the problem.

Benches are frequently placed by tees. The benches should be located far enough from the tee area to provide viewer safety. Benches should also be secured so they cannot be moved or fall over, as seen in the case below.

Panoz v. Gulf & Bay Corporation
208 So. 2d 297 (FL 1968)

Eugene Panoz had played some eight or nine times on the same golf course prior to March 19, 1964. The course had wooden benches placed by various tees for the convenience of waiting players. It was well known that golfers often moved these benches. Panoz and his golf companion arrived at the sixth tee and had to wait a few minutes for the preceding golfers to leave the sixth fairway and green. While waiting, Panoz sat down on a bench that toppled over backwards and caused his head and back to strike the ground.

The defendant had a duty to warn golfers of dangers known or reasonably known to cause injury and a course operator would have to take precautions that would be ordinarily necessary to keep the premises reasonably safe. The defendant was not liable in this case because the bench was not defective and other patrons could have moved the bench to an area that was uneven. Because the benches could have been moved by anyone, the defendants could not control what other golfers did. Similarly, the defendants could not be reasonably expected to protect a patron from being struck by an erratic golf ball or by a golf club thrown by an angry golfer.

To ensure a bench is reasonably safe, the bench should be anchored into level ground (with a cement anchor) to prevent the bench tipping over or patrons moving the bench.

Course Design

A golf course has to be reasonably safe for the business invitees that will be using the course. Normally, a course is rented by an EA for a specific event. A course that is improperly constructed should not be used, no matter how attractive or challenging the course.

Westbourough Country Club v. Palmer
204 F. 2d 143 (8th Cir. 1953)

Sixteen year old Ann Palmer was struck in the head by a golf ball while riding in a car traveling along a highway. The highway ran across Westbourough Country Club's course. She had to cross the highway to reach the clubhouse and swimming pool. The highway was 60 feet from the tee.

Even though three of the 18 local golf courses had similar roads crossing their fairways, that fact did not make a highway crossing a golf course the usual or customary practice for a golf course. The appellate court refused to overrule the lower court's verdict for Palmer and held that the club was negligent in maintaining a road across a fairway. The jury was not bound by the fact that it was more dangerous to run the road parallel to the fairway.

Even if a course is laid out according to customary standards, you could be negligent if the course design is unreasonable. Just because someone else has done something does not mean he/she is correct. Thus, no matter how many individuals engage in a certain course of conduct, if that course of conduct is unreasonable you could be liable. You have to remember that a customary standard is not a fixed law, but becomes evidence for a jury to determine whether you exercised a reasonable standard of care. If you have a feeling that a course is designed in an unreasonable manner, or you are told of prior accidents, you could be acting unreasonably by leasing or using the golf course.

A good example of this point was seen in a 1995 Maine case. A railroad track ran across the first fairway and was visible from the first tee. A golfer hit a ball that hit the tracks, bounced back, and then hit her in her face. The jury awarded her $40,000 and the Maine Supreme Judicial Court concluded that although the tracks did not belong to the club, the club's duty extended to land which it had invited golfers to use ("Court says $40,000 injury award was par for the course," 1995).

Another concern with renting a golf course is making sure the golf cart paths are in a reasonably safe condition. Golf cart paths have to be both constructed and maintained in a safe manner as evidenced in the following case.

Ryan v. Mill River Country Club, Inc.
510 A.2d 462 (CT 1986)

On April 26, 1981, Gina Ryan and Lois Hanson were playing golf at the Mill River Country Club. While driving a three-wheeled golf cart on a paved path from the seventh tee to the seventh green, the plaintiff turned the golf cart in an easterly direction and proceeded downhill along the cart path. While traveling down the path, the golf cart turned sharply to the left, throwing the passenger (Hanson) from the cart. The cart continued in a northerly direction until it turned over. Both Ryan and her passenger were injured.

The jury concluded that the golf course was negligent in having an uneven golf cart path up a hill's slope without any guardrails to keep the cart on the path. The golf course knew about the defective condition, as one of the course employees knew about two other accidents in the same area. The defendants had failed to take any actions to remedy the defect.

In addition to making sure the cart paths are properly situated, the paths should be inspected to make sure they are free from loose gravel, oil or other items that could help cause an accident.

Before deciding to use a golf course, you should inspect the course to make sure all the fairways have enough space between them to prevent errant balls from straying between adjoining fairways. If it is well known that balls often go onto different fairways, and if fairways are unreasonably close to one another, you should provide specific warning to golfers that the fairways are very narrow and very close to each other.

Items that do not seem that important can be very important when an injury occurs. For example, you have to make sure yardage markings on the score cards are written correctly, especially if a pin or green has been moved.

Cornell v. Langland
440 N.E. 2d 985 (IL 1982)

Rita Cornell received a jury verdict for $5,951.55 in compensatory damages and $6,000 in punitive damages against Old Orchard Country Club. The Defendant, Arthur Langland reached the eighth tee and looked at the scorecard to ascertain the distance to the green. The card indicated that the hole was a 315 yard-par four hole. Langland looked down the fairway and saw the plaintiff and her husband approaching the green. Langland waited until they reached the green and then proceeded to tee off. His drive struck Cornell's head, while she was pulling the pin from the hole.

While the scorecard said the hole was 315 yards from the tee, the tee had been moved several times and a laser measurement performed the year after the accident indicated that the center of the tee was 232 yards from the center of the green. The plaintiff's husband also measured the distance shortly after the accident and found it to be approximately 217 yards from the tee to green. The golf course's pro manager stated that they had moved the green two years beforehand, but they had a lot of score cards left over. The manager stated that when they printed the cards again, they would probably change the measurement.

The appellate court agreed that the golf course was negligent in failing to see that the card properly reflected the true yardage. However, the appellate court also concluded that the mismarking of the card was not the type of conduct that justified the imposition of punitive damages. Thus, the punitive damages were overturned.

Equipment

If *golf clubs* are provided for participants, the clubs should be examined for any loose grips, cracks, loose heads or any other forms of club deterioration.

Golf carts are often rented without any inspection. As with a rental car, participants do not examine the golf carts to determine if they are safe; golfers assume they are safe. If golf carts will be used in your event, you should make sure the golf course guarantees that the carts are in reasonably safe condition. Any golf course that does not provide some assurance that they regularly maintain their carts or their carts are reasonably mechanically safe should be suspect and you might want to find another course willing to provide safe carts.

Gifford v. Bogey Hills Golf and Country Club, Inc.

426 SW. 2d 98 (MO 1968)

Arthur Gifford, age 14, was golfing with his father at the Bogey Hills Golf and Country Club. The pair rented one golf cart and their golfing companions rented another cart. No warning about defective brakes were given to the plaintiff or any other foursome member. Gifford's father drove the cart until the fifth hole. During that time he found the brakes would not lock the cart's wheels and would only bring the cart to a rolling stop. Gifford then drove the cart until the third hole of the back nine holes. One foursome member hit a ball down a hill. While Gifford stayed in the cart on top of the hill, the others went looking for the lost ball.

The cart was parked or stopped with the brake fully depressed when the cart started rolling downhill. Gifford removed his foot then stepped on the brakes several times with no results. The cart crashed through a barbed-wire fence at the bottom of the hill, causing Gifford severe injuries.

Defendants normally inspected and lubricated all the golf carts every two weeks. However, at the time of the accident, the cart's brakes had not yet been adjusted. The court found the defendant negligent for not inspecting the brakes. The brake problem existed for several weeks and could have been discovered if the defendant had used a simple routine inspection plan.

Supervision

Golf is a very individualized game. Most golfers do not expect a golf tournament director to provide education, equipment or significant monitoring. However, under certain circumstances you will be forced to provide proper supervision such as when dangerous conditions arise which a golfer might not know about or appreciate the severity. A person in a golf pro shop might hear about a lightening storm, but if they cannot communicate the danger to others then liability can ensue. This issue arose in a New Jersey case where a golfer was struck by lightning. The appellate court reversed the lower court's summary judgment order and the golfer was given a chance to prove that the safety precautions taken by the golf course failed to meet industry standards (*Maussner v. Atlantic City Country Club, Inc.*, 691 A. 2d 826 (N.J. Super. A.D. 1997)).

The 19th Hole

Especially on hot summer days, golfers like to have a little drink before, after and sometimes during play. You should make sure that a "no alcohol" rule is adopted and enforced for all participants during play. You cannot be responsible if a golfer sneaks in a drink, but you can ban coolers (filled with alcoholic drinks) on golf carts. You can also prohibit selling alcohol between holes (except limited sales between the front and the back nine holes).

The famous 19th hole is a different story. Alcohol related issues are discussed in more detail in Chapter 32. However, as the court in *Panoz v. Gulf & Bay Corp.* stated, "a higher degree of care would be reasonably imposed in the area around the club house where there are a large number of people congregated in a limited area and the owner has better means of providing protection for patrons."

Proper alcohol supervision includes making sure individuals that have had a little too much to drink do not wander onto the fairways, interfere with other golfers, play another round or drive motorized golf carts. It is very difficult to determine when someone has had too much to drink, but any individual selling alcoholic beverages should be required to determine whether or not someone appears to have over imbibed. In a Wisconsin case, a golfer had 13 drinks before he fell face first onto a brick path outside the 19th hole after tripping on his own golf spikes. Even though it is rare for a drunken person to win a negligence case, the court awarded the golfer $41,540 based on the gaps between the bricks in the walkway ("Drunken golfer wins $41,540 after fall," 1996).

Conclusion

You can help make sure your golfing event minimizes the potential for injuries by:

- making sure all lakes and ditches are visibly marked off-limits,
- making sure the tee-off area is inspected and repaired if it is in poor condition,
- making sure the course design is reasonable and safe,
- making sure all golf cart paths are appropriately placed and safe,
- making sure all equipment loaned to golfers is in the best condition,

- supervising participants so they do not cross fairways when other people are hitting shots,
- supervising the location and amount of alcohol served.

Chapter 17

Gymnastics

Gymnastics is an elegant and demanding sport requiring great expertise and experience to execute flawless moves worthy of a "10" score. The high flips, dismounts and pounding meted out on various apparatus requires high quality equipment and regular equipment inspection. The major concerns you have in a gymnastics event are the facility, the equipment and proper supervision.

Facility

Special precautions need to be taken whenever children can easily reach dangerous equipment. The doctrine of attractive nuisance, which applies to dangerous equipment or locations accessible to children, applies to gymnastic equipment. You have to make sure children only utilize the equipment when proper supervision is available. This extremely important policy can be implemented fairly easily. *You have to lock up the gym or store the equipment in a locked closet whenever a supervisor is not present.* This warning cannot be stressed enough for such apparatus as trampolines or springboards, which are very attractive for children. The following case highlights this concern.

Grant v. Lake Oswego School District Number 7
515 P. 2d 947 (OR 1973)

Carol Grant was a 12-year-old seventh grader in 1971 when she was injured by jumping off a springboard and striking her head on a low doorway beam. Grant had jumped on the springboard approximately twenty times during the exercise class. The teacher told her and several other students to move the springboard to another location. The teacher testified that she told the girls to lean the springboard on its side when they put it away.

Grant admitted she was putting the springboard away according to the teacher's instructions. However, the girls put the springboard down, but did not tip it onto its side. Grant knew the clearance to the doorway was

213

low, but she tried to propel herself back into the exercise room when she hit her head.

Grant alleged that the defendants were negligent in:

- placing a springboard under a low ceiling and doorway,
- failing to turn the springboard on its side or otherwise make it harmless,
- failing to warn students of the dangers of hitting the low ceiling and/or doorway, and
- failing to supervise the students in using dangerous exercise equipment.

A jury awarded Grant $10,500. The lower court overturned the jury verdict claiming that the evidence showed she was contributorily negligent. The appellate court overturned the lower court's order concluding that Grant's contributory negligence did not bar her suit or her recovery.

Special care has to be taken to make sure any dangerous apparatus is properly locked after being used. Just putting equipment in a corner or warning people not to use the equipment will not work. A reasonable EA would appreciate the risks inherent in trampolines and springboards and would take extra precautions to protect potential users. Another precautionary step could include a light locking mechanism. Several types of locking mechanism are available that do not let anyone turn on or off the light switch after the mechanism is engaged. Such devises are fairly inexpensive and easy to install. Champion America, Inc. (1(800) 521-7000 dept. 300) is one company that sells such devises.

Matting

Adequate matting has to be provided for the entire area both under and around each apparatus. There are numerous types of matting style, shapes and thickness. National or regional associations should be contacted regarding appropriate matting recommended for various competitive levels. However, the following suggested standard can usually be applied to most competitive levels under the elite competitive level. The authors recommend that *Competition mats should be at least 1 to 1 1/2 inches thick, landing mats should be at least 3 1/2 to 4 1/2 inches thick and crash pads should be at least 6 to 12 inches thick.* The matting should be laid out according to the directions provided by the apparatus manufacturer. If no directions are provided with the equipment, you can find out what matting layout will be the most effective from other programs or various gymnastic governing bodies. It is imperative that the apparatus' leg pieces are properly covered. Every location where a gymnast might land should be protected with some form of matting.

Govel v. Board of Education of Albany,
48 N.Y.S. 2d 299 (NY 1944)

On March 5, 1942, Mr. Govel was injured upon alighting after a somersault. The apparatus used was a springboard covered with a mat adjacent to some parallel bars, five feet tall and about twenty inches wide, over which the pads had been draped. Govel ran about thirty feet, gained impetus from the springboard, and while turning in the air his foot struck a parallel bar and he fell on the bare floor. On a prior day, another boy broke his arm in the same exercise and a number of other students had been injured in the past.

Under state law, physical education was a required course. The law required the regents to adopt rules determining the subjects to be included in physical training courses. The acrobatic feat in which Govel was injured was not a recommended exercise, but a combination of two different exercises.

The court concluded that it was the teacher's duty to "exercise reasonable care to prevent injuries; to assign pupils to such exercises as are within their abilities and to properly and adequately supervise the activities." The teacher was negligent in this case because he:

- failed to have mats in place on the far side of the bars (which would have reduced the hazard of Govel's fall following the somersault),
- assigned a student (who was not exceptionally skilled) to an exercise beyond his prowess and which was not recommended on the regent's syllabus, and
- for making the assignment knowing the inherent danger-as several boys had been similarly injured, including one a few days before Govel's accident.

Thus, if you misplace mats or fail to provide adequate protection, you could be liable for breaching a duty to protect participants.

Apparatus that require the gymnast to become airborne has to be adequately surrounded with at least the minimum amount of required matting as illustrated in the *Singer* case.

Singer v. School District of Philadelphia
513 A.2d 1108 (PA 1986)

While performing a gymnastic stunt over a vaulting horse at a district school gymnasium, David Singer fell and broke his elbow when he missed a mat and landed on the hardwood floor.

The lower court granted a judgment on the pleadings for the school based on its conclusion that Singer did not present any facts whereby the school could be held negligent. The appellate court reversed the lower court's ruling. The appellate court concluded that the pleadings alleged negligence concerning the care, custody and control of the landing surface around the vaulting horse. Under the immunity exception, a suit related to the condition of a facility was not barred by governmental immunity. The court concluded that sufficient matting protection is a necessary element of a gymnasium floor. Appropriate matting was within the school district's care, custody, and control. The defendant was also possibly negligent in failing:

- to maintain a proper lookout,
- to warn the plaintiff about possible dangers,
- to adequately supervise the gymnastic activities and
- to properly choose, construct, manage, maintain and control the landing surface.

Ventilation

Any area that is used for gymnastics has to be properly ventilated to prevent the accumulation of humidity or chalk dust in the air. Accumulating humidity or dust can cause an apparatus to become slippery, thus increasing possible accidents.

Many gymnasts use fine chalk to help them get a better grip. Most chalk settles to the floor, but when individuals are running around, the chalk dust could be kicked up into the air and could interfere with someone's vision. Gymnasts should be instructed to brush off excess chalk over the chalk dispenser and the gymnasium floor should be swept after every meet or practice.

Equipment

As stated previously, gymnastic equipment can be very dangerous. Therefore, gymnastic facility owners and managers are held to a strict standard for the equipment's quality. All apparatus has to meet the highest safety standards and be inspected for proper construction. Equipment which needs to be inspected regularly includes rings, parallel bars, high bars, uneven bars, balance beam, pommel horse, women's vaulting horse and a Reuther board.

You should ensure that older, outdated equipment is replaced with the latest, safest models. Parts from one apparatus should never be exchanged with parts from different apparatus. This is especially important when the two parts come from different manufacturers. The only method that you can use to ensure the apparatus is in the best possible condition is to thoroughly inspect and maintain the gymnastic equipment and facility on a frequent basis. A qualified inspector who knows what to look for (regarding wear and tear, stress, etc.) and understands how equipment should be installed, has to inspect the equipment on a frequent and timely basis. An inspection chart should be developed before the event and the inspector should examine all the apparatus used before, several times during and after the event. The inspector should indicate the condition of the apparatus on the inspection chart. After each team or group has used an apparatus, the apparatus should be checked to ensure that nothing was bent or loosened during the previous competitive round.

Whoever fits, adjusts or maintains the apparatus has to be specifically trained in proper maintenance procedures for each apparatus. The inspector's duties should include completing the inspection chart, which could be used as evidence of a regular and thorough maintenance plan.

Wells v. YMCA of Bogalusa
150 So. 2d 324 (LA 1963)

On May 6, 1960 Roy Wells, 14, jumped from a YMCA springboard. While in the air, Wells tried to turn a flip over a rope attatched to the board. Wells broke his arm when he fell over the rope. Roy claimed the YMCA failed to:

- lower the rope for him to properly clear,
- catch him which would have prevented the fall,
- provide qualified instructors, provide safety devises for hazardous operations,

- allowed him to engage in a dangerous operation without safety devises and instructors.

Wells testified that he regularly attended YMCA classes for two years and he was an active member in the leaders club, in which the older gymnasts assisted the younger ones.

Wells had just learned that afternoon how to do a somersault from the board landing on his feet. Two spotters stood on either side of the springboard holding a rope at various heights for the gymnasts to jump over. The spotters were responsible for trying to catch any gymnast who was unable to complete the somersault.

The court concluded that the YMCA was not negligent for Wells' injury because it acted reasonably. The YMCA acted reasonably by:

- providing adequate facilities and safety precautions,
- having adequate equipment,
- following the equipment's protective regulations,
- utilizing a qualified staff.

The court's finding was supported by the fact that Wells had performed several successful flips before he fell, and he was considered a superior gymnast.

Following established standards still might not protect you if a jury finds that the standard is not reasonable.

Tiemann v. Independent School District #740
331 N.W. 2d 250 (MN 1983)

Sandra Tiemann was instructed to run towards a pommel horse, jump on a springboard, put her hands on the horse and jump over the horse with one leg on either side of the horse. However, the pommel (handles) on the horse had been removed, leaving two half-inch diameter holes on the horse's surface. While trying to jump, her finger got caught in a hole, causing her to fall on the wooden floor alongside the horse. Tiemann sustained permanent injuries to her right leg.

Besides the claimed insufficient matting around the horse, Tiemann claimed that the school district was negligent in allowing students to use the horse without the pommels in place. The school district claimed that the prevailing custom among physical education instructors was to use vaulting horses with exposed holes. The court concluded that a jury could find the defendant negligent if removing the pommels fell below the reasonable care requirement.

---

l

Whenever any equipment is used, you have to follow both established standards as well as ensure you reasonably discharge your duty for providing a safe environment.

Three of the specific areas of equipment concerns that have to be examined very carefully are ground attachments, trampolines and moving equipment.

Ground Attachments

All gymnastic facility and equipment inspectors have to examine the floor plates to make sure there is no fraying where the floorboards meet the metal connection plates. Inspectors should also make sure that all guide wires, cables, hook-up wires and/or turnbuckles are properly installed. Only qualified individuals should install gymnastic equipment. Gymnasts are often used to move and set-up equipment. The problem with this practice is that if a gymnast fails to properly secure or inspect any equipment, you could be liable for failing to ensure that properly qualified individuals installed the equipment. Apparatus inspection also cannot be ignored during the event. The previous safe use of the apparatus by other participants might indicate that the apparatus has been safe, but it does not guarantee the apparatus will remain safe.

Trampolines

What once used to be a popular fad and an enjoyable activity for the whole family has almost died in the United States because there are too many suits over dangerous trampolines. Trampolines, in and of themselves, are not inherently dangerous. The problem is that participants often lose their balance while trying to accomplish mid-air twists and turns. However, many trampoline users who lost their balance fell in unusual positions or locations on or off the trampolines. Thus, the problem has not usually been the trampoline itself, but the lack of supervision, which was required for safe trampoline use.

Gary A. Smith, a medical doctor and doctor of public health, released the result of a study relating to children injuries on trampolines. The 1998 report concluded that:

> Injuries related to trampolines, especially backyard trampolines, are an important cause of pediatric morbidity. These injuries have also resulted in death. The rapid increase in the number of trampoline-related injuries to children during the recent years is evidence that preventive strategies are inadequate. Children should not use trampolines at home. The sale of trampoline for private recreational use should be stopped, and a trade-in campaign should be conducted nationally to decrease the number of existing backyard trampolines (Smith, 1998).

Smith's study noted that trampoline related injuries increased from 29,600 in 1990 to 58,400 in 1995 (a 98% increase) (Smith, 1998). The same study concluded that trampoline injuries from 1990 through 1995 sent almost 250,000 children to hospitals (Smith, 1998II). While these numbers are great (almost 83,000 emergency room visits in 1996 by children and adult tramploiners), they still pale compared with the 500,000 ER visits by bicyclists and 103,000 ER visits by roller bladers (Smith, 1998II).

Trampoline use has declined even though many cases against trampoline amusement facilities were won by the facilities. The *Daniels* case represents one case where a facility prevailed using the assumption of risk defense.

Daniels v. S-CO Corp.
124 N.W. 2d 522 (IA 1963)

Ernest Daniels was injured on July 11, 1960, when he fell while using a trampoline at the defendant's trampoline center. Daniels was a 35 year-old accountant who was visiting the trampoline center with his four-year-old daughter. Nobody knew what happened to Daniels or why he fell. The record only showed that two witnesses found Daniels lying by the side of the trampoline after they heard someone fall.

Daniels received a jury verdict for $6,500 in a lower court. The appellate court held that a 35 year-old with a college education was sufficiently warned and assumed the risks as danger signs were posted, there were no hidden dangers and there were signs telling patrons to ask for instruction if desired. The appellate court also concluded that the facility did not breach its supervision duty because it did not need a supervisor at each trampoline. Thus, the lower court's decision was reversed.

The court rationalized that older patrons at these facilities could appreciate the risk of losing their balance in the air, and could ask for instruction if they desired. However, younger patrons have to be warned and supervised more closely as they might not appreciate all the risk or ask for assistance.

Due to all the problems and lawsuits with trampolines, some courts considered them inherently dangerous and required specific warnings for all participants wishing to use them. However, warnings are only effective if they are properly conveyed. The failure to properly post warnings was raised in the *Pell* case, below.

Pell v. Victor J. Andrew High School
462 N.E. 2d 858 (IL 1984)

Lauren Pell was permanently injured in a gym class. Pell was injured while performing a somersault off a trampoline manufactured by AMF. Pell, a 16-year-old sophomore and beginning gymnast, was injured on a mini-trampoline in 1980. The trampoline consisted of a 37-inch square shaped frame with springs and a fabric bed. Affixed to the fabric bed was a warning that stated:

> [C]aution. Misuse and abuse of this trampoline is dangerous and can cause serious injuries. Read instructions before using this trampoline. Inspect before using and replace any warn, defective, or missing parts. Any activity involving height creates the possibility of accidental injuries. This unit is intended for use only by properly trained and qualified participants under supervised conditions. Use without proper supervision can be dangerous and should not be undertaken or permitted.

The problem with the warning was that the trampoline bed, to which the warning was attached, was placed in such a manner that the warning label was on the bottom, facing the floor.

The court concluded that warnings have to be adequate to perform their intended risk reduction function. Warnings are inadequate if they:

- do not specify the risk presented,
- they are inconsistent with how a product should be used,
- do not provide a reason for the warning,
- if they do not reach the foreseeable users.

The defendant high school settled out of court with Pell for $1.6 million. The jury awarded Pell a $5 million verdict against AMF. AMF, Inc., a large sporting equipment manufacturer, appealed the judgment. The appellate court affirmed the lower court's decision because there was sufficient evidence from which the jury could conclude that the warning was ineffective. The warning was ineffective because the warning was placed in a location that could not be seen by the user. The warning also failed to specify that a severe spinal cord injury could result in permanent paralysis if somersaults were performed without a spotter or a safety harness.

If a trampoline is being used, you have to make sure all participants sign a waiver that expressly states all possible injuries that could befall them. All warnings should be plainly visible to the participants.

You must ensure that the springs and the frame covering have sufficient padding to protect participants that might drift from the trampoline's bed.

To cover the springs, many EAs stretch rubber or other fabrics from the mat to the frame, thus covering the springs and protecting participants from falling between the springs. Some manufacturers have developed netting cages to fit around trampolines to help protect people from falling off. These devises are relatively new so there has not been an opportunity to fully track their effectiveness or determine if they will become a potential standard for the industry.

Another major concern with trampolines is the amount of supervision required to protect participants. The *Daniels'* court concluded that a supervisor is not required at each trampoline. However, to provide the greatest amount of supervision, you should place a spotter on each side of the trampoline. As it is often difficult to get a spotter for each side, you could use a trampoline with the assistance of at least two spotters, who could be positioned at opposite diagonal corners.

Supervision

Gymnastics is a sport that requires substantial supervision. Supervisory guidelines have to be established and communicated from the very beginning and covering all activities. All training and competitive sessions have to be closely supervised. No roughhousing can be allowed and no unsupervised children should be allowed to congregate around potentially dangerous apparatus (which is basically any equipment above the floor). Supervision needs to be provided when moving, setting-up and tearing down any equipment and padding. Spotters are needed for more than just somersaults or trampolines. Intricate maneuvers, even by world class gymnasts should not be attempted without having a spotter present. If a spotter rule is in effect, then the participants should be able to rely upon a spotter being there. All spotters should be mature and capable of following the predetermined spotting rules, without being distracted.

One of the keys to providing proper supervision entails having qualified coaches/instructors. Negligent hiring is a critical concern in gymnastics as young gymnasts are often asked to help train even younger gymnasts rather than having a certified coach/instructor with all the proper credentials. Liability can ensue from having a coach/instructor who does not have the skill, qualification and/or experience to supervise complex maneuvers working with children performing complex maneuvers (Greenwald, 1980).

A good example of the principal above was highlighted in a California case from 1992. The 17-year-old plaintiff was injured in the high school gym during open use of the facility after school hours. He was attempting a "front catch" or "Yager" on the high bar when he fell. Supervision was provided by a volunteer gymnast. The plaintiff made several claims including:

- the volunteer was negligent,
- the defendant provided inadequate supervision/instruction,
- the coach did not teach the necessary lead-up skills to the somersault skill,
- the defendant should have required him to wear a safety belt.

The defendant claimed that the volunteer was not an employee, the plaintiff was an experienced gymnast who performed similar, difficult, moves and the plaintiff had already showed enough proficiency with the safety belt that it was time to perform without the belt.

The court concluded that the volunteer was an unpaid employee in the course and scope of employment and that the volunteer's negligent conduct was the proximate cause of the plaintiff's injuries (medical damages were $2.5 million and claimed lost earnings were $2 million). While the plaintiff did not assume the risk, the suit was still resolved in the defendant's favor based on the court's finding that gymnastics constituted a hazardous recreational activity which provided defendant with governmental immunity (*Acosta v. Los Angeles Unified School District*, WEC 133-767, 1992).

During training, or while teaching complex maneuvers, a safety or spotting belt should be used. Supervisors should insist that everyone use a belt for his/her own protection. You or your supervisors have the last clear chance to prevent an injury by requiring someone to use a belt. Thus, if a participant refuses to use a belt or harness for new or hard maneuvers he/she should be prohibited from using the apparatus. To avoid the potential *peer pressure defense*, all the participants should be required to use a belt. A belt rule is especially important for children, as they are usually legally incapable of being contributorily negligent.

Other supervision related concerns include having volunteers or untrained individuals assisting gymnasts. Smaller gymnastics studios often ask older gymnasts, often teenagers to help instruct young children. This practice could lead to significant supervision related concerns as the teenagers, while having significant gymnastics experience, might not have any supervision experience. The most experienced gymnast who cannot teach or properly supervise several five-year-olds represents a serious risk for those children.

Lastly, another major supervision concerns involves moving equipment. Similar to moving heavy pads for wrestling, gymnastic pads and equipment can be very bulky and burdensome. Proper supervision entails properly instructing individuals in both moving and storing equipment. In a New York case, an 18-year-old girl with the help of other gymnasts was moving some equipment when she struck a 16 foot long balance beam leaning against the wall. The beam fell over hitting the plaintiff in the head. The plaintiff claimed negligence and negligent supervision against the coach for allowing the students to move the equipment near the beam. The jury awarded the plaintiff $250,000, but reduced the award ten percent for plaintiff's comparative negligence (*Mora v. Board of Education*, N.Y., New York County Sup. Ct., No. 23257/89, Nov. 2, 1992, ATLA Law Reporter, Vol. 36, June 1993, p. 178.)

Conclusion

A gymnastics event can be produced with a lower risk level by:

- locking up all equipment that is not in use,
- placing adequate matting in and around all apparatuses,
- making sure the facility is adequately ventilated,
- making sure the apparatus is properly constructed and maintained, with appropriate parts and by a qualified individual,
- inspecting the apparatus before, during and after each event,
- providing adequate supervision and padding for trampolines,
- making sure spotters and/or safety belts are used for difficult or new maneuvers,
- providing adequate supervision for gymnasts at all levels.

Chapter 18

Hockey

Hockey is an extremely fast-paced agility sport that has generated more fights than goals during many games. Hockey's image as a rough sport highlights the importance of participant supervision. Hockey is more difficult than basketball to manage because hockey is played on ice. A basketball court can be swept during half time with a broom, however, an ice rink requires a Zamboni machine to scrape ice shavings off and lay a new layer of ice to maintain proper skating surface conditions. With the recent popularity experienced by both ice skating and in-line skating, basketball court related issues should be examined in addition to the hockey risk management techniques highlighted below. The major concerns you may face in putting on a hockey event can include the ice rink, spectator violence, equipment and supervision concerns. The major difference between ice hockey and in-line hockey entails ice related floor concerns where ice related falls often cause less damages than falls on cement.

Rink

Ice rinks are not inherently dangerous, but at least one court in Canada concluded that a waiver was only valid if the ice rink was perfectly safe. A 17-year-old flew into the boards and became paralyzed. He sued claiming the ice was substandard. The final award against the facility was $8.7 million (Canadian) ("Hockey isn't even immune from lawsuits," 1996).

Keeping the surface ice in a reasonable condition and making sure the hockey peripherals are installed correctly are critical concerns. The rink ice surface should be kept at a *temperature of 22–24 F degrees* to allow for the least thawing and the best skating conditions (Krupinski, 1999). If the ice is too soft or if too much ice shavings or water are on the surface, they could cause an injury. After every period of a professional hockey game, a Zamboni should scrape the ice (Krupinski, 1999). Youth level competition only requires a pre-game scraping due to less damage caused by the lighter skaters. The frequency of resurfacing depends on the ice's condition, so you should make sure the surface is checked on a regular basis by supervisors and/or referees. Furthermore, national and regional standards should be researched to determine what specific temperature and ice conditions need to be maintained.

Only a *qualified and experienced Zamboni driver* should be used. An inexperienced driver could make a mistake or fail to properly operate the machine. This could subject you to liability under the negligent hiring/supervision theory. All skating has to be prohibited while the Zamboni is on the ice. All skaters should be cleared from the ice prior to the Zamboni being deployed. A general announcement and warning should be made that the ice has to be cleared prior to being re-surfaced.

Most EAs rent a rink or use a rink operated by an experienced rink owner/manager. You should make sure the owner/manager has taken all the necessary steps to make the facility reasonably safe. Do not be afraid to ask the owner/manager if the rink is safe. If you are told that the rink is very safe, and someone gets injured, you could claim that you asked about the facility's condition and relied upon the owner's/manager's statement. The final facility rental agreement should specify proper ice maintenance obligations of the parties.

The *goal cage and netting* should not be permanently fastened to the ice rink floor (Krupinski, 1999). It should be attached through breakaway posts that allow the whole cage to move if a player skates or slides into the cage. Appropriate hockey association rules should be followed to make sure the standard amount of space between the cage and the boards is present (Krupinski, 1999 normally 12-15 feet). If there is not enough space behind the goal, you should make sure there is enough room for at least several players behind the cage and players need to be warned about any smaller space limitations. The penalty and team boxes should be designed so their doors open in, and not out onto the ice. This would avoid the potential problem of a door swinging open and hitting another participant. Furthermore, all handles, knobs and other potentially protruding objects should be recessed or removed to avoid injury.

Both the *rink and the dasher boards* along the rink's sides have to be examined regularly to make sure the boards are not loose or damaged. A loose runner board can catch a participant's skate blade and send the person flying.

To protect spectators and skaters, you should only use a facility that has plexi-glass or some other form of *protective screening* above the boards. The plexi-glass sheets (or other safety material) that are above the rink boards should be examined before the event to make sure they are not loose or cracked. If there is a net above the plexi-glass, it should also be checked for holes or aging. Spectators need to be protected from pucks flying over or through the screens and participants need to be protected from spectators throwing items at them. Spectator-related issues are discussed further in the guide.

Spectator Violence

As hockey is not immune from violent confrontations between opposing players, heated tempers in the stands can also effect participants in a hockey game. Spectators should not be allowed to bring in cans, bottles, fruits or other objects that may be used to throw at participants. Loudspeaker announcements should also be made regarding the penalty for throwing items into the rink (ejection and possible criminal prosecution, or forfeiture of a game). Similar to baseball games, EAs have to properly manage promotions and give-aways to make sure they are not arming fans in the stands with possible weapons. The Los Angeles Dodgers had to forfeit a game in 1995 when their baseball promotion night went sour and fans threw balls at players on the field (Hummel, 1998). Similar concerns and potential injuries could occur if fans throw hats, squids, octopuses and other items into the rink. Uniformed guards should be posted to help enforce a posted anti-throwing policy. Installing or raising a net over the plexi-glass shields can also make it more difficult for fans to throw items at the players.

Possible violence continuing off the ice can quickly spread to angry fans. In one Canadian case the authors heard about, a hockey player was able to recover damages after he was involved in a fight with another participant. A relative of the person with whom he just had a fight came out of the stands and attacked the hockey player on his way to the dressing room. If a hockey player has been involved in a fight or if the game involves known rivals involving past fan violence, you would be on notice that a scuffle might occur between player(s) and the fan(s). You must take appropriate steps to ensure adequate and qualified security is present and visible to prevent any potential violence.

Equipment

You should make sure all the *pucks* are regulation pucks approved by an appropriate hockey governing organization. If *hockey sticks* are provided to players or if they bring their own sticks, the sticks should be examined for cracks, wear or fraying which could cause the stick to shatter. Especially with children, you should make sure participants are using *appro-*

priate hockey skates (ice hockey or figure skating). It is also a wise idea to check children's' skates to make sure that the laces are properly tied to prevent a possible twisted ankle or collisions.

You should enforce rules requiring *face guards and helmets, chest and leg padding and goalie gloves for all goalies.* All other players should be required to wear a regulation strength hockey helmet with a face guard. It is imperative that only hockey helmets be used, not lacrosse helmets. You only should use equipment that meets or exceeds appropriate standards, as demonstrated in the following case

-----

Everett v. Bucky Warren, Inc.
380 N.E. 2d 653 (MA 1978)

William Everett was a nineteen-year-old post graduate student at New Preparatory School in Cambridge, Massachusetts when he was injured in a hockey game. The game was played in 1970. While playing against Brown University's freshman team, Everett attempted to block a shot by throwing himself horizontally on the ice. He landed in a position that was directly in the puck's line of flight. The puck hit Everett's helmet and caused a skull fracture. The injury required placing a metal plate into Everett's head.

Everett was wearing a helmet specifically ordered by the school's hockey coach. The helmet was a three-piece helmet designed to more effectively fit a participant's head through fasteners and leather strips to tighten the helmet pieces. However, the helmet was designed in such a way that there were gaps between helmet pieces ranging from minimal gaps to 3/4-inch gaps. The puck penetrated the larger gap.

Everett was awarded $85,000 because the jury found that the manufacturer negligently designed the helmet, the school was negligent for supplying the helmet and the helmet was unreasonably dangerous. In reference to the school, the court concluded that the school was required to exercise reasonable care to not provide equipment that it knew, or had reason to know was dangerous. The court also held the coach to a higher standard of care and knowledge in connection with his ordering a dangerous three-piece helmet. Safer one-piece helmets were available for purchase, but the coach purchased the three-piece model.

Helmet selection is a critical concern based on the number of head injuries each year. However, having an appropriate helmet (as well as any other protective gear) is not enough. Skaters need to know how to properly fit, wear and maintain them. In addition, skaters need to be properly taught how to play. Between 1988 and 1994, seven hockey players suffered cervical spine injuries and that number jumped with seven such injuries in 1995 (Conklin, 1998). In one case, a college player was paralyzed during the first 11 seconds of his first college game (Conklin, 1998). Most of these serious injuries are due to aggressive play where one player moves or slips and goes head first into another player or dasher boards.

Supervision

As with all other events, supervision needs to be provided throughout the event, but also during pre-event and training periods. Activities such as free skating can become very dangerous if no rules are applied and players start high sticking or lofting numerous pucks into the air all over the rink. Furthermore, skaters often let their guard down when they are not playing and might not concentrate as much on protective skating.

Because significant contact occurs between participants, ice and in-line hockey participants need to be supervised to ensure that individuals competing against each other possess the same skating ability, age, size and strength. Excellent skaters can be significantly smaller in size than other participants and should be allowed to participate if they are well trained. They should also receive a written warning about hockey's physical nature and all possible injuries inherent in the sport. Young and inexperienced players should always wear protective pads, helmets and mouth guards. Experienced players should also wear all the required protective equipment. However, as experienced hockey players understand the risk inherent in the sport, they could reasonably assume the risk of participating without protective equipment.

Referees can be influential in minimizing potential injuries by calling checks early, and often, to discourage an overly aggressive game. Referees should also be informed about players that are "enforcers" for the purpose of intimidating opposing players. A known enforcer should be warned at the game's onset that any unnecessary and intentional rough conduct could be punished with stiff penalties or expulsion. Enforcers in professional hockey are trained participants and their competition is both well trained and knowledgeable about the risks inherent in hockey. However, most amateur players are not in the same physical condition as professional athletes and are playing primarily for recreation. Coaches should not encourage rough conduct since an injured player could claim that the opposing coach did not act reasonably or encouraged dangerous conduct. When violent acts occur, an injured athlete might have greater latitude for punishment outside the civil justice system. In one 1998 incident a defenseman for the Phoenix Mustangs was forced to post $10,000 for bail to get out of jail after a fight. The player attacked an opponent with his stick as the players were leaving the ice after the second period. The attack resulted in a broken nose and 20 stitches in the other player's face. The injured player pressed charges which resulted in the assailant being arrested during the game and facing a felony assault charge ("Hockey arrest," 1998). Possibly ten years ago, Sports Illustrated highlighted an American hockey player charged with murder in Italy for seriously checking a player into the boards with such force that the player died.

An injured player could also claim that his own coach failed to warn him about certain team's or player's dangerous propensity which the coach knew or should have known were more violent.

Conclusion

It is impossible to prevent collisions in either ice or in-line hockey. Similar to auto racing or skiing, whenever anyone generates momentum and need significant room to stop, they will not always stop in time. If limits were placed on how fast skaters could go, the sport would die. Furthermore, participants and spectators love the contact inherent in the sport. All skaters have to understand the risks they face and need to be prepared to voluntarily accepts all risk which they are specifically told about.

A reasonable hockey administrator should take the following steps to help ensure event safety:

- making sure the rink's temperature is correct,
- making sure the ice is a consistent texture (i.e. not soft),
- having the ice scraped before, during and after the event,
- properly securing the goal cage and net,
- inspecting and repairing the rink and dasher boards,
- inspecting and repairing the protective screening and netting,
- providing reasonable participant protection,
- examining all hockey sticks, ice skates and helmets for defects, hazards or damage,
- supervising and controlling aggressive play.

Chapter 19

Racquet Sports

Tennis, squash, racquetball and badminton can be played both indoors and outdoors, thus providing numerous playing conditions. Tennis has the widest different court surfaces with clay, synthetic, grass and cement courts being used throughout the world. The major concerns that have to be addressed when running a racquet sport event include the indoor or outdoor court conditions, the equipment used and the supervision required.

Indoor Courts

Significant control can be exercised over indoor courts, as nature's elements cannot affect the surface in the same manner as outdoor courts. Natural elements still can damage a court and significantly increase potential injuries. Leaky roofs can often create puddles that might go unnoticed on slick, waxed surfaces. In one case, a female was injured on a wet floor while beginning to play racquetball at a California based YMCA. The plaintiff contended that a YMCA employee wet-mopped the racquetball court floor and failed to post any warning signs. The wet floor was impossible to detect due to the alledged poor lighting. The YMCA claimed it did not know about the wet condition and that an employee did not cause the situation. The jury believed the plaintiff and awarded her $153,000 (*Leake v. Santa Maria Valley YMCA*, SM85064, Verdicts & Settlements, March 24, 1995, p.8).

Besides water puddles, you have to regularly inspect indoor floors for water, sweat, dust and other slippery substances. You also should examine the indoor court to make sure:

- the floor is level,
- no warped or bubbled wood is present,
- the floor is not loose or cracked in any location,
- all floor boards or pieces are secured.

Any height difference in the floor should be repaired immediately to prevent tripping over the hazard.

Waxenberg v. Crystal Baths
129 N.Y.S. 2d 71 (NY 1954)

On May 7, 1948, Waxenberg was injured when an opponent in a hand-ball game collided with him. Crystal Baths in the Woolworth Building operated the four-walled handball court. Waxenberg's opponent had tripped on a portion of the linoleum floor that was raised one inch higher than the other parts of the floor. The raised area had other problems including being wavy, cracked and loose. Waxenberg was familiar with the defect, as he had played on the same court on previous occasions.

Waxenberg's opponent was thrown off balance by the uneven floor, swung at a ball while off balance and hit Waxenberg in the face, causing a portion of Waxenberg's eyeglass to become embedded in Waxenberg's eye. Waxenberg's eye was removed at a later date.

Waxenberg received a jury verdict for $7,500 that was overturned by the appellate court. The appellate court determined that Waxenberg assumed the risk of competing on the defective floor because the defect was neither obscure nor hidden.

Through ordinary inspection, a major floor defect can be spotted very early. Remedying the defect early can save money as well as a possibly preventing a suit. If a height differential cannot be repaired, the court or facility should not be used.

The authors suggest that if a court has glass or wood walls, the walls should have a *three-inch strip of bright color painted at eye level* to help a participant anticipate the wall. *Lights* over the court should be either recessed into the ceiling and covered with plastic, plexi-glass or a wire mesh or the light fixture should be encased in a wire harness to prevent a direct hit from a racquet or squash ball, which could shatter the bulb. *Ceiling panels* should also be securely fastened to prevent panels falling onto the court.

ACSM's Guidelines highlight the following standards for indoor court sports:

- Mercury vapor or warm white fluorescent lights providing at least 50 foot-candles at the floor surface should be used,
- The recommended space between indoor tennis courts is 12 feet on the sides and 21 feet on each end,
- The recommended temperature should be 60 to 65 degrees Fahrenheit, with less than 60 percent humidity and with an hourly air exchange rate of eight to 12 exchanges per hour.

Outdoor Courts

Outdoor courts pose the challenge of having to contend with natural elements. Water, mud and leaves are just some conditions that should prompt you to either repair or prevent using an outdoor court. In the same manner as all other athletic facilities, you have an affirmative duty to make sure the courts are in reasonably safe condition. This duty entails making sure slippery conditions like leaves, mud or water puddles are raked away, rolled out or suctioned off. The court's surface also has to be examined to make sure there are no defects, cracks, height differentials and/or buckles in the surface.

Heldman v. Uniroyal, Inc.
371 N.E. 2d 557 (OH 1977)

Julie Heldman was injured in August 1971, while competing as a professional tennis player in the Wightman Cup tennis championship between the United States and Great Britain. Uniroyal manufactured a special synthetic rubber material, which they claimed was suitable for outdoor tennis courts. Uniroyal warranted their "Uniroyal Roll-A-Way Tennis Court" free of dents, hollow, soft or rough spots which was safe and fit for its intended use as a tennis playing surface. However, during the competition, the surface began to blister and came loose at the seams. A rainstorm during the event caused air bubbles to form under the surface. This made footing uncertain and unreasonably hazardous. Heldman injured her knee on the surface.

The lower court entered a judgment for Heldman, but the appellate court reversed based on evidentiary grounds (repairs made after the accident could not be admitted to show the conditions at the time of the accident). However, the appellate court also felt that Heldman had a higher degree of knowledge and awareness about defects in the synthetic tennis court due to her status as a professional tennis player. The court felt that a professional tennis player assumes and appreciates risks inherent in competing on a synthetic tennis court with bubbles and gaps.

Some courts have concluded that weeds and/or other objects on the court do not represent a concern if they are obvious. In *Lobsenz v. Rubinstein* the court concluded that a 15-year-old assumed the risk of playing on a tennis court with depressions and weeds when the danger was obvious.

The court concluded that the player could have possibly recovered if the hazard was obscure or unobserved by the player (*Lobsenz v. Rubinstein*, 15 N.Y.S. 2d 848 (NY 1939)).

While a professional tennis player might assume the risk, you have to make sure a court with these problems is not used unless it is repaired. Less-experienced players are not held to possess the same knowledge as a professional tennis player.

You should make sure outdoor tennis *lights* are turned on at the correct time and the lights are all the proper wattage/footcandles. Lights should be turned on around an hour and a half before dusk and the lights should produce at least 30–60-foot candles of light at the playing surface ("Sports lighting," 1997). ACSM's Guidelines recommend that light fixtures should be at least 10 feet away from court sidelines/endlines.

An additional lighting related concerns involves proper connection and protection of electrical outlets. Due to adverse exposure issues, any control panels or electrical connectors need to be properly placed out of people's reach and locked. In a Texas based case, a jury awarded $2 million to the family of a deceased 3-year-old boy who was electrocuted by a faulty high-voltage electrical box at a tennis club. The child was watching his brother play when he stepped at the edge of the electrical box and put his hand on a nearby fence. The plaintiff had claimed that the tennis club failed to adequately inspect the electrical system (Flynn, 1995).

Only courts with *adequate space* around the outer lines and between adjoining courts should be used. The following case highlights why spacing is so important.

Morrow v. Smith

198 N.Y.S. 2d 737 (NY 1960)

Sidney Morrow and a tennis partner visited the tennis courts owned by the defendant and operated under the name of Smith's Parkway Tennis Club. The two tennis players were told to take whichever court was available. The two started playing and while Morrow was chasing a ball, he ran into a fence and wall by the court. The wire mesh fence and stone wall were nine feet nine inches from the base at the side of the tennis court. The stone wall was directly behind the wire mesh fence and was partially covered with leaves. Since the wall was built in 1929, approximately 30,000 players used the particular court in question without any accidents.

Morrow sued for the injuries he sustained in the collision, but the court threw out his case because he was not owed a duty and even if he was owed a duty, he would have been contributorily negligent. The court also felt that nine feet nine inches was an adequate amount of space between a tennis court and a fence.

Based on the above case, if a fence or wall is closer then nine feet from the base or sidelines then the court might not be suitable for tennis. Using an unsuitable court is a negligent breach of your duty. Fences should also be inspected to make sure the *fence posts* are adequately reinforced whenever tennis windscreens are used.

Equipment

Because participants are swinging racquetball and squash racquets in close proximity to one another, special concern has to be given to eye protection. Balls and racquets often come in contact with participants and players' eyes are very vulnerable. Participants should not be allowed to play without wearing eye goggles. If participants do not have their own goggles, extra pairs should be available for their use. Another item that should be required for squash or racquetball participants are wrist thongs. Wrist thongs attach to a racket's handle and to the participant's wrist. Wrist thongs prevent a racquet from leaving a participant's general vicinity even if the participant looses his or her grip. If a racquet flies out of a participant's hand and hits another participant, you could face liability *if* a reasonable EA would have required using wrist thongs.

Supervision

One major supervisory concern associated with racquet sports is making sure participants do not use to many balls, or other equipment, at the same time. Participants frequently bring additional balls with them to the court and the addition of these balls can make court movement more dangerous. By supervising the participants and requiring gathering loose balls or equipment before continuing play, you will reduce the possibility of a sprained ankle.

In a facility with individually enclosed courts, it is often difficult for you to see everyone playing. You should continuously check the enclosed courts and monitor participants. Line judges or other officials can also help make sure participants are playing in a safe manner.

Safe instruction is also a critical concern. In a California case, an advanced tennis player was taking a class with a professional instructor. The player was hit in the eye by a ball the instructor hit which first ricocheted of her racket. The plaintiff claimed the two were not co-participants which would have prevented her suit, but were instead in a teacher-student relationship. In a teacher-student relationship, the teacher owes an obligation to not enhance risks faced by those they are teaching. The appellate court overturned the lower court's summary judgment motion and sent the case back to the lower court for a jury to decide liability. The case was send back because there was a factual dispute. The teacher claimed the student was ready to receive the ball and thus assumed the risk of mishitting the ball. The student claimed that she was not ready and the teacher should not have hit the ball when the students was not ready (*Fidopiastis v. Hirtler*, 41 Cal. Rptr. 2d 94, 34 Cal. App. 4th 1458 (CA 1995).

Conclusion

Racquet sports are not the typically dangerous sports which most EAs spend a lot of time preparing for. However, such complacency leads to injuries. Simple concerns such as tripping or slipping hazards are magnified. Thus, attention to the small details will help to prevent many risks found in running racquet sport events. To help prevent injuries, you should take the following steps:

- check the court for cracks, holes, bubbles, warped wood, rough or slick spots and loose tiling,
- inspect the indoor courts for any dust and mop up any spilled liquid,
- check the court and remove any leaves, twigs, mud and/or water puddles,
- check to make sure lights are protected from balls,
- check to make sure glass or wood walls have a visible marker at eye level,
- check to make sure there is adequate space behind the court's base and sideline,
- require participants to use eye guards and wrist thongs,
- supervise the event at the appropriate level required by the situation.

Chapter 20

Soccer

Soccer, arguably the most popular sport in the world, has the same basic risks as those associated with football, but there are numerous unique characteristics that separate the two sports. The major similarity in the two sports is the playing field that has to be inspected to ensure that glass and other debris is not present on the field. The major risk differences that separate the two sports include the goal posts, corner flags and supervision concerns.

While the same field risks are seen in football and soccer, a football player has more protection when they fall. In one case, a soccer player seriously injured his knee when he stepped in a gopher hole while chasing the soccer ball. The plaintiff claimed that:

- the field was infested with gopher holes,
- the gopher holes created a dangerous condition,
- the defendant had constructive knowledge of the holes, but failed to take remedial action, and
- the defendant failed to post warning signs.

While the defendant claimed the plaintiff faced an obvious risk and should be comparatively negligent, the jury still awarded the plaintiff $100,000 which was reduced to $70,000 based on finding the plaintiff 30% negligent (*Martinez v. County of Los Angeles*, Case No. EAC 61726, Jury Verdicts Vol. 36, No. 37, September 11, 1992, p. 25–6).

Goal Posts

Goal posts can be dangerous if athletes run into them, so padding can prevent some potential injuries. In fact, most soccer related deaths during competition occur as a player runs headfirst into unpadded goal posts or trips and hits his/her head against the goal post. Some soccer programs utilize padded goal posts. While not the norm, padded goal posts could become an industry standard in the near future. Some individuals have also suggested using goalie helmets to help protect a goalie's head.

237

The goal post should be checked for splinters, broken or deteriorating welds, loose nuts and bolts and any other deterioration. If a cement-anchored goal post is used, the base should be inspected to make sure the cement anchor is not exposed. Any such exposed section could represent a tripping hazard. Adding additional dirt can cover the exposed cement. The goal posts should also be checked for sturdiness and stability.

There should not be any gap between the net and the goal post frame. Goal nets are usually hung from the back of the goal post over hooks or nails. If hooks or nails are the only option you have for fastening the net, you should bend back the nails into the post to protect a person from being cut or punctured by a nail. Nails or hooks should be checked at the beginning of the soccer season and any rusted ones should be replaced immediately.

Velcro should be the preferable method for fastening a net. No one can get their hand caught on Velcro. In one case, a man was putting up a net when his ring got caught on a nail and he had his finger amputated as a result of the accident. Metal rear net-hooks should be nailed into the ground to secure the back of the net. To help with visibility, a brightly colored net could be used.

Corner Flags

Corner flags seem like innocent pieces of equipment that could not cause any damage. However, even small items have the potential to cause serious injuries. Like down-markers in football, if the corner flags are made of metal or thick wood, running into them could injure a participant. If a red cone is used instead of a metal flag, a participant can possibly trip over the cone. Rubber flag post or flexible/bendable flags are the safest corner flags. The risk of being injured by a corner flag seems to be minimal, but it is still a potential risk that has to be addressed.

Supervision

The major difference between soccer and football is the amount of supervision required. Football is a contact sport where participants benefit from protective padding. Soccer is also a contact sport, but only a minimal amount of protection is available to participants. Most players, wear shin guards to protect themselves from being cleated or kicked during the game. Shin guards should be required for fullbacks, halfbacks and forwards. Male players should also be required to wear athletic supporter cups.

You should try to educate participants and limit heading by younger players. European findings point to potential brain damage for repeated headings over an extended soccer career.

The *goal post* has to be supervised as closely as the participants. Participants should not be allowed to hang on goal posts, especially on portable goal posts. Particpants need to be closely monitored when they move the goal posts. A ten-year-old boy was paralyzed after some players tried to move the goal and it tipped over onto the injured child (Conklin, 1998). Such injuries are not unusual as soccer goals have caused 22 deaths and hundred of serious injuries since 1979 when the Consumer Products Safety Commission started tracking such injuries (Concklin, 1998). When portable goals are not in use, they should be locked together with chains, with their open goal faces facing each other, like a set of parentheses-( ). Goal posts that are implanted into the ground need to be sufficiently secured that they cannot be tipped over or bent if several people hang on the crossbar. Due to the significant threat posed by goals tipping over, every effort needs to be taken to ensure the goals cannot tip over from player misuse through drunk fans hanging on the goal. One last concerns involves metal goal posts which, during adverse weather, could act as a lightning rod for participants standing next to the goal. Lightning warnings should be sounded whenever players are in the field and lighting is within 3–8 miles away.

Participants should use only rubber soled-cleats. You should also make sure participants demonstrating an overly aggressive attacking manner, are carded (yellow or red) early to help control a game's emotions and tempo.

A final concern in supervising soccer matches is *participant or spectator violence* against other participants. This concern is frequently seen in competition between different ethnic or nationality groups. Often talking with participants, coaches and supporters before a match can help reduce altercations. In one infamous case, a coach was heard shouting to his players to "waist him." This comment was made in reference to a star player on the opposing team. One of the coach's players collided with the plaintiff and the resulting injury seriously damaged the plaintiff's two knees. The plaintiff's injuries caused him to lose a college scholarship. The parties did not disagree that the coach yelled from the sidelines. The lower court awarded the plaintiff $277,000. The appellate court reversed the award claiming there was no proof that the coach was heard on the field or that the player acted upon the coach's urging (Marcus, 1997). While such misconduct by the coach might seem extreme, a survey by Purdue University showed the supervision concern is even more serious. The survey showed that 84 percent of teenage soccer players said they would intentionally foul, even at the risk of injury, an opposing player to prevent a goal ("Go figure," 1998).

Tight officiating can also limit the potential for altercations. If you know that a certain event could *likely* lead to a physical confrontation, then you should move the match to a neutral site, bar spectators from the game and/or bring in visible uniformed security personnel to act as a deterrent.

Conclusion

The football chapter should be examined to determine some of the possible risk management actions (field, supervision, etc.) you should take. In addition, you should make sure the following specific actions are taken: check the goal post, net and corner flag for any potential dangers, require protective equipment for all players and closely supervise the participants to prevent potential altercations.

Chapter 21

Track & Field

In the span of six days in 1997, two accidents helped highlight some significant concerns in track and field. One athlete was killed after he was hit in the head by a discus. The culprit was possibly negligent supervision. In a separate case, a pole vaulter landed in part on the mat, but hit his head on some concrete and later died. While the pit was only one-year-old, and the mat exceeded all rules by four feet on all sides, the facility was still possibly negligent for having cement near the landing area. These are just two tragic examples of what can go wrong when poor supervision and inadequate facility inspections occur.

The variety of different events that are going on at any one time at one location can make track events very difficult to supervise. Problems could develop as participants try to warm up in an area that might seem safe, but could easily become dangerous. The classic example involves injuries from an off-course *discus, javelin or hammer* hitting a runner on the track. Care should be exercised to ensure that the weight throwing areas (discus, shot put, javelin and hammer) are roped-off with fences or barricades extending beyond the throwing circle. The authors recommend a multi-panel, U-shaped 15-foot high chain-link or wire-mesh fence to encompass a hammer throw circle. All spectators and officials should be on notice prior to any throws being attempted. Cautious EAs can also utilize a warning horn to warn other participants prior to a contestant throwing their equipment.

Long jump and triple jump pits should be raked or roto-tilled before competition so the pits have fine, loose sand instead of dried out, hard sand that can easily cause an injury.

Any indoor or outdoor track needs to be free of obstructions such as protruding roots on a sand track to proper drainage and sloping of synthetic track surfaces. ACSM's Guidelines suggest that surface material over a concrete foundation should be at least 3/8 inch thick and should be textured for superior traction.

Road and cross-country races have similar hazards to bicycling events. A reasonable EA should examine the event course thoroughly for any potential hazards. Roots and tree stumps should be clearly marked and/or painted a bright color. Event personnel can help supervise the course by being positioned at various intervals along the course. Runner check-points become much more critical in ultra-marathons, grueling triathlons or 100

plus mile runs. **Checkpoints** along with support vehicles tracking participants is the most effective manner for monitoring participants.

Special attention should be given to girl cross-country runners. At the
high school level, girls cross-country has the highest injury rate of all sports
at 61.4 injuries per 100 participants. Boys football has 58.8 injuries per 100
participants in 1993 ("Girls cross-country has highest rate of injury, study
says," 1994).

In addition to examining the track, you should examine the available
equipment that will be used. *Hurdles* need to be examined to make sure
they are all the proper height and without any splinters. Block-locking
mechanisms on *starting blocks* need to be checked to ensure they do not
slip after being adjusted.

You also must make sure that the jumping events (*high jump and pole
vault*) have sufficient crash pads or pits with sufficient padding. National
standards should dictate padding thickness. In a New Jersey case, a pole
vaulter hit part of the mat and his shoulder hit the ground. The mat was
too small and when the jumper was taking a practice jump, the coaches
were debating whether or not to cancel the vault due to the smaller mat.
The smaller mat did not comply with the regulations (Mumma, 1997).
The standards and the bars used in the jumping events also should be examined to ensure safety. Only standards with solid bases should be used.
High jump and pole vault cross bars should have plastic tips at the ends
of the bars.

There is a question, in many events, as to how much supervision is required to ensure the event is safe for all the participants. A good example
deals with the health of the participant. A person could appear to be out-
of-shape, but they could end up winning the most physically demanding
event. It would seem discriminatory and offensive to warn only individuals who might appear out-of-shape. Therefore, it is essential that all participants receive adequate warnings. All participants should also sign
waivers indicating they know their own physical abilities and are in good
physical condition.

Gehling v. St. George's University
School of Medicine, LTD.
705 F. Supp. 761 (NY 1989)

Earl Gehling ran in a 2.5 mile "road race" on the Island of Grenada in
1982. Gehling was a student at St. George's University School of Medicine, in Grenada. The race was held on a road between the school's two campuses in the late afternoon. The temperature was between 80–85 degrees

and the humidity level was high. More than one hundred runners participated in the race. Vehicles equipped with oxygen were used to pick up runners who faltered. Water was available at one spigot alongside the road. Gehling was:

- approximately 75 pounds overweight,
- suffered from hypertension, with a history of elevated blood pressure,
- the left ventricle of his heart was enlarged.

Gehling had also taken an amphetamine-like substance before the race to speed his heart rate. It took him 1/2 hour to finish the race. After the race he collapsed and lost control. It became necessary to restrain him because of his hysterical behavior. Several medical students and doctors tried to assist Gehling. He was rushed to a hospital, but he never regained consciousness and died the next morning of heat prostration or heat stroke.

The court concluded that the student was charged with knowledge of his own condition, especially because he was a medical student, thus he assumed the risk of participating in the event.

Conclusion

Track and field events have several key concerns that need to be addressed no matter if the event is run on a Mondo eight lane track or a city street. Proper supervision from picking the right course to the right number of water distributors and course observers is critical. Furthermore, making sure the equipment and facility meet all appropriate safety standards will be the next item analyzed by a jury. If you can provide proper supervision with a safe competitive surface, you will be in a good position to claim assumption of risk. While it might seem simple enough to provide proper supervision and a safe facility, accomplishing this task will take time for you to become familiar with the little items that can help trigger an accident. For example, a nationally distributed risk management video depicts several officials supervising a shot put event. One of the supervisors is a young lady wearing a dress. The problem with wearing a dress is that if it is a straight dress, it could limit leg movement and her ability to get out of the way. Such a supervision related concern becomes most evident after you start seeing the type of injuries that occur and how people were injured.

Chapter 22

Water Sports

Water sports are more difficult to supervise compared to other sports because water can be a quick killer. Injuries occurring on land might hurt a participant, but the environment normally does not worsen the injury (with the exception of hypothermia, or heat stroke, etc.). However, as we were told as children, someone can drown in even a teaspoon of water. The potential hazards associated with water-related facilities requires constant supervision. The major concerns associated with swimming events include pool construction, water quality, diving boards, water slides and participant supervision. A 1980 article in Trial Magazine highlighted safety related concerns which are just as important today. The concern highlighted include:

- inadequate depth markings,
- inadequate pool illumination,
- inadequate illumination of pool entryways,
- missing handrails,
- undelineated steps,
- untrained pool operators,
- inadequate security for entering/exiting the pool,
- inadequate signage, pool covers, alarms or communication systems to prevent pool entry (Peters, 1980).

ACSM's Guidelines have established significant guidelines/standards concerning swimming facilities including:

- daily cleaning of the scum line, pool duct and strainers,
- daily vacuuming of the pool,
- depth markers must be at least 4 inches in high and a color that contrasts with the background,
- every pool must have an overflow system in place to handle water overflow,
- all pools must follow applicable laws concerning such issues as water clarity, purity and temperature,
- all pool-side wiring must comply with National Electronic Code guidelines, especially for any electrical items within five feet of the pool,
- pools should have at least one elevated lifeguard stand/chair for every 2,000 square feet of pool surface area,

- pools should have at least two entry/exit ladders (with handrails) and set out at a minimum of one ladder for 75 feet of pool perimeter spacing,
- outdoor pools should be surrounded by at least a four foot high fence,
- there should be at least five feet of unobstructed space emanating from the pool edge,
- there should be at least three feet of unobstructed space on the sides and rear of any diving board,
- pool water should be pumped, filtered, heated, treated and circulated at a minimum turnover rate of every eight hours,
- each 10,000 gallons of water should be treated with one pound of chlorine every eight hours,
- chlorine levels should be maintained at 1.0 to 3.0 ppm and bromine levels at 1.0 to 2.5 ppm,
- underwater lights should provide at least one watt per square foot of pool area (Sol and Foster, 1992).

Swimming Pools

You normally do not examine a swimming pool when it is empty. If a visual inspection cannot be made when the pool is empty, you should ask if the facility owner or manager has recently examined the pool's bottom to ensure the pool's sides and bottom are safe and smooth. Swimmers could reasonably assume that the pool is smooth, thus rough spots need to be repaired.

If there are *shallow and deep ends*, the different ends should be painted different colors to create a visual warning. Many pools are now manufactured with a zero entry area and gradually slope down. These pools could utilize several different colors and possible textures to warn users of depth changes. If painting the pool's bottom is impossible, you should make sure the *side depth markings* are legible. The depth markers should be visible both on the pool's side and bottom. While some would not feel painting the depth marking on the bottom is important, it provides just one more weapon to support your claim that a plaintiff acted unreasonably under the circumstances as they could have altered their dive. While some organizations are toying with listing a range of depth markers such as "3–8 feet," there is no guarantee that such markings will become the industry standard (Cohen, 1998). The visibility and accuracy of depth markings cannot be stressed enough.

Rigden v. Springdale Park, Inc.
551 S.W. 2d 860 (MO 1977)

Upon entering the pool area, some young children with Judith Rigden, began diving into the water where the pool deck marking indicated the water depth was three feet. Fearing the depth to be to shallow for diving, the plaintiff directed the children to dive in an area where the water depth was listed as five feet. Rigden stood by the five-foot marker and assumed a diving position. She dove with her hands outstretched over her head and her feet together. The ensuing dive resulted in a startling mishap, as Rigden struck her head on the pool's bottom surface.

Evidence at trial showed that at the five-foot sign, the water's depth was only three and a half feet deep. The water was so murky that patrons were not able to see the bottom. There were no signs prohibiting diving at that spot and no oral warnings were given. The fact that the water was murky justified Rigden's reliance on the pool's marking.

The appellate court concluded that the pool's operator owed its patron the duty to use reasonable care in furnishing and maintaining its facility for the purpose for which it was intended. By having an inaccurate pool marker, which patrons would rely upon, the pool operators breached their duty.

Most pools have steps or rails to help people get in and out. The *steps* should be marked in such a way (painted a different color and with nonslip material) that people can see and feel when they reach the step's edge. You should make sure that railings or hanging ladders are securely attached and not rusty. Rungs on a ladder should be checked to ensure no parts are loose or missing. Individuals injured by falling from loose ladders while exiting pools have brought several cases. Such a hazard could easily be discovered and corrected, and as such, liability would be almost immediately imposed on the pool operator.

Numerous pools, especially private pools, are constructed with a *bottom filter*. Filtration systems need to be inspected regularly to ensure that they are working properly. *Drain covers* have to be checked on a regular basis and should not be broken or rusted. Filter covers should always be securely fastened as demonstrated in the following case.

Henry v. Britt
220 So. 2d 917 (FL 1969)

Eleven-year old Gary Henry drowned in a motel swimming pool when his arm became lodged in the main drain outlet at the pool's deep end. The State Sanitary Code required covering the main drain outlet with a grated cover which swimmers could not easily remove. The combined physical effort of Henry's father and the motel manager was inadequate to release Henry's arm from the pump's suction. Henry's arm was only released after the drain pump was turned off. The drain cover was observed on the pool's bottom-several feet from the drain.

The appellate court concluded that the uncovered drain was *prima facie* (on its face) evidence of negligence due to the statutory violation. The lower court's judgment for the defendant was also reversed, as there was no showing of assumption of risk.

When a pool is being drained or cleaned, swimmers should be prohibited from entering the pool. Furthermore, pool operators need to closely examine state laws as they apply to drainage. Several states have enacted stringent laws in response to various cases including a $30.9 million verdict from North Carolina after a five-year-old girl had most of her intestines sucked out after being caught in a drain vortex (Conklin, 1998). In 1994, North Carolina passed a law that outlawed single drains in certain public pools (less than 18 inches of water). California passed a law requiring pools to be retrofitted with at least two drains. Manufacturing companies are also introducing shut-off valves that stop the pumping when the drain is blocked (Conklin, 1998).

The *lifeguard stand* must be high enough for the lifeguard to see the entire pool. All the required life saving equipment has to be present at poolside. There should be several *ring buoys* ranging in size from 20-inch diameters through smaller sizes for children. The lifeguards should also be equipped with, at a minimum:

- a 16 foot long metal pole,
- some rope for a shepherd's crook or throwing line,
- several kick boards,
- other flotation devices,
- first aid supplies including a backboard.

Some basic rules you should follow in and around swimming pools include:

- all the pool chemicals have to be safely stored in a well-ventilated area,

- rules for proper swimming pool conduct have to be posted around the swimming pool and strictly enforced,
- pool lights should not blind swimmers swimming towards the light,
- debris on the pool deck should be cleaned off regularly,
- any light or electrical outlets, sockets or device in/around a pool have to be safely grounded with ground fault interrupters to prevent electrical shock.

Ropes are erroneously used by some people to separate the shallow-end from the deep-end. These ropes are perpendicularly, hung not the parallel lane markers. These ropes should not be used as tripping or diving onto the rope could injure a swimmer. Lane marker buoys should be used when there are supervisors present who can make sure swimmers do not dive across swimming lanes.

In addition to checking the swimming pool and the water chemicals, the surrounding area also has to be inspected. Some major concerns outside the water include:

- the deck's condition,
- rocks, nails or other items that can injure a participant,
- inadequate pool illumination,
- a locking gate (especially to keep children away from the pool),
- the availability and posting of "pool closed" signs,
- posting warning and pool rules signs throughout the facility,
- installing an above and below water communications system,
- possibly installing a pool cover (preferably a heavy, electronically operated cover that cannot be lifted or moved by a child),
- installing an intruder warning system (if someone climbs over the pool's fence).

Water Quality

Water quality is a major concern in operating swimming pools. Without the right amount and combination of chemicals, the water can cause rashes or other illness from bacteria buildup. The water also has to be clear enough that a six-inch diameter black disc tossed into the deep end can be seen by someone outside the pool. This role is not hard and fast as some other standards also exist for determining water clarity.

Burgert v. Tietjens

499 F.2d 1 (10th Cir. 1974)

Robert Burgert, a 12-year-old boy, drowned at the defendant's Sycamore Springs Recreation Area. On August 24, 1969, Burgert traveled with a church group to Sycamore Springs. Burgert was playing with a friend in the swimming pool through 5:00 p.m. His friend realized that he was missing around 6:00 p.m., but did not tell anyone. At 9:30 p.m., defendant's employees noticed Burgert's clothes were still in his basket. After searching for a substantial amount of time, they found Burgert's body at the pool's bottom. He had died 2 1/2 hours earlier.

The pool was 75 feet wide and 140 feet long. The pool's depth ranged from two to ten feet. The pool's water was supplied by a natural spring. Due to water clarity problems, an observer could only see 2 1/2 feet below the water's surface. The water was described by witnesses as cloudier than usual. The defendants knew about the poor water quality before they opened the pool for business that day.

Under Kansas law, Sycamore Springs was not an insurer of Burgert's safety, but was liable for his death due to negligence. The court concluded that defendants breached their duty of ordinary and reasonable care by opening the pool with such poor water quality. The water was so murky that the lifeguards could not see below three feet. The appellate court affirmed the lower court's award of $30,539.95.

You should have a *maintenance schedule* listing when the pool was last cleaned and all pool cleanings and chemical insertions should be recorded to document a reasonable water maintenance program.

If you have examined the swimming facility and everything is in reasonable condition, then you probably have discharged your duty to provide a safe facility.

McKeever v. Phoenix Jewish Community Center

374 P. 2d 875 (AZ 1962)

Mary Agnes McKeever was a ten-year-old girl playing at the Phoenix Jewish Community Center's swimming pool with other family members. The father left the children playing in the shallow-end and went to a grass area about 100 feet away. McKeever went with some friends to the pool's side near a safety rope. The girls were jumping into the deep end and climbing back out to dive again. There were roughly forty other people in the pool with one lifeguard observing. McKeever's two friends went to another area while McKeever stayed in the deep-end.

The lifeguard had just completed a routine inspection around the pool and did not see anything unusual. Upon returning to his station, the lifeguard was called to assist in McKeever's rescue. Only five minutes had elapsed since McKeever's friends had left her till the time she was discovered. The lifeguard got to the scene as fast as humanly possible and made every effort to revive her. All necessary equipment was available at pool side.

The defendant kept the pool in a safe condition; a qualified person inspected the premises; all the necessary life saving equipment was present; the lifeguard effectively monitored the pool; and the lifeguard responded quickly to the accident. Because the defendant did everything reasonably under his/her control, the court concluded that the drowning was an unavoidable accident for which there was no liability.

Accidents are bound to happen, and unfortunately some swimmers drown. You should always remember that you are not an "insurer of safety." You cannot guarantee that someone will never get injured. All you can do is take reasonable steps and exercise ordinary care while maintaining a safe facility.

Diving Boards

Diving boards have to be positioned properly in an area with sufficient water depth. Competitive diving platforms should provide a launch into water that meets all appropriate national sanctioning bodies' regulations. Recreational diving boards should produce an entry into water at least seven to nine feet deep. A non-slip surface should be applied to diving board's ends. Back in the 1940s individuals used to cut bicycle tires and wrap the rubber around diving boards to decrease the slipping hazard. Non-skid paint does the trick these days.

A dock owner at the lake, marina, etc., who knows individuals dive from the dock, has a duty to make sure the area around the dock is sufficiently deep and that there are no rocks or other objects six feet below the water surface. The following case highlights this point.

Montes v. Betcher
480 F. 2d 1128 (8th Cir. 1973)

Fernando Montes, a 35-year-old, suffered a vertebral fracture after making a running dive off a short boat dock. The accident occurred on a Sunday afternoon in July 1968. Montes was familiar with the area and had executed several prior dives. During prior dives, he never encountered any rocks or other items. In the dive in question, Montes hit a jagged piece of concrete resembling an anchor. The cement anchors had been made for defendant's own boats used in the resort.

Betcher owned the resort since 1963. Defendants charged $10 a day for cabin accommodations and resort usage. Betcher never inspected the dock area or "raked" the shoreline and lake bottom. No warning signs were posted and there was no segregation between the boats and swimmers.

The court concluded that Betcher had a duty to warn users about obstructions on the lake bottom. Defendant was also negligent in not warning the diver, or undertaking active vigilance to protect guests.

Docks in shallow water should be roped-off and warning signs should be posted which prohibit diving into shallow water. The warning should specify risks such as paralysis, quadriplegia or other possible injuries from diving in shallow or dangerous water.

Water Slides

Water slides are a major amusement craze throughout the world. Strict inspection rules have to be established for these slides. Even if the slide's sides are fairly high, the combination of lubricating water, speed and smooth movement makes it difficult to control a participant's movement. Netting could be attached to the slide's sides to help control a participant's shifting. All participants should be warned about the hazards involved in shifting their weight and possibly losing control.

Supervision is needed to move sliders away from a slide's bottom so subsequent sliders will not collide with others. In addition, participants should be given only one option; *sliding down feet first*. A participant sliding down head first cannot control their movements as well, and there is the possibility of running into someone or something head first, thus creating the opportunity for severe head injuries. While no known industry standard exists concerning appropriate sliding techniques, the above recommendation represent a practical risk management solution to head injury cases.

Outdoor Water Facilities and Boating

There are many variables that cannot be controlled at a river, lake or beach. Selecting an event site is a critical step for any event. This step is even more important for outdoor water events as nature can provide numerous surprises for participants and EAs. Before selecting an event site, you should determine whether the site had ever been used for a similar event, if it had been inspected and if there are any maps, charts or other documents showing water depth or other hazards.

Any possible area that could be hazardous, even if not on property you own or have permission to use, has to be supervised. If there is a possibility that participants might enter property not used in your event, you have to take steps to prevent such access. This can be accomplished by providing appropriate warnings or posting individuals to block access to the property. You should always remember that the attractive nuisance theory applies equally to land under your control and all adjoining land that might reasonably be expected to attract children to dangerous areas.

Lastly, special attention needs to be paid to water condition. For example snow-fed rapids in California created higher than usual water levels and more dangerous rapids that led to over 11 deaths and nine deaths in a one week period ("Snow-fed rapids take grim toll in California," 1998).

While traditional river or lake activities often occur close to shore where diving related concerns or drowning issues occur more frequently, boating related activities often present more technical concerns. For example, jet skis are causing a stir in the water and in court rooms. Environmentalists can try to halt an event due to the potential environmental concerns. Accidents can occur from jet skis reaching top speeds of over 60 miles per hour and racing from 0 to 50 in about five seconds. Such speed coupled with an inexperienced rider possibly releasing the clutch to avoid hitting an object can make steering almost impossible (Sward and Doyle, 1997). In California alone, 45 percent of all boat accidents in 1996 were attributable to jet skis. Furthermore, 57 people died in 1996 on jet skis nationwide (Sward and Doyle, 1997). Problems such as these has led some states such as Texas to require mandatory boating safety classes. Passed in 1997, the Texas law requires anyone born after September 1, 1984 to take a mandatory boater education class if they ride a personal watercraft vessel of 10 horsepower or greater or a sailing vessel over 14 feet (Behrens, 1998). Thus, when running an event where watercrafts might be utilized, you should make sure all participants have completed any required coursework, whether local or from the Coast Guard, and can show proof of completion.

Sailing can be dangerous and most sailors assume the risk of injuries such as being hit by a swinging boom (*Stimson v. Carlson* (1992) 11 CA4th 1201, 14 CR 2d 670). However, in a water ski accident case, the heirs were able to show that the boat operator who ran into the jet skier had not exercised due care in operating the boat. The jury awarded $2 million, but reduced that award by 50 percent due to the jet skier's contributory negligence (*Garrison v. Sea World*, FL, Orange County Cir. Ct., No. CI 87—9140, April 13, 1992).

Supervision

While facility related concerns are critical in swimming and diving cases, the key that most courts examine is the supervision provided by the facility owner/operator. Supervision concerns often relate to adequate lifeguard services and enforcement of pool rules. However, other supervision concerns are also critically analyzed such as providing proper and timely medical assistance. In a scuba diving case, a Mexican based resort lost a $3.095 million verdict after a diver brought a negligence suit claiming the resort failed to ensure that he received hyperbaric treatment which failure resulted in the "bends" ("Scuba diver suffers 'bends,' 1997).

Warning participants is a difficult task as each participant might have a different understanding or appreciation of the dangers present in water activities. Thus, warnings have to be tailored to the message receiver's anticipated understanding. Some participants can be warned through warnings prohibiting specific activities or general danger signs while children or non-English speakers might need visual warning signs.

No matter what rules are adopted, all rules need to be properly communicated and enforced. In a school diving case, a school administrator admonished students not to jump from a balcony into the pool. The students were warned that if they continued, they would be sent home. The students continued to jump and encouraged a 14-year-old to also jump. He jumped and fell on to the concrete. The court concluded that the jumping was not an isolated event and the school had notice that it had occurred for a number of years. A teacher admitted that the jumping would not have occurred if a teacher had been at the pool. The court concluded that the school failed to supervise the students and the lack of supervison was the proximate cause of the student's injuries (*University Preparatory School v. Huitt III, et al.*, Corpus Christi Court of Appeals, No. 13-94-439-CV, 9/26/96).

Children under age seven cannot be contributorily negligent. Thus, you have to make sure children swim only if a parent or supervisor is present. A lifeguard could qualify as a supervisor. Fencing should be considered as a viable option whenever it is impossible to control potential swimmers. This solution is frequently seen in remote areas such as beaches, water holes, quarries or river sections. Most states also require publicly and privately owned pools to be fenced.

You should make sure warning signs are posted all around the swimming area. A sign stating "swim at your own risk" is not enough. The warning signs should contain the following information:

- what times the facility is open,
- what dangers are inherent in the activity (drowning, head injuries from diving, cramps, inhaling of water, etc...),
- the facility rules (no running on the deck, no diving in the shallow-end, no swimming while under the influence of alcohol, no alcohol/drinks or food allowed in the facility, only one person allowed at a time on the diving board, divers have to wait for previous diver to surface and clear before diving, no horseplay or fighting in the water, etc...),
- the penalty for violating a rule,
- what dangers are assumed by the participant,
- where first-aid equipment can be found,
- all emergency phone numbers,
- the times lifeguard(s) are on duty,
- when the facility closes.

You should also remember that numerous individuals never read warning signs, thus some facilities try to avoid accidents by closing whenever lifeguards are not on duty.

Lifeguards

You have a duty to furnish an appropriate number of adequately trained lifeguards or supervisors to supervise the facility. Lifeguard-related concerns were highlighted in the *Bailey* case.

YMCA of Metropolitan Atlanta v. Bailey
130 S.E. 2d 242 (GA 1963)

Ronald Bailey died on May 4, 1955. He was only nine-years-old. There was no evidence as to how he died, but his submerged body was clearly visible in the YMCA's swimming pool.

The court stated that a pool operator owes the duty to exercise a great degree of diligence and responsibility when young boys who do not know how to swim are using the pool. The case was sent to a jury to determine whether the YMCA's activities were negligent. The court found that the YMCA's activities included:

- not testing lifeguards for ability,
- not investigating lifeguard qualifications,
- not replacing a broken rope separating the shallow-end from the deep-end which also separated the children who knew how to swim from those that could not,
- having only one lifeguard.

The lifeguard was a 67-year-old man who could not supervise the entire pool by himself. Several witnesses testified that the lifeguard spent some of his time reading a newspaper while 38 children were swimming in the pool.

An EA should hire as many lifeguards as reasonably possible to supervise the participants. Sometimes you can determine the number of lifeguards required through examining state or local statutes. Under California's Health and Safety Code (Section 24101.9), lifeguards are required for any wholly artificial water facilities for which the operators charge a direct fee. Thus, by examining statutes or rules, you can determine whether or not you are required by law to have lifeguards, and possibly the number of lifeguards required. If there is no law setting out a minimum lifeguard requirement, you should look to association standards to make a reasonable decision on the number of lifeguards required. The authors have heard from several sources that two lifeguards for every 25 meters in a swimming pool or one lifeguard for 200 yards of water front property could be an appropriate superviosrial number. These numbers should be increased or decreased depending on the number and type of participants at the facility at any given time. Circumstances and the type of facility help dictate how many lifeguards might be required. A facility should always try to have at least one extra lifeguard available in case there is an increase in attendance or if an accident occupies a lifeguard's time. The extra lifeguard could be a facility administrator or could be someone who lives in the neighborhood and can be contacted with very little notice.

Besides appropriate numbers, the lifeguards have to know their duties and responsibilities. Upon hiring any lifeguards, especially teenagers, you have to make sure the lifeguards adhere to your safety rules. If a lifeguard violates a rule, you should provide them with only one warning. Repeated rule violations can show that you did not take adequate steps to ensure a participant's safety. Lifeguard duties and responsibilities should be posted on or near the lifeguard stand. A lifeguard's major duties are to detect distress signs and act promptly to remedy the situation. The *S & C Co. v.*

Horne case (1977) is an excellent example demonstrating inadequate supervision and the liability attached to hiring poor lifeguards.

Lifeguards should not be allowed to take their attention away from the pool. Lifeguards can talk to their friends as long as they are looking at the pool and the patrons for distress signs. Reading papers/magazines or eating food should not be allowed while a lifeguard is on duty. Personal phone calls, including cellular phones, should also be prohibited.

Lifeguards also have a duty to control participant conduct in and out of the pool. The lifeguards should immediately eject rule violators who do not heed the lifeguard's warnings. The only way the lifeguard can effectively control rule violators is by giving them only one warning before being expelled. Such a policy will eventually become ingrained through patron's minds and will result in less roughhousing.

Quinn v. Smith Company
57 F. 2d 784 (5th Cir. 1932)

Adwina Maria Quinn was a patron at defendant's bathing pool in Miami Beach, Florida. She was attending a water carnival/swimming contest held in a swimming pool, which measured 50 feet by 100 feet. After the event, some patrons started acting in a boisterous manner and pushing one another off a platform. One of the patrons hit Quinn causing her to fall into the pool and suffer serious injuries. Quinn claimed that the defendants did not employ anyone to maintain order at the event.

The court concluded that the defendant owed a duty to provide a safe place and a duty to police and supervise the facility to protect others from wanton and unprovoked assaults. Whether or not defendant breached this duty was a question for the jury.

Conclusion

Water sport related issues can be very diverse. From product liability issues associated with sailing vessels and water skis to diving incorrectly into a pool. As highlighted earlier on in the text, swimming related cases represent the most common activity involved in the analyzed sport related cases. These large awards should send a loud and clear message-water sports are dangerous and any lack of supervision or inadequate facilities will possibly add your event to the registry of large awards.

It is beyond this guide to go into a comprehensive analysis of all the risk management requirements for water related events. Several books provide a comprehensive analysis on this topic. In addition, several organizations such as the American Red Cross offer significant safety programs. The American Red Cross offers an aquatics examiner program that could lead to facility certification. This safety program focuses on education and teaching proper strategies and techniques. Other organizations that offer safety programs include the YMCA, U.S. Lifesaving Association, Boy Scouts of America and Jeff Ellis & Associates.

Chapter 23

Wheels

The key risk management concern associated with wheels is speed. Whether in automobiles, go-carts, bicycles, skates or in-line skating, speed has the ability to cause people to loose their judgment in their euphoric quest for even more speed. While speed is not inherently bad, poor equipment, facilities and supervision can cause havoc in wheel based events.

There are numerous sporting events that involve races or racing. Racing is geared to generate speed and whenever speed is involved, there is the potential for crashes, collisions or wipeouts. This chapter will examine several diverse areas ranging from automobile, motorcycle and go-cart racing, to bike races and in-line skating events. It would be impossible to cover all potential issues in this guide. Thus, only major issues are covered in the following pages. More specific information is available from each activity's national or regional governing organization.

Automobile Racing

As with other event facilities, you have to inspect the facility to ensure it is fit for the intended purpose. Racing surfaces have to be relatively smooth with no significant debris or fluid on the track. Before the event begins, and especially after trial runs, the entire racing surface has to be examined. Special care has to be taken in examining banked turns to make sure no oil slicks, pieces of rubber or any other material are on the track.

Virginia State Fair Association v. Burton
28 S.E. 2d 716 (VA 1944)

Landon Burton was an eighteen-year old spectator at the Virginia State Fair. Burton attended a race at the fair with his brother. When the two arrived, all the seats in the grandstands had been filled. The two joined the large crowd lining the edge of the track. There were no permanent barriers to prevent the spectators from approaching the fence, nor were there any safety signs warning individuals not to be too close to the fence.

The State Fair had posted officers every thirty-feet who tried to keep the crowd away from the fence. The officers repeatedly warned the crowd, but the crowd repeatedly surged to the fence. This would force the police to drive them back again.

There was testimony that some track officials had seen some loose nails on the track before the race, but did not tell anyone. There was also evidence presented that on preceding days a platform and bleachers had occupied that vicinity. Driver John Thompson Cumming was on a trial run around the dirt track when his car ran over a loose nail or spike which punctured a tire. Cumming's car left the racetrack, crashed through a fence, and ran into a crowd of spectators killing Burton and injuring others.

The court concluded that the State Fair Association's failure to properly inspect the track and discover and remove loose nails or spikes, one of which deflated the tire on the car and caused it to go through the fence into the crowd, was negligence. The plaintiff was able to recover for Burton's death.

While dirt tracks and obstacle-course races (including demolition derbies) are designed to present drivers with challenges, the challenges cannot be too difficult or dangerous. A participant in such a race cannot assume the risk when a jump is angled too sharply or the course is set-up in an unexpectedly, unknown, dangerous manner. The key is providing proper and accurate warnings in the most understandable means possible-which might include both oral and visual warnings.

While race cars are designed for *safety*, accidents frequently occur. Thus, participants need to be afforded protection from losing vehicle control. A track's infield, sides and curved banks should be filled with bundled tires, bales of hay or other protective devices to help stop out-of-control vehicles. A track construction/maintenance expert should be utilized to ensure a safe track.

A key protection required for any racing event is a liability waiver signed by participants. The waiver should provide express assumption of risk and comprehensive potential injury language so participants have no doubt as to what dangers they might face as well as the possible results that could occur if they indeed face those dangers.

An effective *waiver* could state that:

> by signing this liability waiver the participant expressly assumes the risk of potential lacerations, burns, broken bones, internal and external wounds, head injuries and any other possible injuries that could occur as the result of a participant's collision with another participant, a fence, or any other part of the facility, a tire blow-out, a malfunctioning car or any other potential hazard.

You must remember that a waiver's wording has to be very specific. This example provides only some basic concerns that should be addressed in a comprehensive waiver. Any waivers should be drafted and reviewed by a competent legal advisor.

Most supervisory concerns in automobile racing involve protecting drivers. Drivers should be required to *wear fire-retardant clothing, gloves, helmets and goggles*. The cars should have at least a *harness restraint system, a fire extinguisher within the driver's reach and a roll- bar*. If possible, a communication device in a driver's helmets should be encouraged.

Pit crew members should wear bright *fire-retardant clothing*. Sponsor logos might be colorful, but visibility is a key concern. Every year news stories show a pit crew member being hit by a driver who did not see them. As pit crew members are often bending down, they should wear bright caps that might be easier to see when they are crouched. There should be an adequate supply of fire extinguishers for chemical fires with everyone trained in how to properly use them. To increase the protection level against fires, the track should have its own fire truck and/or engage local fire and paramedic units to decrease the response time after an accident.

Motorcycles

Your inspection duty is greater for motorcycle racing than automobile racing. The slightest defect in the concrete or asphalt can throw a rider from his or her bike. Because the potential injuries from a motorcycle accident are potentially much greater than from an automobile accident, a motorcycle EA would be held to a higher safety standard. To help prevent a possible tragic accident, you should make sure the track is inspected thoroughly. The track inspection and maintenance program has to: *eliminate all potholes, fill in all surface level cracks and the track should be scrubbed down by a thorough cleaning device (preferably a street cleaner) before a race.* You should take every step possible to make the track as safe as possible for racers. *Bales of hay* or other protective barriers should be situated around curved banks, on the track's sides and in the track infield.

Motorcross races present a unique situation as the goal of the sport is to create the most challenging racing environment possible. For both motorized and non-motorized motorcross racing, you have to make sure there are no rocks or other debris hidden in the dirt mounds and pits which help make up the racing course. A participant can reasonably expect to fall on packed dirt, but a participant might not expect to land on a rock or cement.

Motorcycle racers should *wear leather* or other protective outfits and *knee and elbow pads*. *Motorcycle helmets with goggles or visors* should be required for each rider, in each race and practice lap.

Motorcycles, by their very nature, are much more dangerous than automobiles. While racecars have protective equipment that makes them safer than everyday cars, motorcycles do not provide the same protection. Even though the riders assume the injury risk, you should reinforce the assumption of risk with a specific statement in the participation *waiver*. The waiver could state that:

> due to the lack of restraints or protective equipment on motorcycles, the rider understands that the risk of serious or fatal injury is much greater in motorcycle racing than in automobile racing. Through the rider losing control of his or her motorcycle, the rider is exposed to the risk of permanent paralysis, paraplegia, quadriplegia, and other serious injuries.

Go-Carts

Inspecting a go-cart course is very important because most go-cart races involve children or young adults who might not appreciate racing's inherent risks. You should remember that a more experienced racer, no matter what his or her age, will always be held to a higher standard than less experienced racers. Thus, when young children are participating you have to inspect the course thoroughly and provide additional supervision. Because it might be impossible to examine each racer's ability, parents should sign application forms/permission slips indicating that their child is qualified to operate a go-cart.

Regan v. City of Seattle
458 P.2d 12 (WA 1969)

Michael Regan was injured in a go-cart race at the Seattle Center Coliseum on January 9, 1965. Regan was injured after he had completed several laps. His go-cart went out of control on a curve and veered-off the straightaway into some stacked floor bleachers. Regan testified that on a prior race, another go-cart had trouble with its cooling system and dumped water on the course at the spot where Regan's car crashed. He also testified that someone tried to clean the spilled water before Regan's race. Regan also alleged that the negligent design, construction and maintenance of the "crash wall" around the course created a hazardous situation.

The coliseum lessee agreed to keep the premises clean and generally cared for. The lessee also agreed to prevent damage to the premises by providing shock-absorbing crash barriers. However, the city voluntarily undertook to set the hay bales and clean the course.

In overturning a summary judgment for the city, the appellate court determined that the case should go to a jury because there was a question whether the city was negligent in supervising the placement of the go-cart crash wall in an inappropriate manner. There was also evidence that Regan did not have an opportunity to inspect the course after the prior liquid spill, which precluded summary judgment as he might not have assumed certain risks.

Bicycles

The trails, terrain, streets or velodromes used for a bicycling event have to be inspected for any *slippery areas or loose debris*. Loose debris in the form of pebbles, sand, broken glass and other small objects can throw a rider off a bike. Only dangers that are known to you or which can be easily detected have to be corrected. Participants also have to be warned about any dangerous conditions that were not corrected.

The mindset in mountain bike or off-road races is that the more treacherous the terrain, the better the course. Besides warning participants about the possible dangers, areas that are not in use should be clearly marked and all dangerous areas should be roped or taped off-limits with brightly colored material. You could be liable if the competition path sharply winds under a low tree branch and a rider hit his/her head against the branch because they have no time to react.

As with any other event, you should provide a waiver in the event entry form to protect yourself and anyone else associated with the event from suits by injured riders. You should keep in mind that waivers are only valid for injuries that are reasonably foreseeable by the participant at the time they signed the waiver. Waivers do not allow you to be reckless or to act negligently.

Bennet v. U.S. Cycling Federation
239 Cal. Rptr. 55 (CA 1987)

On June 10, 1984, Albert Bennet entered an amateur bicycle race sanctioned and conducted by the United State Cycling Federation (USCF). Upon entering the race, Bennet signed a release that stated in pertinent parts:

> This release is intended to discharge in advance the promoters, the sponsors...from and against any and all liability arising out of or connected in any way with my participation in said event, even though liability may arise out of negligence or carelessness on the part of the persons or entities mentioned above.

While participating in the race, Bennet collided with an automobile. Bennet alleged that the USCF's agents permitted the vehicle onto the course. The vehicle's driver testified that he drove up to a barrier blocking vehicular traffic. The driver told an attendant that he needed to return a camera to work. The attendant let the car go onto the course. Bennet stated that before the race he saw barriers in place, blocking automotive access to the racecourse. He was not told that an automobile traveling in the direction of oncoming riders would be on the course and he saw no cars on the course before the race.

The appellate court held that the release was valid, but there was a question of material fact whether the presence of an automobile on a barricaded bicycle race course was an obvious or foreseeable hazard contemplated by Bennet when he signed the release. Because it is hard to imagine that a car would get through barricades, a car on the course was probably not reasonably foreseeable.

Waivers are becoming an increasingly integral component of bicycling similar to the importance of waivers in automobile racing. In fact, bike manufacturers and retailers across the country are now asking clients to sign a waiver indicating they know about the bike and simple safety features such as quick release hubs (Sunderland, 1994). Similar to motorcycle racing, bike racing/riding requires head protection for all participants. All partcipants should sign a waiver indicating they have inspected their bike and that it is in a safe condition.

In-Line Skating

Both in-line and roller skating present significant risk of injuries from falls or collisions. The primary culprit for these accidents typically lies with improper supervision coupled with the failure to take necessary protective measures. In 1995, industry executive thought the rate of in-line injuries would jump 184 percent from 1993 due to people not wearing the proper protective gear ("In-line skating injuries projected to soar," 1995). The industry leaders suggested that skaters:

- make sure the boots fit snugly,

- make sure the helmet fits snugly and does not shift,
- make sure the helmet and protective gear are approved by American Society for Testing and Materials (ASTM), American National Standards Institute (ANSI), Canadian Standard Association (CSA) or Snell,
- make sure knee, elbow and wrist pads fit properly and are actually worn ("In-line," 1995).

Actually wearing the safety equipment is a key risk management strategy. According to one study, wearing wrist and elbow guards could reduce the risk of wrist injuries by 84 percent (Rafinski, 1996). Furthermore, 65 percent of skater wear some type of protective equipment, but through 1996, only seven percent of skaters wore all the required protective equipment (Rafinski, 1996).

A key to safety with skates (of any type) entails properly supervising to ensure individuals engage in safe competition or recreational activities. A Georgia case from the 1940's concluded that a skating rink supervisor had warned a patron several times to stop the disruptive behavior. The court concluded that the supervisor had a duty to kick the disruptive person off the ice before they injured someone (*Swope v. Farra* (1941) 66 Ga.App. 52).

Conclusion

Wheel based events cannot be made absolutely safe even in specially designed vehicles. Accidents will happen and people will be injured. Most injuries such as falling of a motorcycle or a bike are assumed risks. However, the risk is not assumed when you have engaged in some type of activity that enhances the risks or creates a new risk where one might not have existed previously. When running any wheel based event you have an affirmative obligation to ensure the track, path, course, etc. is/are in a reasonably safe condition with all hazards clearly marked. Whenever spe-

Chapter 24

Winter Sports

Winter sports, like water sports, present the challenge of nature's ever-changing weather and climate that can instantly destroy an event site. A beautifully groomed ski slope could become a slick sheet of ice very rapidly and your duty to warn about these changed conditions can be a full-time task. Winter sport concerns addressed in this guide center around skiing, bob sledding or tobogganing and snowmobiling. Skiing will be highlighted in a cursory manner due to the divergent state laws affecting the industry and the abundance of skiing law experts available to assist an EA.

Skiing

As discussed in Chapter 5, state laws often shape various duties. In fact, based on the *Sunday* case below, and other similar suits, over 25 states have passed laws outlining the risks of skiing and setting forth specific conduct for skiers (Nelson, 1991). Besides various duties imposed by state laws, you also owe participants the duty to inform them about all known dangers or dangers you should have discovered through a diligent inspection. Inspecting a ski slope is a very difficult and time-consuming process. It is impossible to eliminate all exposed rocks, brush, tree growths, trash and/or any other dangerous items. However if a risk can be removed, then you should remove the risk. To provide a reasonably safe facility you should send ski patrol personnel out on at least several runs down the different trails during the day to ensure the terrain has remained safe during the course of the day.

Wright v. Mt. Mansfield Lift, Inc.
96 F. Supp. 786 (VT 1951)

Florence Wright was injured while skiing in Stowe, Vermont. She and her husband (a professional skier) were transported by a lift to the ski run and had already had one successful run before attempting the same run again. While skiing down a marked trail, Wright collided with a snow-covered tree stump and suffered a fractured leg in the collision.

The ski lift and most of the ski run were owned by Lift, Inc. The defendants hired the five- to six-member Mt. Mansfield Ski Patrol to police the ski trails. It was the Patrol's duty to inspect each trail, every day, and to make sure the trails were suitable for skiing. The Patrol skied down the trails and inspected the trails for any unsafe conditions that appeared on the open trails. When a problem was spotted the Patrol put up warning flags to notify skiers. The Patrol also posted which runs were closed. The unsafe runs were closed-off by chain or rope and warning signs were put up at various points on the trail.

The court concluded that the defendants owed a duty to advise patrons of any trail changes which reasonably prudent persons would have foreseen and corrected. The defendants did everything in their power to make the trails safe. Thus, the plaintiff had to assume the dangers inherent in skiing because the defendants were not negligent in inspecting or warning the plaintiff.

The assumption of risk defense based on the inherent dangers in skiing has been revised by a more recent decision that imposes a higher degree of responsibility on the administrator of a skiing event. The following case was a watershed case highlighting assumption of risk issues in skiing.

Sunday v. Stratton Corporation
390 A. 2d 398 (VT 1978)

Mr. Sunday was a 21-year-old skier when he was injured in a skiing accident on February 10, 1974. The injury occurred at defendant's ski resort in Stratton, Vermont. Sunday sued, alleging that defendant negligently maintained its ski trails and failed to warn skiers about hidden dangers. Sunday became entangled in some brush on a novice skier trail. Due to the accident, he was rendered a permanent quadriplegic. A jury concluded that the defendant was 100% at fault and awarded Sunday $1,500,000.

The defendant showed at trial that they did almost everything that could reasonably be expected. Every effort was made to make the trail a perfect surface for skiing. In making the trails, trees were cut and machines removed all stumps, brush, and stones. The trail was then raked, fertilized, and grass was planted to help create the defendant's world-wide reputation for trail maintenance.

The court determined that the defendant owed a duty to exercise reasonable care in keeping the premises in a safe and suitable condition that would not unnecessarily or unreasonably expose skiers to danger. The court felt that being entangled in some brush was not really a danger inherent in the sport, but inherent in the skiing trail. Thus, even though both parties did not know about the brush, the defendant was still negligent in not providing a safe skiing facility.

With even the slightest hint that there might be a problem on one of the trails, you have to repair or close that run. The major question asked by courts is "Who is in the best position to prevent an accident?" The answer for the courts is normally very easy, the event administrator. Before an event you have to be sure you know all the potential skiing dangers ranging from: man-made to natural conditions, obvious to concealed conditions and new to old conditions. Several courts have held that a natural hazard is assumed, but if the hazard was man-made, the facility is liable. One man-made hazard is a trail shaped to funnel skiers in a certain direction.

The required inspection depends upon how many trails are on the mountain and the mountain's size. It is very difficult to pinpoint how many inspectors might be required. For example, the ski facility in the *Sunday* case had 52 ski patrolmen on duty, plus a trail crew charged with checking for hazards. Novice trails should be inspected frequently because novice skiers do not have as much control or experience to avoid potential hazards. Before using a skiing facility, check with the operators or owners to determine what their accident history is and which runs should or should not be used for your event. You should also find out if they have appropriate insurance coverage for both liability and medical concerns.

In addition to trees and rocks, there are other hazards on the slope that need to be marked to help prevent accidents. Two major items that need to be marked are snow making or moving machinery and lift towers. Large equipment should be stored or situated away from ski runs, but if they cannot be moved, they should be painted a bright color with night-glow paint.

A higher duty is owed when night skiing is allowed. A skier can assume many risks during the day, but the ability to spot risks at night can be severely hampered. Hazards have to be clearly marked and well-illuminated warning signs need to be posted far in advance of any dangerous areas. Lights have to produce sufficient lighting for skiers to clearly see the entire ski run without any substantial dark patches.

As with night skiing, the ability to assume risks in a blizzard is very difficult. If the EA has prior knowledge of a possible blizzard, then the EA has an affirmative duty to inform participants about the impending weather conditions. If a storm hits the facility, the EA should determine whether conditions are severe enough that a skier can not see at least 90 feet ahead, at which point the facility should be shut down until the storm ends. Storms can also raise additional concerns such as deep powder where a skier, or more specifically a snowboarder can get turned upside-down and suffocate in the lose snow. Suffocation can occur if people cannot get out of their boot bindings and just keep sinking into the snow (Sunderland, 1993). An additional concern entails skiers going down closed ski runs. Barriers should be installed at the top of a run to help block access to a closed run. Appropriate warning signs also need to be posted. Skiers need to be specifically told that skiing on closed runs is prohibited, illegal in some states, and considered trespassing on some properties. The courts usually hold against skiers injured when going down a closed run or leaving a trail.

Ski Lifts

Ski lifts represent a significant concern that is often overlooked when inspecting skiing facilities. For many skiers, the ski lifts can pose the most hazardous obstacle on the trails. You have to make sure instructions for getting on and off ski lifts are printed and shown in picture form at the lift's loading and unloading stations. Full-time attendants should supervise lift operations at each station. A ski lift transports people and as such is defined as a common carrier. Common carriers also include busses and airlines. All common carriers have to follow strict state and/or federal safety laws. Therefore, special care should be taken to ensure all laws are followed and appropriate safety personnel are manning the lift.

Supervision

Besides attendants at the ski lift loading and unloading stations, supervisory personnel are required to help curtail dangerous horseplay on the trails and rescue stranded or injured skiers. As with any other skill intensive sport, you should make sure people are skiing at the appropriate difficulty level commensurate with their skill. While it might be hard to prevent someone with weak skills from claiming they are experienced and skiing down a black diamond run, you can always try to educate individuals about skills needed to traverse a given run. You can also ask anyone that might need lessons to register for them before attempting to ski. In one California case, a camp counselor sued and recovered $600,000 claiming the camp should not have let her ski without requiring her to first take lessons ("Novice skier injures knee," 1997).

You should hire or procure ski patrol services affiliated with the *National Ski Patrol System, Inc.* to help rescue stranded or injured participants. The patrol's duties include: supervising participant conduct on the trails, making sure trails are safe and ensuring participants are safely making it down the trails. Controlling participants' speed is essential on crowded trails. Speed becomes a critical issue when individuals do not have complete control of their, or other's reaction times. In one California case a skier settled a suit for $125,000 against another skier claiming the other skier violated the right of way rules called the Skier's Responsibility Code which are prominently displayed at ski areas (*Wersinger v. Cheney* (1994), Nev. Fed. Dist. Ct. No. CV93-00362). Skiing and snowboarding accidents have made significant media attention with the deaths of Sonny Bono and a Kennedy in 1998. In 1999, news reports started reporting more tragedies involving accidents and collisions that could be preventable (Watson and Ruibal, 1999). While accidents will always occur, you have an obligation to conduct your event in the safest manner possible which means taking extra time to ensure individuals know the rules and are capable of following the rules based on their physical ability. Individuals who are allowed to engage in horseplay or other dangerous activities represent a danger to themselves and to others. Remember, you are considered to be in the best position to possibly eliminate a participant related risk.

Controlling drinking before skiing is impossible. However, you should always look for intoxicated or reckless conduct on the slope and assign individual to watch for such conduct and remove dangerous skiers from the trails. In *Freeman v. Hale*, the court concluded that a skier does not assume the risk of injury by another intoxicated skier as drunken behavior is not a common component of downhill skiing (*Freeman v. Hale* (1994), 94 Daily Journal, D.A.R. 17643).

Ski Lodge

In addition to the ski trails, you should inspect the ski lodge. Some major concerns involved in managing a ski lodge include slippery or icy floors, ski storage problems and serving alcohol to participants. Individuals who have just come in from the snow will normally be tracking snow into the lodge. Slippery floors are a major concern if the lodge's floor is not carpeted. Carpeting or other absorbent mats, pads, etc., should be used throughout a ski lodge and especially in aisles and corridors. Water absorbent mats should be placed both inside and outside the lodge. You should make sure the entrance area is mopped up whenever the mats are saturated. Saturated mats should be replaced immediately. The walkways in-and-around the lodge also must be shoveled and treated to prevent icy paths and steps.

Stearns v. Sugarbrush Valley Corp.
296 A. 2d 220 (VT 1972)

William Stearns was injured in January, 1969, at the Wonder Bar owned by the Sugarbrush Valley Corp. Stearns and his companions entered the bar's parking lot and walked up a 600 foot-long steep, icy path towards the facility. Stearns noticed that the condition of the path was icy and slippery. He had several drinks, but he was not intoxicated. Upon leaving the facility, Stearns fell on a relatively level portion of the path that was extremely icy. No sand or salt had been used on the path.

Earlier the same day, a bar employee also fell on the ice and had notified the defendant about the hazardous condition. The court concluded that the facility was negligent in not maintaining the 600 foot, partially steep, icy path, which was the only path between the restaurant and the parking lot.

Thus, all stairs and areas around the lodge and/or the parking lot should be shoveled and de-iced regularly. Shoveling and de-icing steps becomes even more critical when there is only one path to the lodge. Special care should be taken when de-icing any walkway. While salt or de-icers might melt snow, the melted snow can refreeze as ice, which is more treacherous than the snow. Thus, you have to utilize appropriate de-icers that will not solve one problem, and then create an even more dangerous problem.

You should make sure there is a *secure equipment storage area* with enough space for all the individuals that might want to use the lodge. If your event has 100 skiers participating, then there should be enough storage space for over 200 skis and poles. An attendant should be used to help organize stored skis and poles to help participants avoid tripping over or breaking equipment while rummaging through the storage area.

As in golf, the ski lodge often serves as the "19th hole" for skiers. Serving *drinks* to skiers can lead to potentially disastrous results. The limited movements required in golf makes it more difficult, but not impossible, for a drunken golfer to be injured. However, skiing requires additional control and body coordination that could be significantly impaired after several drinks. Participants who have had a few too many drinks, but insist on navigating down steep icy roads represent another significant liability concern for those that sold or provided the alcohol. It is a very difficult decision, but you have to weigh the risks associated with serving alcohol against the pleasure participants will have from coming out of the cold for a drink. By employing responsible bartenders/waitresses, you can control how much alcohol is served to each patron and hopefully avoid some of the host liquor liability problems highlighted in Chapter 30.

Bobsledding

Similar to skiing trails, bobsled and toboggan runs have to be inspected for rocks, shrubs, trash or other items that could throw a rider from a sled. One of the biggest dangers involved in bobsledding is stopping. While skiers can turn to stop themselves, individuals on bobsleds, toboggans or inflated inner tubes normally only stop when their vehicle hits something, reaches ground level or the rider is thrown. To protect participants, obstacles such as rocks, trees or ditches should be removed or rerouted.

Participants should be required to wear helmets and *only one person* should be on a bobsled, toboggan or inner tube. While two people going down a hill together might be more fun, the increased weight can lead to greater speed, less control and the potential for both riders to collide with each other. Equipment should be checked to make sure runners are properly secured. Any brakes or handles should be examined to ensure they are operational and properly attached.

Snowmobiling

Snowmobiles can be dangerous even on flat surfaces. Speed and obstacles represent significant concern. All event participants should follow set speed regulations based on what event is being held. Thus, a lower speed should be enforced for a family event while a higher speed could be allowed when adult racers are the only participants.

A snowmobile can throw a rider after running over a small bump, log or tree stump. Drivers can normally anticipate bumps or jumps, but snowmobile riders might not be able to anticipate bumps as evidenced in the following case.

Isler v. Burman

232 N.W. 2d 818 (MN 1975)

Elizabeth Isler was riding on a snowmobile, and was injured when the snowmobile went into a ditch four feet wide and one to three feet deep. The accident occurred on New Year's Eve, 1969. Darrell Burman was driving the snowmobile. The two were participating in a church-sponsored youth group outing. The church's youth director arranged for using the land and inspected the property's various trails. However, he did not inspect the exact spot where Isler was injured. The youths were not given any specific warnings, but were told to be careful. The group started their activity when it was dark and snowing lightly.

After about twenty minutes, the riders encountered a ditch that intersected the trail at a right angle. Isler was flung forward upon crossing the ditch and then backwards where she hit her back against a rear support bar. The ditch was on an established trail and other snowmobiles had passed the same spot that night without any trouble.

Burman testified that upon approaching the ditch he had slowed down to about five to six miles per hour. Due to the injury, Isler suffered a compression fracture of her lumbar vertebra. Her injuries were permanent.

Isler was able to recover ($40,000) for the injuries she received because the church had assumed the duty to inspect the premises. The church was negligent because it failed to properly inspect the premises and warn the plaintiff about potential hazards in the field.

Besides inspecting the snow's condition, you should inspect the field layout, mark any dangers with a colored flag and closely monitor weather conditions. For the greatest level of protection, the following snowmobile hints should be followed:

- check the machines daily for any problems,
- in wilderness conditions remember to bring a spare drive belt, headlight bulb, tow rope and first aid kit,
- always utilize the buddy system,
- wear the right clothes,
- wear protective helmets and face shield/goggles,
- make sure people keep their feet in the footrest area,
- avoid wearing long scarves that could get tangled on moving parts,
- warn participants to stay away from rivers and lakes where the ice covering might not be known,
- maintain proper distancing when riding with others,
- warn riders about the prohibition against chasing wildlife,
- inform everyone about applicable local, state and federal laws (Young, 1989).

Conclusion

The *Isler* case highlights how important it is to inspect a facility you are using even if you do not own the facility. By renting or leasing a mountain or field, you are under a duty to properly select the area. You can be liable for failing to properly research an area's safety record or failing to provide appropriate warnings for all potential event participants. Anyone leasing/loaning you their property would be more inclined to warn you about all possible concerns they know about in order to help prevent an injury and being dragged into litigation. However, as nature can quickly change, you cannot rely upon what the owner/manager has claimed without undertaking a reasonable inspection prior to starting the event.

Besides facility related concerns, you have to ensure proper equipment usage. Requiring someone to wear a helmet has little value if you do not enforce that rule. Furthermore, you have to make sure every participant understands and follows all applicable safety rules, especially as they relate to alcohol and roughhousing.

Chapter 25

Referees and Officials

It used to be a very simple problem to correct. Without notice, a referee or official might not be able to attend an event, so a spectator was used as a substitute. Those days are over. Now referees and officials are not being developed at a fast enough pace to fill the ranks of those referees and officials who are quitting due to pressure, lawsuits, verbal abuse and even physical attacks. Several states have adopted immunity statutes for referees and other sports volunteers. These statutes will hopefully eliminate some suits against officials, but you could still be sued for a referee's action or inaction. Your potential liability can stem from a *respondeat superior* relationship (employer/employee). Thus, a major concern for any EA is the status of the referee as an employee or independent contractor. Other referee concerns include participant control, crowd management, premises inspection and negligent event supervision.

Employment Classification

As discussed in Chapter 2, there are two worker categories that can be associated with an event, employees and independent contractors. If the referee is an independent contractor then you might not be liable for his/her actions.

Gale v. Greater Washington
Softball Umpires Association
311 A. 2d 817 (MD 1973)

Donald Alan Gale discovered that being a baseball umpire was dangerous when an upset player thought Gale made a bad call and attacked him with a baseball bat. The player hit Gale in the neck, hip and leg. Gale was a member of the GWSUA (the defendant) when he was attacked. The association provided trained and qualified umpires and assigned umpires to officiate various events. Umpires required each team captain to sign a game slip that was sent to the association for verifying the umpire's payment. The association called umpires and offered them the opportunity to officiate some games. Umpires were free to choose which games they wanted to officiate.

The court concluded that Gale was an independent contractor and could not receive worker's compensation. Gale was an independent contractor because he was free to accept or reject game assignments and his conduct was under his complete control.

You should attempt to make the referee's employment status clear from the very beginning. To clarify the employment status, you should enter into a written contract with the referee stating explicitly whether or not the referee controls his or her own work, in the manner they choose and with his/her own equipment. The contract should also clearly indicate whether or not the referee is an independent contractor. An EA would prefer to have the referee classified as an independent contractor to avoid the problems associated with vicarious liability. However, even if a contract states the referee is an independent contractor, if you thoroughly control how he/she performs their job they will be considered an employee (Fried, Miller and Appenzeler, 1998).

Participant Management

While referees are supposed to be peace makers, that job can be made very dangerous by irate coaches, participants and/or spectators. The following examples help highlight the concerns faced by referees and officials.

- In 1885, Charles Comiskey of the St. Louis Brown incited the crowd at the World Series to chase the umpire who scaled the outfield fence and disappeared ("History of disputes," 1996).
- In 1901, a national league umpire was beaten by fans after a controversial call cost a game and police were forced to draw their revolvers to protect the umpire ("History of disputes," 1996).
- Umpire Dave Pallone is spit on by Dave Conception in 1983 and shoved by Pete Rose in 1988 due to calls he had made (Beaton, 1996).
- The manager of a T-ball team is charged with allegedly assaulting a 16-year-old umpire who was trying to stop the manager from berating his own daughter for playing poorly ("Jurisprudence," 1997).

These incidents highlight the plight officials can face and the need to properly control coaches, participants and spectators to avoid harm to officials. You also have to protect officials and referees from misconduct by participants that could injure other participants and/or officials. A referee in 1996 football game removed two chin-strap buckles from a football players helmet as they were causing cuts to opposing players. The buckles were milled by the student's father to razor sharpness to prevent head slapping. The buckles could have injured more players and officials if the referee did not catch the problem ("The razor's edge," 1996).

Referees are responsible for ensuring that participants are competing under appropriate sport rules and our society's laws. If a participant is competing in a negligent manner, then the referee has to stop the negligent action before someone is harmed.

A referee cannot stop all negligent acts. However, if a referee has the ability to stop a negligent event or a dangerous act, but fails to do so, he/she could be liable for nonfeasance. If there is an imminent threat, the referee has to act immediately to eliminate the potentially negligent behavior. Only through proper training and experience can a referee determine when a situation might require his or her intervention. This is most often seen in boxing or wrestling where a referee has to determine, in a rapid manner, whether or not to let a match continue.

Carabba v. Anacortes School District No. 103
435 P. 2d 936 (WA 1968)

Stephen Carabba was injured in a wrestling meet held at Anacortes High School. Mr. Robert Erhart, a state trooper, was the meet referee. Carabba, a senior, wrestled against another senior from Oak Harbor High School in the 145-pound weight division. Near the end of the third round, the opponent, who was ahead in points, attempted to pin Carabba's shoulders to the mat. The opponent utilized a half-Nelson and tried to flip Carabba from side to side to get a pin. This process took the competitors to the wrestling mat's northwest corner.

Erhart noticed a gap between the wrestling mat and a small side mat and moved to close the gap to protect the wrestlers from rolling off the wrestling mat onto the bare floor. Erhart only diverted his attention momentarily. During the diversion, Carabba's opponent applied a full-Nelson for approximately 10 seconds. Almost simultaneously, the whistle blew and the opponent broke the hold on Carabba after a final lunge. Carabba slumped to the mat and was unable to move due to a major portion of his spinal cord being severed. Due to the accident and permanent paralysis, Carabba lost all voluntary function under his neck.

The appellate court concluded that there was an issue whether or not Erhart acted negligently in taking his eyes off the participants. Thus, the lower court's initial ruling for the school was reversed and a new trial was ordered to determine if Erhardt was negligent.

This situation is very difficult for a referee because they must weigh which risk is more severe. The *Carabba* referee probably felt that preventing the wrestlers from injuring themselves on the mat was riskier than an incorrectly applied wrestling move.

Crowd Management

A referee can be liable for not protecting spectators from participants. Referees have to be concerned about spectators being hit by a football or a basketball player who is carried out of bounds. While such a concern would not be as important in a major league ballfield, it would be important at a little league or high school field. To prevent such accidents, referees should not allow spectators to gather too close to the sidelines. An accident can be prevented if the referee stops an event after the spectators pass beyond a certain point. This principle was vividly shown in the *Domino* case (*Page 158*) where the umpire had moved the spectators behind a bench three times, but failed to stop the spectators from pushing the bench into the playing area. If the umpire had kept the spectators next to the fence, the plaintiff would not have been injured. An event should not be resumed until the spectators are in their appropriate places. There is no set distance that would be considered reasonable. However, the authors would suggest ensuring four feet between the spectators and the endlines on basketball courts. Football sidelines and endlines should be at least ten feet from the closest spectators. These concerns are highlighted in greater detail in Chapter 28-spectators

Facility Inspection

Referees should be given guidelines concerning when and under what conditions an event should be stopped or restarted. Guidelines should be established by the event safety committee, based on sound logic (do not use metal objects during lightning storms, etc.). These guidelines should be prepared in advance and all referees should receive the guidelines. The guidelines should require checking playing conditions before, during and after an event. Referees should know current weather conditions as well as the sunset time to help determine how long an event should last. Sunset times will determine when an event should be canceled due to darkness or when lights should be turned on.

Referees should know under what conditions an event should be postponed or canceled. Typically, an event should be canceled if any facility or participant hazards cannot be repaired, removed or avoided.

Forkash v. City of New York
277 N.Y.S. 2d 827 (NY 1967)

Before a city-sponsored youth semi-final softball game for the 1963 Bronx championship started, participants told the umpire that the cement field was not in reasonable playing condition. The umpire had the infield area swept to clear the broken glass, but the outfield was not swept. After the first inning, the participants complained about the outfield's condition. The umpire's response was that the broom had been "put away." The umpire's concluding remarks were, "It is getting dark, so just get out there and play."

Four innings later, when it had become quite dark, plaintiff Gary Forkash tripped on some glass in the outfield and collided with the other plaintiff, Howard Hersh. Based on the authoritative position held by the umpire over the youths (both 18-year olds), the appellate court refused to dismiss the case based on the assumption of risk defense raised by the umpire. Thus, the jury was allowed to hear the plaintiffs' negligence claim.

Event Supervision

The various event supervision concerns relating to participants equally apply to referees and officials. You could be liable for a referee's injuries as well as a referee's decision. A referee could possibly sue you if you failed to adequately protect the referee from participants or spectators. If you know that a certain coach has a tendency to bully or push around referees, then you would have an affirmative duty to warn the referee about the coach's behavior. You can also be liable for a referee's injuries that result from a poorly supervised event at a dangerous facility.

Smith v. University of Texas
664 S.W. 2d 180 (TX 1984)

James P. Smith sued the University of Texas and the National Collegiate Athletic Association (NCAA) for personal injuries Smith received while serving as an unpaid and volunteer official at the NCAA National Track and Field Meet. While officiating at the shot-put event, Smith was hit by a shot-put.

The lower court dismissed Smith's suit. The appellate court reversed the lower court's dismissal because a "genuine issue of material fact existed as to whether the University's employee, the head track coach, and another volunteer official...were negligent in the use of the shot-put area and the shots themselves by failing to properly supervise the...conduct of the shot-put event." The appellate court concluded that the university, the coach and the other officials could be negligent in failing to properly supervise the event and adopt regulations for safely conducting the shot-put event.

Referees can assume the risks inherent in the sport. However, they do not assume the risk associated with a dangerous facility or an event's negligent operation if the referees did not know about the danger(s).

You also have to be aware of laws that might affect the officiating process or those who can officiate. In addition to laws providing for greater penalties for those who assault officials, some laws might aid an official in a claim against an EA for failing to utilize an official. Under the Americans with Disabilities Act (*Chapter* 8), several coaches have brought claims, and won the right to keep coaching even though they might utilize a wheel chair ("League settles lawsuit coach in wheelchair called no hazard," 1998). An umpire could possibly raise the same claim that they could effectively perform their job in a safe manner and as an EA you would have to consider the potential legal ramifications from denying that person the right to officiate.

As an EA, you have to protect referees from spectator retaliation, especially after a close game or a controversial call. To help protect referees, you should escort them out of the facility with uniformed security personnel. Some EAs take the following steps to protect referees: having idling cars ready to drive them away, having decoy referees (normally police of-

ficers wearing referee outfits) leave the stadium first and/or having referees change into street clothes before leaving the stadium.

Conclusion

This chapter has highlighted various concerns associated with officials
ranging from your liability if they are an employee to effective means to help
them escape a hostile crowd. No matter what the employment status might
be for an official, the stories and cases highlighted above demonstrate that
the officiating business is no longer a safe business. Coaches, participants
and spectators are taking the law into their own hands and dispersing "justice" on the proverbial peace making officials. All officials need to be aware
of the potential for violence and you have a heightened obligation to warn

Chapter 26

First Aid

It is exceptional when an event is completed without an injury. The following stories highlight medical and injury related concerns you might face.

- Second impact syndrome is the name given to minor head injury that is followed by a subsequent minor injury-which might result in death. The combined trauma of two separate head impact incidents can lead to catastrophic results (Levy and Manning, 1997). This syndrome is critical as over 100,000 concussions occur each year in football alone and 300,000 in all sports combined.
- A jury awarded $1,171,152 to a California boy who fell on the playground and complained about headaches after he hit his head. The suit claimed the school district employees failed to care for the nine-year-old after the fall ("School fails to care for injured student," 1998).
- On average 12 high school athletes die each year from often hidden heart disorders. In an 11 year study, 158 deaths were analyzed with 134 (120 males) of those deaths being heart problems (Pai, 1996). The most frequent sports the deaths occurred in include basketball (48 deaths), football (44), track (19), soccer (6), baseball (5) and swimming (3).

Based on the serious risk threats inherent in certain sports and the potential for catastrophic injury in everyday activities, EAs have a heightened responsibility to provide effective and timely medical assistance. When a person gets injured at an event, you cannot assume that the person will heal himself or herself. You must assist an injured party to avoid being charged with nonfeasance. This theory was reinforced by a famous college athletics case. The parents of a Gettysburg College lacrosse player sued after their son's death. The court concluded that the college owed a duty to have measures in place at the practices or games that would have "provide[d] prompt treatment in the event that he or any other member of the lacrosse team suffered a life-threatening injury." (Kleinknecht v. Gettyburg College, 1993). While this duty does not extend to all students, the court concluded that a recruited student athlete is owed a higher duty of care. That duty requires the institution to provide prompt and adequate emergency medical services at school-sponsored athletic events (*Kleinknecht v. Gettysburg College*, 989 F. 2d 1360 (3d Cir. 1993)).

Your first defensive strategy against a negligence claim is the implementation of procedures to avoid injuries. Following event rules and regulations, accompanied by thorough supervision and high quality equipment and facilities, helps reduce potential injuries. The second defensive strategy is a strong first aid program. A first aid program needs to be comprehensive and requires providing quick and accurate emergency assistance, as well as documenting all incidents.

First Aid Program

The event safety committee should appoint, is at all possible, an experienced doctor, emergency medical technician (EMT) or athletic trainer to supervise the event's first aid program. The title for this individual could vary, but this guide will utilize the term "First Aid Director." The first priority for the First Aid Director is to develop first aid procedures that clearly sets out what steps need to be taken, and how to take those steps.

You could be liable for the First Aid Director's negligence if he/she is considered an employee, rather than an independent contractor. Because First Aid Directors normally control their own conduct and use their own tools, they are normally considered independent contractors by the courts. A First Aid Director on your payroll and under your control would probably be considered an employee.

The First Aid Director is held to a high standard of care; the standard of care depends on whether or not the first aid director is considered an "expert." The old "locality rule" which requires a doctor to conform to the local standards in the area which they practice has lost judicial favor. The current trend is to consider locale as just one factor necessary to evaluate the doctor's conduct (*Wiggins v. Pirer*, 171 S.E. 2d 393 (S.C. N.C. 1970)). However, there is still a set standard for doctors who hold themselves out to be specialists as they are held to a national standard. That standard compares the doctor's conduct with other specialist in the same field, with the same experience.

The First Aid Director should be familiar with all the latest first aid procedures and have a working knowledge for treating specific sports related injuries. An example of a specific sports procedure entails using bolt cutters to remove an injured football player's helmet, rather than sliding the helmet off, which could cause additional injuries. Such techniques are often developed through national organizations in the sport medicine/athletic training area. As discussed in Chapter 9, the First Aid Director should be familiar with and follow guidelines set by associations such as the American College of Sports Medicine. Team physicians or trainers should also be certified by reputable organizations such as national medical boards or organizations such as the National Athletic Trainers Association.

Trainers and other event personnel are held to a lower standard then doctors. However, they still have to act in a reasonable manner.

Gillespie v. Southern Utah State College
669 P. 2d 861 (UT 1983)

Rickey Gillespie attended Southern Utah State College on a basketball scholarship for the 1977–78 school year. On January 4, 1978, Gillespie sprained his ankle in a practice scrimmage. David Slack, a student trainer, treated Gillespie's ankle by spraying the ankle with a tape adherent, applying a pre-wrap to prevent the tape from coming in contact with the skin and then taping the ankle. Gillespie then immersed his ankle in ice water for fifteen minutes, then removed his foot from the water and walked on his ankle for several minutes. This cycle was repeated several times.

Later that evening, Slack went over to Gillespie's apartment and soaked the foot in ice water for approximately two hours. The next day, Gillespie visited a doctor who felt the ankle had been overtaped and that Gillespie only suffered a sprained ankle. The doctor recommended continued taping and icing of the ankle. That night, Gillespie slept with his ankle submerged in ice water. Gillespie suffered frostbite to his toes, foot and his heel. Gillespie became ninety percent disabled in his lower right leg and foot.

There was a question whether or not Gillespie's ankle could have healed itself if the trainer had not taken any steps. The lower court dismissed Gillespie's claim against the college and the appellate court affirmed that decision. The appellate court concluded that Slack, by providing incorrect treatment, did not become a guarantor of good results therefore, the college was not strictly liable. However, the trainer was not off the hook for his actions.

Even though the First Aid Director could employ inexperienced student trainers as first aid workers for a low price (or possibly as free-beginning interns), the risk of their increasing an injury can out-weigh the financial savings. Student trainers have to be closely supervised and they should not provide any advice/medical treatment. Furthermore, all state laws and national association governing standards need to be closely followed.

If a state law specifically requires CPR certification, and a trainer has their training licensed, but a lapsed CPR card than you cannot use that person until they obtain a valid CPR card. Failure to meet the proper certification requirements could result in a negligence per se claim.

The First Aid Director is responsible for developing and equipping a first aid kit with all the necessary equipment. Simple first aid kits should be available at each event site and first aid personnel should only dispense items in the kit or items previously approved by the First Aid Director.

The following is an equipment list representing typical equipment that should be available in an event first aid kit and/or event site:

- vacuum/wood splints,
- long spine board/ scoop stretcher,
- bolt cutters,
- stethoscope,
- blood pressure cuff,
- crutches,
- neck, shoulder, knee, and ankle immobilizers,
- antiseptic solution,
- sterile gauze, including eye pads,
- Band-Aids and roll gauze in various sizes,
- adhesive tape/scissors,
- tweezers, cutters (rings, etc.), clippers, knife, blades, etc.,
- eye cup,
- sterile water,
- ice or cold packs,
- thermometer,
- blankets and towels,
- universal precaution kit for biohazard spill cleanup.

Additionally, appropriate waste containers need to be available for proper disposal of any hazardous or medical waste, especially when anyone has a bleeding-related injury. Individuals need to be specifically trained in the proper disposal techniques used when handling a bloody cut, blood soaked paper goods, blood soaked clothing and blood smeared equipment. Appropriate cleaning agents need to be purchased to clean any areas that might have been exposed to blood or other bodily fluids. It is a good idea to contact a fire department, ambulance company or local health departments to provide appropriate information and contacts to determine what local health laws need to be followed.

Speed

A procedure list, outlining the steps to follow after an accident, should be given to each person involved with the first aid response program. The procedure list should include the location of any phones, if other communication devices are not available (walkie-talkies are often used as a reliable method of keeping in contact with all the first aid personnel). The list should contain the First Aid Director's phone number and nearest police, fire, paramedics and emergency squads. The list should also contain a street map and a facility map to assist emergency response personnel (paramedics, ambulance) to the exact location where the injured person can be found. The individual who contacts emergency response personnel should give his/her name and specify the exact injury site location to help speed-up response time. You should also have a master list containing the telephone numbers of the emergency contact person for each participant (this information should be requested on applications and waivers).

Timely response can also be maintained by using well-trained first aid personnel at each event site. Before an event, first aid personnel should be shown the facility and equipment layout to develop familiarity and reduce response time. Using a "medical" golf cart or a car can help save traveling time at a large event.

Once an injury occurs, the first aid procedures have to be implemented immediately. Paramedics or an ambulance team at the site should be contacted at the same time the First Aid Director is notified. If there is no standby ambulance team, then the First Aid Director should examine the injured person and determine what steps to take. If the First Aid Director cannot examine the injured person, he or she could still highlight appropriate procedures to follow. The key entails quickly communicating information about the injury to individuals who can make an informed decision. Questions the First Aid Director must deal with include:

- whether or not an injury is life threatening,
- who should administer first aid,
- should the injured person be moved,
- how should the person be moved,
- where and how should the injured person be transported?

If an injury is not an emergency, the First Aid Director should receive either written or oral consent from the injured party before providing any assistance. To avoid a battery charge for unlawfully touching a person, the first aid policy should specify that verbal contact-even screaming-should be utilized prior to touching an injured person. Verbal contact should include an assertion that you are going to touch the injured person. If the injured person does not respond, then you would be acting in a reasonably prudent manner if you physically examine the injured person.

While the injury is being evaluated, all spectators should be disbursed. Spectator congestion around an injured person makes it difficult to help the injured person and the crowd can block emergency vehicle access.

Arriving at the accident scene and administering first aid in the swiftest manner possible cannot be stressed enough. The following case highlights this point.

Wightman v. Town of Methuen
526 N.E. 2d 1079 (MA 1988)

Adam Wightman, a second-grade student, was injured on the school playground in 1983. An older student had picked up Wightman by his legs and spun him around in the air. Wightman pled with the older child to stop, but the bully did not do so. Upon hitting the ground, Wightman injured his arm. Injured and crying, Wightman went to the two supervisors who were on duty. The supervisor did not examine his arm, but sent him to class rather than taking care of his injury. His teacher noticed his pain and sent him to the nurse's office. The nurse was not available, so a physical education instructor administered some first aid and then called Wightman's parents. At the hospital the parents discovered their son had multiple arm fractures and required surgery.

Because the school failed to seek immediate medical attention the school waived its immunity for discretionary functions. However, the Wightman's failed to sue under the theory of failure to seek immediate medical attention. Thus, the school prevailed based on Wightman's failure to sue under the correct legal theory.

Accuracy

The First Aid Director, or appointed representative, must evaluate an injury's nature and severity to determine what action is required. The First Aid Director must protect the injured individual from any further harm which includes comforting the injured to prevent shock. The First Aid Director must stabilize the injury or restore the participant to a reasonable condition. *No matter what happens with the treatment, once first aid is started, treatment cannot be stopped until the person is completely treated or taken to the hospital.* Even if an athlete is going to the hospital, the athlete should not be allowed to drive or go to the hospital alone, especially after a head injury.

Accurate diagnosis and *injury treatment* is the First Aid Director's major responsibilities associated with speed. Both are a necessity. Thus, if there are several first aid personnel working shifts, they should not have shifts longer than five to six hours. If longer shifts are taken, the first aid personnel might become fatigued, which could result in losing accuracy. Losing accuracy can lead to negligence even though the injury response time was quick. It only takes one mistake to turn a treatable injury into a tragedy that will likely lead to a lawsuit as seen in the following case.

Welch v. Dunsmuir Joint High School District
326 P. 2d 633 (CA 1958)

Anthony Welch was a high school football quarterback playing in a scrimmage between Dunsmuir High School and Enterprise High School in California. Welch attempted a quarterback sneak and was tackled shortly after running through the line. As he was falling forward, another player moving to tackle him fell on Welch. After the play, Welch was found lying on his back and was unable to get to his feet. The coach suspected a possible neck injury and asked Welch to grab the coach's finger. Welch was able to move his fingers while he was still on the field.

A doctor was 20 to 25 yards away, but did not provide any assistance until Welch was removed from the field. Four players on each side of Welch lifted him and moved him to the sidelines, without anyone directing the move. The doctor checked Welch and found he could not move his fingers. Welch's removal without the use of a stretcher or backboard was an improper first aid procedure.

The appellate court affirmed Welch's $325,000 verdict ruling that moving Welch off the field was the proximate cause of his permanent quadriplegia. The school could have used a door, a shutter or a bench if a stretcher was not available.

Another accuracy concern involves correctly treating an injured participant. You should make sure the facility used for handling emergencies or treating or rehabilitating injured participants, is reasonably safe. All equipment not in use should always be safely stored and locked. All drugs, even aspirin, should also be locked away with only the First Aid Director having access to the drugs.

Some of the major "nevers" that have to be remembered at all times by all event personnel include:

- never supply any drugs, even aspirin,
- never just wrap joint injuries (thinking they are just strains),
- never allow someone with a head injury to return to competition, drive home or drive to a hospital without medical approval,
- never use cutting tools for blisters, corns, etc.,
- never administer heat, electrical or whirlpool treatments without the consent of a physician and only after proper inspection of the equipment,
- never slap or splash water on an athlete's face to revive the athlete,
- never encourage an injured person to move if they are in pain,
- never move an injured person until they are examined by the First Aid Director or physician,
- never take a helmet off someone's head if they have a possible neck injury,
- never move a neck injury victim without qualified medical assistance.

Documentation

Rudyard Kipling's famous poem reads in pertinent part, "[I]f you can keep your head while all about you are losing theirs and blaming it on you..." This phrase is highly appropriate to the injury documentation process. Documentation is critical for establishing factual evidence that might be required for trial. The best time to record what occurred is right after an injury is detected because the facts are still fresh in everyone's minds and witnesses are in the general vicinity. Thus, even though chaos can surround an injury, you have to act to treat the injury while at the same time completing all relevant documentation.

The information that needs to be recorded on an accident report include:

- the injured person's name and address,
- the person's sex and age,
- the person's next-of-kin,
- the injury time and date,

- the nature of the injury,
- the body part(s) affected by the injury,
- the person's vital signs,
- current medications or known allergies,
- the location where the injury occurred,
- how the person was found or how the injury was discovered,
- who reported the injury,
- what specific equipment or facility was being used,
- an objective accident description,
- which supervisor or volunteer was on duty when the injury occurred,
- who administered first aid,
- what first aid steps were taken (exact time and sequence),
- how the person was transported and to where,
- the treatment or injury aftermath,
- the names and addresses of witnesses and their statements,
- who filled-out the accident report,
- did the person refuse treatment.

A sample injury report form can be found in Appendix B.

Every injury and reported injury should result in a completed injury report form. Whenever possible you should try to obtain a *signed Refusal of Medical Treatment form* from anyone refusing medical assistance. Such a form is contained in Appendix B. All event personnel should offer medical assistance for any injury. The decision whether or not to accept medical assistance rests with the injured person, unless he or she is unconscious. As highlighted above, providing assistance to someone who does not ascent to such treatment is a battery against that person.

Conclusion

No one wants to have an injury at an event, but injuries are inevitable. Knowing that there will be injuries puts you in a position that you can develop a comprehensive response schedule to deal with any injuries. By appointing the right people and setting specific boundaries for conduct you can eliminate most liability concerns associated with providing or failing to provide proper, accurate and speedy medical assistance. The major steps you should take to ensure your first aid program is operating in a reasonable manner include:

- appointing a qualified First Aid Director,
- developing a first aid procedures list (containing procedures, phone numbers, maps and accident report forms),
- only allowing student-trainers to work under tight supervision,
- placing complete first aid kits at each event sight,
- avoid undertaking first aid assistance if at all possible, but if you cannot avoid assisting someone, you have to execute the procedures in a speedy and accurate manner,
- posting emergency service signs,
- strategically placing first aid teams around the site,
- avoiding premature returning of participants to competition,
- avoiding heat stress or other heat threats,
- making sure all event personnel are certified in cardiopulmonary resuscitation (CPR), know basic first aid and recognize emergencies,
- coordinating safety communication through one person or a central post,
- inspecting and maintaining all equipment used for first aid or therapy,
- preventing participants from treating themselves with event equipment or medicine.

Chapter 27

Transportation

One often overlooked concern while running an event is transportation to or from an event. Often it is not necessary to analyze transportation concerns because participants/spectators transport themselves to and from events. But, the event administrators must still concern themselves with transporting various individuals. When dealing with sporting events it may be necessary to transport fans, staff, athletes, families and cheerleaders. The event administrator must determine what the most fitting form of transportation might be for the event. Automobiles, buses and airplanes are the three most common transportation methods.

The event safety committee must determine the easiest and safest transpiration option(s). Government agencies might use government-owned cars and/or school buses. A government agency might not have to worry about purchasing or renting a vehicle, but they might have to follow specific rules concerning: the method of travel, who can drive, where to purchase gasoline and other potential restrictions.

For non-government entities, rented cars or vehicles might be the exclusive transportation option. While negotiating a rental agreement, you should try to negotiate a reduced price for a complete package including insurance coverage. If the rental firm's insurance premiums are too high then you could try to add a rider to the event insurance policy or to a personal car insurance policy. If you have contracted with someone else to handle the event's transportation, then you should make sure they have a safe accident record, well-maintained vehicles and adequate insurance coverage. If an outside contractor does not have a safe record, you could be liable for failing to properly screen and choose the transportation provider. Most legitimate transportation contracting companies willingly provide insurance and accident information upon request.

Anytime that an EA must coordinate transportation, he or she must be aware of potential statutory concerns. "The applicable standards of care are often set by statutes and, therefore, the administration must check all applicable statutes on driver and vehicle eligibility requirements" (Burling, 1992). Liability is a concern regardless of who is selected to transport individuals to and from events. The degree of liability is not entirely reduced, even if the institution hires a private transportation company. Therefore, specific transportation guidelines must be implemented for every event administrator. These guideline must encompass all methods such as: hiring an outside company, public transportation, athletes driving themselves, parents driving athletes, school officials driving and/or assigning students to drive. Included in the actual guideline must be rules concerning such issues as:

- the method of travel,
- who is driving the vehicle,
- where to buy gasoline,
- where to get vehicles inspected and repaired,
- where to park the vehicles.

Specific research must be undertaken before deciding who is transporting the athletes or other individuals. First, the event administrator must ensure that the drivers have a good record. This includes students, government officials and even outside contractors. If an EA hires an outside contractor, liability is not automatically relinquished. The EA could be liable if they hire someone with a bad driving record and did not sufficiently research his/her background. If outside contractors are utilized, you should make sure they have appropriate insurance coverage commensurate with the total number of people that will be transported. A $1 million aggregate policy does not go as far if 20 people are injured in comparison with a policy limit of $1 million per claim.

Automobiles

In situations where automobiles must be used, the cars, vans or trucks must be in good condition. This is true for not only government owned vehicles, but for personal vehicles too. For government owned vehicles, there must be regular check-ups performed by certified mechanics, to ensure good running condition. Safety concerns (not including the driver's qualification or appropriate insurance coverage) that must be examined include, but are not limited to:

- condition of tires,
- condition of brakes,
- overall vehicular condition,
- when the car last had a professional check-up,
- the vehicle's legal capacity.

Often times, government agencies use vans, which allows for larger capacity. These vans are not only loaded with people, but also with equipment. The weight of the equipment must also be taken into consideration when determining if the vehicle is loaded to capacity.

Adams vs. Kline
239 A. 2d 230 (DE 1968)

In 1964, at the University of Delaware, a 19-year-old student named Gary Adams was injured in an automobile accident. The accident occurred when the van Gary was driving collided with another vehicle owned by the school. Adams was injured in the accident, while helping to transport a portion of the university's soccer team. He sued the coach who was driving the other vehicle, and the university who owned the vehicles. Adams was driving a University owned van with six players and the team's equipment. He was following the other van driven by Kline, when he collided into the rear-end of Kline's van. Adams failed to stop in time, because when he attempted to stop, the brakes on the vehicle failed.

According to the school there had been no previous problems with the brakes, therefore no cause to warn Adams of a faulty vehicle. Up until that point, Adams had never mentioned any problem with the brakes. In Adams suit against the school and the coach, he claimed that he was supplied with a van that had defective brakes, or they allowed him to overload the vehicle. The van Adams was driving was carrying between 1300 and 1400 pounds, although its capacity was only 900 pounds. The coach, who was overseeing the trip made the mistake of allowing the van to be loaded above its capacity weight. Before the trip, Coach Kline should have checked the records on the vehicles to see their capacity weights.

While the coach should have warned Adams about the overloading, he was not responsible for notifying Adams about the brakes because there had been no previously known break problem(s). Although Adams did sustain injuries, it was believed that they were not caused by the overloaded vehicle, but rather the breaks. Kline was not responsible for checking the brakes, to see if they were defective. Thus, the coach was not negligent.

In orchestrating a plan for transporting to and from an event, the vehicles are not the only aspects that must be researched to avoid liability. It is also necessary to check out who will be driving the vehicle or the chosen mode of transportation. If the EA is aware of a driver who has a bad record, then it is his or her duty to find another driver. The passengers rely on the protection from the EA or whoever is in charge of transporting concerns to select a safe driver. Otherwise the EA could be found negligent for knowingly endangering passengers' lives.

Hanson vs. Reedly Joint Union School District
111 P. 2d 415 (CA 1941)

In May 1938, Ruth Hanson, a student at Reedly Junior College was killed in an automobile accident. All students at Reedly were required to take at least one physical education course such as tennis. A vehicle accident occurred on her way home from tennis practice. Since the school bus left the school grounds at 4:00, and practice did not begin until around 4:15, many of the students were forced to find other means of transportation. Since 1933, the school made it a practice to allow the students who had cars to drive those who did not have cars home from practice. It was up to the teacher in charge to make the decision concerning who would be doing the driving. The students who drove were given one gallon of gas for every ten miles they drove.

Another student named Theodore Eschwig, had been driving Hanson and some of her friends for the majority of the second term. Eschwig's car was a 1930 Ford sports roadster, which had no top, horn, fenders or running boards. The car was in very poor shape, having numerous faulty accessories such as: lights, speedometer, steering column, brakes and tires. Since the car was obviously in poor condition, the teacher should not have allowed Eschwig to drive his car. Hanson was the only student killed in the accident, with six others being injured.

In court, the tennis teacher testified that he was aware the car was not in good condition, and that Eschwig was in fact a reckless driver. Therefore, the tennis teacher was negligent in allowing the students to ride with Eschwig in his faulty vehicle.

These two cases highlight the importance of policies and guidelines concerning vehicle inspection and driver certification. On a regular basis all vehicles should be carefully examined by a competent mechanic who knows what the vehicles will be used for and under what conditions they will be used.

Buses

Often times, government agencies either have their own buses or hire chartered buses from independent contractors. Hiring independent contractors is practical because they usually will have their own insurance policies. Even though the carrier should have sufficient insurance coverage, it is still necessary to ensure that the contractor has a good record. It is also necessary to make sure that the company hired is a reputable company. While most independent contractor agreements are easily established through a contract, any potential confusion needs to be resolved before any participants/spectators are transported.

Lofy v. Joint School District #2
166 N.W. 2d 809 (WI 1969)

On March 18th, 1965 an accident occurred in Wisconsin involving a bus rented by Cumberland High School. An independent contractor had been hired to transport students and faculty to see their team perform in the state high school basketball tournament. Each passenger on the bus was charged a percentage of the total cost the school had paid to rent the buses. The high school principal arranged for two 41-passenger buses and one 37-passenger bus to transport the faculty and students to and from Madison. As one of the buses was traveling down the highway it struck a car from the rear. Coincidentally, Matthew Lofy who was an employee of the Cumberland schools drove the car that the bus hit Mr. Lofy's wife and children were injured and he was killed in the crash. Mrs. Lofy sued not only the independent contractor, but also the school district.

The question in the suit against the school district was whether the bus company was acting as an agent or as independent contractor. An independent contractor is defined as, "a person employed to perform work on the terms that he is to be free from the control of the employer as respects the manner in which the details of work are to be executed" (I 66 N. W. 2d 809). The only instructions from the school were the scheduled departing and arriving times, the return departure time and the best possible route. Almost all other issues were handled by the bus company. Due to the lack of significant control, the company was an independent contractor and not an actual agent for the school. If the courts had found that the company was acting as an agent, rather than an independent contractor, then the school might have been negligent.

Regardless of whether or not an independent contractor is utilized, safe transportation entails establishing conduct rules for both drivers and passengers. A good driver would be significantly hindered by poor participant/spectator conduct. Individuals throwing items or running in a bus can help distract even an experienced driver. The following case represents another rider supervision concern.

Brewer v. Hatcher Limousine Service, Inc.
708 So.2d 163 (AL, 1997)

On September 4, 1992, Paige Brewer a student athlete at John Carroll High School in Alabama, was injured in a bus accident. Brewer was riding a rented bus from school to an athletic event when she decided to hang out the bus window. As the bus moved backwards her head was pinned between a utility pole and the bus window. Brewer was killed in the incident.

The principal of John Carroll High School, Dr. Rebecca Sullivan, arranged the bus rental. She contacted Hatcher Limousine Service, who only had one bus for the school's use. So, Hatcher contacted White Limousine, Inc. to get one more bus. The buses were to carry student athletes to and from an athletic event.

The Brewer family alleged that Hatcher Limousine had negligently breached their duty to provide safe transportation services. They also claimed that there was some kind of agency relationship between Hatcher and White (the bus driver). The court concluded that the duty to transport the atheletes was non-delegable once assumed. Thus, summary judgment was denied as the issue of whether or not the defendant assumed the duty to transport was still in dispute.

In situations such as the *Brewer* case, the EA should demand a certificates of insurance naming the school as additional insured on every transportation provider policy. The certificates should also include the names of any potential subcontractor. If a transportation contractor is going to seek the assistance of another company, the transportation contract should require the EA's consent for any such assignment.

Airplanes

Airplanes are another increasingly common transportation method in traveling to and from sporting events. With the long distances many college teams have to travel, airplane travel has become much more common. When choosing to fly, it is common practice to use commercial airlines. It is the EA's duty to make sure that a reputable airlines is chosen. The same concerns associated with choosing a reputable bus transporter apply to a potential airlines carrier. Besides making sure the carrier has appropriate insurance, you might want to examine specific travel insurance policies that might cover player deaths or event interruption if you miss a flight.

Transportation Hierarchy

The following hierarchy lists the best to worst strategies for transporting individuals. The best strategies present the lowest risk level while the worst strategies present the greatest potential exposure to risks.

1. Out Source (Hire Independent Contractor)

If an independent contractor is hired, then liability is usually transferred away from through contracts. Contractors are often required to follow very strict federal and state transportation regulations designed for common carriers.

2. Public Transportation

Having participants utilize public transportation such as city buses is a safe option because it will also limit possible liability towards the school.

3. EA Drives the Athletes

Although probably one of the most common practices, this is an option that many schools wish they could avoid because they are taking on significant potential liability in this situation. However, some liability risks can be reduced by the fact that the EA would be making all the transportation decision. The added degree of control can help ensure risk management practices are implemented.

4. Participants/Spectators Drive Themselves

This practice should be avoided, if possible, but is still not as risky as assigning parents, participants or spectators to drive. Liability can still be razed if the participants/spectators leave from event grounds to go to a different facility or any other travel arrangement. Similarly, a group of athletes might decide to carpool from a school to an athletic event. If any such car pools are organized, the EA should avoid being involved in the process. The second the EA identifies a specific driver they will asume a duty to provide safe transportation as athletes rely upon the EA to steer them in the right direction.

5. Parents Drive Athletes

While parents or other non-participants driving athletes might seem to be as strong a choice as outsourcing, an injured plaintiff can claim that the EA (especially if the EA is with a school) had a duty to provide safe transportation and cannot delegate that responsibility to others who are not common carriers.

6. Assign Students to Drive (Worst)

Assigning students to drive is probably the worst option in the transportation hierarchy. This is because the EA or school is putting themselves at a liability risk by essentially handing over the responsibility to a select few students. Questions that could arise include:

- whether or not the driver was a safe driver,
- whether or not the driver or vehicle owner had adequate insurance
- when the vehicle was last serviced,
- were the brakes and other essential components recently inspected, repaired or replaced,
- whether the driver had any prior tickets,
- whether the vehicle had safety devises such as air bags,
- whether the driver enforced safety precautions such as wearing seat belt?

Conclusion

While transportation is traditionally not considered the biggest concern in running an event, it can be the critical link between a safe event and a disaster. Special attention needs to be paid to analyzing safety records of anyone or any vehicle in the transportation process. While you might be able to control an athlete's use of equipment, transportation entails countless variables which cannot be controlled, such as other drivers and road conditions. Only through developing a comprehensive transportation safety plan can you attempt to make the transportation process safer. A transportation safety plan should address the following concerns:

- developing a transportation policy and distributing it to all personnel associated with the event,
- making sure all responsibilities are clearly defined (Burling 1992),
- making sure all employees, volunteers, participants and spec-

tators understand the transportation procedures and policies (Burling, 1992),

- obtaining insurance certificates from each common carrier and determining if they have appropriate permits and licenses (Burling, 1992),
- keeping meticulous vehicle records which should include a complete list of repairs, accidents and a yearly evaluation of each vehicle's condition (Burling, 1992),
- creating appropriate policies for those who utilize personal vehicles to transport participants/spectators (Burling, 1992),
- creating a policy for accident reporting (Burling, 1992),
- making sure everyone has copies of all appropriate accident forms, mileage charts and road maps,
- providing specific written rules and instructions to each driver,
- prohibiting vehicle overcrowding, whether with people or equipment. This is especially important if the overcrowding will reduce visibility.

Section III
Event Spectators

Chapter 28

Spectator Management

The following cases and incidents help highlight the magnitude of crowd liability concerns.

- Cases filed by 18 plaintiffs against the University of Wisconsin in response to a crowd rush in 1993 were dismissed due to government immunity. The plaintiffs claimed the university knew about the potential danger, but failed to take appropriate actions. The defendants claimed they did everything in their power to protect the fans (Balousek, 1996).
- A woman sued the Atlanta Braves and Terry Pendleton for injuries she received when Pendleton tossed a ball to her in the stands. She dropped the ball and a mad scramble ensued where she was injured (Rosenberg, 1996).
- New York city high schools have placed a limit on the number of fans that could attend basketball games ("Schools rule rowdy crowds off-limits at sports events, 1991).
- A brawl in the last minutes of a high school football game led to eight police being officers injured and four arrests ("Four arrests after football game brawl," 1992).
- A soccer match brawl in South Africa led to 42 deaths ("Soccer match deaths bring inquiry," 1991).
- The parents of a boy who got his foot stuck in an escalator at Giants Stadium sued the facility claiming they failed to install an inexpensive safety device that would have prevented the injury (Zambito, 1996).
- An Ohio jury awarded a photographer $906,000 (reduced 35 percent for plaintiff's contributory negligence) for injuries he suffered when he was following regulations (kneeling behind a set line), but was hit by two players. The videotaper claimed that the policy forcing him to kneel mad it impossible for him to quickly move out of the players' way (*Gallagher v. Cleveland Browns Football Co.*, OH, Cuyahoga County, C.C.P., No. 178718, Dec. 11, 1991, Law Reporter, September, 1992, P. 266).
- The Michigan Speedway race track added 2-feet of fencing to one turn (for a total of 17 feet) after a crash sent a wheel into

the stands killing three and injuring six others ("Track heightens fence in wake of fatal crash," 1998).

- In a monster truck accident, the truck overturned killing a teenager on the sidelines ("Teen killed at truck show," 1997).

These represent just some of the vast number of cases or incidents where fans seeking a good time left with injuries or suffered more serious injuries possibly due to the negligence of the event administrator.

The duties owed to event participants are as diverse as the number of sports people can enjoy. Besides participants, you and the safety committee also owe a duty to spectators. Even if only one spectator is at the event, that person needs to be supervised. The more spectators present at the event, the greater the likelihood of an accident. Thus, no matter how many spectators are present, you owe them a duty to provide a reasonably safe environment. Providing a reasonably safe environment is not just a risk management concern, but a marketing concern. Spectators are interested in attending and spending money at a safe facility.

Every sport has its own unique characteristics that can influence the duty you owe. Fans at a professional wrestling match might be very boisterous, but they normally only shout at the participants. On the other hand, some baseball and football fans can get into fights over their favorite teams.

A basic assumption in this section is that the facility used for the event has been constructed before the event by a third party. The requirements associated with constructing safe athletic facilities are not within the scope of this guide. However, just because another person constructed the facility does not absolve you of a duty to provide a safe facility. You could be negligent if you are on notice that the facility has or had a defect that has not been repaired. Unfortunately, many facilities have potential problems that you may only discover through inspecting the premises after you have already agreed to its use. Thus, a contract provision should be included allowing you to inspect the facility and to back out of the contract if significant defects are discovered.

The written rental agreement received upon renting a facility should also specifically provide that the facility lessor has informed you of all known, reported or repaired hazards. You should also try to review maintenance records, accident reports or incident reports to help determine problem areas. If the lessor is unwilling to provide any information, you should be suspicious that possible problems might exist. The refusal to provide documentation could put you on notice that there is a potential facility defect. If you cannot inspect a facility's documentation, you should have the facility owner or manager sign a declaration indicating that you have been warned about all dangers they reasonably could have discovered.

The major duties you have are inspecting the facility to ensure safety, warning spectators about potential dangers and properly managing the crowd.

Inspection

The basic duty you owe to spectators was stated best in the *Johnson* case. In *Johnson v. Zemel* (160 A. 2d 356 (NJ 1932)) the court concluded that when an owner lets out a facility for a public purpose, he thereby holds out to the public that the facility is safe; he is bound to use reasonable care to see that the facility has been properly constructed and maintained in fit condition for the purpose for which it is used; and he is responsible for injuries resulting from his failure in that regard. In essence, the court concluded that the facility owner has an affirmative duty to make sure the facility is safe for the activity for which it is being used.

If spectators are expected at your event, you should make every effort to ensure the area where the spectators will be situated is hazard free.

Bleachers

Because bleacher benches can be perched high off the ground, you should make sure all steps, seats, hand rails, restraining rails, stadium "top rows" and seat backs are in a reasonably safe condition.

Stoud v. Bridges
275 S.W. 2d 503 (TX 1955)

Husband and wife, Horace and Essie Bridges, sued J.C. and Vernon Stoud, owners of the Tyler Baseball Club, for the death of their son Louis Bridges. Louis Bridges, a minor, fell backwards off the top of the stadium grandstand at the Tyler East Texas ball park. The minor landed on his head on the concrete walkway several feet below.

The parents alleged that the Stoud's failed to provide a safe backrest or one sufficiently strong enough to prevent a patron from falling backwards, or in the alternative, the grandstand was defective. The lower court's jury held that the Stouds were negligent because the seat back could have been inspected and repaired with only a minimal amount of work. The appellate court affirmed the jury verdict.

Special care has to be taken with steps, gaps in floorboards and gaps between the seats and floorboards because a child or a person's leg could fall between these gaps. If such gaps exist, small children should not be allowed to walk through the bleachers unsupervised. On a regular basis, all seats, floor boards, seat-backs, overhanging (mezzanine) or double tiered bleachers and other facility seating features should be inspected for structural aging, soundness, warping, cracking, loose or exposed components and general deterioration.

Walkways and aisles should be clearly marked, painted with non-skid footing material, have no cracks or splinters and be free of debris or spilled liquids. Seating and riser boards should not contain any splinters, broken boards, exposed hardware (bolts/screws) or jagged metal. Bleacher handrails should be firmly attached, smooth and without any corrosion.

Bleacher location is also very important. Especially with movable bleachers, the authors recommend that you should make sure the bleachers are at least six feet away from the playing area. If possible, 12 to 15 feet would be an even safer distance. Unfortunately, many high school gyms were constructed in such a manner that the seating area can be less than three feet from a basketball court's endlines. It is often impossible to change this potentially hazardous set-up. If the gym floor is being resurfaced, new lines could be painted that allow additional room to help provide additional space for spectators. If this option is not available, you should block-off the first row or two. The empty seats would allow a player to stop at the bleachers without running into or tripping over any fans.

Walkways

Over the past thirty years, many stadiums have been built with concourses or walkways where fans can purchase concession items while still watching the competition. Walkways around the stadium should be constructed with shatterproof plastic extending over the top of any half-walls. If there is no protection over the half-walls, especially in baseball, a spectator in line to buy some food or use the restroom could get hit by an unseen projectile. While this possibility is quite remote, it has occurred.

Jones v. Three Rivers Management Corporation
394 A. 2d 546 (PA 1978)

Evelyn Jones was injured while attending the opening day game at Three Rivers Stadium on July 16, 1970. Built into the concourse wall above right field, were large openings through which pedestrians could look out over the playing field and stands. Jones was standing near one large opening when she was struck in the eye by a ball hit during batting practice. Jones had diverted her attention from the opening to go to a food concession stand when the ball hit her.

The lower court's jury held for Jones. However, the appellate court reversed the lower court's ruling. The appellate court's ruling was based on the ordinary rules applicable to all risks that may be present in a baseball stadium. These risks include the risk of being hit by a foul ball.

Walkways should be clean, free of holes or cracks and adequately lighted. Any protrusions or obstructions in the walkways should be eliminated. A good, smooth, unobstructed surface is especially important when people are rushing in or out of the facility. As highlighted earlier on in the text, trip and fall cases are the most common type of claim brought against sports facilities. Special attention should be spent looking for protruding fixtures such as fire extinguishers, water fountains or other items that can block or hinder traffic. During an emergency, when people start to scramble, a rough or slippery walkway could trip-up someone, leading to that person being trampled by other spectators. Walkways should be inspected throughout the event. Specific individuals should be assigned to pick-up trash, clean liquid spills and monitor passageways throughout the event.

Warnings

Warnings are critical for any activity, but courts can be used to help determine whether or not a warning was indeed adequate or effective. In one recent case a woman sued the Texas Rangers after she fell from the upper deck and claimed the railing was inadequate and there existed inadequate warnings about the railing. The railing was 30-inches high and city code only required the railing to be 26 inches high. Furthermore, the Rangers claimed an usher warned the woman three times not to sit on the railing (Shurmaitis, 1996). Even if you have someone providing oral warnings, a plaintiff can still claim that they were not provided with any written warnings.

Even with foul balls in baseball which are considered an inherent risk in the game (see below), individuals can claim that they still need a warning for what others might call an open and obvious danger. A spectator sued the Chicago White Sox after being hit by a foul ball. The White Sox pointed to the law in Texas, Michigan, Missouri and Pennsylvania that clearly states that a fan assumes the obvious risk of being hit by a foul ball and baseball clubs in those states do not need to provide any additional warnings. However, the Illinois court held that that was not the rule in Illinois and that the club needed to provide a warning that would be adequate to enable the fan to avoid the harm or to otherwise protect themselves. The Sox claimed they provided warnings on three separate occasions including:

- flashing a warning on the scoreboard,
- the caveat printed on the back of the ticket (even though the part with the warning was taken at the admission gate),
- a public address announcement which provided that:

> Also, the White Sox ask that all fans be alert and aware of thrown or batted balls. And bats that may leave the field of play and enter the seating area. The risk of injury to a spectator is greatly increased by those who do not pay attention to the play in progress. Thank You!!(at 50).

The court concluded that the three warnings might be adequate, but it was up to a jury to determine if they in fact were adequate to discharge the club's duty to warn (*Coronel v. Chicago White Sox, Ltd.*, 595 N.E. 2d 45 (ILL.App. 1 Dist. 1992).

The duty to warn typically applies to risks the spectators might not know about. Typically, you do not owe a duty to warn someone about risks that are so obvious that any reasonable person would know about the risks. Most people in the United States have at least seen one baseball game (on television, at a ballpark or at the movies), thus most courts hold this prior experience provides the spectator with notice that foul balls are often hit into the stands. However in other sports where the knowledge of the risks is not as widespread, more people have recovered due to their limited risk knowledge. Hockey is one such sport where traditionally there has not been as much public knowledge concerning the spectator risks inherent in the sport. Since you can never assume how much knowledge someone might have, you should always provide the highest quantity and quality of oral, visual and written warnings.

The key question is how much warning must you provide to discharge your duty to warn?

Keys v. Alamo City Baseball Company
150 S.W. 2d 368 (TX 1941)

Frieda Keys was attending only her second baseball game. A large crowd was in attendance at the Alamo City Baseball Club game due to a special "Ladies Night" promotion. Only 300 to 400 seats remained unoccupied. Patrons had a choice of sitting in the screened or the unscreened sections. Keys was at the game with her 14 year-old son, and had watched her son play baseball on numerous occasions. Keys had been sitting in the unscreened section for five or six innings and had seen several foul balls enter the stands. At the time Keys was hit by a foul ball, she was not paying any attention to the game, but was talking to a friend several rows behind her.

The lower court judge granted a judgment not withstanding the verdict for the baseball club. The appellate court affirmed the lower court's decision and also specifically indicated that it would be absurd to require the ticket seller or other employees to warn each patron that he or she would be imperiled by a "vagrant baseball" if they sat in the unscreened section. Thus, a patron who chooses to sit in an unscreened section assumed the risk of being struck by a batted ball.

Most spectators have turned over an admission ticket and seen some writing on the back. The value of these ticket-back warnings has been debated because some courts feel these warnings are too general. Even with additional warnings such as signs and pre-game announcements, some courts still feel that additional warnings might need to be provided. The *Coronel* court reasoned that spectators cannot and do not always watch where a foul ball is going as the spectator might be talking, eating food, buying items from a vendor or looking in another direction. In response to *Coronel* case and a similar case against the Chicago Cubs, the Illinois legislature passed special legislation changing the law and creating the assumption of risk standard for baseball fans hit by foul balls in Illinois.

Courts have concluded that to be effective, warnings have to inform spectators about the widest possible risk to which a spectator may be subject. Thus, specific warnings, not general warnings, are required for effective ticket backs or any other warnings.

Falkner v. John E. Fetzer, Inc.
317 N.W. 2d 337 (MI 1982)

Kathy Falkner was injured on May 11, 1975 at Tigers Stadium in Detroit, Michigan when she was hit by a foul ball. Falkner claimed that Fetzer failed to make the stadium safe by:

- failing to provide screening in the area in which she sat,
- failing to inform her about the availability of screened seats,
- failing to offer her the choice of screened or unscreened seats,
- failing to provide a sufficient number of screened seats,
- failing to warn her by sign(s) about the hazard of being hit by a foul ball.

The lower court jury ruled for Falkner in the amount of $250,000. Fetzer contended on appeal that even if they owed a duty, that duty was discharged through the warning on the back of the ticket and by a pre-game announcement. The appellate court concluded that the warnings on the back of the ticket along with an announcement at the start of the game might not be enough, and a jury could determine whether Fetzer's conduct was reasonable. The appellate court realized there was no duty to warn spectators about the obvious risks in baseball, but a jury could determine that a warning might be required for plays with a high degree of risk. The appellate court reversed the lower court's verdict because Falkner failed to show that if a proper warning was given, she would have moved to a screened seat. Thus, the proximate cause element of a negligence claim was missing.

Each event has a different spectator-warning requirement. Some well-documented warning requirements have been established for baseball, hockey, football and motor sports. These requirements and safety issues are discussed below.

Baseball

There is generally no duty to warn spectators about the obvious risks faced by baseball spectators. One of the most obvious risks involved in baseball are foul balls hit into the stands. Courts assume that since baseball is America's "favorite pastime," everyone should know that foul balls are often hit into the grandstands. Most spectators assume the risk of being hit by a foul ball because they *have witnessed foul balls in previous baseball games. Spectators also assume the risk of being hit by a foul ball when they sit in an unscreened area.*

Kavafian v. Seattle Baseball Club Association
181 P. 679 (WA 1919)

Kavafian sat in the grandstands owned and operated by the Seattle Baseball Club. He was entitled to sit wherever he wanted. He chose a seat in an unscreened section. There were numerous screened seats available for his use.

The court concluded that he assumed the risk of sitting in the unscreened area when he had the opportunity to safely sit behind the screened area. Thus, a precedence was established that spectators normally assume risk associated with being hit by foul balls in the grandstand and cannot recover for such injuries.

While the *Kavafian* court held for the defendants, another issue arises when there exists an inadequate number of seats in a protected area. In *O'Neil v. City of Newark*, a young infant and his mother were watching a softball game. There were no more seats behind the backstop where a 20 foot high fence stood. The two sat in another section they thought was protected, but the fence where the ball came over and hit the todller was only five feet six inches high. The case settled for $900,000 (*O'Neil v. City of Newark*, CA, Alameda County, H-154451-0, 1995, Jury Verdicts and Settlements, Vol. 39, No. 5, Feb. 3, 1995, P. 4).

There is no set standard for how much *screening* is required. If less than 30 feet of screening is provided at a professional baseball park, you could anticipate that the screen might be too small. However, a 30-foot screen at a Little League field might be more than adequate. The courts have adopted a flexible standard for the amount of baseball screening required. You have to *provide enough screening for the number of spectators that might want protection (Coronel*, 1992). If you know that more spectators want screening, then you have to provide additional screening. If a spectator wished to sit behind a screen, but there were no available seats, you could be negligent in not providing enough screened seats.

Providing enough screened seats is not, by itself, enough. The screen has to be in excellent condition. A screened area can almost ensure a patron's safety. Thus, safety conscious patrons should sit behind a screened area with the knowledge that no foul ball can penetrate the screen.

Edling v. Kansas City Baseball and Exhibition Co.
168 S.W. 908 (MS 1914)

Edling visited the ballpark owned by The Kansas City Baseball and Exhibition Company on May 31, 1911 for a game against the "American Association." Edling paid the fifty-cent admissions price and took a seat behind home plate. A screen made with chicken netting was behind the plate to protect patrons from foul balls. The stadium had a seating capacity of 7,000 fans. The court concluded that approximately 700 balls are pitched during a game (and warm-ups) and on average 10 balls were fouled into all directions (the reader should remember that this was a baseball game in 1911; the game has changed tremendously over the past 80 plus years).

The stadium owner claimed to have inspected the netting on a daily basis and made any repairs whenever a defect was found. However, Edling was able to show that the netting was old, worn and rotten. The ball that hit Edling had passed through a hole about a square foot in area, and there were other holes of various sizes throughout the screen. The court felt that the screen had not been repaired in over two seasons.

The court concluded that while the ball club was not an insurer of a patron's safety, however, when they undertook to provide screening, they had to provide reasonably safe screening. The owner did not provide reasonable protection because the hole in the screen was not fixed before the game.

In addition to checking screen size and condition, you should make sure a screen is in place to protect patrons from foul balls hit straight back. Most screens protect patrons behind home plate, but if a foul ball goes straightback over the screen, then the ball could come down behind the screen and hit an unsuspecting spectator. A second screen could be added from the top of the stands or press box to the screen behind home plate to provide additional protection. Netting underneath or on top of the press box can prevent foul balls from hitting the press box and ricocheting down onto fans sitting below. Since the press box can be hit by a foul ball, only shatterproof glass or similar material should be used for the press box.

Hockey

The amount of warning required for hockey games is more difficult to determine because the warning varies with the event's location and the fans' experience. A fan in the New England area would have a broader base of hockey knowledge than someone from New Mexico. Location however, is not the only criterion.

Normal warnings on tickets or public address systems might not be enough for an inexperienced spectator so additional specific warnings would be required.

Shurman v. Fresno Ice Rink, Inc.
205 P.2d 77 (1949)

Marvel Shurman visited the Fresno Ice Rink with her husband on October 28, 1947 to watch a Pacific Coast Hockey League game. This was the Shurman's first hockey game and they knew nothing about the sport. The couple asked for the "best seats in the house." The defendant seated them in the front row immediately adjacent to the ice. A 40-inch railing was below them and just to their side was a protective wire screen used to protect certain seats, especially behind the goal. A player took a shot which became airborne and struck Mrs. Shurman on her chin. She spent eight - 10 days in the hospital, and received 25 or 30 stitches and had several teeth loosened.

The ice rink had 22 signs posted in and about the building, reading: "Warning, Danger from Flying Pucks...Patrons Assume all Risk of Injury from Flying Pucks." Other signs stated that protective screen seats were available to those who asked. Two public address announcements about flying pucks were made during the game.

The court concluded that when a spectator picks his/her own seat and is familiar with the risk of a flying puck, then they could assume the risk of sitting in an unprotected seat. However, in this case the Shurman's asked for the best seat in the house and the management selected the seats for them. Mrs. Shurman did not know the dangers inherent in sitting in an unscreened section. Because she was not familiar with the game, she required additional warnings and the warnings provided by the ice rink was inadequate. The court rejected the common knowledge rule (like baseball, where it is common knowledge that foul balls enter the stands) because at the time of this case (1947) the general public was not that familiar with hockey.

Once a protective screen is present and spectators get accustomed to the protection, then you have to make sure the protective device remains there.

Sawyer v. State
485 N.Y.S.2d 695 (NY 1985)

Joanne Davis a 13 year-old spectator, (her mother, Mrs. Sawyer brought the law suit) was injured when a puck struck her while she watching a hockey game at the State University of New York at Oswego. Davis's lip was injured when a puck shot over the rink's glass barrier hit her. Dasher boards three and one-half feet in height enclosed the rink. Behind each goal and along the sidelines, tempered glass protective barriers, five feet and three feet in height respectively, were mounted on top of the dasher boards. There were no signs posted warning spectators about flying pucks.

The tempered glass barrier was installed in February 1983, approximately one month before the accident. The game was a playoff game and there were over 600 spectators; more than the arena's seating capacity.

The game was Davis's first game at the arena since the tempered glass protector was installed. Since the protective barrier was reduced when the tempered glass replaced the old netting, the University had a duty to tell patrons that there was less protection.

Davis did not assume the risk of being hit by a puck. Thus, the appellate court upheld her $9,000 verdict. The court concluded that the new glass screen was unreasonably used because, at 8 1/2 feet, it was one foot lower then the previous screen. Spectators were not informed about the height change.

Football

Some of the same concerns that affect football spectators also affect basketball games. One concern spectators have in both these sports is being hit by a player going out-of-bounds. Some EAs erect a rope around a football field and allow spectators to stand behind the rope. The problem with roping-off a field is that spectators can push past, under or around the ropes and participants can be tackled out-of bounds past the ropes.

Perry v. Seattle School District #1
405 P.2d 589 (WA 1965)

Louise Perry was a 67-year-old grandmother watching a football game in which her grandson was playing. The game was between the Garfield and West Seattle High Schools third string teams. Perry was not familiar with football games. There were no bleachers provided on the West Seattle sidelines. Since her grandson played for West Seattle, she did not want to sit on the opponent's side, which had two sixty-person bleachers.

Perry was standing on the sidelines at about the 30-yard line when a ball carrier made a wide-end run, running close to the sidelines. Two opposing players threw him out of bounds, and he collided with Perry. Perry was violently thrown to the ground and suffered permanent severe injuries. Perry was not watching the play when she was knocked over.

The court concluded that Perry was contributorily negligent for standing so close to the field. The court also concluded that she was contributorily negligent because she was involved in conversation, instead of watching the play, and she was the only one who did not move away from the oncoming players. Perry claimed that the spectators could have been protected from injury if the school had put up a rope or a fence around the field.

The court rejected this argument because an athlete could be injured running into a barrier or an athlete might roll beneath a rope and injure a spectator.

Spectators should be informed about seat availability. Spectators who stand within a certain area need to be informed that they are viewing the game from that location at their own risk. If you sell all the bleacher tickets, and only sideline tickets remain, an injured spectator on the sidelines might not assume the risk of injury because there are no alternative seats available.

Most football games are played in outdoor stadiums and playing football games in winter can lead to weather-related complications such as snow and ice created hazards.

Hartzell v. U.S.
539 F. 2d 65 (10th Cir. 1976)

Edson Hartzel was a spectator at the United States Air Force Academy stadium for a football game between Air Force and Stanford. The game was held on November 14, 1970. The previous Thursday, a 30-person snow removal crew worked to eliminate snow-related hazards. On Friday, 26 people worked at snow removal. Snow continued to fall on Friday night and a crew of 25–30 people plus 75 high school students worked on snow removal Saturday morning. By 8:00 a.m., over 125 people were trying to remove snow within the stadium. Saturday morning, six people were spreading "Snowmelt" around the stadium. Just prior to the game's start, 10 people were involved in spreading "Snowmelt."

Prior to Hartzel's fall, another spectator slipped on the same stairway and fractured his hip. No announcements about the slippery condition were made over the public address system. Nor were there any warning signs posted.

Hartzel knew there was a lot of snow around the stadium, but he entered the stadium and watched the game through the third quarter. Upon exiting the stadium, Hartzel slipped at the bottom of the stairway and fell down injuring his back and head. The court concluded that the defendant's attempt to remove the hazard was reasonable and the risk of icy steps was so obvious that Hartzel and other spectators did not require a warning about the risk.

Icy conditions and/or slippery surfaces caused by spilled liquids regularly occur throughout stadiums. That is why you should use non-skid paint/tape and special de-icing agents whenever icy conditions present themselves to potential spectators.

Motor Sports

Spectators at a racing event should be warned about the potential hazards present in the grandstands, behind concrete or other protective barriers and in the infield or pit area.

Risks present in the grandstands include cars crashing into or through barriers and car parts (especially tires) flying into the stands after a collision. Luckily, most racetracks have sufficient barricades and netting. Insurance companies often pre-walk a racetrack to ensure the track is safe and the stands are properly protected. If portable grandstands are used, they should be moved back from the track a safe distance. Additionally, each spectator should be given the option of sitting in a location with more protection, and frequent warnings should be given on ticket backs, over loudspeakers and inside the racing program. Similar to baseball or hockey, you should provide enough safe seats for those who might wish to sit in protected seats.

Rogers v. Black Hill Speedway, Inc.
217 N.W. 2d 14 (SD 1974)

Patty Jean Rogers, Dianne Knigge, and Steven Knigge brought separate actions against Black Hill Speedways based on an accident that occurred on July 24, 1970. The three were spectators at the one-half mile, banked, oval racetrack used primarily for stock car racing. A grandstand that held 2,500 people was located on the track's west side. Over 3,700 fans were in attendance on the race date. The track's east side had a fence ranging in height from approximately five to 15 feet. The track management placed spectator benches behind the fence sections that stood fifteen feet high. Track management made no significant effort to dissuade spectators from breaching the so-called restricted area that was located five feet behind the fence. The security force kept moving the spectators out of the restricted area, but the spectators would always move back to a spot right behind the fence.

During the evening's last race, a car went out of control on the Number 2 curve. The car went through the fence and injured the plaintiffs. The plaintiffs thought the area was safe because other spectators were sitting on the grass right behind the straightaway fences.

The racetrack owner was found negligent by the court because even though the area was designated as a "non-spectator" area, track managers did not physically go to the grass area to enforce the "non-spectator" warnings given over the loudspeakers.

Security personnel are not supposed to be used just for show. If spectators need to be moved, security personnel should not just ask them to move and then leave the scene. Security personnel have to take affirmative steps to prevent the spectators from returning to a dangerous area. If that means remaining there for the entire event or calling in the police, the security personnel should take those steps. This principle applies across the board to all sports facilities. One allegation raised in the various lawsuits stemming form the stampeded at Camp Randall Stadium (after the 1993 Michigan v. Wisconsin football game) centered around the security personnel failing to properly clear aisles and keep them clear (Murphy, 1998).

A car going out of control in the infield is fairly common, but many fans and people associated with racing still like to watch the action from the infield or pit area. To protect yourself, you should require an infield spectator to sign a waiver before entering the area. The waiver should inform a spectator about the dangers associated with a car going out of control, exploding or catching fire and the possibility of death or serious injuries due to such an accident.

Waivers can be effective for adults who can assume obvious risks, but they are not effective for children. Thus, children should not be allowed in the infield, as they cannot fully appreciate the inherent risks associated with being in the infield, even if warned. On the other hand, most adults in the infield or pit area assume the risk of injury because the location is considered inherently dangerous.

Miscellaneous Sports

Golf, wrestling and skiing can also provide unique warning requirements. The risks a golf spectator might face include being hit by a ball, tripping in or over a hole or ditch and/or other course dangers. All golf spectators should be warned about different tee-off locations and times, and where shots will be coming from. You should make sure all holes (gopher holes through ditches) and sprinklers are either clearly marked or recessed into the ground. Water hoses should also be properly stored to eliminate a tripping hazard. As with all other sports, you do not have to make the course perfectly safe. Thus, a spectator would probably not win a suit for tripping over a small rock in the rough.

Other potential golf dangers that could require warnings are spectator bridges or grandstands. While the potential for injuries from structures like bridges or grandstands is small, accidents involving these structures have occurred on several occasions.

Rockwell v. Hillcrest Country Club
181 N.W. 2d 290 (MI 1970)

James and Ann Rockwell were injured on July 27, 1963, when a suspension bridge covering the Clinton River and located on the Hillcrest golf course collapsed. Immediately before the bridge gave way, there were approximately 80–100 spectators and a golf cart on the bridge. The spectators were on the bridge to watch a golf tournament on defendant's course. Mrs. Rockwell sustained serious injuries when she fell 25 feet.

The Rockwells' claimed that there were no warning signs stating that the bridge had a maximum 25-person spectator capacity and no oral warning about the potential collapse was given. The plaintiff also claimed that there was no site supervision. The lower court returned a $75,000 verdict for the plaintiff, which was affirmed by the appellate court.

A question that is often asked, is whether or not a golf spectator can sue for being hit by a golf ball while watching an event? The answer to this question would be the same as for a baseball spectator. It is common knowledge that golfers have a hard time controlling their shots. Most spectators at a golf event are accustomed to seeing several shots enter the crowd. Even though most spectators understand this risk, it is still a good idea to place a warning on all admission tickets, in the event program and posted signs around the course.

The EA of a *wrestling* match should make sure all spectators sitting around the ring's apron or barricades are warned that a wrestler could be thrown out of the ring. Similarly *ski* spectators, wishing to watch the race from behind the course fences or ropes should be warned that a skier could lose control and crash through the fence or leave the course boundaries.

Crowd Management

EAs must arrange facilities to promote effective spectator movement while avoiding the potential for injuries caused by overcrowding spectators. The right balance has to be reached between these two goals, but it is often hard to find. For example, ropes, cones or barriers can help direct traffic, but they should not be used in a manner that unduly hinders traffic or causes a tripping hazard.

Roping-off an area can be dangerous because someone could be pushed or trip over the ropes. A low-slung rope might be dangerous because spectators could be injured attempting to jump over the rope. It is more effective and safer to use yellow police or construction style "hazard" tape or other flexible markers. All exits should be freely accessible, unlocked and clearly marked. Blocking an exit could also lead to potential injuries or a stampede.

The safety committee should develop and implement specific strategies and policies for dealing with potential crowd problems. Most crowd control issues deal with the conduct of security personnel. For example, security personnel for football games should:

- keep the fans content,
- maintain order,
- reduce tensions,
- prevent fence scaling,
- prevent fans from rushing the field,
- prohibit the raising of goal posts.

The risk of not stopping destructive behavior can be seen in the previously mentioned *Cimino* case where a torn down goalpost injured a spectator. While preventing a field rush or scaling goalposts is an important concern, the safety committee also has to determine when the crowd is just too large and that more injuries would occur if security personnel prevent rushing the field. In the previously mentioned Camp Randall Stadium stampede, the police pulled back to the goal posts once the student onslaught occurred. This tactic helped reduce the total number of injuries (Murphy, 1998).

Crowd control policies should also discuss how to treat fans when they are a threat to other spectators or themselves. This potential problem frequently occurs with drunk and or boisterous fans seated in an opposing team's spectator section.

Kiser v. City of Anaheim, No. 88-6125

April 26,1990 Ninth Circuit Court of Appeals

The plaintiff and a friend were causing a disruption in the stands. The police, who were trying to avoid a violent confrontation, escorted the two out of the area. The police felt the plaintiff could become violent. Thus, when his friend pushed one of the officers, the police were forced to use a painful finger-hold on the plaintiff. The court upheld the lower court's decision concluding that the finger-hold was reasonable and justified due to the potentially "very volatile and explosive" situation involving hostile fans.

Besides policies for handling problem spectators, the event safety committee can reduce crowd problems by:

- using separate and distinct spectator sections,
- positioning visible security officers,
- moving the event to a neutral sight,
- not having any spectators at the event,
- playing the event at an unusual hour (i.e. early afternoon basketball/football games for high schools)
- monitoring the crowd with surveillance cameras,
- utilizing foot- and bike- patrols.
- utilizing undercover officers,
- requiring all fans to pass through metal detectors,
- canceling events and/or prohibiting larger crowds than what the event staff can handle.

Conclusion

While sport participants understand the repercussions of not following the rules, spectators often do not have the same appreciation. Participants will know that they will possibly be tested for drugs so they will not try to engage in any activity that can jeopardize their ability to participate. Spectators on the other hand might consider sneaking alcohol into a facility a game. Spectators might think about outsmarting the security and staying one step ahead of others. While some participants try to navigate around the rules, the group-think mindset in the stands could make some fans feel like they are invincible and will not be caught.

The key to spectator safety is proper communication. Spectators need to know the safety rules and be warned about both obvious and hidden hazards. Fire, weather, evacuation and related safety plans need to be posted and communicated on a regular basis. Besides just developing and communicating policies, you need to practice what you preach. Fire drills and evacuation procedures need to be tested on a regular basis to learn what concerns might arise. Concerns could include how to extract a wheelchair user from the facility and when should that person be removed to avoid any traffic congestion issues which could lead to a greater potential loss of lives. Furthermore, exits can become clogged if traffic patterns are not studied and event staff trained on how to help clear a facility. These are only some of the basic concerns associated with facility spectators issues. Numerous additional issues can arise such as spectator free speech, the right of disabled spectators and even non-spectator concerns raised by those not attending an event (such as neighbors suing for nuisance because the facility lights are too bright). It is beyond the scope of this guide to deal with every single spectator related concern. However, you can be certain that the same risks faced by any business from those using their facility such as slipping in the store or tripping on the sidewalk in front of the store represent the same concerns raised by spectators. A possible rule of thumb would be for an EA to spend as much time (or more) on the safety of spectators as they do on the safety of event participants. The greater the number of spectators.....the higher your duty.

Additional areas of concern that need to be addressed when dealing with spectators include operating a concession stand(s), selling alcohol at the event, and monitoring the event's parking lot. These three areas have been separated from the other duties associated with event spectators because they are often overlooked and they deserve special attention.

Chapter 29

Concessions

Most sports fans are accustomed to attending their favorite sporting event and purchasing their favorite Polish sausage from either a stadium hawker or a concession stand. You should make sure all the food products sold are of the highest quality and without any defects.

Some potential food concerns include:

- spoiled food,
- ineffective refrigeration systems,
- the use of old or dirty oil in deep fryers,
- using unclean utensils,
- insufficiently heated food (*simonella* threat),
- using dented cans,
- using poor quality food.

These are only some possible concerns associated with selling food-related items. You could be negligent if you sell hot dogs that have been exposed to inappropriate temperatures, were cooked on dirty rollers or were served with spoiled relish. Because a reasonable food seller would not serve food in such a haphazard and dangerous manner, your actions would indicate a reckless disregard to the health of spectators, which only means one thing—negligence. The existence of dirty equipment or old food can become an easy case of negligence if a fan receives food poisoning from eating food cooked under such dangerous conditions. If however, the equipment was clean, the hot dogs were freshly thawed and all the condiments were fresh, then the *fan would have to prove that it was not something else they ate*, that caused their illness.

You should make sure all food is properly stored and fresh. All the equipment should be regularly cleaned and covered at night to protect the equipment from bacteria, dirt or other health hazards. Deep fryers and other equipment that use oil should have the oil changed on a regular basis. Cooking oil should be changed based on how often the equipment is used, what foods are cooked in the oil, how often the manufacturer recommends changing the oil and how often the health department requires oil changes.

To help establish a record for the proper concession operations, you should develop and use a checklist to determine when new food is purchased, old food is thrown away, equipment is cleaned and when oil is changed. A sample checklist can be found in Appendix K.

To supplement a checklist, you should make sure a health inspector examines the food preparation and service areas on a regular basis (according to appropriate statutes or codes). Most concession operators fear health inspectors, but if the operation is clean there should be nothing to fear. However, if the operation is unclean the health inspector can require changes before spectators forces a change through an injury. An inspector's report indicating clean premises can be an important tool in fighting a suit claiming negligent food handling/processing. Conversely an inspector's report indicating poor conditions and documenting health hazards could be a key evidentiary fact in a spectator's suit.

Non-Food Items

Manufacturers of defective souvenirs can be liable for any injuries resulting from their defective products. However, you could still be named in a suit for a defective product, due to your duty to sell safe products. You should closely inspect all products sold and determine whether the item unduly exposes a purchaser to harm. If you know a product is dangerous or have heard about a potential hazard with a product, that product should not be sold any under circumstance. It cannot be stressed enough that you should make sure souvenirs and food items are not packaged in plastic bags that a child could suffocate on. All plastic bags should be clearly marked that they represent a potential choking hazard to children.

As concession operators and hawkers are normally employed by an EA or are volunteers working for an EA, you should make sure they conduct their work in a safe manner. While it might be a crowd-pleasing show when a vendor throws a bag or item to a purchaser, if they cannot control the object they are throwing, someone hit by the object might not feel their injury was humorous. An EA would not have to be as concerned about independent contractors as long as the contract contains an indemnity clause.

Concession stands should be designed to avoid patron congestion or pushing and shoving to get in line. Some authorities suggest that concession stands should be closed during competition and only opened during intermissions. Other authorities recommend leaving the concession stand open at all time. Either way, you have to make sure there are a sufficient number of trained, uniformed security personnel visible during intermissions and at the end of the event to help manage the spectator traffic flow.

Areas around the concession stand can quickly become very dirty. Sodas and beer can spill, greasy food can be dropped on the ground, napkins or containers can be dropped or trash can cover-up a dangerous area. Special care should be taken to ensure all areas in and around concession stands and bathrooms are cleaned-up at regular intervals during the event. Sticky or slippery areas should be cleaned up as soon as possible, especially in and around stairs. *A clean facility can help ensure spectator safety.*

Conclusion

While concession related concerns might not be the greatest potential threat you might face as an EA, attention to details throughout an event are the hallmark for running a safe event. Serving fresh and safe food from a hazard free concession area are the starting point for reducing concession related risk. Other concession related risks could include: employee theft of products and money. Parking attendants and concessionaires need to be closely monitored for employee theft as the loss of money is a significant risk for any event. Some facilities have installed surveillance cameras to stop criminal mischief and these cameras have often become most useful in identifying criminal conduct of a facility's own employees rather than the criminal act of third parties.

Numerous facilities are now instituting new policies for the sale and/or distribution of beverages. Bottled beer used to be sold in many stadiums, but the threat of an empty bottle being used as a projectile or a weapon has ended that practice. Selling alcohol at a sporting event presents some additional concession-related liability concerns.

Chapter 30

Alcohol

Most stadiums and arenas across the United States have realized the problems associated with intoxicated spectators. Some spectators do not know their drinking limit that creates a very touchy supervisorial situation. Some colleges and national fraternities have banned beer kegs to help reduce drinking related concerns (Dodge, 1991). Each EA has to weigh the additional supervisory responsibilities against the potential income and enjoyment that are possible from selling alcohol at an event. Furthermore, the same concerns that are often raised with spectator drinking at an event also apply to participants who can cause the same injuries (i.e. getting into an accident while leaving the facility).

The amount of supervision required when selling or allowing alcohol at an event is hard to pin-point. It is almost impossible to determine how an intoxicated person will act. Thus, anybody that has had too much to drink should be watched for possible aggression or violence. Unfortunately, it is normally very difficult to determine who is drunk and whether they will become violent.

Ollison v. Weinberg Racing Association
688 P. 2d 847 (OR 1984)

Mary J. Ollison was attending a "Fan Appreciation Night" in January 1980 at defendant's racetrack, Portland Meadows Race Course. Beer was sold on the premises for less than half the ordinary price. A patron named Thurman, fired a gun, causing a stampede which caused Ollison's injuries.

The appellate court remanded the case back for trial because Ollison could conceivably prove that the racing facility could have know that such an event (a shooting by a drunk fan) could occur. The court also concluded that the lack of adequate security could have been a substantial factor in the injury; and even though the exact act (shooting) might not have been foreseen, an injury could be reasonably foreseeable from the facility selling alcohol at less then half price.

To help make the difficult decision concerning whether or not to serve alcohol, you should carefully examine all the duties that will be assumed by selling alcoholic beverages at the event. Facility managers across the country have examined whether or not to serve alcohol to patrons. This has led many facilities to prohibit alcohol sales after a certain point in the event. Facility apprehension to selling alcohol after a certain point during an event can be traced back to regulations called "dram shop" or social host liability acts. A dram shop is defined as a drinking establishment. These acts allow a person injured by an intoxicated individual to receive financial compensation from the person or institution that served alcohol to the intoxicated individual. These acts normally prohibit selling alcohol to someone under the legal drinking age, or serving alcohol to someone who was already intoxicated before being served another drink.

Beseke v. Garden Center, Inc.
401 N.W. 2d 428 (MN 1987)

Daniel Modert and Daniel Holmquist were students at Alexandria Vocational Technology Institute when they signed up for a "Bowl-A-Thon" held at Garden Center Lanes. Approximately 130 students attended the event held from 11:00 p.m. to 2:30 a.m. The school's agents supervised the event. The two students were intoxicated and were asked by defendant's manager to leave the event. The manager and the school's agent removed the two from the bowling alley. Shortly after leaving, the police found the two in a car that had been involved in a rollover accident. Modert died in the accident and his guardian Arlene Beseke brought suit, claiming Garden Center illegally sold alcohol to the two knowing they were already intoxicated.

The court concluded that the school had no duty to supervise the activity of its students who were over the legal drinking age. The school acted as a social host and did not give or furnish any alcohol. Beseke tried to use a Minnesota statute that created liability for anyone selling alcohol to someone illegally or who caused intoxication. However, the court did not accept that argument because the school did not sell any alcohol. The court opinion *did not* mention whether or not the bowling alley was held liable for providing drinks.

In a fraternity related case, the court's conclusion was different as there was direct proof that the fraternity served the alcohol. A lacrosse club was sued after an initiate died after consuming a significant amount of alcohol at a club sponsored event. The court concluded that the club did not have to force someone to drink to be liable. Rather, the court concluded that as long as the initiate thought he was required to drink to join the club and joining the club was valuable to the person, there exists pressure to drink. Thus, the court allowed the suit to proceed against the club members (*Haben v. Anderson*, 597 N.E. 2d 655 (Ill. App. Ct. 1992).

Alcohol Screening

If you decide that no alcohol can be carried into or sold at the event then you have to make sure that all event personnel follow the policy very closely.

Allen v. Rutgers, State University of New Jersey
523 A. 2d 262 (NJ 1987)

Tom Allen was a fraternity member participating at a party during a Rutgers University football game. The game was held on October 18, 1980. Prior to the game and during the game, Allen had a large quantity of "grain punch" which was a mixture of fruit punch and 180 proof grain alcohol. The University had a policy against drinking alcoholic beverages during football games. The University checked packages before spectators entered the stadium, but security was loose. Due to slack security, the fraternity brothers were able to smuggle in a five to ten gallon grain punch container.

At one point in the game the fraternity brothers attempted a "Rude Gaver" in which, dressed in costumes, they would enter the track at half time and run a 1/4-mile race. Security personnel prevented the students from entering the track area. Allen along with several other fraternity brothers attempted to enter on the other side of the stadium. After being stopped again, Allen tried jumping over a four-foot wall. Allen did not realize there was a 30-foot drop from the wall and he sustained serious and permanent injuries from hitting the cement.

The question sent to the jury was whether or not the University breached its duty by failing to prevent the admission of alcohol in the stadium. The jury returned a verdict for the University because Allen was unable to prove that his injuries were proximately caused by the University's failure to enforce its policy. Allen also tried to impose the duty of a tavern owner (under a dram shop act) to the University, but the court felt that this analogy was inappropriate. The University was not similar to a tavern because it did not sell beer, thus they could not control the plaintiff's drinking.

This case could have been avoided if the university security personnel had followed the regulation and checked all packages for alcohol. No bottled or canned alcohol drinks should be allowed into your event. Event personnel should be on the lookout for hidden flasks, drinking pouches, fake binoculars with beverage compartments and any other means by which fans try to sneak in drinks. You should inspect the facility and parking lots to make sure beer kegs are not brought to the event. You should also keep an eye out for individuals serving alcohol to minors.

Conclusion

The point to remember when examining whether or not to have alcohol at an event is whether you can effectively supervise alcohol or exercise reasonable control of alcohol drinkers. If you cannot, then ALCOHOL SHOULD NOT BE SERVED! However, one way to avoid most alcohol-related concerns is to contract with an outside vendor to be responsible for all alcohol sales. The contractual arrangement can specifically indicate that they will assume all alcohol-related liability.

Chapter 31

Parking

Parking provides a unique blend of circumstances that at times are under your control and at other times open to influenced from people both within and external to your event. For example, baseball fans park and watch a game while football fans make a day of the game including tailgate parties. Game time affects the parking lot as day games for football produce crowds for most of the day while afternoon baseball games have a more condensed time window ("Outside the arena, parking is the name of the game," 1997). Traffic congestion problems can be a big problem. For example, baby boomers arrive at a concert right before it starts while country music fans arrive early and rock fans leave later than all other concert fans ("Outside," 1997).

Parking is an unusual topic compared to decisions about potential athletic equipment, how much supervision is required or the gym floor to be used. However, parking lots are essential for any event expecting a large crowd. There are specific duties you have when using parking lots. The duties are established based on who owns or controls the parking area. If spectators or participants find parking on the street or in parking lots not under your control or supervision, then they normally park at their own risk. However, you owe a duty to protect individuals in authorized parking lots from all known or reasonably foreseeable risks. You also owe a duty to inform spectators about risks associated in adjoining lots or facilities if the area is a high crime area.

The criminal acts of a third party are often unpredictable, but you can learn significant information from the mindset individuals have when dealing with parking. Males examine safety in terms of the safety for their vehicle while women analyze their personal safety. Furthermore convenience is more important than safety for male customers and vice-a-versa for females ("Survey shows customers have dim view of parking," 1998). Parking garages and parking lots can represent significant opportunities for criminals to hide and attack an individual. The liability for such assaults can be immense. Over 40 percent of all security claims filed against retail and mall owners involve parking lot related crimes (Pitorri, 1998). Another study indicated that 20 percent of all facility security claims involve parking facilities and the average award for those cases was $575,000 (Monahan, 1997). One jury awarded a woman attacked and killed in a mall parking garage over $3.5 million for inadequate security (Pitorri, 1998). One point raised in a similar case with a $2.1 million award was the fact that the garage attendant had worked a 14-hour shift and fell asleep and did not hear the woman's screams (Pitorri, 1998).

Various techniques from survailance cameras to security guards can be utilized to make parking safer. Wal-Mart conducted a test at a Tampa site which had previously experienced 226 car thefts, 25 purse snatchings, 32 burglaries and 14 armed robberies. By adding a security golf cart and a uniformed employee they cut down the parking lot crime to zero (Lee, 1997).

Another concern is fights between individuals that start in an unsupervised parking lot. The "lets take this outside" mentality often leads to fights in facility parking lots.

Bishop v. Fair Lanes Georgia Bowling, Inc.
803 F.2d 1548 (11th Cir. 1986)

The Bishop group of three bowlers were bowling at the Fair Lanes Bowling Alley when they noticed their pitcher of beer was missing. The group was attending a "Midnight Madness" bowling extravaganza and arrived at approximately 1:00 a.m. The Bishop group asked several other bowlers (Burke group) whether or not they took the beer. The other group denied the accusation and became belligerent and confrontational. A heated exchange lasted for up to 30 minutes. The Burke group suggested they go outside to settle the matter, but no fists were raised and no punches were thrown. The Burke group was visibly intoxicated when they were at the alley, but they were still sold additional beer.

Members of the Bishop group complained to the bowling alley manager, but nothing was done and the Burke party was not moved to other lanes. The Burke group proceeded to harass and taunt the Bishop group until the alley closed at 2:30 a.m. The Bishop group waited until the Burke group left the alley and then exited. A violent melee occurred in the parking lot when the Burke group attacked the Bishop group. Bishop was beaten unconscious.

The court concluded that the alley's management was negligent in not anticipating the potential physical altercation between the two groups. The court's decision was based in part on the fact that the bowling alley manager did not make the facility safe (i.e. by expelling the Burke group or watching/escorting the parties in the parking lot).

In a contrasting case at a baseball stadium parking lot, a patron was jumped by two drunks. The court held against the plaintiff and indicated that no security measures could have prevented the drunks from attacking someone (*Noble v. Los Angeles Dodgers, Inc.*, 168 CA3d 912 (1985)).

Conclusion

Based on the size, terrain and surrounding environments, parking lots can be a significant injury threat. This chapter has primarily addressed assault related issues. However, there are countless additional concerns such as trip and fall issues, negligent valet service, thefts from vehicles, broken windshields from foul balls and a host of additional concerns. One of the best means to handle such concerns is appropriate signage to educate everyone about specific risks and to let them know about what risks they assume by parking in the lot/garage.

In addition, you should post security personnel around the parking lot after an event to make sure spectators can reach their vehicles safely, and to spot intoxicated individuals that should not be allowed to drive. Unlike a personal dinner party where the host can control his or her guests, during an event you might feel uncomfortable telling an intoxicated adult not to drive. However, you might have a duty to make sure the intoxicated person does not injure themselves or someone else. Police officers can help make your job a little more comfortable. The presence of police officers at the event parking lot can possibly influence an intoxicated person to forgo driving or a possible ticket.

Chapter 32

Putting the Pieces Together for an Effective Risk Management Program

The duties owed to spectators are similar to the duties owed to participants. Your major duty is to make sure the facility is reasonably safe for its intended use. The major difference between the duties owed each group is that participants participate under the assumption that they might face a risk of being injured while competing. On the other hand, spectators normally do not assume they will be injured while attending an event. Because spectators are not expecting an injury, you have to take additional precautions to ensure the facility is reasonably safe.

You should coordinate your efforts with the safety committee to make sure:

- the facility is properly inspected,
- the parking lot is inspected,
- adequate warnings (printed and oral) are given to the spectators,
- adequate crowd control policies and strategies exist,
- all spectator policies are implemented,
- concessions operations follow the highest safety standards,
- adequate supervision is provided for parking lots.

One of your most important decisions is whether or not to serve alcohol to spectators. Local laws and ordinances can play a major part in deciding if alcohol can be served and under what conditions alcohol can be served. If you decide to have alcohol at the event, then you should make sure:

- alcohol is served in paper/foam/plastic cups,
- alcohol is not served after a certain time,
- cabs are available to drive intoxicated spectators home,
- there is adequate supervision of spectators leaving the event.

You should always remember that developing and implementing sound management policies for protecting spectators is normally based on cir-

339

cumstances, past history and similar facilities. Unfortunately, effective risk management sometimes rests in the hands of chance.

Accidents occur even in the best-managed events. Every event includes an element of chance and if an accident occurs, it does not mean you are not a good event administrator.

This guide was written to present some of the major risks you should recognize when running an event. There are numerous specific and unique risks associated with running an event that did not find their way into this guide. It is beyond the scope of this text, or any other text, to identify each and every concern you might face.

Experience provides the greatest resources for developing risk management plans. Communications and sharing information with other EAs is highly beneficial. To get the best liability picture possible you should try to enlist quality individuals, and if at all possible, an attorney to serve on the event safety committees.

You should always remember that it is better to err on the side of over-supervision than to have inadequate supervision. Over-supervision will not take the glamour from an event. On the contrary, tight supervision puts the event in control so the athletes and spectators can respectively participate in and view the event safely. There is no glamour in receiving an injury that could have been prevented.

The intent and concepts within this guide are synthesized in Appendix L which is a comprehensive risk management facility/program review for a martial arts studio. Every facility/program is different and different risks would be identified throughout the world. Thus, never take a risk management plan developed at one facility and assume that it would apply to every risk a different facility might face.

Appendices

Appendix A

Sexual Abuse
Prevention Manual

The following appendix is a sexual abuse prevention manual utilized by several nonprofit organizations in the United States. The manual first discusses the severity of sexual abuse to help encourage the adoption of a sexual abuse prevention program. The manual then provides specific direction for developing and implementing a sexual abuse prevention program.

Sexual Abuse Risk Management Manual
For Youth Sports/Activities Organizations
Gil B. Fried, M.A., J.D.
University of New Haven
Copyright © 1999

Table of Contents

Introduction 346
Sexual Abuse in Youth Sports (Article) 347
Prevention Manual 368
    Goals, Objectives & Strategies 369
    Policy Statement #1 372
        Forms — List of Contacts for Reporting Suspected
           Cases of Child Abuse, Sexual Abuse, or Neglect ...380
           Child Abuse, Sexual Abuse & Neglect Form 381
           Chart of Child Behavior and Indicators of
           Potential Abuse 382
           Processing Guidelines After A Child Reports
           Sexual Assault/Abuse 384
           Some Interview Do's and Don'ts 385
           Working with the Parents of a Sexually
           Abused Child 386
           Program Checklist 387
    Policy Statement #2 388
    Acknowledgment 391
        Form — Acknowledgment 391
Prevention Program 392
    Volunteer and Employee Screening 392
    Job Description 393
        Form — Model Job Description 395
    Application Form 396
        Forms — Application #1 (employee) 397
           Application #2 (volunteer) 398
           Release 399
    Candidate Selection 400
        Interview 400
           Form — Interview Response Form 403
        References 405
           Form — Reference Interview Form 406
    Placement 408
    Training 409

Supervision 410
Suspension 411
Termination 412
Education 414
Developing Educational Programs for Children 414
Definitions 415
Topics 418
Questions to Ponder 419
Some Practical Steps 420
  Forms — Pre-Test/Post-Test 422
    Key 423
    Sample Letter to Parents 425
    Follow-up Letter to Parents After Program
    Completion 426
Conclusion 427
References 428
Organizations 430

Introduction

Various terms are used to discuss the horrors that can happen to children. Sexual abuse, child abuse, neglect, verbal abuse, negative peer pressure and a host of other terms describe the current state of affairs affecting countless children on a daily basis. The issue is real, the damages are significant, yet we have not been able to produce or develop an immunization to protect children. As long as there are children, there will be individuals who abuse them.

The question is not whether or not we can stop these violations. Rather, the question is how can we arm children, and ourselves with the appropriate skills and information necessary to protect them. This manual is not unlike a variety of other manuals in print. However, this manual focuses primarily on the sports, recreation, and activities industries which present a significant risk due to a variety of factors. These factors include numerous children, numerous adults, emotionally charged environment, educational environment and an environment with a significant amount of physical contact between a participant and other participants and/or supervisors.

This manual was deigned to discuss the issues associated with sexual abuse prevention in the sports context. The manual starts with a recent article adapted from another article written by Gil Fried and published in the Journal of Legal Aspects of Sports (1997). All readers are encouraged to critically read the article which provides specific examples of risk reduction strategies that have proven effective in a variety of programs. The article further provides additional guidance regarding affirmative steps that can be taken both at the local and national level to pass laws which are more "user friendly" for organizations interested in screening applicants.

The manual then provides specific steps to help implement an effective sexual abuse prevention program. Emphasis will focus on developing a specific policy statement to be adopted throughout the organization. Sample policy statements are included to facilitate ease in implementing and preparing a policy statement. Additional information and forms are provided dealing with employee screening and educational programs.

The secret to an effective risk management program designed to reduce the chances of sexual abuse focuses on developing and fostering an organization wide mindset that preventing sexual abuse is critical for the organization's success. There are no easy solutions to protecting our children. However, this manual can be used as the starting point for informing individuals of the problem's magnitude and generating productive discussion within an organization.

Sexual Abuse in Youth Sports

Gil B. Fried, M.A., J.D. [1]

Newspaper headlines throughout the past eight years focused on abuses meted out to female athletes and non-athletes. A notable example of abuse by an athlete was seen in the O.J. Simpson trial which highlighted Simpson's past record of spousal abuse. Media attention also focused on numerous additional cases ranging from abusive coaches, sexual attacks by athletes, sexual harassment between students (even students as young as 5 years old) and sexual assaults and improprieties against athletes.

One incident in Texas highlights the importance of protecting youth engaged in sports, recreation or outdoor activities from a multitude of risks. A nine-year-old girl was abducted from a soccer match, sexually molested and killed. The man refereeing the game was charged with the murder. However, while police were investigating the crime they had a chance to review several video tapes of the game. The police were able to identify four convicted pedophiles who were watching the game in addition to the referee, who was also a known pedophile. Such soccer games are not unique to just Texas. Similar occurrences are happening on a daily basis throughout the United States.

While these events have garnered significant media attention, organizations have begun to be aware of the need to develop comprehensive solutions to the ever increasing problem of sexual abuse in athletic settings. Historically, organizations have often swept sexual improprieties under the carpet, if possible, and then only act to censure such conduct when the incident becomes publicized. Millions of young athletes from youth leagues through interscholastic athletics are at risk to rape, battery, child abuse, sexual assault and molestation. However, significant steps can be taken to reduce the chances of sexual abuse in youth sports through the implementation of a comprehensive sexual abuse prevention program, the implementation of relevant risk management strategies and legislative assistance from a variety of governmental agencies.

Child abuse is a national epidemic affecting over 3 million children in 1994.[2] Approximately 500,000 of these cases involve sexual abuse.[3] Ac-

---

1. Gil B. Fried, Esq. is an Associate Professor at the University of New Haven teaching sports law, sport management, and sports marketing. Mr. Fried received his Masters Degree in Sports Administration and Juris Doctors from The Ohio State University. Prior to joining the University of New Haven faculty, Mr. Fried was the director of the San Francisco based Sports Law Center.

2. NATIONAL COMMITTEE TO PREVENT CHILD ABUSE, NCPCA FACT SHEET, Chicago, IL (1995).

3. John Patterson, CHILD ABUSE PREVENTION PRIMER FOR YOUR ORGANIZATION 1

cording to a 1994 survey, twenty-one percent of all reported child abuse cases involved physical abuse while eleven percent of the reported cases represented sexual abuse against children.[4] Studies of the general adult population show that anywhere from 6 to 63 percent of females were sexually abused as children.[5] In 1992, twelve states reported to the Federal Bureau of Investigation 20,824 forcible rapes of females, of which, 51 percent were juveniles under age 18.[6] While sexual assault usually implies physical confrontation, sexual abuse will be used throughout this text to refer to a wide spectrum of interactions including: rape, physical assault, sexual battery, unwanted physical sexual contact, unwelcomed sexually explicit or offensive verbal communication, coercive or exploitive sexual contact, verbal sexual harassment and/or sexualized attention or contact with a minor by a person in a position of authority.[7]

Why the emphasis on youth sports in particular? Whenever there exists a parental or nurturing environment, children are much more likely to acquiesce to activities they normally would never undertake. Similarly, when

---

Nonprofit Risk Management Center, Washington, DC (1995).

4. National Committee, supra note 2.

5. National Committee, supra note 2. While the exact magnitude of sexual abuse is not known, a Los Angeles Times survey found that 27 percent of women and 16 percent of men claimed to have been sexually abused prior to reaching majority (18). Id, citing Finkelhor, D. A SOURCEBOOK ON CHILD SEXUAL ABUSE (1986). The American Medical Association reported that over 700,000 women are sexually assaulted each year. Richard Saltus, *Doctors Urged to Learn Signs of Sexual Abuse*, HOUSTON CHRONICLE, November 7, 1995, 5A. The AMA's research also concluded that an act of sexual assault occurs throughout the United States every 45 seconds. Id.

6. Patrick Langan, and Caroline Wolf Harlow, *Child Rape Victims, 1992*, CRIME DATA BRIEF, U.S. DEPARTMENT OF JUSTICE, June 1994, 1. The same data provided an estimate that 17,000 of the 109,062 women raped in 1992 were under age 12. Id. at 2.

7. Patterson, supra note 3, at 17-18. See also, Diane DePanfilis and Marsha K. Salus, A COORDINATED RESPONSE TO CHILD ABUSE AND NEGLECT: A BASIC MANUAL 7, National Center on Child Abuse and Neglect, U.S. Department of Health and Human Services, Washington, DC (1992). Abusive sexual assault is clinically broken down into three differential categories: power (where one party controls the other either through power or position such as a teacher or coach), knowledge (where one party cannot appreciate the consequences of the relationship) and gratification differential (where only one party will be gratified by the sexual encounter). Kathleen Coulborn Faller, CHILD SEXUAL ABUSE: INTERVENTION AND TREATMENT ISSUES 10-11, National Center on Child Abuse and Neglect, U.S. Department of Health and Human Services, Washington, DC (1993). The National Center on Child Abuse and Neglect has identified the potential for sexual abuse by a coach in an example of non-contact sexual abuse as follows: "[A] coach told a team member he had a fine body, and they should find a time to explore one another's bodies. He told the boy he had done this with other team members, and they had enjoyed it." Id. at 12.

the expertise of one person places them in a position of authority over another, the expectation of compliance is clear. Such an environment is the norm between a coach and an athlete. One athlete described the relationship as follows: "When I look at my coach, I look for someone who is doing the right thing, someone who can show me how to do the right thing. They are like surrogate parents who you look up to. I never felt that way about a teacher. It's a different relationship, and so the standards are different."[8] Furthermore, the more the coach is admired and held in awe by the athlete, the more his or her wishes will be followed.[9]

Another reason why stopping sexual assaults in youth sports is so important can be found in the empirical research which shows that 70%-80% of adult sexual offenders, were sexually victimized as children.[10] By providing a safer environment for children to learn socialization and teamwork skills without being exposed to possible sexual assault in that specific sports environment can hopefully reduce the number of future abusers. While helping to curtail sexual assault in youth sports organizations is a start, children can face sexual assault in countless environments and surroundings which are impossible to control.

This guidebook will present potential risk management strategies that can be deployed by a youth sports organization to reduce the chances of sexual assault occurring within their programs. The guidebook consists of a brief article discussing critical issues in sexual abuse prevention and then provides the appropriate material to help implement a sexual abuse prevention program. The article will examine the laws currently in place, civil liability examples, specific prevention strategies currently utilized by some youth sports organizations, specific risk management strategies and finally proposed legislation that could assist youth sports organizations fight the problem of sexual abuse.

The Law

Criminal sexual assault cases often revolve around school settings and the special relationship that exists between teachers, coaches, administra-

---

8. Debra Blum, Coaches as Role Models, CHRON. HIGHER EDUC., June 2, 1995, A36. See also Gil Fried, *Applying the First Amendment to Prayer in a Public University Locker Room: An Athlete's and Coach's Perspective*, 4 MARQ. SPORTS L. QUAR. 2, Spring 1994, 301, at 311-312.

9. D. STANELY EITZEN, *The Dark Side of Coaching and the Building of Character*, SPORTS IN CONTEMPORARY SOCIETY 133 (1989).

10. Gail Ryan, *Victim to Victimizer*, 4 JOURNAL OF INTERPERSONAL VIOLENCE 3, September 1989, 325-341, at 326.

tors and students. Several states have laws that specifically provide criminal penalties for individuals who use their position of authority or trust to seduce or coerce a child into sexual activity.[11] Sexual battery is defined, in part, by Mississippi statute as:

> "(2) A person is guilty of sexual battery if...the person is in a position of trust or authority over the child including without limitation the child's teacher, counselor,...scout leader or coach."[12]

Laws prohibiting a coach from abusing his/her position of authority have been upheld in court decisions involving a coach and a player he/she was coaching. One such case is *Scadden v. State*, where a high school volleyball coach was convicted of second-degree sexual assault against a volleyball team member.[13] The coach violated Wyoming Statute Section 6-2-30 by using his position of authority to force submission to sexual intercourse; which submission would not have occurred, but for the coach's position.

Cases highlighting sexual assault in youth sports produce sensational news stories. Newspaper headlines regularly contain articles involving coaches, volunteers and individuals affiliated with a sports program being prosecuted, convicted or pleading guilty to criminal acts of sexual improprieties.

As is often the case, incidents that spawn newspaper headlines are often replicated in court opinions. A typical case is *People v. Rossi*, which involved a Little League baseball coach who sexually abused three children. The children testified that Rossi had them stay overnight at his house. During these overnight stays, Rossi would sleep with the boys in the same bed and then would fondle and sodomize them. Rossi was convicted and sentenced to consecutive 1 to 3 year terms for each of the six sodomy convictions, 1 to 3 years for each of the sexual abuse convictions and 1 year for the conviction for endangering the welfare of a child.[14]

---

11. States with authority abuse statutes include: New Hampshire (State v. Collins, 529 A.2d 945 (N.H. 1987)), Michigan (People v. Usman, 406 N.W.2d 824 (Mich. 1987)), and New Mexico (State v. Gillete, 699 P.2d 626 (N.M. Ct. App. 1985)). States that have case law creating a duty for individuals in a position of authority include: Alaska (Skrepich v. State 740 P.2d 950 (Alaska Ct. App. 1987) involved a karate teacher who abused his position of authority), North Carolina (State v. Gilbert, 385 S.E.2d 815 (N.C. Ct. App. 1989)), Ohio (State v. Penton, 588 N.E.2d 951 (Ohio Ct. App. 1990)), and Rhode Island (State v. Burke, 522 A.2d 725 (R.I. 1987)).

12. Mississippi Codes, § 97-3-95 (2) (1972). See also Page's Ohio Revised Code Annotated, § 2907.03 (1994). The Ohio Revised Code specifies criminal sexual battery involving sexual conduct with a parent, guardian, custodian or person in loco parentis. Ohio Revised Code § 2907.03(A)(5).

13. Scadden v. State, 732 P.2d 1036, 1038-1039 (Wyo. 1987).

14. People v. Rossi, 585 N.Y. Supp. 2nd, 816 (S.C., 1992).

Civil Liability

Often, criminal convictions or investigations foster civil litigation. Possibly the most notorious civil suit involving a coach and young athletes is the Linda Van Housen case.[15] Michael Ipsen, a local running coach, started a sexual relationship with Linda when she was 13-years-old. Linda claimed her coach stated that: "he was her coach and next to God and knew what was in God's mind..."[16] Two other members of the same running team also claimed to have their first sexual encounters with the coach when they were only 15. While Linda's mother tried to go to the police with the two other victims, the Redwood City Police dropped their sexual abuse investigation. Several years after moving out of Ipsen's house and suffering a nervous breakdown, Linda filed a civil suit against Ipsen, who was found guilty of sexual abuse of a minor and ordered to pay $1.1 million in damages.

The Housen case differs from traditional sexual abuse civil cases because most civil suits focus on the "deep pocket" rather than the coach.[17] Traditionally, the "deep pocket" with enough money to pay a judgment is the coach's employer or the organization for which the coach volunteered his/her service. Even non-profit organizations are considered "deep pockets" because the organizations typically have insurance coverage. Cases against employers or supervising organizations can be broken down into two legal categories; failing to prevent a coach's alleged acts of sexual abuse,[18] and negligent employment practices.[19]

---

15. Eric Goodman, *The Coach and His Girls, A Dangerous Bond*, GLAMOUR, October, 1993, 248. See also S.L. Wykes, *Coach Tells of Runner's Suicide Threats*, SAN JOSE MERCURY NEWS, August 12, 1992, B1.

16. Goodman, at 249

17. 1996 witnessed the first filing of a civil suit under the 1994 Violence Against Women Act. The act allows victims to sure their attackers for civil damages if the attack was fostered by the victim's gender. The case was brought by a student from Virginia Polytechnic University allegedly raped by two freshman football players from the same school. Nina Bernstein, *Rape Victim Turns To Federal Law*, HOUSTON CHRONICLE, February 12, 1996, A1.

18. See generally, Hagan v. Houston Independent School District, 51 F.2d 48 (5th Cir. 1995) alleging the school's principal failed to prevent the coach's sexual assault which was a violation of the students' constitutional and civil rights. Recently successful civil cases have focused on a school's obligation to provide an environment free of sexual abuse under Title IX, rather than a negligence cause of action. Leija v. Canutillo Ind. School Dist., 887 F. Supp. 947 (W.D. Tex. 1995) and Rosa H. v. San Elizario Ind. School Dist., 887 F. Supp. 140 (W.D. Tex. 1995). While claims can be brought under Title IX for suits brought by students in program receiving federal funds against program personnel (teachers and coaches), courts refuse to extend Title IX coverage to student-on-student or partic-

Plaintiffs in sexual assault civil cases often allege that the school district or youth organization should be liable for the negligent act of their employees or volunteers. Several terms such as vicarious liability or respondeat superior can be used to describe the employment relationship in which the coach's negligence is imputed to the employer. For liability analysis, a volunteer, acting in the scope of their specified volunteer duties, is considered similar to employees.

Bratton v. Calkins, involved a 17-year-old high school student, who had a sexual relationship with a science teacher who was also her softball coach.[20] Two years later, she sued her former coach and school district alleging negligence.[21] The school district successfully prevailed based on the fact that no respondeat superior (and therefore no employer liability) liability existed because the sexual conduct was outside the coach's scope of employment.

Besides being sued as the abuser's employer, school districts and sports organizations have been sued for their alleged failure to determine that a volunteer or prospective employee had a propensity to engage in sexual misconduct. In *Thurmond v. Richmond County Board of Education*, the parents of a six-year-old student sued a physical education instructor and his employer for sexual abuse.[22] After affirming summary judgment for the school, the court noted that there was no evidence of any prior criminal behavior by the teacher and the school had successfully screened the teacher through the Georgia Criminal Investigation Center.[23] Thus, while a school or youth organization has a duty to investigate an applicant's

---

ipant-against-participant sexual harassment. Judy Wiesler, *High Court Won't Hear Texas Case*, HOUSTON CHRONICLE, October 8, 1996, 1A.

19. Negligent employment practices include negligent hiring, failing to supervise an employee, failing to properly train an employee, and negligent retention of an employee. The term negligence infers the failure to act reasonable under the circumstances. Thus, while no employee screening process is 100% accurate, it is considered a reasonable business practice to screen applicants and identify any potential problem applicants. JOHN PATTERSON, STAFF SCREENING TOOL KIT 10, Nonprofit Risk Management Center, Washington, DC (1994).

20. Bratton v. Calkins, 870 P.2d. 981 (Wash. App. Div. 3 1994).

21. Bratton alleged the school district was negligent in failing to: control, supervise and regulate extracurricular activities; properly investigate or take corrective measures; and anticipate dangers and take precautionary measures. Id. at 983.

22. Thurmond v. Richmond County Board of Education, 428 S.E.2d. 392 (Ga. App. 1993).

23. Id. at 395. See also Big Brother/Big Sister of Metro Atlanta, Inc. v. Terrell, (359 S.E.2d. 241 (Ga. App. 1987)) wherein the court held that screening was sufficient when the applicant's family history was reviewed, three references were contacted and the applicant went through several extensive interviews.

background, no liability could be attached to the background check if the applicant had a clean criminal history.

Preventing Sexual Assaults

While some programs have successfully defended civil suits alleging sexual assault by an employee or volunteer, the old adage that 'a strong offense is better than a strong defense' applies in sexual assault cases. This adage is especially appropriate when organizations develop and implement comprehensive risk management programs. One organization that has undertaken several measures to protect athletes in its charge is USA Gymnastics.[24] USA Gymnastics has authority over its 11,100 member coaches and 120,000 gymnasts. There are an estimated 30,000 gymnastic coaches and 500,000 gymnasts competing in school or park and recreation programs. Over the past six years, USA Gymnastics has expelled 11 coaches for sexual abuse involving approximately 20 boys and girls. To stifle the problem before more children are victimized, USA Gymnastics urges gym owners to conduct criminal background checks before hiring, distribute educational material and encourage the reporting of sexually deviant conduct. USA Gymnastics' actions represent the start of a comprehensive risk management program which could possibly be expanded in the future to cover other types of abuse such as negligent coaching and abusive coaching practices.

US Youth Soccer has made child abuse prevention a top organizational objective which included the production of a "Kidsafe" brochure and program.[25] The Kidsafe program requires all US Youth Soccer affiliates (serving approximately 2,000,000 children age 5 to 19) to have written policies concerning child abuse, a point person for handling assault claims, a law enforcement liaison and approved practices for hiring, training, supervising, investigating and dismissing individuals. Kidsafe requires all coaches and administrators involved in US Youth Soccer to be registered and questioned concerning conviction for crimes of violence or crimes against persons. All individuals possessing specific criminal histories are excluded from participating as a coach, volunteer or administrator. Organizational policies designed to eliminate abuse and applicant screening are the cornerstones of the Kidsafe program.

---

24. Maryann Hudson, ... On the Dark Side, Sexually Abusive Coaches a Major Concern, HOUSTON CHRONICLE, May 28, 1995, 14B.

25. US YOUTH SOCCER, KIDSAFE, A RISK MANAGEMENT PROGRAM, Richardson, TX (1994).

Screening applicants is rapidly becoming the major tool for identifying individuals who might have a greater propensity to engage in sexually inappropriate activities. In a study of 197 convicted child molesters released from prison between 1958 and 1974, the recidivism rate for those reconvicted of subsequent sexual crimes was 42 percent.[26] These figures have not gone unnoticed by elected officials. Legislative bodies throughout the United States have passed various laws helping to identify and track individuals convicted of sexual assaults due to the high risk of recidivism. Due to the greater than normal likelihood that someone previously convicted of sexual assault crimes might reengage in the same or similarly abusive activity, a criminal history background check provides one method for identifying individuals who are more likely to engage in illegal sexual activity. Furthermore, although sexual abusers often demonstrate a long, pervasive and active abuse pattern, four-fifths of child sexual abuse cases in one study resulted only in court ordered probation.[27] Nine states specifically require coaches or physical education instructors working with schools to be screened for prior criminal convictions.[28]

While background checks for potential employees is appropriate in a variety of circumstances and positions, the harder question involves criminal background checks for individuals interested in volunteering their time. Most youth sports programs rely heavily upon and are regularly seeking volunteer assistance. While an organization cannot offend potential volunteers, the organization has to protect children in their charge. Thus, all volunteers should be told the reason why their backgrounds will be checked and that the organization's policy is designed to protect the children.

In Washington, individuals interested in volunteering with non-profit organizations can be required by the nonprofit organization, as a condition

---

26. Karl Hanson, Richard Steffy, and Rene Gauthier, *Long-term Recidivism of Child Molesters*, 61 JOURN. CONSULTING CLINICAL PSYCHOL. 4, 1993, 646-652 at 646. Among child molesters, those with male victims have the highest recidivism rate while those with unrelated female victims had a lower recidivism rate. Vernon Quinsey, Marine Rice, and Grant Harris, *Actuarial Prediction of Sexual Recidivism*, 10 JOURNAL INTERPERSONAL VIOLENCE 1, March 1995, 85-100 at 86.

27. Barbara Smith, THE PROBATION RESPONSE TO CHILD SEXUAL ABUSE OFFENDERS: HOW IS IT WORKING?, 1 and 9, A Study of the American Bar Association, Criminal Justice Section (1990).

28. Connecticut Gen. Stat. Ann. § 10-221d(a) (Supp. 1995), Florida State Ann. 231.02 and 231.15 (Supp. 1995), Georgia Code Ann. § 20-2-211 (Supp. 1995), Nevada Rev. Stat. Ann. § 391.033 and 391.100 (1991), Ohio Revised Code Ann. § 3301.541 (Supp. 1994), Oregon Rev. Stat. § 342.223 (1993), Rhode Island Gen. Laws § 16-48.1-5 (1988), Tenn. Code Ann. § 49-5-413 (Supp. 1994), and Washington Rev. Code § 28A.410.010 (Supp. 1995).

of volunteering with that organization, to sign an informed consent form allowing a criminal history background check.[29] The background checks are conducted by the state patrol which researches whether the applicant has a record for conviction of offenses against children or other persons. The legislation is designed to benefit non-profit organizations and goes as far as to provide that no non-profit organization can be charged a fee for a background check.[30]

While Washington does not charge nonprofit organizations for background checks, most organizations interested in conducting background checks in any other state have to pay a state agency or a private organization to perform a check. The YMCAs in Houston have access to a city run information data base, but the YMCA also utilizes a private organization to conduct a more thorough check throughout Texas and sometime nationally. The cost for a private agency background check can range from $45 to $100 for each applicant and are conducted utilizing various data bases throughout the nation. The California Youth Soccer Association has over 40,000 volunteers in Northern California alone. Based on an average cost of $50, the cost for conducting a thorough background check for California Youth Soccer Association would total $2 million. The expense of conducting background checks on the estimated 3 million youth coaches would be staggering. Such a financial burden would cause most nonprofit sports organization to stop providing sports activities. Even with some drawbacks (timeliness of the information, geography (if a former convict moves between states either during or after parole) and privacy rights concerns), employment background checks remain the primary tool for weeding out potential bad apples. The key to any screening process is the signed consent to release information form.

An effective employment or volunteer disclosure form should, at a minimum, contain the following requests and statements: first, last and middle name, any prior names or aliases, social security number, complete address, date of birth (only request from volunteers, not potential employees), home and work numbers, driver's license number, state and expiration date, any coaching certificates or diplomas, prior background in-

---

29. Washington Revised Code § 43.43.830 et seq. (Supp. 1995). Information can be released if it pertains to either an employee or a volunteer who will have regularly scheduled unsupervised access to children under sixteen, and other specific groups.

30. Wash. Rev. Code § 43.43.838(2). The research is only performed to assist in making initial employment or engagement decisions. An insurance company cannot require, as a prelude to receiving insurance, that all new employee or volunteers have their records checked. Lastly, the nonprofit organization requesting the background check shall be immune from civil liabilities for failing to request a background check, unless the failure to do so constitutes gross negligence. Id. at § 43.43.834(7).

formation concerning involvement in youth athletics, personal and business references including current phone numbers, all prior residences for the past ten years, any convictions for crimes involving violence, sexual assault, child molestation, or crimes against persons, a description of the organization's policy concerning the handling of individuals with prior criminal histories, whether an appeal process is available for those rejected, the period of time the form is valid and when it will be updated. A signature and date line next to a statement indicating the applicant voluntarily gives the organization the authorization to check the applicant's criminal background is critical.

While convictions for sexual offenses might appear in a sex offender registry open to numerous sources, Child Abuse Central Registries usually list alleged (and convicted) incidents involving any claim of child abuse. These records are strictly controlled with access only provided to specified groups such as schools and foster-care agencies. Volunteers might not be listed under a sex offender registry, but may have been accused of alleged child abuse. Thus, organizations should require all volunteers (and employees) to contact a state's central registry and request a copy of their own information. An applicant without any allegations in their records could then produce a registry's reply stating they are not listed.

In addition to establishing a policy to review each applicant and creating an application form, organizations should consider developing an appeals process available for individuals rejected for any reason including past criminal history. The appeal process, as well as the screening process, needs to be confidential. At least three individuals should sit on an appeal board. The appeal board should operate under equitable guidelines to allow individuals with clean records the opportunity to prove they can be trusted. The appeal process is even more important with volunteers because if volunteers feel the organization does not give them an opportunity to be heard, the organization might have a difficult time recruiting additional volunteers in the future.

Checking backgrounds requires more than just a criminal history check. Some programs are adopting extensive interviews to search for prior conduct which might not appear in a criminal history check. Additional screening steps include having in-depth phone interviews with all references, interviews with current or previous work supervisor and requiring all applicants to read and sign a form agreeing to abide by the organization's sexual abuse policy. The sexual abuse policy form should include a pledge that the applicant will adhere to the organization's policy or hold the organization harmless and indemnify the organization for all costs associated with a sexual abuse allegation which leads to a conviction or plea bargain.

Screening should not be limited to just applicants or volunteers. Whenever an overnight activity is scheduled at an individuals house, all individuals residing at the premises or who will participate in the activity should also submit to background checks prior to the event, and a database of approved families should be created. Some individuals might feel that such a measure is taking risk management strategies to an extreme. However, a jury would not be sympathetic to a sports organization that did not take any steps to discover that an overnight activity was taking place in the house of a convicted sex offender. Due to the difficulty in tracking and investigating any and all adults and youths involved in overnight activities, all overnight activities should be prohibited by the organization.

Additional Steps Needed to Protect Young Athletes

Most organizations that employ sexual abuse prevention programs do not preach background checks in a vacuum. Background checks are only one component of a comprehensive sexual abuse prevention plan that includes, first and foremost, an organization's sexual abuse policy reinforced throughout the organization. The organization's sexual abuse policy should be developed by individuals aware of the research in the sexual abuse field. Imagining where a potential abuser might attack children or what an abuser might look for in choosing a victim becomes the cornerstone from which to build an effective policy designed to deter potential abusers. A recent study of 91 men from England, convicted of sexual offenses against children, helps highlight an abuser's mindset.[31] The survey discovered that a majority of offenders pick their victim based on the child's appearance, how the child was dressed and they often looked for children with low self-esteem or a child with whom they have had a special relationship. The abusers overall preferred a pretty, young, small and provocatively dressed child.

In the aforementioned study, the offenders primarily used the following strategies to access a victim: play or teaching activities (including sports), developing isolated contact through baby-sitting and bribes, outings, or a lift home. A majority of the offenders were between the ages of 30 and 42 years when they committed the act, 35% were professional, 48% were married, 66% of the offenders knew their victims through family, friends or caretaking opportunities and the sexual assault most often occurred at the offender's home. Some suggestions offered by the survey participants included: staying away from secluded remote places, being wary of public toilets, never going into public toilets alone, always walking to or from

---

31. Michelle Elliot, Kevin Browne, and Jennifer Kilcoyne, *Child Sexual Abuse Prevention: What Offenders Tell Us*, 19 CHILD ABUSE & NEGLECT 5, pp. 579-594 (1995).

events or school with at least one other child, never accepting rides from strangers and never teaching children that a person that looks a certain way is bad because abusers come in all shapes, ages, colors and professions.

After analyzing how offenders try to assault children, an organization can start implementing a prevention program designed to eliminate specific dangers. One suggested sexual abuse prevention program stresses the four P's; personnel, program, premises and participants.[32] The following recommendations can form the basis of a risk management program incorporating the four P's.

Personnel

In addition to screening and securing qualified personnel, an organization has to make sure everyone involved has adopted the organization's mindset. By carefully drafting precise job descriptions and setting forth what is and is not acceptable conduct, a potential volunteer or employee will know what types of activities are unacceptable. Acceptable activities could include monitoring children, teaching sports skills and helping to adjust football equipment. Unacceptable activities could include entering a bathroom stall with a child or helping undress a child who already knows how to handle their personal hygiene/care. Job descriptions should include the job title, purpose, duties, responsibilities, required qualifications, training and position restrictions. Applicants should be required to sign-off on the application, indicating that they meet all the job description requirements. After thoroughly analyzing the application, the applicant has to be interviewed. Interviewers should be well trained to identify danger areas. For example, many child molesters have limited contact with members of their own peer group.[33] An interviewer can discover this information by asking legally appropriate questions about the applicant's social life. Interviewers should also look out for mannerisms, gestures, vocabulary or other external indicators which might show a potential problem or inconsistency with statements contained in an application.

One contact person should be appointed in each organization as the sexual abuse (and child abuse) resource person who can handle confidential screening material, handle all claims and be a liaison with police and social services professionals. This person should be given a title such as "Special Friend."

Supervisors should be properly trained in recognizing signs of sexual abuse and signs that someone within their charge might be undergoing significant family changes which could possibly lead to sexual abuse. Sud-

---

32. Faller, supra note 7, at 27.
33. Patterson, supra note 3, at 39.

den changes in a volunteer's or employee's personal life can signal potential problems which should be monitored. Emotional situations such as marital strife can often weaken an individuals temptation to engage in a sexual relationship.[34]

The organization's "Special Friend" can develop specific policies concerning what steps are taken to investigate a claim of sexual abuse, how to confront and who should confront an individual identified as a possible abuser, how to suspend an individual until the allegations are resolved and how to terminate a person's involvement in the organization after being convicted of a sexual offense. The organization has to take all appropriate measures to prevent retaliation against the child making a sexual assault claim. Retaliation can be prevented by reassigning the accused, putting the accused on leave (paid leave if he or she is an employee) or by formally warning the accused and/or others that anyone caught retaliating will be dismissed immediately.

Program

Organizations should schedule a coaches/parent meeting prior to starting each season. This meeting should focus on explaining the organization's sexual abuse prevention program, soliciting assistance from parents to support the program and educating parents on some of the subtle signs of abuse. Parents should also be informed about specific organizational policies. For example, if an organization prohibits overnight activities, parents should know the organization strictly enforces such a rule. Thus, parents should not acquiesce to someone claiming they work for the organization and wanting to take a child on a special overnight excursion. Even if the parents of other children within the organization are promoting an overnight activity, parents would have been warned from the very beginning that such activity is not an approved organization activity.

Other specific rules should include: prohibiting photographing partially clad or naked children, prohibiting one coach from taking individual athletes or a team alone on excursions or overnight trips, having a buddy system in place, only allowing kids to ride home with specifically designated drivers and prohibiting coaches, volunteers, officials and visitors from assisting children in removing any clothing; except for sport specific equipment such a football shoulder pads.

Special rules should be adopted concerning specific sports, such as gymnastics, where physical contact is unavoidable. Current gymnastics clothing permits a spotter's hands to slide up a gymnasts body with relative

---

34. Stephen J. Bavolek, *Sexual Abuse and Exploitation of Athletes by Their Coaches*, CHILD CENTERED COACHING NEWS, Spring 1995, 5.

ease. All participants and parents should be informed of the potential for significant bodily contact. Any individuals wishing to avoid such contact can be provided an opportunity to participate in other activities. Parent(s) and children should sign a statement indicating they have received information concerning the extent of bodily contact and that they and their child(ren) willingly accept such risk by continued participation.

Parents should be encouraged to drop-in unannounced to practices or games. Noted sexual abuse researcher Finkelhor and his associates discovered lower rates of abuse in child care programs that encouraged parents to drop in for unannounced visits.[35] Parents should also be allowed access to their children at all times.

Sports organizations have to develop a mindset which filters down to the athletes and is adopted by the athletes. Children have to be actively involved in developing the sexual abuse prevention program and prevention strategies so that the children understand that sexual abuse against their peers is unacceptable conduct. Approximately one-third of sexual molestations are perpetrated by children.[36] Thus, educational campaigns should target both sexual abuse prevention techniques and steps to take if a child engages or might engage in sexual molestations. It should be noted that virtually all elementary and high schools currently provide sexual abuse prevention education to students. Education can include assertive steps by the athletes themselves to reduce sexual abuse between athletes and other individuals. A good example at the adult level was established in 1995 by Rollins College where the schools baseball players wrote a date-rape contract for the women at Rollins and published the contract in the College's newspaper. The contract required the baseball players to treat all women with respect and to not make sexual advances without their partner's approval.

Premises

The key to protecting premises is access. By limiting facility access an organization can drastically reduce access to children. All facilities should be designed or retrofitted to provide only one entrance and exit. It is very difficult, if not impossible, to secure all entrances and exits or conduct significant screening at large stadiums or arenas. However, in smaller facilities, visitors could be asked for a photo identification card to verify their address. If a facility cannot be designed to eliminate unauthorized access (such as a soccer field in a public park) a designated person should periodically go through the stands and sidelines to monitor the spectators.

---

35. Faller, supra note 7, at 32.
36. Patterson, supra note 3, at 25.

Additional attention should be given to securing locker rooms, bathrooms, and changing areas. Some programs and schools have designed showers and bathrooms with viewing areas and mounted cameras that can help spot potential abusers, while providing privacy for children using the bathrooms or showers. While cameras can help prove a case of sexual abuse, they can also be used inappropriately. Access to cameras or viewing areas should be strictly limited.

Adjacent facilities, including parking lots, might also pose security problems. Inadequate premises lighting is a major concern for night activities. Children should not be allowed to wander in parking lots or wait in public areas without supervision. Parents should be encouraged to pick-up their child(ren) directly from the facility or a program volunteer should escort children directly to waiting cars or busses.

Participants

A central component of an organization's sexual assault prevention program is the participant education program. Such a program emphasizes a child's rights and helps them understand that they have a choice. The prevention program has to be carefully presented to avoid scaring children while effectively communicating safety tips. Children should be taught that it is okay to say "No" to children or adults. Children should also be taught the difference between good and bad touching. Touching should: be in response to the needs of the child, be given with the child's permission, avoid private areas, be open and not secretive and be regulated by the participants age, experience and understanding. While an organization should not engage in sex education instruction without parental consent, children can be taught that they have private areas which others should generally not touch.

All participant education programs need to discuss the concerns associated with unwanted or unwelcomed advances or actions by strangers, coaches, administrators and parents. Furthermore, participants need to be educated on the harms associated with peer sexual abuse and assault. Participants need to understand the legal repercussions for sexually assaulting a fellow participant. Parental consent should be solicited and obtained in writing prior to any educational component on preventing sexual abuse.

Participants should receive assertiveness training which will hopefully assist a child in resisting an abuser. Appearing confident has been shown to help discourage a would be attacker. Organizations should develop policies requiring all players to report unapproved or uncomfortable conduct to the "Special Friend" immediately after an incident arises. The "Special Friends" would then take all necessary steps to protect the child, report the incident to appropriate authorities and gather information critical for any future legal needs.

Preventing a potential offender from knowing a child's name can reduce the chances of the offender endearing him or herself to the child. Steps to reduce the chances of identifying participants include: taking names off their uniforms, not publishing lists of player names/addresses, listing parent's work phone numbers-rather than home numbers and cheering teammates on by using their jersey number, rather than their name.

Lastly, if possible, children should be taught to sign-in and sign-out of practices and competition, provide their parents with specific times they will be home after practice or competition and carry some change in case they need to make a phone call.

Organizations are not required to implement any and all sexual abuse prevention strategies. Each organization has to evaluate their own goals and objectives before implementing any risk management program. While some strategies might dehumanize the athletic process, that threat has to be weighed against the fear that failing to implement that strategy could possibly contribute to a sexual assault.

The Need for Further Protection

Legislation

While the 1978 Child Abuse Prevention and Treatment Act had been repealed, the Personal Responsibility Act (HB 4), was being considered by the U.S. Senate which would have relaxed the confidentiality laws surrounding criminal records.[37]

New laws are also being passed requiring organizations to prevent sexual harassment which can lead to sexual assault. Sexual harassment has traditionally been litigated in the employment law context between an employee and an employer. However, under California law, sexual harassment has been extended to apply to a teacher-student or similar relationship.[38] Sexual harassment is defined as sexual advances, solicitations, sexual re-

---

37. J. Randolph Burton, *Justice for Children—Legislative Objectives*, 1 THE TEXAS LAW REPORTER 4, August 1995, 10. See also 42 U.S.C.S. § 5119(b).

38. California Civil Code § 51.8 (Supp. 1995). Allowable damages under the statute include emotional distress, treble damages, punitive damages, and attorneys' fees. California Civil Code § 52.

quests or demand for sexual compliance that were unwelcomed and persistent or severe and which continued after the victim requested that the conduct stop. If similar legislation is adopted by other states, more organizations will be required to develop policies and procedures to prevent both sexual assault and sexual harassment.

While new laws are being adopted, there are a variety of laws which have yet to be adopted, but would be very beneficial in the fight to prevent sexual assault in youth sports. Members within youth sports organizations should be encouraged to lobby for legislation to provide enhanced penalties, sentencing or revocation of parole for any volunteers and/or employees who lie on application forms and do not mention past convictions or provide false names or other misleading information.

Legislation should also be supported providing for enhanced penalties for youth coaches convicted of these crimes. Enhanced penalties are warranted by the authority position exercised by coaches and teachers which can force sexual compliance.

Currently, 41 states require the registration of convicted sexual offenders upon their release.[39] These laws normally require registration if the individual had been convicted in any jurisdiction throughout the United States. These laws also normally require the implementation of a database to help disseminate information about past offenders to local law enforcement agencies. However, as of January, 1996, only eight states allow public access to

---

39. Ala. Code § 13A-11-200(1975), Alaska Stat. § 12.63.010(1994), Ariz. Rev. Stat. Ann. § 13-3821 (1993), Ark. Code Ann. § 12-12-902 (1987), Cal. Penal Code § 290 (1994), Colo. Rev. Stat. § 18-3-411(1) (1991), Conn. Gen. Stat. Ann. § 54-102r (1994), Del. Code Ann. tit. 11, § 4120 (1994), Fla. Stat. § 775.22 (1994), Ga. Code Ann. § 42-9-44.1 (1994), Haw. Rev. Stat. § 706-603 (1991), Idaho Code §§ 18-8303-8306 (1993), 730 Ill. Comp. Stat. Ann. § 150/2 (1992), Ind. Code §§ 5-2-12-5 through 5-2-12-11 (1994), Kan. Stat. Ann. §§ 22-4903-4910 (1994), Ky. Rev. Stat. Ann. §§ 17.510-530 (1994), La. Rev. Stat. Ann. § 15:535 (1991), Me. Rev. Stat. Ann. tit. 34-A § 11002 (1993), Mich. Comp. Laws §§ 28.721-730 (1994), Minn. Stat. § 243.166 (1994), Miss. Code Ann. § 45-33-1 et seq. (1994), Mo. Rev. Stat. Ann. §§ 566.600-625 (1994), Mont. Code Ann. § 46-23-502 (1991), Nev. Rev. Stat. § 207.151 (1991), N.H. Rev. Stat. Ann. § 632-A:11 (1993), N.J. Rev. Stat. §§ 2C:7-1-5 (1994), N.D. Cent. Code § 12.1-32-15 (1993), Ohio Rev. Code Ann. § 2950.01 (1974), Okla. Stat. tit 57, § 582 (1993), Or. Rev. Stat. §§ 181.518 and 181.591 (1991), R.I. Gen. Laws § 11-37-16 (1992), S.C. Code Ann. §§ 23-3-400-490 (1994), S.D. Codified Laws. Ann. § 23-5-14 (1990), Tenn. Code Ann. § 38-6-110 (1989), Tex. Rev. Civ. Stat. Ann. Art. 6252-13c.1 (1993), Utah Code Ann. § 77-27-21.5 (1994), Va. Code Ann. § 19.2-298.1 (1994), Wash. Rev. Code § 9A.44.130 (1994), W.Va. Code §§ 61-8F-2 through 61-8F-8 91993), Wis. Stat. § 175.45 (1993) and Wyo. Stat §§ 7-19-302-306 (1994). See also 42 U.S.C. § 14071 (1994).

registration material, and access is normally only allowed if it is a necessary for public protection.[40] Current legislative trends involve the newspaper publication of a released sexual offender's age, gender, street name and zip code.[41] While some states are making this information available to citizens who request it, in at least one state, Texas, a convict's name will not be published for fear of vigilante actions against the parolee.[42] Legislation should be adopted allowing the publication and dissemination of a parolee's name and other information to all school, day care centers and other specified non-profit organizations to help screen potential applicants/volunteers.

Currently, 49 states require various specified individuals to report child abuse cases.[43] This reporting requirement is primarily an obligation for

---

40. The State Statutes Project, *Child Abuse and Neglect Statutes at a Glance Fact Sheet*, 1 undated. California established a 900 number so citizens could determine if an individual is registered as a child molester. Mitchel Benson, *Parents Given Safety Line*, SAN JOSE MERCURY NEWS, July 1, 1995, 1A. Callers can request up to two names for $10.00, but callers need to give their name, provide a good reason for why they are calling, identify the number of children at risk and provide the subject's name and additional information (date of birth, social security number, address, driver's license number or exact physical description). Id. at 18A.

Due to the lack of a national data base that would allow law enforcement authorities to track sex offenders between states, legislation was introduced by Senator Phil Gramm entitled the Sexual Predator Identification and Notification Act of 1996 which required convicted sexual criminals to register with the FBI when they cross state lines. Eric Hanson, *Law Aims To Track Sex Offenders*, HOUSTON CHRONICLE, March 17, 1996, A37.

41. Similar bills have been adopted in Delaware, Louisiana, Oregon, Washington, New Jersey and most recently, Texas. Eric Hanson, *Authorities Prepare to Publicize Release of Sex Offenders*, HOUSTON CHRONICLE, December 16, 1995, 37A.

42. In Colorado, anyone can walk into a police station and ask to see the offenders' list maintained by the police.

43. Ala. Code § 26-14-3, Alaska Stat. § 47.17.020, Ariz. Rev. Stat. Ann. § 13.3620, Ark. Code Ann. § 12-12-507, Ala. Code § 26-14-3, Alaska Stat. § 47.17.020, Ariz. Rev. Stat. Ann. § 13.3620, Ark. Code Ann. § 12-12-507, Cal. Penal Code §§ 11165.7, 11165.8, and 11166, Colo. Rev. Stat. § 19-3-304, Conn. Gen. Stat. § 17a-101, Del. Code Ann. tit. 16, §§ 903 and 904, D.C. Code Ann. § 2-1352, Fla. Stat. Ann. § 415.504, Ga. Code Ann. § 19-7-5, Haw. Rev. Stat. § 350-1.1, Idaho Code § 16-1619, Ill. Ann. Stat. Ch. 325, Para. 5/4 , Ind. Code §§ 31-6-11-2.1 and 31-6-11-3, Iowa Code §§ 232.68 and 232.69, Kan. Stat. Ann. § 38-1522, Ky. Rev. Stat. Ann. § 620.030, La. Rev. Stat. Ann., Ch. C. arts. 603 and 609, Me. Rev. Stat. Ann. tit. 22, § 4011, Mass. Gen. L. Ch. 119, § 51A, Mich. Comp. Laws Ann. § 722.623 Minn. Stat. § 626.556 Subd. 3, Miss. Code Ann. § 43-21-353, Mo. Rev. Stat. § 210.115 Mont. Code Ann. § 41-3-201, Neb. Rev. Stat. § 28-711, Nev. Rev. Stat. § 432B.220, N.H. Rev. Stat. Ann. § 169-C:29, N.J-. Rev. Stat. § 9:6-8.10, N.M. Stat. Ann. § 32A-4-3, N.Y. Soc. Serv. Law § 413, N.C. Gen. Stat. §§ 7A-543 and 115C-400, N.D. Cent. Code § 50-25.1-03, Ohio Rev. Code Ann.

teachers, social workers, police and health care professionals. This reporting requirement should be extended to coaches and sports administrators. While this will require some additional work from coaches, the end-result would be extremely beneficial.

Legislation should also be adopted to provide immunity for organizations that publish or disseminate information concerning an individual who has been terminated or resigns because of sexual inappropriate behavior, allegations and/or convictions. Many youth organizations are fearful of being sued if they tell the real reason for a coach's departure. Even though truth is a defense to any defamation claim, organization do not want to waste valuable time and energy embroiled in litigation. Thus, many organizations will tell someone accused of misconduct that if they leave town, the organization will not press charges nor tell anyone what happened. This practice has to stop. In fact one insurance company recently lost a several million dollar verdict in Florida for failing to tell a subsequent employer that a former employee had violent tendencies. The employee was known to carry a gun and had his hit list of who he wanted to kill. This information was not given to the new employer when the new employer called to check his reference. The new employee shot and killed several people shortly after being hired. Thus, an organization can face a lawsuit if they tell the reason for dismissing a coach or if they fail to tell others why the coach was dismissed. Only through immunity laws protecting the release of such information will organizations feel comfortable disclosing that someone was dismissed for violating an organization's sexual abuse policy. Similar laws already provide immunity for individuals who report cases of alleged child abuse, which might be inaccurate.

National Campaign

A national campaign involving federal and state authorities along with all youth sports organizations is needed to coordinate various currently existing or planned programs. A coordinated campaign will reduce the chances of a convicted abuser affiliating with different organizations in

---

§2151.421, Okla. Stat Ann. tit. 10, §7103, Or. Rev. Stat. §§419B.005 and 419B.010, 23 Pa. Cons. Stat. Ann. §6311, R.I. Gen. Laws §40-11-6, S.C. Code Ann. §20-7-510, S.D. Codified Laws Ann. §26-8A-3, Tenn. Code Ann. §37-1-403 Tex. Fam. Code Ann. §34.01, Utah Code Ann. §62A-4a-403, Vt. Stat. Ann. tit.33, §4913, Va. Code Ann. §63.1-248.3, Wash. Rev. Code Ann. §26.44.030, W. Va. Code §49-6A-2 Wis. Stat. Ann. §48.981, Wyo. Stat. §14-3-205, P.R. Laws Ann. Tit. 8, §406, V.I. Code Ann. Tit. 5, §2533

different states or different sports. The hallmark of such a campaign could involve a national computer database assessable to all youth organizations. Once an employee or volunteer has been cleared they should be issued a photograph identification card. The card could be valid for several years. The card could be presented to any sports or youth organization and automatically qualify that individual to work with any youth organization. Only certified individuals would be allowed to work with children. Such a system can track individuals convicted of sexual abuse and other crimes against people. It could also be used in conjunction with coaching education programs. The identification card can indicate what coaching level the coach has reached and what type of training they have completed.

One component of a national effort is the development of educational materials. VideoNet has produced a video "Special Report" entitled "Somebody Told."[44] The video conveys several steps to reduce sexual assault in youth programs including: developing organizational written policies, designating a contact person to coordinate efforts with government agencies, immediately reporting and handling all alleged cases of sexual assault, utilizing a previously produced press release and not interrogating either the victim or the alleged assailant.

One educational campaign entitled "Keep Child Abuse Out of Child Sports" was launched by Parents and Coaches in Sports, a program of the National Institute for Child Centered Coaching based in Park City, Utah.[45] The campaign revolves around various types of abuse, but provides two important points to consider in developing a sexual abuse prevention plan. Some children who have experienced abuse do not like to be touched. Thus, a coach should be sensitive to this fact. Additionally, while numerous coaches congratulate an athlete by tapping them on their buttocks, individuals who have experienced sexual abuse in the past can perceive such touching as a bodily violation.

Lastly, sexual abuse prevention materials and courses have to be included with athletic strategies and conditioning material typically provided to coaches. As role models, coaches can use their persuasive clout to encourage children to say no, assert their rights, protect their privacy and to report any unwanted verbal and non-verbal communications. Coaches can only teach necessary skills if they understand the problems and solutions. Coaches also have to take their role as an educator very seriously and concern themselves in the lives of each athlete.

---

44. VideoNet, *Somebody Told* a 23 minute video and accompanying Leader's Guide, undated.

45. STEPHEN J. BAYOLEK, COACHES' MANUAL—HAVING FUN AND FEELING GOOD ABOUT ME (1993).

Conclusion

Sexual abuse is not an easy topic for most people to talk about. However, the increased reporting of sexual abuse cases involving youth sports participants signals a call for more thorough safeguards. Currently existing laws provide an opportunity to weed-out some potential "bad apples" wishing to affiliate with youth and youth programs. Case law has highlighted the need for youth sports organizations to implement comprehensive sexual abuse prevention programs to prevent extensive liability exposure. Thus, youth sports organizations have to undertake the development and implementation of comprehensive risk management plans to secure their participants, program, personnel and premises from potential abusers.

Prevention Manual

The following manual provides the framework with which a youth sports (and non-sports) organization can implement a comprehensive sexual abuse prevention program. The manual has little value if the organization does not take a serious look at its goals and objectives for implementing a sexual abuse prevention policy ("SAPP"). No organization should undertake a SAPP just because everyone else has a similar plan. Every organization is different and each has to be treated differently. Thus, the first step in developing a SAPP is to identify the organizational goals and objectives pertaining to prevention and education as they apply to the four P's discussed in the article (program, personnel, place and participants). Each P should have it's own set of goals, objectives and strategies. Goals are broad statements concerning ideals the organization wants to pursue. Objectives should be more concrete and represent the best method for determining if the goals are being met. Strategies represent specifics tasks which, when completed, will result in obtaining the objectives. Goals, objectives and strategies are critical in the formation process of a SAPP policy statement.

Each organization should appoint one person who has the time, sensitivity and patience to serve as the organization's "Special Friend ("SF")." There are no set guidelines concerning who should serve in this capacity. Some girls feel more comfortable talking to women. However, boys are also subject to significant levels of sexual abuse. Thus, ideally there should be two SFs, if possible. If there is only one SF, an alternate SF should be designated if a child feels more comfortable talking to someone other than the SF. The SF's first order of business is to establish the organization's SAPP statement. The SAPP statement will be grounded upon the various goals, objectives and strategies developed by the organization. The SF should convey a planning meeting with organization administrators, select parents and select children to help establish appropriate goals, objectives and strategies.

Program goals, objectives and strategies are designed to further the organization and its general programs. The primary purpose of a youth sports organization is providing sports and recreational opportunities. However, an additional major focus is providing safe programs. Thus, specific identifiable and measurable criterion should be established to determine if progress is made to operate safe programs. Similarly, all aspects of personnel, facilities and participants involvement have to be analyzed to develop appropriate goals, objectives and strategies. Some potential goals, objectives and strategies are listed below. This is not an exhaustive list and represents some typical goals, objectives and strategies. Sample goals, objectives and strategies could include:

Program

Goals—
> Run as safe a program as possible.
> Provide the most appropriate environment for children to enhance their skills and learn sportsmanship.
> Do what ever it takes to eliminate sexual abuses by volunteers.

Objectives—
> Reduce the number of reported injuries from last year.
> Evaluate all programs on a yearly basis.
> Provide a screening method to screen volunteer applicants.

Strategies—
> Train children to properly use the organization's "SF."
> Hire an independent reviewer to annual evaluate programming.
> Screen every applicant for a volunteer position on a yearly basis.

Personnel

Goals—
> Hire the most qualified employees possible.
> Train employees and volunteers to identify signs of abuse.
> Terminate volunteers who do not follow the rules.

Objectives—
> Make sure all employees have been screened for past criminal histories.
> Make sure all employees have participated in a sexual abuse prevention course.
> Make sure all volunteers are properly trained and screened prior to any contact with program participants.

Strategies—
> Every applicant for either a paid or volunteer position has to complete an application form which contains a release for the inspection of criminal background information.
> Every employee and volunteer has to attend a mandatory two hour training session on our SAPP at least every other year.
> Post-tests should be administered to ensure comprehension.

Place

Goals—

Ensure the facility does not provide opportunities for
pedophiles to attract children or allow access to children
in unsupervised locations.
Secure the facility perimeter from unauthorized access.

Objectives—

Facility surveillance should be undertaken on a quarter-hour
interval.

Strategies—

One administrator, coach or volunteer should be assigned each
day to help patrol the facility on a quarter-hour basis.
Surveillance should include inspecting restrooms, offices and
closets to make sure they are either locked or clear of any
unauthorized or unacceptable use.
All individuals assigned to surveillance duties shall carry an
organization issued cellular phone with pre-programmed
numbers for the police, family services and the SP.

Participants

Goals—

Teach children how to prevent sexual abuse.
Teach children how to avoid engaging in sexual abuse.

Objectives—

Provide each participant with at least one hour of educational
training to identify and overcome hurdles associated with
sexual abuse.

Strategies—

Each parent should sign a waiver, if interested, allowing their
child to attend SAPP educational programming.
Two individuals should be utilized to teach various safety and
touching rules.

After a complete list of goals, objectives and strategies has been developed, the organization has to incorporate these thoughts into a workable, living document that will guide the organizations' SAPP. This document is commonly called the organization's Policy Statement or Policy Notice. A policy statement is a document setting forth the rules which govern the conduct of all members within the organization. The policy statement clearly defines what is expected by members and what punishment is given for violating expressed rules. It is not enough just to have a written policy.

To be effective, and legally binding, the rules set forth within the policy statement have to be communicated to the individual responsible for following the policy. Thus, the policy statement should be handed out to each employee and volunteer. Each employee and volunteer should be asked to read the policy statement and sign a form indicating they have read, understood and accept all the terms, rules and conditions set forth in the policy statement.

Sexual Assault Prevention
Program Policy Statement #1

Purpose

To establish policies and procedures to be used by all employees and volunteers, to educate parent(s), participants, coaches, employees and volunteers about concerns, to develop and implement specific risk management strategies and to coordinate the filing of oral and written reports to the local department of social services/law enforcement agency for suspected cases of child physical abuse, sexual abuse, sexual assault or neglect.

Definitions

A. *Administrator*: The term administrator refers to any paid employee or volunteer who has a position of authority, can exercise control over program units and/or has the power to coordinate the activities of other individuals within the organization. For purposes of this Policy Statement, administrators include coaches, referees and team officials.

B. *Child*: A child refers to any individuals under the age of majority (18).

C. *Abuse*: (1) The physical injury of a child by any administrator, or other person who has permanent or temporary care, custody or responsibility for supervision of a child under circumstances that indicate that the child's health or welfare is significantly harmed or at risk of being significantly harmed or (2) sexual abuse of a child, whether or not physical injuries are sustained.

D. *Sexual Abuse*: Any act or acts involving sexual molestation or exploitation, including but not limited to incest, rape or sexual offense in any degree, sodomy or unnatural or perverted sexual practices, on a child by any administrator or other person who has the permanent or temporary care or custody or responsibility for supervision of a minor child. Sexual molestation or exploitation includes, but is not limited to contact or conduct with a child for the purpose of sexual gratification, and may range from sexual advances, kissing or fondling to sexual crime in any degree, rape, sodomy, prostitution or allowing, permitting, encouraging or engaging in the obscene or pornographic display, photographing, filming or depiction of a child as prohibited by law.

E. *Neglect*: Child neglect means the leaving of a minor child unattended or other failure to give proper care and attention to a child by the administrator or any other person under circumstances that indicate that the child's health or welfare is significantly harmed or placed at risk of significant harm.

A neglected child is one who is:

- left unattended or inadequately supervised for long periods of time.
- showing signs of failure to thrive, or psycho-social dwarfism that has not been explained by a medical condition. There may be other evidence that the child is receiving insufficient food.
- receiving inadequate medical or dental treatment.
- significantly harmed or at risk of harm as a result of being denied an adequate education due to administrative action or inaction.
- wearing inadequate or weather-inappropriate clothing.
- significantly harmed due to a lack of minimal health care.
- ignored or badgered by the administrator.
- forced to engage in criminal behavior at the direction of the administrator.

IMMUNITY COVERAGE

Any person who makes or participates in the making of a good-faith report of abuse or neglect or participates in the investigation or in a judicial proceeding resulting therefrom shall in so doing be provided with complete and absolute immune from any civil liability that might otherwise be incurred or imposed as a result thereof by the organization.

WHERE COACH(ES), ADMINISTRATORS OR VOLUNTEERS ARE UNSURE WHETHER ABUSE OR NEGLECT HAS TAKEN PLACE, THE SITUATION NEEDS TO BE DISCUSSED WITH THE ORGANIZATION'S SPECIAL FRIEND AND LOCAL AUTHORITIES.

Program Policies

Special Friends

The organization shall nominate, hire or elect at least one individual to serve as the organization's special friend. Such individual should receive or have received specific training in identification, evaluation, diagnosis, investigation and disciplining procedures established by local and national authorities in the sexual abuse, child abuse and child neglect arena from local and national authorities.

The special friend is responsible for developing specific educational programs to be taught to the organization's members. The educational programs shall focus on prevention, education and reporting a variety of inappropriate behaviors. The special friend is the first contact for processing any claims of inappropriate behavior raised by children or administrators. Upon being notified of any inappropriate behavior, the special friend will immediately meet with the victim and initiate counseling, contact with proper authorities and appropriate investigation to insure protection and preservation of all evidence.

In addition to handling all claims or allegations of inappropriate behavior, the special friend shall be the only individual within the organization with the express authority to review criminal background information on any and all applicants for administrative positions. The special friend shall review all releases of criminal background information, process the releases through the appropriate law enforcement agencies, review the results and then properly store all such records in a confidential manner. The special friend is responsible for maintaining an active list of approved administrators. All individuals denied employment or volunteer opportunities based on criminal records shall be identified and cataloged for future reference.

Buddy System

It is this organization's policy that no activities shall ever take place wherein there is any one-on-one contact between an administrator and child, if such activities can practicably be avoided. All activities, if practicable, shall be conducted utilizing a buddy system wherein two or more adults are used during all organization sponsored activities. Thus, at least two adults are required to conduct practices, team parties and any competition.

Sleep Overs

Any sleep over activities whether parties at parent homes, overnight parties or traveling away games are expressly prohibited by this organization. The organization expressly prohibits such activities and can never endorse or support such activities. All sleep over based activities are the sole and exclusive responsibility of children or their parents with all administrators being barred from either coordinating or endorsing such activities.

Conduct of Activities

All activities of this organization shall be conducted with the needs and concerns of the children in mind. All policies, programs, personnel and procedures should be focused on providing quality programs in a safe environment. Any steps which advance the safety of all children shall be implemented if approved by the organization's board of directors.

Employment/Volunteers

On the recommendation of the organization's most senior administrator, the organization's board of directors may suspend or dismiss an administrator, coach, volunteer or other professional assistant for misconduct in office or other inappropriate activities, including, but not limited to, knowingly failing to report suspected child abuse. Upon the filing of any complaint alleging sexual abuse, child abuse and/or sexual assault, the organization's special friend will gather all pertinent facts and present such facts to the board of directors after reviewing all factual findings with the accused to hear both sides of the stories. If the alleged abuser admits to the conduct, the board of directors will employ the most appropriate punishment allowed above. If the alleged abuser denies the conduct, the board of directors can conduct any necessary further investigations deemed necessary prior to rendering any appropriate punishment or exonerating the alleged abuser.

Reporting Procedures

When any coach or administrator suspects child physical or sexual abuse or neglect, he or she must report their suspicions immediately to the special friend and local social services agency or the appropriate law enforcement agency, orally and in writing as prescribed by law. In a case of suspected neglect, the oral report should only be made to the local department of social services. The responsibility of an employee or volunteer to report suspected cases of child abuse or neglect is mandatory. All reports must be made as soon as possible, not-withstanding any provision of law, including any law on privileged communications. In addition to making an oral report, the employee or volunteer shall also inform the special friend that a case of suspected child abuse and/or neglect has been reported to the department of social services or law enforcement agency. It is the special friend's obligation to ensure that cases of suspected child abuse, sexual abuse or neglect brought to his/her attention are duly reported and monitored until each and every case is resolved in its entirety.

The employee or volunteer making the oral report to the department of social services or appropriate law enforcement agency is also responsible for submitting a written report to the special friend (see Suspected Child Abuse/Neglect Form). The written report must follow the oral report and be made within forty-eight (48) hours of the contact which disclosed the existence of possible abuse and/or neglect.

Copies of the written report for abuse or neglect should be sent to the local department of social services. Copies of the written report for abuse also should be sent to the local State's attorney office. Additional distribution shall be determined by special friend, but shall be limited to persons who have a true need-to-know and should not violate the confidentiality requirements discussed below.

The written report should contain as much of the following information as the person making the report is able to furnish in suspected cases of child abuse and/or neglect:

1. The name, age and home address of the child;
2. The name and home address of the child's parent or other person who is responsible for the child's care;
3. The current whereabouts of the child;
4. The nature and extent of the abuse/neglect inflicted on the child, including any evidence or information concerning previous injury possibly resulting from abuse or neglect; and

5.   Any other information that would help to determine the cause of the suspected abuse or neglect; and the identity of any individual responsible for the abuse.

Confidentiality

The identity of the employee or volunteer reporting a case of suspected child abuse and/or neglect should not be revealed. All records and reports concerning investigations of child abuse and/or neglect and their outcomes are protected by various confidentiality laws. Unauthorized disclosure of such records is a possible criminal offense which could subject the violator to fines and/or imprisonment. Under various laws, information contained in reports or records concerning child abuse and/or neglect maybe disclosed only:

1.   Under court order,
2.   To personnel of local or State departments of social services, law enforcement personnel, and members of multidisciplinary case consultation teams who are investigating a report of known or suspected child abuse or neglect or who are providing services to a child or family that is the subject of the report;
3.   To local or State officials responsible for the administration of the child protective service as necessary to carry out their official functions;
4.   To a licensed practitioner who, or an agency, institution or program which is providing treatment or care to a child who is the subject of a report of child abuse or neglect; or
5.   To a parent or other person who has permanent or temporary care and custody of a child, if provisions are made for protecting the identity of the reporter or any other person whose life or safety is likely to be endangered by disclosing the information.

Investigation

The organization is not in the business of investigating inappropriate behavior which should properly be handled by appropriate governmental agencies or justice officials. However, the organization's special friend is responsible for identifying which organization is the proper organization for referring the case and what steps need to be taken to protect other children within the organization. The special friend may briefly question a child to determine if there is reason to believe that the child's injuries resulted from physical or sexual abuse, by the child's caretaker and/or household member or from an organization administrator, (e.g., What happened to you? How did this happen?). However, in no case should the child be subjected to undue pressure in order to validate the suspicion of abuse and/or neglect. Any doubt about reporting a suspected situation is to be resolved in favor of protection the child and the report made immediately.

In the event a child is questioned by the protective services worker and/or police during an investigation of either child abuse and/or child neglect within the organization, whether the child is the alleged victim or a non-victim witness, the special friend should determine after consultation with the individual from the local department of social services or the police officer whether they should be present during the child's questioning. The special friend's sole role would be to provide support and comfort to the child who will be questioned.

Parent Notification

Although the organization expresses a preference for parental notification, the special friend is not required to notify parents or guardians of investigations during organization activities involving suspected child abuse, sexual abuse or neglect. The special friend, in consultation with the protective service caseworker, may decide whether the parents should be informed of the investigative questioning. It may be determined, for example, that disclosure to the parents would create a threat to the well-being of the child.

In the event that a child is in need of emergency medical treatment as a result of suspected abuse, assault or neglect, the special friend, in collaboration with an appropriate health professional, when available, shall arrange for the child to be taken immediately to the nearest hospital. The protective services worker or law enforcement officer should be consulted before taking the child to the hospital when feasible; in cases where the emergency conditions prevent such consultation, the protective services worker should be notified as soon thereafter as possible. In all other instances, it is the role of the parent(s), guardian(s), protective services worker and/or law enforcement officer to seek medical treatment for the child.

Parental Awareness

Parents should be advised of the legal responsibility of the organization to report suspected cases of abuse and/or neglect. In order to facilitate positive interactions between the organization and home/community, it is necessary to inform parents of this requirement before a problem arises. A letter should be sent to all parents at the beginning of the year setting forth educational programming and investigative procedures.

Information on child abuse and neglect should be disseminated as follows:

1. Provide annual training information dissemination sessions to all administrators on child abuse/neglect policies and procedures, symptoms, programs and services and prevention curriculum.
2. Implement, as part of the curriculum, an awareness and prevention education program for all children.
3. Initiate a public awareness program for children, parents and the community at large. Information may be disseminated in organization newsletters or independent educational programs.

Approved Organizational Forms

The forms attached hereto and incorporated herein by reference represent the official forms approved by the organization's board of directors. Any future additions, modification, deletions, substitutions and/or new forms can be adopted only if approved by a majority of the board of directors at a regularly scheduled board meeting.

List of Contacts for Reporting Suspect
Cases of Child Abuse or Neglect

Organization's Name: _____

Organization's Address and Telephone Number: _____

_____

Special Friend: _____

Date Form Completed: _____

1. Department of Social Services
    Name: _____
    Address: _____
    Contact Person: _____
    Phone Number: _____
    Facsimile Number: _____
2. Local Police Department
    Name: _____
    Address: _____
    Contact Person(s): _____
    Phone Number: _____
3. Local State Attorney's Office
    Name: _____
    Address: _____
    Contact Person(s): _____
    Phone Number: _____

Child Abuse, Sexual Abuse & Neglect Form

To: Local Department of Social Services
From: Special Friend _____
           Address: _____
           Phone Number: _____

Suspicion of Child Neglect
Suspicion of Child Abuse   Circle all that apply
Suspicion of Sexual Assault

* *

Name of Child: _____
Address where child can be found: _____
Birthdate: _____
Name of Person(s) Responsible for Child's Care: _____
Address: _____
Phone Number: _____
Relationship to Child: _____
Person(s) Suspected of Abuse or Neglect: _____
Address: _____
Phone Number: _____
Relationship to Child: _____

Describe in objective detail the nature and extent of the alleged injury, neglect, abuse and/or sexual assault to the child in question. _____
_____
_____

Describe in objective details the circumstances leading to this report and any and all facts identifying the suspect as the alleged perpetrator: _____
_____
_____
_____

_____   _____
Signature and Title of Person Making Report   Date

Chart of Child Behavior and Indicators of Potential Abuse

Child's Name _____

Parent's Name _____

Home Address _____

Home Phone _____

Today's Date _____

Reporter's Name _____

Answer the following questions with a "Y" for yes and an "N" for no:

Does the child:

receive a lot of spanking(s) at home _____

receive any spanking by teachers or coaches _____

complain that his/her parent(s) is/are always angry _____

complain that his/her coach(es) is/are always angry _____

come to school early and finds any reasons to stay late after
school/practice _____

hesitate when going to practice or want to leave practice early _____

role-plays abusive parent(s) or dramatizes abusive situations with
puppets, toys, sporting goods or in artwork _____

abuse or pick on younger children _____

frequently miss school without any explanations _____

frequently miss practice without any explanations _____

wear clothing inappropriate to the weather (usually long sleeves and
pants to hide bruises) _____

show physical evidence of abuse _____

describe incidents of abuse _____

show aggressive behavior, is self-abusive or expresses suicidal ideas _____

Follow-up questions:

Were there any witnesses _____

Who were the witnesses (name(s)/address(es)) _____

_____

How was information obtained (volunteered, reported by others) — describe:

_____

_____

Was any investigation made _____

Was any report prepared _____

Chart of Child Behavior Page 2

Please provide comments on any question in which you responded "yes."

_____
_____
_____
_____
_____
_____
_____
_____
_____
_____
_____
_____
_____

I have personally completed this form and affirm that all responses provided above were given to me by the child or observed on the date listed above.

Reporter's Signature

_____

Processing Guidelines After a Child Reports Sexual Assault/Abuse

1)   All alleged instances of abuse, signs of abuse, physical indicia of abuse, verbal confirmation of abuse or just hunches concerning abuse that occurred within the organization or associated with an organization's event(s) should be reported immediately to the organization's "special friend" who can be reached at _____.

2)   Complete an intake form concerning the initial assessment (See page 382). No further steps should be taken by a coach, administrator or volunteer after this point. All further actions should only be taken by the organization's "special friend", the police or child protective services ("CPS"). Parents or other individuals responsible for the welfare of the child should be referred to the "special friend" if they have not yet been contacted by the "special friend."

3)   Absolutely no investigation or confrontation should be made by the administrator, coach, volunteer, or "special friend." No retaliation should be made against an accused abuser/assailant. Anyone accused or suspected of abusing or assaulting a child should be relieved of all child related program contact until an investigation can be made by the police or CPS concerning the substantiation of a child's claim. Specific procedures should be established to allow an appeal for any employee who is suspended due to an alleged abuse/assault. Volunteers do not have to be afforded any special considerations, however, for public relation benefits and to prevent future problems recruiting volunteers, it is recommended that volunteers receive the same type of treatment received by employees.

4)   The following represents some considerations that should be followed when the "special friend" reports alleged instances of sexual abuse/assault.
  a.   If the child suffered maltreatment or is threatened with harm-report to CPS.
  b.   If a crime occurred-report to the police.
  c.   If the parent/guardian is the abuser-report to CPS.
  d.   If you do not know who is the perpetrator-report to the police
  e.   If there is evidence to arrest the abuser/assailant-report to police
  f.   Is the child safe-report to CPS.
  g.   Will the family require any emergency assistance/counseling-report to CPS.

5)   After a thorough investigation has been completed by the police and/or CPS, the organization has to review all documentation available to them and determine what measures, if any, could be implemented to prevent future similar circumstance from occurring during the organization's programs.

Some Interviewing Do's and Don'ts

When Observing or Talking With a Potentially Abused Child

DO:
- Make sure the "Special Person" is someone the child trusts.
- Make sure the "Special Person" is the person most competent to talk with children.
- Conduct all discussions in private,
- Sit next to the child, not across a table or desk.
- Make sure the child understands that the discussion is confidential.
- Reaffirm the need to report child abuse, sexual abuse and neglect.
- Conduct the interview in a language the child understands.
- Ask the child to clarify words/terms that are not understood.
- Tell the child if any future action will be required.
- Tell the child that retaliation will not be accepted.
- Explain all future proceedings.

DON'T:
- Allow the child to feel "in trouble" or "at fault."
- Disparage or criticize the child's choice of words or language.
- Suggest what answers the child should give.
- Probe or press for answers the child is unwilling to give.
- Display horror, shock or disapproval of parents, coach, child or the situation.
- Pressure or force the child into removing clothing.
- Conduct the discussion with a group of people.
- Leave the child alone with a stranger (e.g., a Child Protective Services caseworker).

When Talking With the Parents

DO:
- Select the most appropriate person to talk with concerning the situation.
- Conduct the discussion in private.
- Tell the parent(s) why the discussion is taking place.
- Be direct, honest and professional at all times.
- Reassure the parent(s) that they have the organization's complete support.
- Tell the parent(s) if a report was made or will be made and who will receive the report.
- Advise the parent(s) of the organization's abuse/sexual assault policy statement.
- Reassure the parent(s) that the organization strictly prohibits any retaliation.

DON'T:
- Try to prove abuse or neglect; that is not the "Special Friends" role.
- Display horror, anger or disapproval of organization, parent(s), coach, child or situation.
- Pry into family matters unrelated to the specific situation.
- Place blame or make judgments about the parent(s) or child.
- Try to provide legal advice.
- Make value judgment concerning the organization's conduct and whether anyone was negligent.

Working with the Parents of a Sexually Abused Child

1.   Provide as much information as possible to the parents

    a.   indicate that your organization has a legal and moral obligation to report suspected sexual abuse.

    b.   indicate that your program has a sexual abuse prevention policy

    c.   indicate that children rarely lie about sexual abuse,

    d.   indicate that offenders are usually acquainted with the victim.

2.   Encourage the parents to cope with the situation. Clarify your organization's role in the process. Always reiterate that your organization will always advocate actions that will benefit the child. However, be sensitive to the fact that all parties involved may be angry, in denial or grieving.

3.   Stress the positive steps the family, parents and child have already taken. Indicate the strength and character of the child in reporting the abuse and the parents or relatives support through believing the child.

4.   The parents can be reassuring the child by:
    a.   believing the child
    b.   supporting the disclosure
    c.   empathizing with the child
    d.   not blaming the child,
    e.   protecting the child.

5.   Differentiate the parental concerns from the child's concerns. The parents might be concerned about social or legal ramifications. The parents might blame themselves for failing to prevent the abuse. But, at the same time, the child might feel guilty for breaking up a family, turning-in a loved one or feel guilty for hurting his/her parents.

6.   Share ideas with the parents on techniques that could protect the child in the future such as the touch continuum, self-esteem development, empowering children, self-defense and basic sexual abuse prevention taught in your organization's sexual abuse prevention curricula.

7.   Provide informational resources such as phone numbers and contacts within the police department, social services, child protective services and other governmental agencies. Also provide information on non-government agencies and discuss the resources they can provide both the parents and the child.

8.   Let the parent(s) know that you are a resource and an advocate for them and the child. If they run into any problems, let them know that they can always follow-up with your organization for any additional assistance that might be required.

Program Checklist

The following checklist represents items that need to be incorporated in any organization's comprehensive sexual abuse prevention program. The checklist should be reviewed on a continuous basis to make sure employees and volunteers are always following the organization's policies and procedures.

Description of activity	*Being applied*	
	Yes	No
Job descriptions are available for every paid position	——	——
Job descriptions are available for every volunteer position	——	——
Each applicant has to complete an application form	——	——
Each applicant has to sign a criminal record release	——	——
Interview forms are completed for each applicant	——	——
Have all the references been interviewed	——	——
Have you obtained criminal records from all applicants	——	——
Have all applicants reviewed the organization's sexual abuse policy statement	——	——
Are all the interviewer trained in proper and legal interviewing techniques	——	——
Are policies in place to handle sexual abuse allegations	——	——
Has a "special friend" been appointed	——	——
Has the "special friend" received specific training in sexual abuse	——	——
Do you hold a parents meeting prior to each season	——	——
Are parents given a copy of the organization's sexual abuse police	——	——
Are parents told that the organization does not allow overnight events	——	——
Are parents informed of the organization's educational program	——	——
Do you use pre-test and post-test to determine knowledge levels	——	——
Are all coaches trained in sexual abuse education techniques	——	——
Are sexual abuse prevention strategies applied to all activities	——	——
Are children taught about good v. bad touches	——	——
Are children taught that they have the right to say no	——	——
Are children taught how to contact the organization's "special friend"	——	——
Are children taught to use the buddy system	——	——
Are all members of the organization required to work with children utilizing a buddy system	——	——
Are all members of the organization, children and parents told which activities are and are not permitted by the organization	——	——
Do you allow photographing of children outside the activity setting	——	——
Do you control facility access	——	——
Do you control access to restrooms or changing rooms	——	——
Has you facility identified or eliminated all areas in which a child could be assaulted or kidnapped	——	——
Are all areas well lit	——	——
On road trips, do you require separate sleeping accommodations	——	——
Are policies in place to reduce the chances of out-of-program contact between children and coaches/administrators	——	——
Are all suspected cases of abuse reported to the proper authorities	——	——

Sample Policy Statement #2

It is this organization's policy to provide a safe, abusive-free environment for our children, employees and volunteers. Therefore, all individuals interested in volunteering their service within this organization are required to complete the volunteer application form. Furthermore, all volunteers must attend required sexual assault prevention training sessions.

Purpose

The purpose of this policy is to establish guidelines and procedures regarding volunteer responsibilities. This policy contains information on program objectives, responsibilities, recruitment, screening, education, evaluation and other elements necessary to ensure quality and safe programming.

The primary goal of this policy statement is to reduce the chances of battery, sexual abuse, molestation and other sexual offenses of a youth by a volunteer within this organization.

Overview

Scope

This Policy Statement establishes guidelines and standards for compliance by all volunteers and potential volunteers. Every volunteer and employee should be familiar with the general and specific guidelines of this Policy Statement.

Objectives

1.   To establish guidelines for the volunteer screening process.
2.   To delineate standards for this organization.

Definitions

For this Policy Statement, the following definitions will apply:

Facilities: Recreational or athletic facilities used primarily or temporarily to house recreational or sports activities.

Personnel: Volunteers, custodians, contract employees, recreation supervisors, facility managers, program managers/administrators, coaches, athletic directors and/or all others providing services to children within programs sponsored or administered by this organization.

Volunteers: (a) persons providing services without pay. (b) Citizens from various economic, ethnic, social and political backgrounds who apply for volunteer roles within the organization. Volunteers may be, but are not restricted to, professional men and women, senior citizens, students, families and community restitution workers.

Volunteer Application: Forms that must be completed, signed, submitted and processed before a volunteer is allowed to work with children.

Background Check: A procedure conducted by this organization through various law enforcement agencies which have access to a volunteer's criminal history records, if any. The criminal history information is provided to the organization only after a signed release for disclosure of such records is received from the volunteer. The screening procedure is confidential and only one person within the organization will have access to these records.

Volunteer Appeal Process: An appeal process is available for individuals rejected for any reason included past criminal history. At least three individuals from the organization's board of directors sits on the appeal panel. Appeal panel members can utilize law, equity or the best interest of the organization in affirming or rejecting the results obtained from the initial background check. Appeal panel decision could include probationary periods or other reasonable conclusions. the appeal process shall remain confidential.

Sexual Abuse: The term "Sexual Abuse" will be used throughout this Policy Statement to refer to a wide spectrum of interactions including: rape, physical assault, sexual battery, unwanted physical sexual contact, unwelcomed sexually explicit or offensive verbal communication, coercive or exploitive sexual contact, verbal sexual harassment and/or sexualized attention or contact with a minor.

Child Abuse: Verbal abuse (ridicule or put-downs), physical abuse (any hurting touch or excessive exercise used as punishment), emotional abuse (threats to perform unreasonable tasks) and sexual abuse.

Training Sessions: Any scheduled session for staff or volunteers designed to provide comprehensive sexual abuse prevention education.

Procedural Outline

The organization's "Special Friend" will have primary responsibility for the management of and ensuring compliance with this policy statement.

Additionally, all organization employees, volunteers and representatives must be knowledgeable of all policies, procedures, rules and regulations and responsibilities as set forth within the Policy Statement. All personnel and volunteers must attend the scheduled training sessions.

The Special Friend will be responsible for scheduling training sessions for staff and volunteers, maintain a database of all volunteer applicants and session attendees, review all applications for completeness, verify the true identity of applicants, process all applications through designated law enforcement agencies, collect all criminal background results, issue rejection notices to volunteers who fail to meet the organization's clean background requirement, coordinate appeal panels and coordinate the overall policies and procedures as set forth in this policy statement. The Special Friend will maintain confidential files on all applicants for at least five years after they have left the organization. Final volunteer placement and acceptance will be made by the Special Friend and approved by the organization's board of directors.

Any criminal background check which produces a record of any crime involving violence against children or people will be barred from volunteering with the organization. Any individual with any other felony convictions for which prison time or jail sentence has been served or will be served are also barred from volunteering. Any individuals who has served their time for any felony not involving crimes against children or person and who has successfully completed parole can be offered conditional volunteer assignments until their conduct demonstrates they can handle additional volunteer duties and obligations.

Regulations

Volunteers are required to follow the following rules and procedures:

Truthfully complete an application form.

Sign a release for the disclosure of criminal records.

Volunteers must complete the entire screening process prior to placement.

Volunteers must always demonstrate exemplary behavior.

Contact a supervisor if they are unable to attend or will be late for a designated activity.

Notify a supervisor prior to taking any vacations.

Resolve all problems with a supervisor.

Report any and all suspicious activity to a supervisor or the Special Friend.

Report any alleged abuse or assault to the Special Friend.

Dress appropriately for the activity.

Be evaluated annually by their supervisor.

Expected not to intimidate, harass or bother participants, families and other facility users or activity participants.

Must be at least 16 years of age to qualify as a volunteer.

All volunteers who engage in illegal or immoral acts, including, but not limited to child molestation, theft, drug abuse, sexual assault, etc., will be automatically dismissed from their duties and reported to appropriate local authorities.

Shall not be left alone and in charge of a facility or activity without receiving prior approval from a supervisor.

Exceptions

There will be no exceptions to the policies, procedures and guidelines of this Policy Statement unless issued by the organization's board of directors, in writing.

Non-compliance with any provision of this Policy Statement will result in automatic disciplinary action.

Acknowledgment

After a comprehensive policy statement has been prepared, the statement has to be circulated throughout the organization. Every employee and volunteer within the organization should receive a copy of the statement and sign the form below indicating they have received the statement, read the statement and will abide by the statement's rules and regulations. A policy statement is meaningless if it is not communicated effectively to those required to follow the policy. Thus, all new employees and volunteers have to receive a copy of the policy statement and acknowledgment's receipt. Furthermore, existing employees and volunteers should re-read the policy every year and acknowledge they have reviewed and understand the statement.

Acknowledgment

I _____ acknowledge that on _____(Date) I was given a copy of the organization's sexual abuse policy statement and that I have read the statement and voluntarily agree that as a condition of further participation, employment or involvement in this organization, I will abide by all the terms, conditions, policies and procedures contained within the statement.

I willingly sign this form on _____(Date) in _____ (Place).

_____
Signature

After receiving a signed acknowledgment from all employees or volunteers, it is critical to undertake the next step in the sexual abuse prevention process, the screening of current and future employees and volunteers.

Prevention Program

Volunteer and Employee Screening

Managing employees and volunteers forms one of the most effective barriers to help prevent sexual abuse. The hallmark of an employee of volunteer management program is the screening process. Timeliness, cost, geography and accessibility to specific databases are critical issues in the screening process (see article page 354). But screening will not identify every potential abuser. Most abusers have molested, accosted and/or assaulted numerous children before they were caught-if they were caught. It is impossible to pick every bad apple, however, through utilizing a comprehensive employee and volunteer management program, an organization can identify numerous concerns and create a solid defense to any wrongful hiring or negligent supervision claim.

In order to implement the most effective program, the SAPP can be tailored for both employees and volunteers. There are numerous differences between employees and volunteers. These differences primarily rely upon legal rights and an organization's responsibility. An organization might have to follow the American with Disabilities Act, equal employment opportunities, affirmative action, sexual harassment, Age Discrimination in Employment, federal and state constitutions and a host of other legal concerns when searching for, interviewing, hiring and terminating an employee. On the other hand, volunteers have no rights. There is no constitutional rights to volunteer with an organization. There is no property right to continued participation as a volunteer, nor are there any due process right that have to be followed if you wish to terminate a volunteer's involvement.

The SAPP can cover a variety of issues, with screening being just one component of the SAPP. Other components include developing proper job descriptions, candidate selection, placement, training, supervision, suspension and termination. As with an policy or organization rules, the rules have to be established, clearly communicated and strictly enforced on a consistent basis.

Screening is required to identify individuals who could create unacceptable risks if placed in a position supervising or dealing with children, prevent the inappropriate and/or incorrect placement of a known abuser/assailant within your organization, reduce your organization's chances of being held responsible for negligent hiring and protect all individuals within your organization. Screening cannot identify all potential abusers. This is especially appropriate when abusers are fellow athletes. It is impossible and impractical to screen all participants. However, all participants can be asked if they have ever been convicted of any crimes against people such as assault, molestation, indecency with a minor, child abuse, sexual abuse, etc. Anyone convicted of such crimes can be excluded from participation within the program if the organization's policy statement specifically allows for their exclusion. If the policy statement does not mention exclusion for specific reasons, a rejected applicant can sue claiming they were discriminated against on other grounds (i.e., gender, race, nationality, etc.). However, if there is a specific exclusion on paper, such exclusion could be introduced to a court to show the real reason why the individual was rejected.

While some organizations prohibit the involvement of anyone with a record of past abuse, some organizations only prohibit such a person's involvement when they are actively involved with children or are in some manner engaged in a custodial or supervisorial capacity. Some organizations utilize a scale of allowability based on the proximity to, or vulnerability, of the participants. Some additional concerns include how much solitary time the applicant might spend with children, the dependency inherent in the relationship between the applicant and the participants, the frequency of contact and the length of time the program lasts. As a general rule, stricter screening rules are required when the frequency and intimacy of the contact increases. To help determine what types of contact will be allowed, it is critical to create appropriate job descriptions.

Job Description

Many people have some familiarity with job descriptions from their current employment position. It is quite customary to have job description established in the corporate or government sectors. However, it is less likely to see written job descriptions for nonprofit organizations. However, job descriptions are just as critical in the nonprofit sector as in the corporate or government sectors. Job descriptions form the basis for determining what work would be required by the hired or retained individual. In the corporate sector, you would never see a chief executive officer (CEO) performing the tasks established for a janitor. Their roles are clearly delineated and anyone can refer to their respective job descriptions and determine who should be undertaking specified tasks. Similarly, in the youth sports arena, you would not expect to see a janitor performing the tasks assigned to a coach. Thus, would a janitor be allowed to help children dress and undress for an activity? The answer is not that simple. If there is no one else to help the children change into their swimming suits, and all the children are under age five, then such actions by the janitor might be appropriate (as long as the actions are specified under the job description). If however, there is a coach or other supervisor available who can help watch the children and the children are over 10-years-old, then the janitor's conduct would appear to be highly inappropriate and a possible sign of sexual abuse/assault. Through the job description development process specific duties, obligations, functions and parameters for conduct can be established. The process should be haphazard or done by the seat of the pants. Significant thought and detail should be given for each position. Besides being an effective tool to eliminate unnecessary excess contact with children, the process can streamline operations within the organization and ensure that everyone know what they need to do in order to accomplish the organization's goals.

To develop appropriate job descriptions, start by reviewing what current employees or volunteers do. Ask specifically the various tasks they undertake on a daily, weekly, monthly and yearly (or seasonal) basis. Write down all the various activities that are undertaken to help produce your organization's goals. These various activities should be analyzed to determine if they are properly being allocated to the right individuals. Group all the activities in appropriate positions listing the most important activities first and subsequent activities which are less critical in descending order. Add to the list of activities appropriate job title, specific status (volunteer or paid), job purpose, specific duties/responsibilities, qualifications, supervisor, time commitment, training provided/required and any additional information which will help clarify the job description. Specific detail should be placed on the amount of "hands-on" involvement with children. The following represents a sample job description for a part-time soccer coach. The description includes the key components listed above as well as measurable criterion to help evaluate performance.

Job Description

Job Title:	Head Soccer Coach
Job Status:	The position is a part-time paid position. The coach will be directly employed by XYZ Soccer Organization. The position does not provide any full-time benefits, nor any entitlement to future employment.
Salary:	The salary for this position is $4.25 per hour.
Supervisor:	The Coach will report to _____, XYZ's Vice President of Operations.
Purpose:	The purpose of this position is to provide children age 10-15 with the opportunity to fully develop their soccer skills. The coach is responsible for providing mentoring, educational opportunities, skill enhancement, a safe recreational environment and a wholesome recreational experience.

Duties:

1) Supervise one assistant coach and at least twelve (12) players for a 14 week schedule starting June 7, 1999.
2) provide physical, emotional and intellectual stimulation to all participants
3) promote good sportsmanship.
4) Provide guidance, support and counseling-when appropriate-to all participants in the XYZ program.
5) Be a good listener to verbal and non-verbal communications.
6) Develop and promote new activities that will challenge and motivate children.
7) Provide soccer specific instructions appropriate with the skill, motivational and mental capabilities of each participant.
8) Strictly follow XYZ's soccer coaching program.
9) Develop and maintain a relationship of trust with all participants.
10) Provide any necessary assistance to parents of the participants
11) Supervise the playing environment to prevent non-participants from enteracting with participants during XYZ games, practice or official activities.

Qualifications:	All potential candidates should, at a minimum, have a high school diploma, four years of prior soccer coaching experience, completion of a national coaching certification program (such as American Coaching Effectiveness Program), complete an application form including the signing of a background investigation release form and have prior demonstrable youth counseling experience. Review and accept all the terms of XYZ's sexual abuse policy statement. All references provided on the application form will be checked.
Evaluation:	All assigned children will be provided a pre-test and post-test to ascertain skill development and emotional growth resulting from participation in the program. Such results can be used to determine future employment with XYZ.

Once you know what specific activities you need performed by each employee and volunteer you have to actively recruit the right individuals. There is no one best way to recruit potential employees and volunteers. Word of mouth and personal referrals often form a strong base for discovering prospects. Children that have participated in the organization in the past and adults who were involved on prior occasions also represent a good source. If all else fails, an organization can resort to traditional recruiting tools such as classified advertisements, local colleges, local adult leagues, church groups and employment agencies.

No matter where future employees or volunteers are found, each person has to go through the formal application process. An organization cannot rely on the fact that they have known someone for an extended period of time. The formal application process begins with the completion of an application form.

Application Form

Application forms contain the traditional necessary background information such as name address, phone number, education and work histories. However, the ever increasing need to properly screen individuals to ascertain if a criminal history exists now requires additional information ranging from consent to release criminal records to fingerprinting. The primary application form can contain a release form allowing the release of criminal background information, if any, or a separate release from can be used just for criminal records. The following forms represent an employment application form, a volunteer application form and a sample release which can be used with any application form or separately. All applications, especially employment applications, should be reviewed by an attorney. There are a multitude of questions ranging from birthdate, birthplace, marital status and related concerns which could be asked on a volunteer application and be legal, but be illegal on an employment application. These legal concerns are addressed in greater detail in the interviewing section. However, as this is in essence a risk management manual, it is incumbent not to create an additional liability risk in an effort to eliminate another risk.

Employment Application

Full legal name: _____

Prior names or aliases: _____

Complete address: _____

Home and work numbers: (___)_____ (___)_____

Social security _____

Driver's license number, state and expiration date: _____(or other I.D.)

List all coaching certificates or _____

List all prior involvement in youth athletics: _____

List three personal and business references including current phone numbers:

Personal   (1) _____

            (2) _____

            (3) _____

Business   (1) _____

            (2) _____

            (3) _____

List all prior residences for the past ten years: _____

Have you ever been convicted of any felony, in any state or country: _____

If yes, please describe the felony committed and your current legal status (parole, probation, etc.): _____

I understand and agree that:

1) It is the policy of this organization to deny employment opportunities for individuals who have been convicted of any violent crime or any crime against any person(s).

2) This organization has a strict confidentiality and appeals process concerning the handling of the applications of individuals with prior criminal histories.

3) This application is valid for two years and a new application has to be completed immediately thereafter.

4) By submitting this application I, the applicant, affirm that all the foregoing information I have provided is true and correct.

5) By submitting this application I, the applicant, agree (in return for being allowed to work) that if any of the foregoing information is incorrect, I will forever indemnify and hold this youth organization harmless for any acts or omissions on my behalf solely as it relates to the incorrect information I have provided.

6) By submitting this application I, the applicant, voluntarily waive my privacy rights only to the extent necessary for the youth organization to verify the foregoing information through any reasonable means, including, but not limited to local, regional, state, national or international criminal background check(s).

Printed Name: _____

Signature: _____

Date: _____

Affirmative Action/Equal Employment Opportunity Employer

Volunteer Application

Full legal name: _____
Prior names or aliases: _____
Complete address: _____
Home and work numbers: (___)_____ (___)_____
Social security _____
Driver's license number, state and expiration date: _____
Date of birth: _____ (only for volunteers)
List all coaching certificates or _____
List all prior involvement in youth athletics: _____
List three personal and business references including current phone numbers:
Personal   (1) _____
            (2) _____
            (3) _____
Business   (1) _____
            (2) _____
            (3) _____
List all prior residences for the past ten years: _____
Have you ever been convicted of any felony, in any state or country: _____
If yes, please describe the felony committed and your current legal status (parole, proba-
tion, etc.): _____

I understand and agree that:

1) It is the policy of this organization to deny volunteer opportunities for individuals who have been convicted of any violent crime or any crime against any per-
   son(s). This organization can deny any applicant for any reason or for no reason
   at all.

2) This organization has a strict confidentiality and appeals process concerning the
   handling the applications of individuals with prior criminal histories.

3) This application is valid for two years and a new application has to be completed
   immediately thereafter.

4) By submitting this application I, the applicant, affirm that all the foregoing information I have provided is true and correct.

5) By submitting this application I, the applicant, agree (in return for being allowed to
   volunteer) that if any of the foregoing information is incorrect, I will forever indemnify and hold this youth organization harmless for any acts or omissions on my behalf solely as it relates to the incorrect information I have provided.

6) By submitting this application I, the applicant, voluntarily waive my privacy rights
   only to the extent necessary for the youth organization to verify the foregoing information through any reasonable means, including, but not limited to local, state, national and international criminal background check(s).

Printed Name: _____
Signature: _____
Date: _____

Release

I, _____ (name) hereby authorize *ORGANIZATION* to obtain any and all pertinent information pertaining to any charges, allegations and/or convictions of any kind I may have had or are currently pending relating to any state, federal or international criminal law violations. Such information can include, but is not limited to, any allegations, charges or convictions for crimes committed against children, people and crimes involving moral turpitude. Such information can be obtained from such sources as any and all law enforcement agencies of this state, other states, federal agencies and international law enforcement agencies to the full extent permitted by law.

Social Security Number _____

Driver's License Number _____ State _____

All states and counties which you have lived in over the past ten years _____

_____

Have you ever been convicted of any felony? _____

If yes, please describe the conviction and when you were convicted _____

_____

I affirm, under the penalty of perjury, that the following is true and correct information and I would testify accordingly if called to testify in any court of law.

Signature _____

Date _____

In order for application forms to be effective, all applicants have to write neatly and complete the entire form. Any incomplete or illegible forms (including names or dates written illegibly within the application form) should result in automatic rejection of the application. Individuals receiving applications should review applications for completeness and legibility immediately upon receipt to reduce the time required to send applications back to the applicant for corrections.

Candidate Selection

There are a multitude of questions that can be asked for the best applicants depending upon the region, sport(s), organization, state laws, federal laws and a host of other variables. There are standard interview and job application subjects that have to be avoided as a matter of law. These questions apply only to job applicants. Questions such as what is your age, what is your birthdate, are you American, are you Catholic, are you married, how many children do you have, are you disabled and where were you born all pose significant legal problems. However, the very same questions are acceptable and not a problem when asked to a volunteer. The difference lies in the fact that there is no constitutional right to volunteer, while there is a constitutional right to be free from bias when applying for, working at or being terminated from a job.

Interview Guidelines

The following pointers are practical suggestions to be used when interviewing an applicant. There is no one correct method. Some individuals like to used a structured, formal interview where all questions are written in advance so there could be standardized evaluation of all candidates. Others like to use a less formal unstructured or semi-structured interview process. Whichever method is used, the key for all interviewing revolves around being as thorough as possible in obtaining critical information. Even if you feel very comfortable with an applicant and you might talk informally for a good portion of the interview, you cannot forget to ask the critical questions or to look for the keys that a problem might exist. The following interview rules, suggestions or cues for further investigation represent a partial list of issues that all interviewers should follow.

1) Interviewing is only effective when everyone is thoroughly screened.
2) If at all possible, try to have at least two people at each interview so if a discrimination claim is raised, you could possibly

have two witnesses who can testify as to what happened. Furthermore, you can base decisions to hire or utilize someone based on the opinions of two people rather than one individual.

3) All interviewers should be intimately familiar with the organization's sexual abuse policy.

4) If possible, receive permission from the interviewee to videotape the interview.

5) Utilize all available resources such as police for investigation or fingerprinting, school districts for employee records and any other potential source of information concerning position applicants.

6) Prior to starting the interview, check at least two pieces of identification-at least one with a picture, to make sure the person interviewed is in fact the person that is applying for the job.

7) Ask more intense questions regarding an applicants background when there exists frequent, unexplained moves.

8) Ask more intense questions regarding an applicants background when there exists gaps in employment or education dates.

9) Ask more intense questions regarding an applicants background when there exists any criminal convictions or serious motor vehicle violations. Determine the specifics concerning the convictions or violations including specific dates, jurisdictions, exact charges, exact adjudication and the exact resolution of the conviction.

10) Follow-up with what hobbies are listed and if they are appropriate for someone of similar age and background.

11) Follow-up with what the applicant's attitudes are toward children.

12) Be cognizant of appropriate and inappropriate nonverbal queues.

13) Be cognizant of potential problems if the applicant is single with no "age-appropriate" romantic relationships.

14) Be cognizant of potential problems if all activities and interests center around children.

15) Be sensitive, but also cautious, when an applicant was sexually abused as a child.

16) Be cognizant of potential problems if the applicant is fearful of adult the world.

17) Be cognizant of potential problems if the applicant sees children as "pure," "innocent" and/or "clean."

18) Be wary if the applicant is overanxious to get the position.

19) Deny any applicant who is willing to bend the rules to allow overnights or other prohibited actions.

20)   Deny any applicant who abuses alcohol or drugs.

Interview Questions

Besides developing some general guidelines for interviews, all interviewers should understand what questions they can ask and what questions will solicit the requisite information sought from the applicant. The
following represent some acceptable questions that will provide useful information in analyzing the qualification of any candidate. It should be remembered that you should not ask leading questions, yes or no questions,
nor questions that are too general. Provide the applicant with questions
that allows them to elaborate on responses and provide information voluntarily that could not have been requested through traditional questioning. Additionally. all questions should be relevant and further the informational needs required to make a final decision concerning the applicant.

1)   Why are you interested in the position?
2)   How would you describe yourself?
3)   Have you ever had to discipline a child, and how did you do it?
4)   Why do you like to work with children?
5)   What traits do you think you have that qualifies you to su-
     pervise children?
6)   What about the position/job appeals to you the most/least?
7)   Are you familiar with the issues associated with child sexual
     abuse?
8)   Have you read XYZ's Organizational policy statement con-
     cerning sexual abuse?
9)   What do you think about the policy?
10) Have you ever been convicted of a criminal offense including
     criminal driving violations?
11) Have you ever worked in a position for which you were bonded?
12) How do you interact with children?
13) Are you aware of any problems or conditions that could in-
     terfere with your ability to care for children or in any way en-
     danger any child under your care?

All responses should be recorded in a response form to provide evidence
concerning what questions were asked and relevant responses.

Interview Response Form

Name of Applicant _____

Interviewer(s) _____

Date _____

Position Title _____

Was the applicant given a copy of the job description? _____

Did the applicant read and sign the organizational sexual abuse policy statement and complete job application including authorization to release records? _____

Did the applicant indicate if they needed any accommodation to perform the job's essential functions? _____

Personal Questions

Education _____

Past work experience _____

_____

Last salary (if appropriate) _____

Discipline actions at work _____

school _____

military _____

Military experience _____

Social security number _____

Can they provide proof of residence if they are hired _____

DO NOT ASK—age, race, nationality, religion, sexual orientation, marital status and related questions if the applicant is applying for an employment position.

How did you learn about this position? _____

Why are you interested in the position? _____

What things have you done that have given you the greatest satisfaction? _____

_____

What have been the biggest disappointment in your life? _____

_____

Where do you see yourself in 1 year, 5 years and 10 years down the road? _____

_____

Describe your temperament? _____

Have you know anyone that has been abused? _____

Tell me about that person and your relationship to him or her? _____

_____

How would you describe yourself? _____

Have you ever had to discipline a child, and how did you do it? _____

_____

Why do you like to work with children? _____

What traits do you think you have that qualifies you to supervise children? _____

Are you familiar with the issues associated with child sexual abuse? _____

Have you read XYZ's Organizational policy statement concerning sexual abuse? _____
What do you think about the policy? _____

Have you ever been convicted of a criminal offense including criminal driving violations?
_____

Have you ever worked in a position for which you were bonded? _____

How do you relate with children? _____

Are you aware of any problems or conditions that could interfere with your ability to care
for children or in any way endanger any child under your care? _____

Why do you like working with children? _____

Have you ever had any unsupervised supervisorial obligation with children in any past employment of volunteer position? _____

Is there any information you would like to share about yourself? _____

General observations as they apply strictly to candidate's qualifications _____

Areas possibly necessitating further investigation _____

Notes _____
_____
_____
_____

Have all references been contacted? _____
Any necessary follow-up? _____

References

The rules related to reference checks are not as complicated as interview rules, but the rules are just as important. The primary concerns while checking references deal with defamation. Defamation is the communication of untrue statements about a person to others which, whether or not malicious in nature, which injure a person or hold him or her to ridicule. Relying upon untrue statements from prior employers to make your employment decisions can subject the former employer to a defamation action that would likely involve your organization as well. Based on the potential for numerous defamation claims, many employers only release specific information about a former employee such as the dates they worked, their first position with the company and their last position with the company. The primary defense to a defamation claim is the truth. That is why it is critical to ask only factual questions (if possible) and to ask the person you are contacting to leave out any personal bias or opinions.

In addition to only requesting truthful information, your organization has an obligation to provide truthful information concerning an employee or volunteer who left due to suspect conditions. If an employee was convicted of sexual assault, and you failed to pass this information on to another organization, you could be liable for any harm for failing to warn.

The following form should be completed upon checking every reference check.

Reference Interview Form

Applicant's Name _____ Position Applied for _____

Interviewer _____ Date _____

Reference Being Interviewed _____ Position _____

Company/Organization Name _____

Company Phone Number (_____) _____

How long have you known the Applicant? _____

In what capacity did you know the Applicant? _____

Please describe your relationship with the Applicant. _____
_____

Please describe the Applicant's relationship with people in general. _____
_____

Please describe the Applicant's relationship with children. _____
_____

To the best of your knowledge, has the Applicant ever been convicted of a crime? _____

Would your company/org. ever rehire the Applicant? _____

Was the Applicant ever disciplined by your company/org. and why was he/she _____

Do you know of any traits, conditions, tendencies or problems which would be detrimental to his/her working with children? _____
_____

Comments _____
_____
_____

Interviewer's Signature _____

After all the references have been checked and the initial interview process has been completed, a list of all qualified individuals should be established from those individuals that had passed all initial screening steps. From that point, any needed follow-up interviews should be scheduled. Thereafter, all equally qualified applicants should be grouped in the final approved applicant pool. A final decision can be based on a multitude of variables including an applicant's personality. However, personality can only be used as a deciding factor among equally qualified individuals. Thereafter, the applicants should be sent the organization's standard and approved rejection/hiring letter. The rejection letter should just indicate that after careful consideration of all applicants, another candidate was chosen for the position. It should be reiterated that the applicant should reapply for any future positions that might open within the organization.

Acceptance letters should specify that the organization is interested in hiring the individual. The letter should be as simple as possible and should not contain any terms or conditions of employment. Any such terms could become part of the employment contract, even if such terms are inconsistent with prior negotiations. New employees should be asked to sign specific employment contracts containing all the terms and conditions of employment. A competent attorney should be consulted regarding the necessary terms and conditions to include in such a contract. However, one key provision needed is a clause indicating that the new employee has read and agreed to all the terms contained in the organization's sexual abuse prevention policy and the new employee will indemnify and hold the organization harmless if he or she violates the policy.

Volunteers

Volunteers need to go through the same basic screening process as potential employees. Thus, all the forms above are appropriate for both applicants seeking employment or a volunteer position. However, as noted previously, a volunteer has no employment right so there is a greater latitude regarding what questions can be asked. This does not mean that an organization has carte blanche authority to ask any question it wants. Common sense should dictate what questions are asked. Personal questions could offend some potential volunteers. Volunteers who are insulted might decide not to volunteer and can tell others how they were treated. Thus, questions should be focused only on necessary issues and volunteers should be told why specific questions are being asked. If applicants are told from the very beginning that the organization is interested in protecting the safety and well being of children, most applicants will willingly cooperate. Those who are outraged or refuse to sign a release for criminal records should be told individually what the organization is interested in doing by checking individuals' backgrounds. If the applicant is still not satisfied with your explanation, you should not dismiss the individual as crazy or someone you definitely do not want to associate with your organization. It might be necessary to discuss the appeals process, what exact offenses are examined in criminal records checks and/or how is confidentiality ensured for handling criminal records. Some individuals have been concerned about criminal background checks because some minorities have a greater likelihood of having criminal histories which could lead to discrimination or under representation. By explaining to such skeptics that any criminal convictions not entailing crimes against persons will be dealt with differently, skeptics could hopefully be won over. It should be assumed that no matter how much you explain the importance of screening procedures, some individuals will always feel you are invading their privacy and will refuse to cooperate with your organization. It is impossible to please everyone all the time and an organization has to determine when they have gone far enough in attempting to appease a potential applicant.

There are a variety of questions that can be added to questions traditionally asked to applicants for paid positions. The following questions can be asked during an interview and the answers recorded in the notes section on the Interview Response Form.

1)   Why do you want to volunteer with children?
2)   What questions or concerns do you have about being a volunteer?
3)   How much time do you have to devote for volunteer work?

Placement

Placement refers to putting the volunteer or employee in the proper position. Most individuals are hired or recruited to fill a specific void. In those circumstances, it is easy to place the individual in the appropriate position or job. However, it is a different story when the individual turns out not to be what was expected or the individual was recruited or hired to fill one position and, due to extenuating circumstance, is forced to fill another position. Under such circumstances, an organization might be forced to conduct a salvage operation which might entail reassigning certain tasks or modifying some positions.

Special attention should be focused on any position that requires special contact with a child. If the volunteer or employee is not qualified or has not been properly screened, he/she should not be allowed to assume a position that he/she should not fill. This is not just a hypothetical issue. This situation arises frequently in youth sports organizations. A coach might not be able to make a practice one day because he/she has a doctor's appointment. Because the appointment is sudden, he/she had no chance to plan for a substitute coach. In order to make sure the kids still have a practice, the coach calls his next door neighbor and asks him or her to substitute and supervise the practice. The problem with such an arrangement is that the coaching placement had been approved for the coach, not the neighbor. The neighbor could possibly be the sweetest person, but also could be on probation for sexual abuse. To avoid this situation, a back-up list of approved coaches or referees should be created which a coach or referee could call at any time and obtain an approved substitute.

Only through proper training and educational programs will coaches and administrators fully understand and appreciate their placement and appropriate substitutions options.

Training

Once an individual has been properly placed, that individual has to be trained. Training can be something as simple as introduction to appropriate personnel and procedures. However, to make sure every individual is properly trained requires significant effort, time and commitment. It is estimated that it costs approximately $20,000 to train a new employee in the business sector. This amount constitutes lost time, salaries for the trainee and the people training him/her, losses due to mistakes and similar costs.

There is no way to avoid training costs or responsibilities. Even if the most experienced individual is hired, they still need to be trained in the proper procedures of the specific organization. As would be expected, training is most effective when instituted immediately after hiring or retaining the employee or volunteer. Thus, training actually starts through the interview process. Immediately after hiring or retaining an individual, the organization should provide as much available material as possible to help educate him/her about his/her role and responsibilities. This process can save significant time and energy and provide clear indications of what work will be required. Thus, if the applicant is not that serious about the position, he/she might drop out before wasting valuable time, energy or money.

The introductory material should contain a list of all appropriate personnel, their phone numbers, key board members, the organization's sexual abuse policy statement, a contact list for police and other agencies and information concerning the organization's special friend. Any appropriate policies could also be included in the introductory materials. Such policies could include information concerning the use of office equipment for personal matters (facsimile, phone and/or photocopiers), duplicating keys, allowing access to restricted areas, employee benefits, required paperwork and reporting channels and related policies.

Once an individual reports for his/her first day on the job, time should be dedicated beforehand that certain individuals would dedicate a percentage of his/her day to training. The basic approach to training involves walking an individual through the position. Individuals are shown the various tasks they will need to perform and are introduced to the individuals with whom they will regularly work. There is no one correct method to train individuals. The key to an effective training program involves making sure individuals know the right tasks to perform, the policies they are expected to follow and the individuals with whom they will be interacting on a regular basis.

A key concern with training involves the lack of continued support. Individuals often undergo extensive training during their first week on the job, but do not receive any subsequent training. To successfully implement a comprehensive sexual abuse prevention program, training needs to become an annual activity. New research, techniques and strategies are always being developed to combat sexual abuse and similar concerns. As the organization's key person on sexual abuse, the special friend should regularly update all employees and volunteers on the latest strategies or procedures. A yearly meeting with all employees and volunteers is an effective means for providing additional training and possibly protecting the organization from a suit claiming negligent training of employees or volunteers.

Supervision

Just because individuals have been properly screened and trained does not mean they will not get into trouble or they have not been able to fool the system. An individual could have utilized a fraudulent identity to avoid identification during the screening process. Furthermore, an individual could, even after extensive training, not perform the required job requirements.

Control is a managerial term often utilized to make sure a business is following proper procedure to accomplish the business's goals. Similarly, an organization has to have sufficient controls to supervise employee and volunteer conduct. An organization that has a sexual abuse policy statement already has a framework from which to control and supervise conduct. While supervision entails all aspects of an employee or volunteer's involvement with the organization, this section will only address issues associated with supervising the SAPP.

Supervision entails identifying specific policies within the SAPP and utilizing those policies as guidelines for future conduct. Thus, if the SAPP prohibits any overnight events, supervision requires determining whether or not any employee or volunteer is following the policy. How can an organization properly supervise and control while at the same time not appearing like police investigators? There are several easy steps to take which are nonintrusive and efficient. The special friend can regularly ask children and adults what is going on with their program, team, coaches, facilities and volunteers/employees. The organization has to always be vigilant to watch for trouble signs such as posted flyers advertising unapproved activities, individuals not following the required buddy system, publishing player rosters with home address and phone number and other concerns which directly contradict the SAPP. Constant vigilance is the only means by which an organization can supervise personnel and programs to ensure SAPP compliance.

It should always be anticipated that there might be minor or unavoidable situations which might result in breaching the SAPP. Someone might call in sick leaving only one person to work with children at a given facility. Such an occurrence should not automatically lead to a negative review or suspension. Rather, once such a problem is identified, proper supervision requires determining if such conduct occurs on a regular basis and what steps can be taken to prevent further policy violations. Some solutions to the problem of a sick employee leaving one person alone with children might be terminating the sick employee, switching employees, requesting that another employee spend part of the day at the facility or requesting that parents come early to help with the children.

Suspension

Once a problem has been identified risk management becomes the primary concern for the organization. Risk management does not just imply trying to lower potential monetary judgments against an organization. Risk management also refers to strategies designed to prevent future harm. If an employee or volunteer has violated the SAPP or other organizational rules, that individual needs to be informed about the specific policy(s) that had been violated and given a chance to explain. If the violation is not egregious, the organization might act appropriately by reiterating the SAPP and specifically requesting that the individual continue to follow the policy. If the violation was more egregious, the organization has to determine how egregious the violation was and what harm occurred or could have occurred from the violation. Less egregious conduct could force the organization to issue a written warning or reprimand to the individual. Such a warning or reprimand would be ineffective if there was no set policy as to how many reprimands or warnings will trigger termination or expulsion proceedings.

If the conduct is more egregious, the employee or volunteer should probably receive both a reprimand and a suspension. A suspension is critical to prevent further contact between the individual and the child or children that are involved in the underlying matter. The organization has to develop specific policies as to what steps need to be taken to suspend an individual and whether or not an appeals process is provided. While legally, an appeals process is not needed for volunteers, an appeals process would be very beneficial in helping to retain the confidence of other volunteers. Employees that have a property right in continued employment (based on a legitimate expectation of continued employment from a contract or other sources) cannot be terminated without any reason whatsoever without drawing legal scrutiny. Employees of federal or state programs have a constitutional right to due process prior to being terminated or suspended. Thus, programs that receive any federal or state funding need to carefully examine all employment relationships to determine what rights are provided to each employee. Prior to suspending state/federal employees, employees need to know what charges are being raised against them, what evidence or witnesses will testify and be given a right to examine witnesses. Providing such due process rights is critical for ensuring fairness and truthfulness. However, most organizations are not properly equipped to provide proper adjudication and review of serious incidents involving children. Thus, if at all possible, the organization should defer to other authorities. If other authorities such as criminal courts or child protective service organizations conclude that abuse has occurred and can clearly identify an abuser, the organization can possibly rely upon those conclusion to suspend or terminate an individual. Since the rules and laws relating to further employment and the right to work are very specific, organizations should contact an attorney to determine what specific policies should be followed when suspending or terminating an employee.

Termination

While suspension with or without pay for employees or program suspension for volunteers can limit liability and risk exposure, sometimes an individual has left no other option for the organization, but termination as the last resort when no other options exist.

If the SAPP specifically provides that any employee or volunteer who violates the SAPP faces termination, then any policy violation can result in termination. However, termination, similar to suspension, should be used cautiously to avoid alienating and antagonizing current and future employees or volunteers.

The easy case involves terminating an individual that has been adjudicated guilty of sexually inappropriate behavior. A slightly harder case involves an individual that has been charged, but not adjudicated guilty of any crime. Suspension is a more appropriate measure to take with such an individual until the matter is finally adjudicated.

Termination would appear less appropriate when an individual has just been charged with a possible criminal violation, just arrested without any charges being filed and/or just being investigated for improprieties.

While many people would like to remove any problems from their organization, such a response represents a mob mentality and cannot be condoned. Termination should only be considered after carefully evaluating all the facts and determining how the facts fit within the SAPP policies. The advise of competent legal counsel will help ensure that terminations follow proper legal protocol. There is no guarantee that a terminated employee or volunteer will not sue for wrongful termination. However, with proper intention, following written policies concerning termination procedures and reasons and consulting with an attorney prior to finally terminating and individual's involvement with the organization, the chance of successfully defending the suit rise dramatically.

Once specific screening and employment procedures are developed and implemented, other program components need to be developed to properly implement the SAPP. The SAPP is not just an employment program. A comprehensive SAPP will utilize a variety of techniques to educate employees, volunteers and program participants about sexual abuse and steps needed to avoid or prevent such abuse. The following section provides specific components of an educational campaign that will provide a thorough base for developing and implementing a sexual abuse prevention program.

Education

Developing Educational
Programs for Children

One key to any educational program is the determination of program success. That is, did the educational program achieve its goal(s). There are several goals which could possibly form the cornerstone of your educational program. These goals include: the knowledge that was learned, the attitudes that had been changed, what skills had been acquired or refined, how long the program lasts and is the information transmitted in the most effective manner. Prior to launching any educational program, your organization has to determine what you want to accomplish with the educational program. Your educational goals should be a component of your organization's sexual abuse prevention policy statement. The pre-test and post-test offer a valuable tool to determine if you have accomplished your educational goals. While fifteen sample questions are provided in this monograph, more specific questions can be designed to determine whether the educational program has achieved its goal(s).

It is imperative that all coaches or administrators who teach the educational courses adhere to the program content and process. The educational program should be managed by a motivated parent, or organizational member, rather than an organization administrator. Community awareness and support for the educational program can be maximized when the program is spearheaded by one of "their own" rather than being imposed from "above." In order for the educational program to work. The organization has to foster interagency and/or community support. You will need the support of child protective services, social services, mental health agencies, police department, probation/parole department, schools and a host of other agencies and organizations in order to recruit other instructors and obtain the most appropriate educational materials. All presenters and educators should be specifically trained in sexual abuse prevention education. Presenters need to be able to present the material in a manner children can understand without scarring them. Providing inaccurate information will produce counter productive results. Presenters, at a minimum, need to know: what indicators (physical, behavioral, emotional) are typical of sexual abuse, what reporting requirements exists and how the reporting process works, how to talk to a child who might need help and how to respond to a child who asks for help. This minimum knowledge also needs to be taught to coaches and administrators.

Prior to initiating any education program, parents should receive a letter explaining that the child will receive training in identifying and understanding sexual abuse/assault (see page 425). Any parents not interested in exposing their child to the program should be requested to keep their child out of practices during the instructional period. All other parents should sign the parental consent form attached to the parents' letter.

Educational programming should not be considered in a vacuum. Abusers regularly change their tactics and approaches. New information is available on a continuous basis. Therefore, the organization has to develop a long term plan for the educational program. The plan should be reevaluated every several years to make sure it is as current as possible and still achieving the organization's goals.

Definitions

Prior to starting any educational program, it is incumbent on everyone in the organization to understand the various terms and concepts which will be utilized in the educational program. The following definitions and signs of abuse are useful for everyone in the organization to understand and be able to relate to children in the educational process.

Sexual abuse is commonly defined as any sexual conduct harmful to a child's mental, emotional or physical welfare. Sexual abuse also entails the failure to make a reasonable effort to prevent sexual conduct with a child (Texas Family Code). Sexual abuse may consist of a single incident or numerous acts over an extended period of time.

Child sexual abuse includes fondling, sodomy, oral copulation, child pornography, child prostitution, lewd or lascivious exposure or behavior, intercourse, penetration of a genital or anal opening by a foreign object and any other sexual conduct harmful to a child's mental, emotional, or physical welfare. Noncontact acts (sexual comments, exposure, voyeurism, etc.) might not technically be classified as sexual abuse, but might be characterized as improper sexual activity with a child. The absence of force or coercion to accomplish any act of sexual abuse does not diminish the abusive nature of the conduct.

Sexual abuse is often defined as acts committed by a person responsible for the care of a child (a parent, baby-sitter, day care provider, coach or other person responsible for a child). Sexual assault is usually defined as sexual acts on a child committed by a person who has no responsibility for the care of that child.

Child is used throughout this SAPP to refer to any individual under the age of eighteen. As sexual abuse can happen to anyone, the term child is used to refer to both boys and girls.

Signs of Abuse

Most children will not come right out and say they have been sexually abused. Normally, an adult has to observe either physical or emotional signs of abuse. However, oral indicators still remain the best method for determining sexual abuse. Children might report sexual abuse in an oblique and tentative manner. A child might ask a questions such as, "I have a friend…" A child could also pose a hypothetical such as "what if…."

Physical Indicators

Sexual abuse can, but is not frequently, evidenced by physical injury. A child injured as a result of sexual abuse might:

display difficulty sitting or walking,
report pain/itching when urinating,
report pain/itching when defecating,
complain of stomach aches
report pain or itching in the genital area
experience a secretion or discharge from the genital area
demonstrate unexplained bruises, welts, fractures, or lacerations
demonstrate poor hygiene
appear often tired with no energy
lags in physical development
demonstrate speech or communications disorders
possess torn, stained or bloodied underclothing
have venereal and other sexually transmitted diseases
demonstrate frequently unexplained sore throats
become pregnant
have bruised genitalia

Never perform a physical examination of a sexually abused child. Always bring a child to competent authorities so a qualified physician can perform a thorough examination.

Behavioral Indicators

Behavioral manifestations of sexual abuse can include:

frequent expressions of sexual activity (verbal references, pictures, pretend games)
knowledgeable of sexual relations beyond what is normal for the child's age

frequent masturbation
sexually suggestive behavior
showing infantile behavior
showing extreme fear of being alone with adults of a particular sex
the child's subsequent victimization of other children
being wary of any adult contact
being apprehensive when other children cry
being afraid to go home
exhibiting anxiety concerning normal activities such as toileting or
     napping
complains of soreness and moves awkwardly
arrives at practice early and stays late to avoid going home
wears clothing that covers the body when the clothing is seasonally
     inappropriate
showing little or no distress when separated from parents
being apt to seek affection with any adult
not tolerating any physical contact
being a chronic runaway
exhibiting habit disorders such as sucking, biting fingers, rocking
     back-and-forth
developmental lags (mental, emotional, friendships, etc.)
the inability to concentrate
frequent absences from school or practice
abrupt changes in a child's behavior
a lack of self-esteem
a reluctancy to undress for physical examination or swimming
being overly concerned for vulnerable siblings
poor peer relations

Emotional Indicators

Generalized psychological indicators of sexual abuse include:

withdrawal
depression
sleeping disorders
eating disorders
self-mutilation
phobias
school problems (absences, tardiness, lower grades)
attention problems
poor hygiene
alcohol dependency

drug dependency
suicidal threats/attempts

Once the following definitions and signs are understood, the information can be utilized in developing the topics and curriculum that will form the basis of the educational program.

Topics

While every sexual abuse prevention program is different, and programs should be structured to fit specific audiences (i.e., age appropriate, language appropriate), the following represent topics typically included in educational programs:

Introduction of lesson plan
Pre-test to determine their knowledge base (see p. 422)
Curriculum on types of touching (good v. bad) (see article p. 24)
Question and answer sessions
Role playing different encounters
Behavioral rehearsal of prevention strategies
Puppet show to demonstrate different touch that are good and bad
Explore ways to say "No" without hurting someone's feelings
Review safety rules relating to strangers (see article p. 25)
Utilize a "what if…" game to teach proper responses to dealing
    with strangers
Teach children their rights in their home and how to contact appropriate authorities
Teach children that they are not to blame themselves
Define terms such a crime, victim, sexual abuse/assault (see p. 415)
Discuss methods used to trick or trap children (see article p. 19)
Teach children that abusers or attackers do not necessarily have to
    be strangers
Teach prevention rules/safety strategies such as assertive behavior, decision-making skills, and communication skills (see article p. 24)
Utilize Hula Hoops to teach children about their personal space
Discuss acquaintance rape (see article p. 25)
Discuss assault against co-participants
Discuss how to be a supportive friend
Discuss appropriate displays of affection
Discuss sexual boundaries and limits during a date (i.e., the need
    for communication)
Provide a resource list (see p. 428)

Perform post-test (see p. 422)

Teach parents how to further their child's education or knowledge and how parents should and can protect their children

Send letter to parents reiterating the major points discussed with the children (see p. 426)

Questions to Ponder

Some questions that need to be answered concerning your sexual abuse education program include:

1) How is sexual abuse defined and does the definition give enough information to understand the concept?

2) Are the definitions age/intelligence appropriate?

3) Is sexual abuse defined in terms of touching (positive versus negative touching)?

4) Does the definition cover all types of sexual abuse and provide for examples?

5) Are children taught that the typical abuser is someone they know?

6) Are children taught that abusers typically use a form of coercion to get their victims (bribes, threats, authority, age), not physical force?

7) Are children taught their body parts in a manner that they are then knowledgeable to effectively report sexual abuse?

8) Are children taught that they are never to blame for being sexually abused?

9) Are stereotypes (old, strange, ugly, scary-looking, etc.) of abusers avoided?

10) Are children aware of which situations can possibly turn into potentially abusive situations?

11) Is the self-protection, self-defense or self-esteem components adequate for the age and intelligence of the children?

12) Have the children increased their ability to avoid abusive situations?

13) Do children know who is the organization's "special friend?"

14) Have children utilized role playing and other educational techniques to help their learning process?

15) Are children encouraged to always report sexual abuse or inappropriate contact?

16) Is the instruction provided in a threatening or frightening manner?

17) Is the educational material culturally appropriate?
18) Are children taught that any child, from any race, sex, age, nationality or religion can be sexually abused?
19) Is the material presented in such a manner that it does not further traumatize a child who might have been previously abused?
20) Are children taught that other children can be abusers?
21) Are children taught the penalties associated with the crime of sexual abuse and the repercussions if they sexually abuse a fellow program participant?
22) Does the educational program involve the parent(s)?
23) Does the program have an evaluation mechanism to measure effectiveness?

Some Practical Steps

1) Find out what is already available in your community in terms of prevention programs, educational programs, governmental programs, and support groups.
2) Determine the scope of your program. What ages, activities, personnel and other issues have to be decided before establishing your program. Set specific goals and objectives for your program (i.e. to inform, prevent, educate, etc.).
3) Utilize an advisory board of local experts to assist you in program development and implementation.
4) Implement components of the program in a test run to assure everyone can complete their assigned tasks and responsibilities. Utilize feedback from children, parents and administrators to modify and fine tune the program.
5) Make sure the instructors are properly trained to deal with the specific age group they will be working with.
6) Make sure you have sufficient funding to purchase necessary materials.
7) Make sure you develop community support and awareness. Be prepared for questions and/or criticism from individuals who might not understand the purpose of your program or think you are dehumanizing sports for children who need a nurturing environment.
8) If possible, try to coordinate the program with local school officials or school programs.

9) Emphasis should be placed on creating a safe environment for all participants.

10) All personnel should be aware of, and understand, reporting requirements and their responsibility to always follow the express letter of the law.

11) Staff screening is critical for any sexual abuse/assault prevention program. However, staff screening is just the beginning and should always be used in conjunction with additional safety procedures.

12) Never exploit or inappropriately use past victims of sexual abuse to help promote your program.

13) Be sensitive to the needs of children and their desire to be loved. Regulations and policies should address harmful situations, not a five-year-old giving an innocent kiss to a fellow kindergartner.

Pre/Post Test Questions

1. A bad person is _____
2. I think I am a good person (check one). Yes _____ No _____
3. Should you tell our organization's "special friend" if someone touches you in a way that is upsetting or confusing (check one). Yes _____ or No _____
4. Sex offenders are:
    a. crazy.
    b. weird.
    c. are alcoholics.
    d. individuals with a problem.
5. Sexual abuse means:
    a. someone talking to me using suggestive words.
    b. someone touching me in a upsetting way.
    c. someone asking me to take pictures without any clothes on.
    d. all the above are possible examples of sexual abuse.
6. Sexual assault:
    a. only happens when you do not listen to your parents.
    b. will never happen if you do not talk to strangers.
    c. happens when you are in the wrong place at the wrong time.
    d. could occur at any time and in any place.
7. Any touching I do not approve is sexual abuse (check one). Yes _____ No _____
8. Sexual abuse victims:
    a. are always over 10 years old.
    b. always girls.
    c. always boys.
    d. could be a boy or girl of any age.
9. If I do not like the way someone is touching me:
    a. I should tell my coach.
    b. I should tell a classmate.
    c. I should tell the "special friend".
    d. I should tell no one.
10. I should never trust anyone (check one). Yes _____ No _____
11. Sexual assault only occurs to children who:
    a. are pretty.
    b. are alone.
    c. both a and b, above.
    d. none of the above.
12. Someone who reports a sex offender:
    a. usually will have their name printed in the newspaper.
    b. may have to go to jail.
    c. needs supports from friends and family members.
    d. is a trouble maker.
13. A person is more likely to be sexually abused/assaulted:
    a. at their own home.
    b. in a locker room.
    c. after practice.
    d. at night.

14. To protect yourself from sexual abuse:
    a. never do anything alone.
    b. learn self defense.
    c. trust your feelings in situations that just do not feel right.
    d. do not talk to people that look strange.
15. If a friend told you he was sexually assaulted you would:
    a. think the person was asking for it by the way they dressed.
    b. report the incident to the organization's "special friend."
    c. think if you want that person to be your friend.
    d. tell them not to report the incident or they might get hurt.

Key

Question 1—There is no correct answer to this question. Everyone perceives "bad" differently. A "bad" person can be a mugger, murderer, abuser or in a child's eyes-a parent who does not let the child have dessert. Children have to be taught the difference between good and bad behavior. Emphasis has to be placed on a person's behavior and not personal traits, mannerism or characteristics. Thus, while a person might generally be considered a great person, they also might engage in bad behavioral traits such as beating a spouse or abusing a child.

Question 2—Yes should be the correct answer. Children should perceive themselves as generally being good. Even though they might engage in activities that could be considered bad, children should always consider themselves good. Children that respond "no" should receive some private time to discuss their answer. Abused children often suffer from low self-esteem and might consider themselves a bad person. Such children should be referred to the organization's "special friend" for immediate assistance.

Question 3—Yes. The hallmark for unwanted touching is touching that either upsets or confuses a child. Requested or encouraged touching does not result in a child being upset or confused unless the touching extends past the approved duration, method or location.

Question 4—(d.) Sex offenders are not just drunks, crazies or weirdoes. Offenders are not just old men. Offenders can be anyone. There is no one type of person which children should fear. Children should not be taught to fear everyone. Rather, children should be taught that there are several methods which could be used prevent harm no matter where, when or from whom the threat arises. Utilizing the buddy system, purposeful walking, not being scared to say "no" and not talking to strangers are typical defensive tactics no matter who approaches a child.

Question 5—(d.) There is no one set definition for sexual abuse. The commonly used definition of sexual abuse is defined above on page 372 and 415.

Question 6—(d.) Sexual assaults can occur at night, during the day, even if you listen to your parents, even if you do not talk to strangers or can happen in your home. Abusers can be a friend, family member, baby sitter, coach or an individual who hangs around your team.

Question 7—No. Sexual abuse often involves touching that is unwanted, upsetting or confusing. However, not all unwanted touching is sexual abuse. Parents, teachers or coaches often have to touch a child to prevent them from getting injured or to discipline the child. Thus, while a parent might push a child down, it is impossible to determine whether the action constitutes child abuse unless all the circumstances are analyzed. If, upon subsequent inspection, it is determined that the child was pushed to avoid being attacked by a dog, then the parent's action would seem appropriate and warranted by the circumstances.

Question 8 — (d.) Sexual abuse can affect any child, of any sex, race, age, nationality, religion or socio-economic background. See article page 357 for some key traits abusers search for in their victims.

Question 9 — (c.) See generally discussion concerning question number three, above. Children should be aware that if, for some reason, they cannot find the organization's "special friend," the child should report the touching to a parent, teacher, librarian, policeman, fireman, coach or school principal.

Question 10 — No. Children can trust most people. Most people are interested in protecting and nourishing children. See generally discussion concerning question number four, above.

Questions 11 — (d.) Assaults are not confined to any one group or type of child. See generally discussion concerning question number eight, above.

Question 12 — (c.) There are no repercussions from reporting abuse or assault. The organization's "special friend," police, child protective service personnel and other involved in the process are required to provide as much protection as possible to the child reporting abuse. The organization has to implement as many rules as possible to prevent retaliation. The organization has to provide guidance and information to family and friends of an abused child to ensure they understand what the child is going through.

Question 13 — (a.) Years of sexual abuse/assault reporting has cemented the hypothesis that a child's home is the most likely place in which a child will be sexually abused/assaulted. See generally discussion concerning question number six, above.

Question 14 — (c.) Sexual abuse/assault education has to focus on the child as an individual who can make sound decisions when push comes to shove. Children have to be empowered with the knowledge to make the appropriate decision at the appropriate time. By learning the touch continuum and how/when to say "no," children should be well prepared to trust their own feelings.

Question 15 — (b.) See generally discussion concerning question number three and 12, above. Furthermore, do not rely on a friend reporting the problems to the Special Friend. If you know your friend is in danger, you have an obligation to help by going yourself to the Special Friend.

Letter to Parents Introducing The Educational Program

Dear Parents,

We are starting to introduce your child(children) to a topic of great concern for administrators of youth programs. Sexual abuse/assault is a serious issue in our society. We are extremely concerned about your child's safety. Unfortunately, each year, over 100,000 young people are sexually assaulted in our country. These children are often under ten years old.

As a component of weekly practices, our coaches will be presenting a safety concern program with the assistance of trained administrators. We will discuss the law, sexual abuse, types of bad and good touches and the importance of reporting confusing or improper behavior to the organization's "special friend" (Mr. _____ or Ms. _____)
We will also discuss specific steps children can take to prevent harm, assertiveness training and communications skills.

For anyone that want additional information please do not hesitate to call me. Furthermore, we will have a parents meeting to discuss our organization's sexual abuse/assault policy and program on _____. We hope you can attend. If you would like your child to receive our *free* training to prevent sexual abuse/assault, please complete and return the permission slip below.

Sincerely

_____

I, _____, the/a parent of _____ who/whom competes in _____, do hereby give permission for my child/children to attend the sexual abuse/assault training program. I freely give permission for _____ to discuss issues pertinent to educating my child/children in strategies to reduce the risk of my child/children falling victim to a sexual attack.

_____ _____ _____
Signature   Print Name   Date

Follow-Up Letter After Program Completion

Dear Parents,

Your child/children have just completed a sexual abuse/assault prevention program. You are your child's most important teacher. It is imperative that you reinforce the information your child has learned on a daily basis. To assist you in this task, we have set forth below some issues your child learned. You should stress these points to your child on a regular basis.

1) Touching is special and should be reserved for people you trust or you allow to touch you.

2) Touching can be good, bad, uncomfortable and/or confusing.

3) If you feel confused or do not understand a touch, contact the organization's "special friend."

4) It is okay to say "no" if you do not want to be touched or if someone asks you to do something you either know, or think, is wrong.

5) Anyone can be a victim of sexual abuse/assault. It does not matter what your age, sex, nationality, religion or sexual preference: anyone can be a victim.

6) You should never blame yourself if someone tries to touch you in an inappropriate manner.

If you have any questions or would like additional information, please do not hesitate to contact your team coach or our office.

Sincerely,

_____

Conclusion

It is impossible to rid the world of sexual abuse and child abuse. There will always be individuals interested in fulfilling power or control objectives through abusing children. Youth organizations cannot eliminate sexual abuse. What can be done is reduce the risk of sexual abuse occurring in tightly monitored and administered programs. The starting point of analysis involves education. Education involves more than just educating program or organization participants. If an organization itself (including all administrators, employees, board of directors and parents) is not educated concerning the SAPP, it is impossible to prevent sexual abuse. Once an organization has determined that sexual abuse represents a legitimate and critical concern, the next step involves making sexual abuse prevention a key organizational goal.

The key components of an effective SAPP entail:

1) Developing appropriate goals, objectives and strategies.
2) Incorporating the goals into an official policy statement.
3) Receiving support and "buy-in" to follow the policy statement.
4) Implementing a comprehensive employee/volunteer screening program including a review of criminal background history and checking all references.
5) Insuring all employees and volunteers follow all policies and those that violate the policies receive appropriate punishment.
6) providing a comprehensive educational program for participants.

By implementing the above steps, an organization can significantly reduce the chance of sexual abuse occurring within their programs. The same steps will also become critical in the defense of any suit brought by a program participant sexually assaulted in a program related activity.

References

Books/Pamphlets/Teaching Aids

The Amazing Spider-Man, National Committee for Prevention of Child Abuse 332 S. Michigan Ave., Suite 1250, Chicago, IL 60604-435 (312) 663-3520 (1990). Comic book format designed to teach tips on what to do about physical abuse.

Are Children with Disabilities Vulnerable to Sexual Abuse? Minnesota Program for Victims of Sexual Assault, 430 Metro Square Building, St. Paul, MN 55101 (612) 296-7084. Discusses sexual abuse and prevention techniques for parents of a disabled child.

Basic Facts About Sexual Child Abuse, National Committee for Prevention of Child Abuse 332 S. Michigan Ave., Suite 1250, Chicago, IL 60604-435 (312) 663-3520. Pamphlet discusses definitions, offenses, statistics and reporting requirements.

C.A.R.E. KIT, Child Abuse Research and Education, Productions Association of British Columbia, P.O. Box 183, Surrey, B.C., Canada V3T 4W8 (604) 581-5116. A complete teacher's guide with training manuals, parent's book, puppets, posters, etc..

Child Abuse and Youth Sports, A Comprehensive Risk Management Program, National Alliance for Youth Sports 2050 Vista Parkway, West Palm Beach, FL 33411 (561) 684-1141 (800) 729-2057 (1996). Discusses various techniques to reduce child abuse and sexual abuse in youth sports.

Child Sexual Abuse Prevention: How to Take the First Steps (By Cordelia Anderson) Distributed by Network Publications, a division of ETR Associates, P.O. Box 8506, Santa Cruz, CA 95060 (408) 429-9822. A guide for developing and implementing a child sexual abuse prevention program.

The Educator's Guide To Preventing Child Sexual Abuse, Editors Mary Nelson and Kay Clark (1986) Network Publications, a division of ETR Associates, P.O. Box 8506, Santa Cruz, CA 95060 (408) 429-9822.

Empower-Child Sexual Abuse Education and Prevention Manual. Big Brothers/Big Sisters of America, 230 North 13th St., Philadelphia, PA 19017 ($55.00)

Feelings and Your Body, Coalition for Child Advocacy, P.O. Box 159, Bellingham, WA 98227 (206) 734-5121. Prevention program for preschoolers.

Hey Coach, Winning Ways with Young Athletes, National Committee To Prevent Child Abuse (1994). This pamphlet discusses issues relating to proper coaching technique, player motivation and athlete's rights.

Keep Child Abuse Out of Child Sports, Parents and Coaches in Sports (undated). Small folding pamphlet providing information on preventing abuse.

Kidsafe, A Risk Management Program, US Youth Soccer, (1995). Handbook which describes US Youth Soccer Sexual abuse prevention program and provides a sample volunteer application form to help review past criminal records.

Natural Dolls, Migma Design, P.O. Box 70064, Eugene, OR 97401 (503) 726-5442. Anatomically correct dolls.

Preschool Sexual Abuse Study Cards, Sexual Assault Program, Beltrami County, Box 688, Bemidji, MN 56601. A series of card showing different types of touch to children.

Preventing Sexual Abuse (By Carol A. Plummer) Distributed by Network Publications, a division of ETR Associates, P.O. Box 8506, Santa Cruz, CA 95060 (408) 429-9822. Designed to assist in the development of specialized sexual abuse prevention programs.

Puppets, Krause House, P.O. Box 880, Oregon City, OR 97045. Puppets, books and film strips entitled "Speak Up, Say No."

Safety Kids Set, Brite Musical Enterprises, Inc., 611 Ernest Drive, Godfrey, IL 62035 (618) 466-1442. Utilizes a musical approach to teach children how to safeguard themselves.

A Time to Tell, Boy Scouts of America (Attn: Marilyn Herrington) 1325 West Walnut Hill Lane, Irving, TX 75015-2079. 28 minute video on sexual abuse prevention for boys 11-14 years of age.

Touch Continuum Study Cards, by Cordelia Anderson, Network Publications, a division of ETR Associates, P.O. Box 8506, Santa Cruz, CA 95060 (408) 429-9822. Twelve useful laminated cards depicting sexual abuse prevention principals.

Trainer's Manual: Prevention of Child Sexual Abuse (By Ann Downer) Committee for Children, P.O. Box 51049, Wedgewood Station, Seattle, WA 98115 (206) 322-5050. A manual for those who will train children in preventing sexual abuse.

Organizations

AAHPRED (American Alliance for Health, Physical Education, Recreation and Dance), 1900 Association Drive, Reston, VA 22091 (703) 476-3400.

ACTION for Child Protection, 4724 Park Road, Unit C, Charlotte, NC 28203 (704) 529-1080.

Child Welfare League of America, 440 First Street, NW, Suite 310, Washington, DC 20001 (202) 638-2952. CWLA offers a three video series entitled Confronting Child Sexual Abuse: Video Training Series.

Clearinghouse on Child Abuse and Neglect Information, P.O. Box 1182, Washington, DC 20013 (703) 385-7565

C. Henry Kempe Center for Prevention and Treatment of Child Abuse and Neglect, 1205 Oneida Street, Denver, CO 80220 (303) 321-3963.

National Alliance for Youth Sports (Fred Engh, Executive Director), 2050 Vista Parkway, West Palm Beach, FL 33411 (407) 684-1141 (800) 729-2057

National Association of Counsel for Children, 1205 Oneida Street, Denver, CO 80220 (303) 321-3963.

National Center on Child Abuse and Neglect, U.S. Department of Health and Human Services, P.O. Box 1182, Washington, DC 20013.

National Committee for Prevention of Child Abuse, 332 South Michigan Ave., Suite 1600, Chicago, IL 60604 (312) 663-3520.

Parents and Coaches in Sports, 3160 Pinebrook Road, Park City, UT 84060 (800) 748-4843.

US Youth Soccer, 899 Presidential drive, Suite 117, Richardson, TX 75081 (800) 476-2237.

Women's Sports Foundation, Eisenhower Park, East Meadows, NY 11554 (800) 227-3988.

Youth Sports Institute, Room 210, IM Sports Circle, Michigan State University, East Lansing, MI 48824.

Appendix B

Incident Reporting Manual

The following appendix presents a sample safety manual that focuses on proper education and documentation procedures, Through proper documentation, many risks can be avoided and that is why the following manual was developed by the author for the City of Houston Park and Recreation Department.

Incident Reporting Manual

Gil B. Fried, M.A., J.D.
University of New Haven
Copyright © 1999 Gil Fried

Incident Reporting Policy

1. Definitions

A) *Parks and/or City Parks*—City parks is a term used to describe any facility, open space, field, playground or other man-made or natural condition that exists within the confines of an identified park and recreation property. Included within the definition of city parks are sidewalks, parking lots, bathrooms, port-a-potties and related areas. City parks also should be used to describe any community center. City parks can be substituted for any other term used to describe the programs or facilities in which the incident(s) occurred.

B) *Incident*—An incident references any activity that results in an injury or damage to either a person, structure or property. Incidents include, but are not limited to criminal activity (assaults, thefts, burglary, rape, molestations, vandalism, etc.), inappropriate conduct (violation of park rules, threats, lost children, bringing guns to a city park, etc.), injuries (any personal, structural, vehicle, or property which might include broken bones, contusions, cuts, broken windows, unlocked doors, auto accidents, stolen cars, lost items, broken equipment, etc.), dangerous conditions and any other events or conditions which appear or could appear to warrant documentation for future reference. Anytime police activity (arrest or investigation activity) and/or fire/paramedic activity is noted at a city park, an incident has occurred and should be documented.

C) *Investigate and/or Investigating*—Investigating refers to the formal process of preparing and filing an incident report and the resulting process which determines what steps were taken and the appropriateness of those steps. Investigating a potential incident is a critical component of the incident reporting process and requires a thorough analysis of all the facts and the accurate reporting of objective findings, and not subjective findings.

D) *Reporting*—Reporting involves the formal process of filling an incident report with supervisors or the Department Director's office.

E) *Counsel*—Counseling refers to discussing an incident with an individual park patron or program participant and providing critical information to assist them in resolving any outstanding issues. No Houston Park and Recreation Department employee can ever provide any medical or legal advice or assistance.

F) *Contact Supervisor*—Contacting a supervisor involves the process of reporting an incident or perceived incident to an immediate supervisor. A supervisor should be contacted at the first available point in time after any emergency has passed. Under no circumstance should a supervisor be contacted more than three hours after an incident has occurred which requires a supervisor to be contacted.

G) *Accident*—An accident refers to any unexpected or unintentional event that results in physical injury or damage. Accidents do not involve any type of moving vehicles (see below).

H) *Auto Accident*—An auto accident refers to any accident involving an HPRD vehicle or damage caused by an HPRD vehicle (or personnel) to a civilian vehicle(s). Examples include a vehicle crashing into a tree, a highway collision involving an HPRD vehicle or a weedeater operated by an employee shooting a rock at a car which breaks the car's windshield.

I) *Fire*—The act of burning any item to any degree. Examples include trash fires, electrical fires, grass fires, or a burning facility. The term fire refers to both active and extinguished fires.

J) *Lost Child*—A lost child is any youth under age 10 that is separated from their parent/guardian or from a supervising adult. There is no set time that a child has to be left alone to be considered "lost." A child is only lost if the child specifically indicates they cannot find their parent or guardian. A child also is considered lost if a parent or guardian reports a missing child to any HPRD employee.

K) *Inappropriate Conduct*—Inappropriate conduct refers to any improper conduct displayed by a participant, visitor, employee, or volunteer which threatens the safety of others. Examples include intoxicated conduct, yelling at individuals, threatening others, misusing facilities or equipment, etc.

L) *Violation of Park Rules and Regulations*—All employees, volunteers, participants and visitors have one opportunity to be informed of the park rules and regulations. If such rules or regulations are subsequently violated or there is an initial egregious rules violation, then there is a violation of the rules and regulations as set forth in the Park and Recreation Rules and Regulation Manual available at each park. Examples of such violations include a person selling anything on park property without a valid permit, using glass container in a park, littering park areas or parking in unauthorized areas.

M) *Theft*—Theft refers to the taking for possession of something which is not rightfully owned by the person who took possession. Theft can be categorized as auto and non-auto theft.

N) *Burglary*—Burglary refers to the breaking into and entering a building not open to the general public with the intent to steal.

O) *Assault and Battery*—Assault and Battery occurs when a person intentionally or knowingly causes bodily injury, threatens to cause bodily injury or causes physical contact with another when the person knows or should reasonably believe that the other person will regard the contact as offensive or unwanted. Examples include fighting, pushing another person, threatening someone with a knife or any conduct that puts someone in fear of imminent unwanted bodily contact.

P) *Vandalism*—Vandalism entails any willful or malicious destruction of property. Examples include breaking windows, spray painting a building, destroying plants or overturning park equipment.

Q) *Illegal Acts*—Illegal acts refers to any other illegal conduct which could include: rape, murder, molestation, public exposure, embezzlement and any other illegal activities not covered in the above definitions.

R) *Employee*—An employee refers to any full-time or part-time worker employed by HPRD and engaged in any activity which occurs during regular park operational hours or required work hours, and which directly benefits HPRD.

S) *Volunteer*—Any individual who performs any services or provides assistance to HPRD and any of its programs without remuneration.

T) *Youth*—A youth means any individual under the age of 18-years-old.

U) *Trespass*—A person has trespassed on land when they do not have an express or implied right to be on the land. While city parks are owned by the people, HPRD exercises control over all facilities and grounds and can explicitly exclude anyone from facilities at different times. An example of trespass involves someone jumping over a fence to swim in a pool or opening a window to enter into a facility when it is closed to the public.

V) *Injury/Damage*—The terms injury or damage will be used throughout these procedures to refer to any physical injury to someone or property damage to some thing.

W) *Provide Aid*—Normally referred to as first-aid, provide aid is a more descriptive term concerning how employees or volunteers should handle an injured person. Provide aid refers to providing necessary equipment such as toweling or band-aids, but does not entail the administration of medical techniques or procedures to assist an injured person. More comprehensive assistance can be provided for very serious injuries (while waiting for Medical/EMT assistance), but minor injuries should be handled by the injured person themselves or their own physician.

X) *Request Assistance*—Requesting assistance refers to contacting any internal (i.e., maintenance) or external (i.e., police, fire, etc.) entity to provide guidance or assistance in resolving an incident. A list of qualified sources from which to request assistance is provided in the procedure section for Incident Reports.

Y) *Medical/EMT*—Medical/EMT refers to various providers of emergency service whether it is a county or city run paramedics unit or a private ambulance service.

Z) *Parent or Guardian*—A parent or guardian refers to an individual or entity (i.e., school or day care center) which has either full or temporary responsibility to care for the welfare and safety of a child or youth.

2. Purpose

Incidents will occur within the confines of city parks. These occurrence, if not handled properly, could cause significant losses, injuries, service interruption, damage to city property or personnel and potential large liability concerns for our department and the City of Houston. These guidelines are designed to help all employees, managers and supervisors understand their requirement to properly investigate, accurately complete and timely submit incident reports.

3. Responsibility

All employees, managers and supervisors are responsible for timely investigating and reporting all city park incidents which might occur during their assigned shift—whether or not the incident occurred at a city park or any other location. The morning shift is responsible for reporting any incidents or activity that occurred anytime after the prior night's last shift ended. All incident reports have to be submitted within 24 hours of the incident to the appropriate person responsible for processing such reports. The appropriate contact persons are as follows:

   All personal injury incident reports should be submitted to: _____
   All fire or criminal incidents should be submitted to: _____
   All incidents involving vehicles should be submitted to: _____
   All incidents involving facilities should be submitted to: _____
   All employee injuries should be submitted to: _____

4. Procedures

Once an incident has occurred, all employees, managers and supervisors must exercise responsible and appropriate judgment to determine what action is appropriate and satisfactory to handle the incident and minimize the future impact on employees, volunteers, park visitors, park patrons, the Park and Recreation Department and the City of Houston.

It should be clearly stated that if an injury has not yet occurred, all employees need to take appropriate risk management steps to prevent the injury. Thus, if an employee sees several participants shoving each other, the game should be stopped prior to a fight breaking out between the participants. Likewise, if a basketball rim is broken, no one should be allowed to play with that backboard or rim. Such proactive steps are the required course of action in our department's proactive risk reduction program.

The following steps should be taken when responding to any incident or potential incident.

Step 1 Determine the appropriate action needed in response to the incident keeping mind the safety of employee(s), volunteer(s) and visitor(s). In response to all incidents listed below, a supervisor has to be contacted immediately to notify them about the incident. The following list gives specific suggested responses to various incidents which might occur during a shift:

Incident type	_Response_
Assault and Battery	
Assault involving weapons	Contact Police
Assault during programs	Contact Police, possibly cancel program
Auto Accident	
Auto accident, no injuries, slight damage	Contact Police, exchange insurance info, file report
Auto accident, no injuries, major damage	Contact Police, exchange insurance info
Auto accident, slight injuries	Contact Police, exchange insurance info, possibly administer first-aid
Auto accident, major injuries	Contact Police, Medical/EMTs
Burglary	
Burglary in progress	Do not intervene, contact Police
Other, under $100 value	Contact supervisor, then contact Police
Other, over $100 value	Contact Police, then contact supervisor
Dead Body	Contact Police, then contact director
Fires	
Fire, active	Call Fire Department
Fire, extinguished	Report and repair
Illegal Activities	
Abuse-suspected child abuse	Call Police and Child Protective Services
Abuse by employee or volunteer	Call Police, contact Director's office
Assault, see above	
Burglary, see above	
Murder	Contact Police
Rape	Contact Police/Medical/EMTs
Theft, auto	Contact Police
Theft, non-auto, under $100 value	Contact supervisor
Theft, non-auto, over $100 value	Contact Police
Trespass, willing to leave	Contact supervisor
Trespass, unwilling to leave	Contact Police
Vandalism, minor and suspect known, youth	Contact parents/supervisor
Vandalism, major and suspect known, youth	Contact parents/supervisor and Police

Vandalism, minor, perpetrator unknown	Contact supervisor
Vandalism, major, perpetrator unknown	Contact Police/supervisor

Illness

Fever	Send person home/contact parents
Flu	Send person home/contact parents
Seizure	Call Medical/EMT provide blankets and try to help prevent choking on victim's tongue

Injuries

Broken bones	Call EMTs, provide comfort and blankets to prevent shock, then contact parents
Cuts, minor	Provide toweling and band-aids then contact parents
Cuts, major	Call EMTs, provide toweling, then contact parents
Head or neck injuries	Do not move body, call EMTs, then contact parents

Inappropriate Conduct

Dangerous	Contact Police, then contact supervisor
Disruptive, but not dangerous	Contact supervisor

Intoxicated Individual

Willing to leave park	Contact supervisor
Unwilling to leave park	Contact Police
Bothering park patrons or employees	Contact Police

Lost Child — Look for parent/guardian then contact Police

Property

Lost property, under $100	Contact supervisor
Lost property, $100–$500	Contact supervisor, investigate
Lost property, over $500	Contact supervisor, possibly contact Police

Vandalism, see above

Structural

Broken Door	Contact maintenance
Broken Windows	Contact maintenance
Other Damage	Contact maintenance or supervisor

Violating Park Rules — Contact supervisor

These are typical responses to various incidents. There is no one perfect manner in which to respond to an incident. Based on severity or danger, other authorities might need to be notified for additional assistance. The best rule of thumb to utilize when responding to any incident is that a supervisor is only a phone call away and you should never hesitate to contact a supervisor whenever a new or unique incident arises.

Key Rules for Providing Appropriate Response

After reviewing the appropriate responses outlined above, all employees and volunteers should always keep in mind that the following golden rules should never be violated, under any circumstances.

Never provide anyone with any drugs, even aspirin.
Provide first-aid when no other course of action exists.
Never provide medical advice.
Never let an intoxicated person wander around or drive if they are too intoxicated to control their own actions.
Always provide Police, Fire and EMT dispatchers with accurate directions including cross-streets.
If an incident occurs in a non-HPRD location, all the procedural steps outlined herein should still be followed.

Step 2 After providing a relevant and appropriate response (whether providing assistance or calling for assistance from Police, Fire, EMTs or supervisors) immediately contact the Supervisor who will evaluate your actions and provide any additional insight or contact other necessary persons for further assistance. At no time during the process of contacting the Supervisor should the injured individual be ignored or treated as if they are not special and that their injury or harm is trivialized.

Step 3 Take time whenever the urgency of an incident has subsided to complete an Incident Report. Special care needs to be taken to contact witnesses prior to them leaving the park or incident location. The following overview and procedure section helps describe the necessary steps in the incident reporting process.

Incident Reporting Notice/ Overview and Procedures

Policy Statement

It is the policy of the Houston Park and Recreation Department to maintain a consistent method of reporting and tracking incidents occurring either on, adjacent, near or away from city park property or involving persons engaged in HPRD related facilities or programs.

Policy Amplification

This policy is provided as a framework by which all incident reporting by employees will follow and is not intended to replace and/or circumvent any city, state or federal reporting procedures. Any such policy, forms or procedures should be completed along with an HPRD incident report.

Overview

Scope

This policy applies to all operational phases of the HPRD with particular emphasis on facilities, structures, property and programs where an incident is more likely to occur. Therefore, all employees need to known, understand and follow this policy.

Objectives

1) To provide a standardized method of reporting incidents for use throughout HPRD and the City of Houston.
2) To outline circumstances by which incidents will be reported
3) To develop a basis by which incidents can be tracked and used for analytical studies.

General

This policy details the guidelines, procedures and responsibilities for reporting incidents. Incident reporting is a critical means of recording events that disrupt, damage or destroy city park activities or property. Therefore, a duty exists in every employee position to timely and accurately complete and submit Incident Reports. The failure to follow this policy can result in termination and/or any other response deemed reasonable by HPRD administration.

Primary Responsibility

The office of the Director will have primary responsibility for management and oversight for monitoring this policy and will insure policy compliance.

Procedural Outline

Incident Report

All employees, managers and supervisors are required to report all incidents whether such incident occurred, was reported, was discovered or was witnessed. Reporting is accomplished by timely completing and filing an Incident Report with the proper department representative. If any employee or volunteer is notified of an incident that he/she determines to be severe, then that individual should immediately notify their immediate supervisor. It is the supervisor's ultimate decision whether the incident is severe enough to notify the Department Director. However, any incident involving felonious conduct such as rape, molestations, guns at city parks and related criminal activity should be immediately reported to the Department Director or his/her designee. Addenda A represents a sample Incident Report with proper completion instructions.

Call ins

HPRD has a "call in" system whereby any citizen or employee can report any incident or dangerous condition no matter whether or not a city park is operating during regular business hours. All "call in" dispatchers are responsible for contacting the proper individual should a severe incident arise during non-business hours. The dispatcher will be supplied with the necessary phone numbers and contact persons with all other city departments and emergency service providers. All incidents that are called in should be logged in on a log-in sheet (see Addenda G). Additionally, an Incident Report should be completed for all incidents and submitted to proper individuals the next business day. All Repair Request (see Addenda

F) should be submitted to the Maintenance Department. The dispatcher should complete the incident report after contacting the appropriate park employee(s) to determine the full extent of the incident.

All call in incidents should be analyzed at the most one week after the incident to determine if the incident was resolved and/or if the incident or other dangerous conditions are still present. If any requested repairs or procedural changes are requested, but not completed, such information should be immediately provided to the Department Director or his/her designee.

Submitting an Incident Report

The incident report consists of an original and three attached copies. Once completed, the form should be routed in the following manner:

White (original)	Submit to the Office of the Director
Yellow (copy)	Submit to designated Division Head overseeing the area wherein the incident occurred.
Pink (copy)	Submit to immediate supervisor
Gold (copy)	Retain at the site.

All Incident Reports have to be submitted within 24 hours of the time the incident occurred, was discovered, was reported or was witnessed. If the incident occurred on a weekend or holiday, the incident report has to be submitted on the very next business day. Within 48 hours of the incident, a designated employee within HPRD shall follow-up with appropriate authorities, or the injured individual to determine how the incident was resolved and if there is anything that HPRD can do to prevent further similar incident. Such follow-up is critical in reducing future risks. The information obtained during this follow-up process shall be used to make future risk management decisions. For example, if an individual has been involved in a violent assault, the Police Department should be contacted concerning how the matter was resolved. Through contacting the Police Department or judicial process it can be determined whether or not the individual should be allowed to engage in any future HPRD programs. HPRD can open itself up to a lawsuit for failing to prevent an individual's participation in an activity when his/her violent tendencies were known. That is why it is imperative to follow-up every significant incident.

Supplemental Reports

Incident Reports often need to be supplemented with a variety of forms that are designed to provide additional critical information. All forms should be completed in a timely manner and submitted to appropriate Department officials (i.e., supervisors or the Director). The type of supplemental forms available are listed below.

A) *Supplemental Report*—A Supplemental Report should be used whenever additional information is required. For example, if eight people were involved in an altercation, it would be impossible to clearly and legibly write all the necessary information on one Incident Report form. A Supplemental Report is especially important when further explanations are required or when there are numerous witnesses. A Supplemental Report should be completed when any additional information is obtained after an initial Incident Report has been filed. For example, if a participant engaged in inappropriate conduct and was counseled, any future inappropriate conduct can be recorded in a Supplemental Report that references the prior Incident Report. This referencing process is critical to inform other employees and city parks about certain individuals or events that should raise concern.

Supplemental Reports should be utilized to describe any incidents that occur "off site," such as when children are injured while they were attending a HPRD sponsored away event. You should attach to the Supplemental Report any incident or related reports which were prepared by the visited institution, facility or program. Addenda B represents a sample Supplement Report.

B) *Participant Injury/Medical Assistance Reports*—The Participant Injury/Medical Assistance Report (PI/MAR) is only used to report participant injuries. While an injury can be reported on an Incident Report, the PI/MAR provides additional critical information and both should be completed when any injury involves a more severe injury such as broken bones, heart attacks, concussions, etc. All employee injuries should be reported using the Supervisors Injury Investigation Report. All PI/MARs should be completed and returned to the Office of the Director (or his/her designee) within 24 hours after the injury. A separate PI/MAR has to be completed for each individual injured. PI/MARs are filed in addition to the Incident Report which describes how the injury or incident occurred while the PI/MAR reports on the medical condition and disposition of the injured. If at all possible, the injured individual(s) should sign-off on the PI/MAR indicating that they agree with all the assertions and statements made in the Report. Addenda C represents a sample PI/MAR.

C) *Witness Statement*—The Witness Statement will be used when an incident has been witnessed or observed in any manner, and where a witness is willing to supply a written statement including their current name, address and phone number. Every effort should be made to obtain witness statements after every incident. If a witness is unwilling to provide their name or other information for fear of retaliation or reprisal, any employee can arrange for complete confidentiality by checking the confidential box which will guarantee that the witness statement will be given directly to the Department Director and every effort will be made to ensure confidentiality. Addenda D represents a sample Witness Statement.

D) *Inventory Loss/Damage Report*—An Inventory Loss/Damage Report is used anytime there is any property loss or damage to property. Examples include loosing keys, loosing a pager, a lawn mower breaking down, a phone not working, a building being hit by a car or any other similar incidents wherein there exists specific monetary or physical losses associated with HPRD property or facilities. The report should be completed with the best available information and an employee's best judgment as to the estimated loss or repair value. Addenda E represents a sample Inventory Loss/Damage Report.

E) *Repair Request*—A Repair Request should be filed with appropriate Maintenance Department after any property has been damaged that cannot be appropriately and correctly repaired by a city park employee. The Repair Request should be completed as soon as possible after the damaged property has been discovered. If the damaged property represents a risk of injury to possible patrons, the areas around the property should be roped off using yellow warning tape available at each city park. If the requested repair is a serious matter, contact the Department Director's office to evaluate repair options. If the matter is not a serious matter, appropriately rank the priority for the needed repairs. A follow-up phone call should be made after the appropriate time if the repairs had not yet been completed. Addenda F represents a sample Repair Request with appropriate completion instructions.

F) *Log-In Sheet*— A Log-In Sheet records all phone calls received by the call in dispatcher and/or the Department Dispatcher referencing or discussing incidents or potential incidents occurring at city parks.

Addenda A

Incident Report

Section A

Location—specifically identify where the incident happened. Do not just list the park name, the community center name or indicate that the incident occurred at the building/ball field. Write out exactly where the incident occurred. If you cannot adequately describe the location, utilize a Supplemental Report to more thoroughly describe where the incident occurred. The following represents a sample location description.

"The participant slipped and fell underneath the north-side indoor gym basket at Memorial Park. The participant was found at the approximate site of the fall which was eight feet from the north wall and directly underneath the basketball rim."

Every city park office has extra maps which can be used to locate where an incident occurred. Utilizing a red pen, place an "x" where the incident occurred. You can utilize any other descriptive marks which might provide useful information. Useful information can include where a piece of equipment was located, where the injured person was found (if in a different area from where they were injured) and related facts. Any additional information should be specifically described on the map.

Describe any strange or unusual conditions at the location such as water puddles, dust balls, broken glass or other items which affect the location and which might have contributed to the incident.

In addition to writing a brief description, check the appropriate box concerning what location was involved. The choices are: surface street, fields, parking lot, gymnasium, offices, other indoor structures (i.e., closets or bathrooms), outdoor structures (shacks, port-a-potties), playground, zoo, unknown or other (please describe).

Fill in the appropriate Park Identification Number (PIC) in the appropriate spot. Also write in the appropriate operating division (ORP Div.).

Check-off the type of incident that is being reported. The incident types include Assault, Theft (auto and non-auto), Burglary, Vandalism, Trespass, Auto-accident, Personal Injury, Fire, Lost Child, Illness, Inappropriate Conduct, Violation of Park Rules or Other (please describe).

Check-off how you were notified about the incident. Possible means of notification include Call-in, Reported in person, Discovered, Witnessed, Responded to Incident, Other (please describe).

Briefly describe the incident using purely objective language. For example if someone was involved in an altercation during a basketball game the following would be an <u>appropriate</u> description of the incident: "On March 18, 1997, John Williams was playing basketball when, he was hit in the head by Bob Jones. Williams complained of blurred vision and had two cuts on his cheek." *Never* try to put your own subjective opinions into the incident reporting. Thus, the following is an *<u>inappropriate</u>* description of an incident: "On March 18, 1997, John Williams was playing basketball when he was hit by Bob Jones who I have told several times not to get into fight. The two players had been at it all night and the referees screwed-up by not ejecting Jones earlier in the game."

In addition to describing the incident, take the time to examine surrounding circumstances and note any conditions or factors which might have influenced the incident. For example, what was the weather like (did the weather help cause the incident), what type of shoes was the person wearing (were the soles worn out), was the person wearing any knee, ankle, elbow braces, was there any broken equipment around, was the person wearing glasses, did the injured person state they had been injured before and a host of other potential clues you might spot or hear while responding to an incident should be specifically mentioned.

List the exact time and date, if known, when the incident occurred.

Describe the injury or damage in the appropriate "Injury/Damage" space. You should clearly state what medical condition or symptoms were reported or observed. Likewise if property, an automobile or a structure was damaged you should specifically indicate what damage occurred.

Section B

Response section. The response section is designed for you to specifically indicate what you or other people did in response to the incident. There are three sub-section to Section B. The first sub-section deals with the specific actions taken. The second sub-section refers to any assistance requested from either internal or external sources. The last sub-section provides an opportunity to list key individuals who provided assistance in either handling the incident or following-up after the incident.

Action taken should be checked-off at the appropriate action area. The appropriate action steps include Investigate, Counsel, Report, Provide aid, Request assistance or Other (please describe). Counsel means to talk with the injured person or the individual(s) involved in the incident and then to provide appropriate feedback to help resolve the incident. Report means to file an official incident report or other official reports which serves to notify the Department about the incident. Provide aid refers to first-aid assistance with the understanding that employee are not medical professionals and can only provide the injured person with critically necessary first aid assistance. It bears repeating that no employee should ever provide any drugs or medical opinions. Request assistance refers to contacting a variety of internal or external sources to help handle an incident.

Assistance requested should be checked off at the appropriate descriptive box. Appropriate assistance can include Fire Department, Police Department, Medical-EMTs, Parent/guardian, Supervisor or Other(please describe). The Fire Department should be contacted on any and all active fires, except for fires that are contained in small areas such as bar-b-que pits or similar areas where fire extinguishing equipment and experience is readily available. The Police Department should be contacted whenever there exists any potential for significant injury to people or property. Likewise, the Police Department should be contacted when any conduct occurs that is outside the scope of any employee or volunteer's control and can lead to violence. Any violence towards children including rape, fondling, molestation, lost children (when a parent or guardian cannot be contacted) or similar occurrence requiring police expertise should be handled exclusively by the Police Department. Medical-EMTs should be contacted whenever: a cut occurs which cannot be stopped through the application of pressure, when an individual faints, goes into convulsions, is delusional, or cannot take care of themselves, a person suffers heart/chest pain, a person receives a sharp blow injuring their head or if any other condition arises which in an employee's or volunteer's best judgment requires quick professional medical assistance. A parent or guardian should be contacted whenever a youth (under age 18) engages in any conduct that violates the law or park rules/regulations or creates a dangerous condition for that youth or for any other patrons, visitors, employees or volunteers. The parent or guardian should be told to immediately pick-up the youth in question and to meet with a designated representative from the Department. If a parent or guardian refuses to pick-up the child or meet with a Department representative then the Department Director's office should be contacted for further assistance. A supervisor should be contacted if there is more than an estimated $500 worth of damage, whenever the Police or Fire Department is contacted or whenever special medical assistance is required. The term "Other" refers to other potential internal or external sources that might be contacted. Such sources include, but is not limited to, child protective services, truancy officer, school officials, probation department or internal affairs.

When any internal or external assistance arrives, indicate arrival time. If no one responded to the request for assistance, that box should be checked.

The last sub-section should provide information on the person who responded such as their name, employee or badge number, address, phone number and a brief description of what action they undertook and if they prepared any written reports such as an arrest, fire incident, medical assistance and/or a reprimand report.

Section C

Personal- This section provides critical information concerning the people involved in the incident. Thus, if a HPRD vehicle collides with another non-HPRD vehicle both drivers would be listed. If one individual is injured in the incident then only that individual should be listed in this section.

Individuals completing the Incident Report should indicate whether the injured individual is a participant, visitors, employee, volunteer or other. It should be indicated if they were or weren't injured. It should be indicated whether or not the individual was a minor (under 18-years-old) or an adult by listing the person's age. The following information should be entered into the form: the individuals full name, address, phone numbers (work and home) and if appropriate-insurance information (for auto accidents only).

Section D

This sections specifically indicates which documents form the entire incident report. All appropriate boxes should be checked. Potential documents that could accompany the incident report include Police, Fire, Supervisor's, employee injury, Supplemental, PI/MAR, Witness Statement, Inventory Loss/Damage, Repair Request and other reports (please specify).

Section E

This section should contain the name, title, employee number, signature and date.

Sample Incident Reports

Incident Report

Incident Report # _____

LOCATION _____ PIC _____ ORP Div. _____

Time _____ a.m./ p.m.　　　　　　Date _____

Describe Location _____

_____

_____

_____. [] See attached map

__ Field, __ Surface Street, __ Parking Lot, __ Gymnasium, __ Office,
__ Indoor Structure, __ Outdoor Structure, __ Playground, __ Zoo,
__ Other (specify) _____

INCIDENT TYPE

__ Assault, __ Auto Theft, __ Non-auto Theft, __ Burglary, __ Vandalism, ___ Trespass,
__ Auto Accident, __ Personal Injury, __ Fire, __ Lost Child, __ Park Rules-Violation,
__ Illness, __ Inappropriate Conduct, __ Other (specify) _____

INCIDENT NOTIFICATION

__ Call In, __ Reported, __ Discovered, __ Witnessed, __ Responded, __ Other _____

INCIDENT DESCRIPTION

_____

_____

_____

_____

_____

_____

INJURY/DAMAGE

_____

* *

RESPONSE SECTION

ACTION TAKEN

__ Counsel, __ Report, __ Provide Aid, __ Request Assistance, __ Investigate,
__ Other (specify) _____

ASSISTANCE REQUESTED

__ Fire Dept., __ Police Dept., __ Medical/EMT, __ Contact Parent/Guardian,
__ Contact Supervisor, __ Other (specify) _____

ASSISTANCE RESPONSE

Responded __ Yes (time _____ a.m./ p.m.) ___ No response

RESPONDING PARTY

Name _____
Employee or Badge Number _____
Department _____
Phone (____) _____
Action Taken _____
Was a written report made? ___ Yes ___ No (report/case number _____)

****

PERSONAL

__ Employee, __ Volunteer, __ Participant, __ Visitor, __ Other (specify) _____
Personal Injury ___ Yes _____ No _____ Age _____
Name _____
Address _____
Phone (____) _____ Work Phone (____) _____
(for auto) Insurance Company _____ Policy # _____

Second Party, if applicable

__ Employee, __ Volunteer, __ Participant, __ Visitor, __ Other (specify) _____
Personal Injury ___ Yes ____ No _____ Age_____
Name _____
Address _____
Phone (____) _____ Work Phone (____) _____
(for auto) Insurance Company _____ Policy # _____

****

ATTACHED DOCUMENTS

___ Police Report, ___ Fire Report, ____ Supervisor's Report,
___ Employee Injury Report, ___ Supplement Report, ____ PI/MAR,
___ Witness Statement, ___ Repair Request, ___ Inventory Loss/Damage Report,
___ Other (specify) _____

****

COMPLETED BY

Name _____ Title _____
Employee Number _____
Signature _____ Date _____

****

Addenda B

Supplemental Report

Indicate the Incident Report Number (top right hand corner of the incident report) that the Supplemental Report supplements. Reiterate the site location, the PIC location, the incident date, and any other appropriate information. Contemporaneous means that the Supplemental Report was prepared at the same time the Incident Report was prepared. If the Supplemental Report was prepared any time other than at the same time the Incident Report was prepared, then the Follow-Up Report section should be checked. Other appropriate information that could be reported in the lined area might include the names of other individuals involved in the incident, further details obtained by other agencies such as police or fire departments, additional objective information about the incident such as weather conditions (rain, snow, etc.) and facility condition(fire destroyed port-a-potty leaving only one port-a-potty to service an entire park or the facility was recently cleaned and no wet spots were noticed, etc.). *No subjective interpretation* should be given concerning the incident. Furthermore, no potential liability or fault analysis should be provided. Any follow-up should be noted including additional contact with the injured, further information concerning an injury and its resulting disposition, any criminal proceedings and any serious condition that had not been repaired after submitting a prior incident report and work order.

The individual who completes the Supplemental Report should sign their name, employee number, and date the report.

Supplemental Report

Incident Report # _____

Contemporaneous _____ Follow-Up Report _____
Location _____ PIC _____ Incident Date _____

_____
_____
_____
_____
_____
_____
_____
_____
_____
_____
_____
_____
_____
_____
_____
_____
_____
_____
_____
_____
_____
_____
_____
_____

Name _____
Employee Number _____
Signature _____ Date _____

Addenda C

Participant Injury/Medical Assistance Report

This critical report is designed to help determine the extent of any injury and any resulting treatment or assistance that was provided. One report should be prepared for each person that is injured. The critical information needed include prior Incident Report number, date and time. As much information should be obtained from the injured person including name, sex, age, address, phone numbers and next of kin contact person information.

The next section relates to the injury and requires both analysis of current medical conditions/injuries and any known or communicated past problems or medications/allergies. This information is critical because a person might be coherent and responsive immediately after an incident, but thereafter go into shock. If a person is allergic to Penicillin, and they told an employee this information prior to going unconscious, the information can be conveyed to the Medical/EMT personnel. The next section refers to treatment provided by the employee or volunteer. Additionally, any treatment provided by others or hospital transportation should be listed in this section.

The last two sections deal with following-up to determine how the injury was resolved and information concerning the person who completed the Report.

If the person is conscious, try to obtain an Approval statement signature, approving all the information contained in the PI/MAR. If no treatment was requested or if treatment was needed, but refused, the individual should be asked to sign the Refusal of Treatment statement. If possible, try to get a witness to sign the Approval or Refusal of Treatment statements to verify that the injured person willingly signed either statement.

Participant Injury/Medical Assistance Report

Incident Report # _____ Date _____ Time _____ a.m./p.m.
Injured person:
Name _____ Sex (M. F) Age _____
     Last   First   MI
Address _____
     Street   City   State   Zip code
Phone number (___) _____ (___) _____
          Home   Work

Next of Kin/Contact Person:
Name _____
Address _____
Phone number (___) _____ (___) _____
Injury info:
Nature of injury: _____
Body part(s) affected: _____
Vital signs: Breathing (Yes / No), Pulse (Yes / No)
Current Medications _____
Known Allergies _____
How did injury occur: _____
_____
Where did the injury occur: _____
Who discovered/reported the injury: Name _____
Address _____ Phone # (___) _____
Treatment:
Was any first-aid provided: (Yes/ No)
What first-aid was provided: _____
_____
What was done with any first-aid items used (gauge pads, blood soaked tissues, etc.): ___
_____
First aid administered by: _____ employee # _____
Was any assistance requested: (Yes / No)
Assistance requested from: ___ Police, ___ Fire, ___ Medical/EMT, ___ physician
What assistance was provided: _____
Was the injured sent to a hospital (Yes/ No): Which Hospital _____
How was injured transported to the hospital: _____
Follow up:
How was the injury resolved: _____
Name of person completing the form: _____ Employee # _____
Signature _____
APPROVAL
I, _____ hereby accept all the above statements as true and correct and accurately represent my medical condition and the information I gave or was observed by others.
Name _____
Signed _____ Date _____
Witness _____

* *

REFUSAL OF TREATMENT
I, _____ was injured at a facility, structure, property or program/activity run by the Houston Park and Recreation Department. While HPRD staff or volunteers offered to provide first-aid assistance or Medical/EMT assistance, I have willingly refused all such assistance and voluntarily assume any subsequent complications or further injury.
Name _____
Signed _____ Date _____
Witness _____

Addenda D

Witness Statement

The Witness Statement should be used whenever there are witnesses who saw any part of the incident or came upon the incident after the fact. Thus, if someone found damage to a building, they should be classified as a witness. Employee or volunteers are not witnesses, but should be mentioned in the Incident Report.

The Witness Statement should refer to the proper Incident Report number and date. The name of the person who acquired the witness statement should be recorded. It should be indicated whether the Witness Statement was written by the witness him/her self or by someone else. The witness should always be encouraged to write the statement themselves, even if it needs to be written in Spanish or another language. The witness should use their own words in describing what they saw, noticed, heard or did in response to the incident. Never try to influence the words that a witness might use. Have the witness write their name, address, phone number and then sign the statement. If a witness is uncooperative, try to obtain any name or address and write down any information they might have mentioned, trying as best as possible to write down only what the witness said. it is very important that you only write what was said, and not what you think they meant or might have wanted to say.

The confidential box should be checked whenever anyone is cautious about giving their name/information. Confidentiality cannot be guaranteed, but the Department Director will do everything in his/her power to protect the witness's identity.

Witness Statement

Incident Report # _____ Date _____
Witness statement obtained by _____ Employee/Volunteer # _____

Dear Witness: Please use your own word to write exactly what you saw, heard, smelled or any other facts concerning what happened or what you discovered. We appreciate your assistance in helping to make the Parks a better place for all of us.

Written By: _____

_____
_____
_____
_____
_____
_____
_____
_____
_____
_____
_____
_____
_____
_____
_____
_____
_____
_____
_____
_____
_____
_____
_____

Witness's name: _____
Address: _____
Phone number (   ) _____ (   ) _____

Signature: _____ Date: _____

If you wish your statement to be confidential, check the confidential box below. If you check the confidential box, we will make every effort to protect your statement and will not provide a copy of this statement to anyone other than a representative of the City of Houston, without a court order.

[ ] CONFIDENTIAL

Addenda E

Inventory Loss/Damage Report

This report is critical to assist in identifying and repairing lost or stolen items. Any appropriate Incident Report Number should be listed as well as the date the item was discovered lost or damaged. There are occasions when an Incident Report Number is not available. In those cases, contact the Departmental Asset Coordinator and utilize a product or inventory tag number in place of the Incident Report Number.

Contact the Departmental Asset Coordinator by phone for item numbers (PARD #, Shop #, Inventory TAG # or Serial #), purchase price, replacement costs, repair costs or repair time. After completing and signing the report. Submit copies with all appropriate department divisions. If the damage is not repaired after the specified priority period has ended (see Addenda F-Repair Request), an additional Inventory Loss/Damage Report should be filed, indicating this is the second form and should be submitted to the Department Director's office or his/her designee.

Inventory Loss/Damage Report

Location _____ PIC Number _____ Incident Report # _____
Date of Inventory Loss _____

Item # _____
Description _____
Item's Age_____
Item's Purchase Price _____
Estimated Replacement Price _____
Estimated Repair Cost _____
Estimated Repair Time _____

Item # _____
Description _____
Item's Age _____
Item's Purchase Price _____
Estimated Replacement Price _____
Estimated Repair Cost _____
Estimated Repair Time

Item # _____
Description _____
Item's Age _____
Item's Purchase Price _____
Estimated Replacement Price _____
Estimated Repair Cost _____
Estimated Repair Time _____

Item # _____
Description _____
Item's Age _____
Item's Purchase Price _____
Estimated Replacement Price _____
Estimated Repair Cost _____
Estimated Repair Time _____

Item # _____
Description _____
Item's Age _____
Item's Purchase Price _____
Estimated Replacement Price _____
Estimated Repair Cost _____
Estimated Repair Time _____

Name _____ Employee Number _____
Signature _____ Date _____

Addenda F

Repair Request

A repair request is the first step needed to notify the Maintenance Department that some needed repairs have to be made and the time frame within which those repairs need to be made. There is a priority for all repairs based on usage, money, time and related concerns. The following guidelines help establish the repair priority for various items.

Priority 1-Items which are essential for the functioning of a city park. Examples include: furnaces, front doors, lighting and other structural or facility concerns without which the facility cannot operate in a safe manner. All Priority 1 matters have to be repaired within one day.

Priority 2-Items which need to be repaired to ensure the immediate safety of patrons or park visitors. Examples include holes in a sidewalk, missing or broken windows, a broken lock on a swimming pool gate and similar concerns which need to be addressed immediately to ensure patron safety. All Priority 2 matters have to be repaired within two to three days. Any area prioritized as a Priority 2 area should be roped off with yellow or other colored warning ribbon/tape. Furthermore, all facility or program participants, employees, spectators and volunteers should receive either oral or written warnings about the hazardous condition.

Priority 3- Items which are important for the operation of a facility of program. Examples include broken door hinge, broken phones, inoperable security system, and related concerns. All Priority 3 matters have to be repaired within one-two weeks.

Priority 4-Items which pose the lowest priority. A program can operate safely and effectively, but would be better if the repair was made. Examples include unsanded wood benches which might have splinters, a missing tile on a closet floor, etc. All Priority 4 matters have to be repaired within one month.

Any area in need of repair should be marked in such a manner that the hazardous condition is readily apparent and not to be used. This can best be accomplished by using red "road way" cones and yellow "hazard" tape in and around the hazardous area.

Repair Request

Incident Report # _____   Date _____

Priority Number _____

Description of item needing repair _____

_____

Location of item needing repair _____

Describe the damage _____

_____

_____

Name _____   Employee # _____

Signature _____

Follow-up Action (If any) _____

_____

Date _____

* *

Incident Report # _____   Date _____

Priority Number _____

Description of item needing repair _____

_____

Location of item needing repair _____

Describe the damage _____

_____

_____

Name _____   Employee # _____

Signature _____

Follow-up Action (If any) _____

_____

Date _____

Addenda G

Call-In Log

The call in log provides a means to track and record all phone calls received by the Department Dispatcher or Call-In Dispatcher concerning an incident or hazardous condition.

All phone call reports should reference the date, time, person calling, reference location, phone number where caller can be reached, the incident or danger, what action was requested (if any), actions already taken prior to the phone call, suggested action and any appropriate or newly assigned Incident Report Number. For convenience, the person calling can be identified with just an individual's name or employee number. The incident or danger should be specifically described as well as what steps had already been taken (i.e., Assault by a basketball player; police called). Lastly, if the dispatcher suggests any action or course of conduct, all such suggestions should be recorded even if the caller did not follow the suggestion.

Call-In Log

Dispatcher's Name _____   Employee Number _____

Date _____   Time _____ a.m./ p.m.

Caller's Name _____

Caller's Employee # (if applicable) _____

Incident Location _____

Phone Number Calling From ( ) _____

Description of Incident or Danger _____

_____

Action Requested _____

Action Already Taken _____

Dispatcher's Suggestions _____

Incident Report Number _____

Conclusion

It is impossible to eliminate all accidents. Furthermore, incident reports are not designed to eliminate accidents or prevent all hazards. Incident reports and related supporting documentation are designed not to prevent injuries and hazards, but to inform individuals as to what hazards are present and what steps have been successful in reducing or eliminating various injuries or incidents. This data can be useful in developing safer programs and facilities as well as better trained employees and volunteers.

You play an important and critical role in the process. By taking time to properly complete all necessary forms you can help prevent injuries and make park and recreation programs and facilities safer for all users. Complete, accurate and timely reports also help reduce liability concerns and promote our risk management efforts. You are thanked in advance by your superiors for helping to make the incident reporting process work.

If you have any questions concerning any reporting issues, please contact your supervisor. The Incident Reporting Manual should be kept at each city park and available for use by all employees to assist them in completing various reports. Additional copies of any necessary forms can be requested from your supervisor.

Appendix C

Facility Rental Contracts

Note: The following rental agreement contains components typically found in contracts written by the individual or group renting a facility. If you are renting the facility (LESSEE), you should try to bargain for components that could provide you with some additional protection (i.e. a warranty that the facility has no defects, you have been warned about all defects, the facility owner carries insurance on the facility, etc.). Attached to this appendix is a listing of 31 key contractual clauses/provisions that you should try to incorporate in all contracts.

This agreement made this _____ day of _____, 19 __ is between __(Facility Owner/Manager)__ (hereinafter referred to as LESSOR) and __(Renter)__ (hereinafter referred to as LESSEE) whose address is

_____.

Witneseth:

AREA/FACILITY RENTED — DATES RESERVED

1. In consideration of the sums hereinafter specified, LESSOR grants to LESSEE the use of the following facilities:

_____

_____

for the following event: _____
on the following date(s): _____

RENT

2. The LESSEE agrees to pay LESSOR $_____ for the afore-mentioned facility. (You can also have provision(s) for deposits, percentage of gross receipts, final settlement of account, breach of the agreement, facility cleaning, signage, lease assignments, etc. based on your needs, the facility and its intended use).

INSURANCE AND INDEMNITY OF LESSEE

3. The LESSEE shall be liable for all damages to building(s), field(s), and equipment, normal wear and tear excepted, and agrees to indemnify and hold LESSOR harmless from any and all claims or suits arising out of injury or death to any person or damage to property resulting from the

use of building(s), field(s), and equipment. LESSEE will be required to furnish an appropriate certificate of insurance showing that there is in effect, and will remain in effect throughout the term of the Lease, comprehensive general liability insurance, including public liability and property damage insurance, written by an insurer, authorized to do business in the State of _____, in the following amounts:

Comprehensive General Liability (Including Personal Injury,
Contractual, and Product Liability _____
Bodily Injury (each occurrence) _____
Property Damage (each occurrence) _____
Aggregate _____
Worker's Compensation (statutory) _____

The LESSEE should name as additional insured, __(Name of Other Parties to be Insured)__, its officers, agents and employees. At least fourteen (14) days prior to the commencement of this Lease, the LESSEE shall deliver to the LESSOR certificates of insurance, with the limits specified above, evidencing that the policies hereby required by LESSEE will be in full force and effect through the lease term. LESSOR may obtain copies of said policies at LESSEE's expense or cancel the subject event(s).

COMPLIANCE WITH LAWS AND REGULATIONS

4. (a) Compliance with Laws: LESSEE shall comply with all laws of the United States, of the State of _____, and all local statutes and ordinances and all regulations established by any authorized officer or department of said entities; LESSEE will not suffer or permit to be done anything on said premises in violation of any law, statutes, ordinance, rules,or regulations.

(b) Licenses: LESSEE shall obtain all necessary permits or licenses required by such laws, statutes, ordinances, rules and/or regulations. If required licenses and permits are not obtained by the LESSEE, then LESSOR may obtain same and LESSEE will be responsible for reimbursing all associated costs.

(c) Compliance with rules and regulations: LESSEE shall, and shall cause its servants, agents, employees, licensees, patrons and guests, to abide by such reasonable rules and regulations as may from time to time be adopted by the LESSOR for use, occupancy and operation.

CONTROL OF BUILDING

5. The LESSOR and premises, including keys thereto, shall be at all times under the control of the general manager, and he/she or other duly authorized representative of the LESSOR's shall have the right to enter the premises at all times during the period covered by the contract. LESSEE

at its own expense must at all times place proper watchman at all entrances and exists when the same are unlocked. LESSEE is also responsible for securing parking lots and all surrounding areas adjacent to the premises

LICENSOR/LICENSEE

6. It is expressly understood that LESSOR shall not be construed or held to be a partner, agent or associate by joint venture or otherwise of LESSEE in the conduct of its business, it being expressly understood that the relationship between the parties hereto is and shall remain at all times that of licensor and licensee. It is understood and agreed that no agent, servant or employee of LESSEE or any of its subcontractors shall under any circumstances be deemed an agent, servant or employee of LESSOR.

NO REPRESENTATION BY LESSOR

7. Neither LESSOR or LESSOR's employees, agents or servants have made any representations or promises with respect to the premises and LESSEE has examined the premises and is satisfied with the condition, fitness and order thereof. Commencement of the premises use by LESSEE shall be conclusive evidence against LESSEE that the premises were in good repair and satisfactory condition, fitness and order when leased.

_____   _____
LESSEE's Signature   Date

_____   _____
LESSOR's Signature   Date

The above contract is a rudimentary facility contract, The following contract is a more comprehensive facility contract.

FACILITY CONCESSION AGREEMENT

THIS AGREEMENT made this ___ day of _____, ____ by and between _____, a municipal corporation, having its main office _____, (hereinafter "Facility"), and Facility Operator, Inc., whose mailing address will be _____ (hereinafter "Operator").

WITNESSETH:

WHEREAS, the Facility is a multiuse sport facility; and, **WHEREAS,** Operator is qualified and knowledgeable in the field of concession operation; and,

WHEREAS, the Facility desires that Operator provide concession service at the Facility during sporting events.

NOW, THEREFORE, the parties agree as follows:

1 . *Service To Be Provided.* Operator shall, during the term of this Agreement during the hours of operation herein below provided, shall provide concession items as mutually agreed upon by both parties.

2. *Fees.*

a. **Occupancy Fee.** The Operator agrees to pay a concession fee of $_____ for permission to sell concessions at the Facility. This payment of $_____ must be received by _____to be valid.

3 . **Term.** This Agreement shall apply from the date hereof through December 31 _____. The Facility and Operator may by mutual agreement extend this Agreement for two successive one year options, with modifications to this Agreement subject to the approval of both parties. Such renewal shall be in writing and signed by both parties.

4. **Permits.** Operator shall be responsible for obtaining all appropriate and necessary licenses and permits for the sale of its products. Appropriate and necessary permits and certificates for food service from the County Health Department must be obtained and exhibited prior to serving customers. Repeated health code violations or other poor performance leading to Health Department citation(s) shall result in this contract's termination.

5. **Insurance.** During the term hereof, Operator shall maintain in full force and effect bodily injury, property damage and comprehensive public liability insurance of not less than $ 1,000,000. Operator shall deliver to the Facility a certificate issued by the insurance carrier naming the Facility as an additional insured.

6. **Indemnification.** Each party shall indemnify and hold harmless the other and their respective successors, assigns, officers, directors, agents, affiliates and employees from and against all costs, liabilities, damages, expenses, claims and demands whatsoever, including reasonable attorneys' fees, suffered by or asserted against the other party which results directly or indirectly from any negligent, willful, reckless or wrongful act or omission of the other party, its employees, representatives or agents, under this Agreement, or from any breach of its representations and warranties herein. If a claim arises, upon receiving notice or knowledge of any claim, event, or loss for which indemnity is sought hereunder, the indemnified party shall tender the matter to the defending party and cooperate with its defense as that party may reasonably request, and permit the defending party to defend, try, settle, arbitrate or appeal such matter as the defending party shall determine. After tender and acceptance of defense have occurred, the indemnifor shall not be responsible for further defense costs or further attorneys' fees.

7. **Trash Removal.** The Facility shall provide trash receptacles for Operator's operation at no additional cost or expense to Operator. It shall be the Operator's responsibility to empty trash receptacles at the end of each

day, located inside each concession and eating areas, and place outside the facility for final trash removal.

8. **Uniforms.** Operator's employees will use Operator's standard uniform designating them in a manner that sets them apart from security personnel.

9.**Conduct.** Courteous and polite behavior is required and expected of Operator's employees.

10. **Applicable Laws.** Operator shall observe all laws, ordinances and regulations applicable to its operation hereunder, and shall promptly pay when due, all sales, employment, income and other required taxes.

11. **Acts of God and Force Majeure.** Neither party shall be liable for damages for its failure to perform due to contingencies beyond its reasonable control, including, but not limited to, war, fire, strikes, riots, storm, flood, earthquake, explosion, accidents, sabotage, public insurrection, public disorders, lockouts, labor disputes, labor shortages or any other acts of God.

12. **Attorneys' Fees.** In any action to construe or enforce the terms and conditions of the Agreement, the prevailing party (as determined by a court of competent jurisdiction, if necessary) in such action and in any appeals taken therefrom, shall be entitled to recover all reasonable attorneys' fees and costs.

13. **Waiver.** Failure or delay on the part of either party to exercise any right, power, privilege or remedy under this Agreement shall not constitute a waiver thereof .

14. **Severability.** The provision of this Agreement shall be severable and the invalidity of any provision, or portion thereof, shall not affect the enforceability of the remaining provisions.

15. **Authorized Signatures/Effectiveness.** The persons signing this Agreement shall have all legal authority and power to bind Operator and Facility.

16. **Entire Agreement.** This Agreement constitutes the entire understanding between the parties and supersedes all previous agreements or negotiations, whether written or oral, and shall not be modified or amended except by written agreement duly executed by the parties.

17. **Binding Agreement.** This Agreement shall be binding upon and inure to the benefit of the parties, their heirs, successors and assigns.

18. **Pricing and Signs.** All display signage and advertising and promotion located in the Facility must be approved by Facility prior to display and shall not conflict with current Facility sponsors.

19. **No Competition.** During the term of this Agreement, the Facility agrees that it will not enter into an Agreement with any other entity permitting any concession operation at the Facility.

20. **Security.** The management staff at the Facility and the local police shall have keys to each concession location. The Facility is responsible for

hiring, training and managing the activity of all facility security personnel. Security personnel should make regularly scheduled visits to Operators sites and help with securing money deposits after each event.

21. **Default.** In the event the Operator shall fail to comply with all the terms contained herein or fails to remain open for business at the times provided, or fails to abide by any of the terms and conditions thereof, the Facility may at its sole discretion through providing written notice of any such breach/default.

In the event the facility gives written notice of any claimed breach/default the Operator shall be allowed 72 hours after hand-delivery receipt of such notice within which to cure the breach or breaches specified therein. If the breach(s) take longer than 24 hours to correct, the Operator will keep the facility Manager informed of the daily progress being made to correct the breach(s). No breach(s) will take longer than five (5) days to cure and if the breach(s) cannot be cured the Agreement will automatically terminate.

IN WITNESS THEREOF, the parties hereto sign this Agreement on the date below and hereby acknowledge acceptance of all the terms and conditions set forth herein.

Contractual/Lease Concerns for Auditorium Management

The following points should be considered by anyone entering into a contract. A contract is like a marriage; only enter into a contract if you intend to consummate the marriage. Never enter into a contract anticipating reneging or terminating the contract before the actual completion of the contract. This can normally lead you in one direction: to the courthouse.

These points are presented to encourage sports facility operators to revue their currently existing contracts and contractual procedures. By utilizing sound contractual procedures facility operators can help prevent miscommunications or misunderstandings which often cause contractual disputes. The other major cause for contractual disputes is the differing interpretations given by each side to contractual terms/provisions. While a lessee might interpret one obligation to belong to the facility owner, the facility owner could have intended compliance by the lessee for the same obligation. It should be noted that a contract, and any vagueness about the contract terms, will be construed against the contract's author.

The following points are some of the major concerns faced when attempting to create unambiguous and enforceable contracts.

1) What restrictions are needed to keep the other side from adding any *unwanted terms* or conditions? Any and all *changes to the contract* need to be in writing, signed by both parties and signed by individuals with the authority to bind the parties.

2) Are all *prior communications* merged and integrated into the written agreement?

3) Are all *oral modifications* precluded by the contract? If certain individuals are to be specifically excluded from *revising the contract*, you should insert a clause specifically excluding them from changing conditions of the agreement. (This is especially important to prevent non-managerial employees from verbally altering portions of the contract.)

4) What *future acts* can be construed as a waiver or forfeiture of contractual rights?

5) If the other party's representations are being relied upon, are the representations stated as an *express warranty*, rather than a mere "whereas" recital in the contract? If it is merely a recital, fraud must be proved in order to get relief if the facts are different; if the misrepresentation is innocent, the contract may be voided (terminated) if the representation is set up as a warranty.

6) Does the party signing the agreement have the *authority to sign/and bind* the individual or organization they are representing?

7) If a facility is rented "as is,"does the contract expressly exclude any *implied representations* about the facility's condition? Make sure to include a provision that each side has made his/her *own investigation of the facility* and has not relied on any statements or preliminary representations made by the other side.

8) Provide for an express *duration of contract* (one year, one event, etc...) and the right to terminate the contract. If it appears likely that the parties will maintain an ongoing business relationship beyond the express terms of the contract, consider providing for automatic renewal of the contract, but make sure you always preserve your right to terminate the contract after providing appropriate notice.

9) Spell out exactly what constitutes *performance*. Specify who is responsible for taking all steps necessary to complete performance, as well as the time for completion.

10) Insert a *time-of-the-essence clause*. This clause can provide for canceling the contract if the other party fails to perform in a timely manner.

11) Guard against liability from unforeseeable contingencies by inserting a *force majeure* ("act-of-god") clause.

12) In the absence of contrary provisions, delivery and payment are *concurrent provisions*. If the intention is to sepatrate payment and delivery, express provisions might be necessary. If payments are to be made in installments, consider acceleration and prepayment provisions.

13) Always include *indemnification and hold-harmless provisions* to protect you from potential legal action. These clauses are essential for determining who will have the legal obligation to defend a lawsuit.

14) If a deposit is made, consider using the deposit as a *liquidated damages* provision for the other party's default or breach. However, the liquidated damages should not be so heavy or harsh as to be considered a penalty. If no deposit is given, a liquidated damages clause should none-the-less be included in the contract.

15) Protect against inadvertent *defaults* by providing for notice and a subsequent time period within which any default may be cured. Provide a provision relating to whether notice of default becomes effective upon mailing or upon receipt and whether it has to be given by registered or certified mail.

16) If the *governing law* can be specified (i.e. the laws of California will be governing in any dispute) include this provision to help avoid any potential conflict of laws problems.

17) Determine whether or not the contract is *assignable*, and whether or not the original party is relived of liability upon assignment. Provide a clause that assignment is not effective until the assignee assumes the assignor's obligations in writing. You also might want the party who assigned the lessee or the new party to add an additional amount of security as a further deposit against any defaults.

18) You should try to include a clause requiring *arbitration* as the first recourse upon any unresolvable dispute under the contract. Arbitration is usually quicker, more efficient and cheaper than other traditional legal means.

19) You should try to specify the exact *consideration* (i.e. "for the sum of $1...") that makes the contract binding. Even though some states do not require consideration to be specified in a written agreement, if the consideration is specified, it could provide additional proof that a contract was indeed entered into.

20) Always make it clear during preliminary negotiations that there is no agreement until a *final document is signed*. Mark all preliminary documents as "DRAFT" copies.

21) If a party is to have the *right to cancel* the agreement, because the other party breaches the contract, it is advisable to include such a clause in the contract. If such a clause is not included in the contract, it may be necessary to establish a serious breach to defeat the purpose of the contract (i.e. cancel the contract).

22) Is there a provision whereby the parties have the *rights to inspect the books* and records of another party? This is especially appropriate when you are sharing a percentage of the gate receipt with a promoter. You should also provide for reasonable, time, place and manner regulations for inspecting the financial record.

23) Specify who is to carry the *risk of property* loss during the contract period. Also specify who is to carry the insurance, which insurance to purchase, the amount of the insurance coverage and when proof of insurance, or cancellation of insurance, needs to be provided.

24) It should be determined whether the *illegality* of any provision of the contract invalidates the whole contract or just that clause.

25) If the agreement allows certain terms (price, delivery date, insurance requirements) to be determined at a later date, as conditions change, make sure "*escape*," arbitration, liquidated damages and cancellation clauses are included.

26) Before utilizing an escape clause, you should decide if you want the other party to be able to back out of the deal. A good one way *escape clause* should, fix a period and method of notice, leaving no doubt about liability for expenses or benefits that have accrued prior to the lease's termination.

27) Include a *definitions section* so complicated or confusing terms can be defined based on the understanding of both parties.

28) Provide a clause stating who's duty it is to comply with accessibility and accommodations requirement under the <u>Americans with Disabilities Act</u>. This can be accomplished with a clause requiring the lessor to comply with all local, state and federal laws. If any modifications are nec-

essary, the contract should explicitly state who is financially required to make those modifications.

29) A clause should be included relating to who has the right and authority to <u>sell/lease signage</u> at the facility. It is also important to specify if the lessee can post signage of competing companies against currently sponsored signs.

30) The contract should include a clause indicating who is responsible for providing <u>waivers, release or warning to facility users.</u>

31) The contract should have specific clauses dealing with all ancillary services such as security, parking, concession, clean-up and related services.

While this is in no way an exhaustive list, and should not substitute for the competent advice of an attorney, the list does give a flavor as to the multitude of contractual provisions that could be required to produce a comprehensive contract. Some individuals are intimidated by long contracts. It should be remembered that a long contract is not necessarily a difficult contract to understand. If your contract is written in plain English, even if the contract is long, both parties will be able to understand their rights and obligations.

Appendix D

Facility Inspection Schedules

Area Inspected	Inspection Date	Inspected By	Comments	Follow Up
Locker/Dressing Rooms				
_____	_____	_____	_____	_____
_____	_____	_____	_____	_____
_____	_____	_____	_____	_____
Restrooms				
_____	_____	_____	_____	_____
_____	_____	_____	_____	_____
Showers				
_____	_____	_____	_____	_____
_____	_____	_____	_____	_____
Trainer's Room				
_____	_____	_____	_____	_____
_____	_____	_____	_____	_____
_____	_____	_____	_____	_____
Gymnasiums				
_____	_____	_____	_____	_____
_____	_____	_____	_____	_____
_____	_____	_____	_____	_____
_____	_____	_____	_____	_____
Swimming Pool				
_____	_____	_____	_____	_____
_____	_____	_____	_____	_____
_____	_____	_____	_____	_____
Weight Room				
_____	_____	_____	_____	_____

Facility Inspection Log   Page 2

Area Inspected	Inspection Date	Inspected By	Comments	Follow Up
Outdoor Fields				
_____	_____	_____	_____	_____
_____	_____	_____	_____	_____
_____	_____	_____	_____	_____
_____	_____	_____	_____	_____
_____	_____	_____	_____	_____
_____	_____	_____	_____	_____
Concession				
_____	_____	_____	_____	_____
_____	_____	_____	_____	_____
_____	_____	_____	_____	_____
Parking				
_____	_____	_____	_____	_____
_____	_____	_____	_____	_____
_____	_____	_____	_____	_____
Misc.				
_____	_____	_____	_____	_____
_____	_____	_____	_____	_____
_____	_____	_____	_____	_____
_____	_____	_____	_____	_____
_____	_____	_____	_____	_____

Recommendations/Observations: _____

_____

_____

_____

_____

Inspection Approval: I, _____, declare that I approve the completed inspection of _____ on _____.
          (facility)   (date)

_____
Signature

_____
Title

On at least a weekly basis an individual capable of detecting potential hazards should inspect your entire athletic or recreational facilities. Any required follow-up inspections and/or repairs should be clearly indicated and acted upon to ensure a reasonably safe facility. If a facility will be used for a single event, a thorough inspection should be completed prior to the event and afterwards.

Appendix E

Facility and Equipment Repair Logs

Facility Repair Log

Area Inspected _____

Date Inspected _____ Inspected By _____

Follow-up Requested (Y/N)?___

Condition _____

Comments _____

Repair Order Number _____

Repairs Needed _____

Action Taken _____

Follow-up Required (Y/N)? ___ Check again on _____

Repairs made by _____ Date Repaired _____

Equipment Repair Log

Equipment Inspected _____

Date Inspected _____ Inspected By _____

Follow-up Requested (Y/N)? ___

Condition _____

Comments _____

Repair Order Number _____

Repairs Needed _____

Action Taken _____

Follow-up Required (Y/N)? ___ Check again on _____

Repairs made by _____ Date Repaired _____

Appendix F

Job Description

Job Title: Head Soccer Coach

Job Status: The position is a part-time paid position. XYZ Soccer Organization will directly employ the coach. The position does not provide any full-time benefits, nor any entitlement to future employment.

Salary: The salary for this position is $4.25 per hour.

Supervisor: The Coach will report to _____, XYZ's Vice President of Operations.

Purpose: The purpose of this position is to provide children age 10-15 with the opportunity to fully develop their soccer skills. The coach is responsible for providing mentoring, educational opportunities, skill enhancement, a safe recreational environment and a wholesome recreational experience.

Duties:

1) Supervise one assistant coach and at least twelve (12) players for a 14-week schedule starting June 7, 1999.
2) provide physical, emotional and intellectual stimulation to all participants
3) promote good sportsmanship.
4) Provide guidance, support and counseling-when appropriate-to all participants in the XYZ program.
5) Be a good listener to verbal and non-verbal communications.
6) Develop and promote new activities that will challenge and motivate children.
7) Provide soccer specific instructions appropriate with the skill, motivational and mental capabilities of each participant.
8) Strictly follow XYZ's soccer coaching program.
9) Develop and maintain a relationship of trust with all participants.
10) Provide any necessary assistance to parents of the participants
11) Supervise the playing environment to prevent non-participants from enteracting with participants during XYZ games, practice or official activities.

Qualifications: All potential candidates should, at a minimum, have a high school diploma, four years of prior soccer coaching experience, completion of a national coaching certification program (such as American Coaching Effectiveness Program), complete an application form including the signing of a background investigation release form and have prior demonstrable youth counseling experience. Review and accept all the terms of XYZ's sexual abuse policy statement. All references provided on the application form will be checked.

Evaluation: All assigned children will be provided a pre-test and post-test to ascertain skill development and emotional growth resulting from participation in the program. Such results can be used to determine future employment with XYZ.

Appendix G

Employment

Employment Application

Full legal name: _____

Prior names or aliases: _____

Complete address: _____

Home and work numbers: (___)_____ (___)_____

Social security _____

Driver's license number, state and expiration date: _____(or other I.D.)

List all coaching certificates or _____

List all prior involvement in youth athletics: _____

List three personal and business references including current phone numbers:

Personal   (1) _____

           (2) _____

           (3) _____

Business   (1) _____

           (2) _____

           (3) _____

List all prior residences for the past ten years: _____

Have you ever been convicted of any felony, in any state or country: _____

If yes, please describe the felony committed and your current legal status (parole, probation, etc.): _____

I understand and agree that:

1) It is the policy of this organization to deny employment opportunities for individuals who have been convicted of any violent crime or any crime against any person(s).

2) This organization has a strict confidentiality and appeals process concerning the handling of the applications of individuals with prior criminal histories.

3) This application is valid for two years and a new application has to be completed immediately thereafter.

4) By submitting this application I, the applicant, affirm that all the foregoing information I have provided is true and correct.

5) By submitting this application I, the applicant, agree (in return for being allowed to work) that if any of the foregoing information is incorrect, I will forever indemnify and hold this youth organization harmless for any acts or omissions on my behalf solely as it relates to the incorrect information I have provided.

6) By submitting this application I, the applicant, voluntarily waive my privacy rights only to the extent necessary for the youth organization to verify the foregoing information through any reasonable means, including, but not limited to local, regional, state, national or international criminal background check(s).

Printed Name: _____
Signature: _____
Date: _____
Affirmative Action/Equal Employment Opportunity Employer

Volunteer Application

Full legal name: _____

Prior names or aliases: _____

Complete address: _____

Home and work numbers: (___)_____ (___)_____

Social security _____

Driver's license number, state and expiration date: _____

Date of birth: _____ (only for volunteers)

List all coaching certificates or _____

List all prior involvement in youth athletics: _____

List three personal and business references including current phone numbers:

Personal   (1) _____

              (2) _____

              (3) _____

Business   (1) _____

              (2) _____

              (3) _____

List all prior residences for the past ten years: _____

Have you ever been convicted of any felony, in any state or country: _____

If yes, please describe the felony committed and your current legal status (parole, probation, etc.): _____

I understand and agree that:

1) It is the policy of this organization to deny volunteer opportunities for individuals who have been convicted of any violent crime or any crime against any person(s). This organization can deny any applicant for any reason or for no reason at all.

2) This organization has a strict confidentiality and appeals process concerning the handling of the applications of individuals with prior criminal histories.

3) This application is valid for two years and a new application has to be completed immediately thereafter.

4) By submitting this application I, the applicant, affirm that all the foregoing information I have provided is true and correct.

5) By submitting this application I, the applicant, agree (in return for being allowed to volunteer) that if any of the foregoing information is incorrect, I will forever indemnify and hold this youth organization harmless for any acts or omissions on my behalf solely as it relates to the incorrect information I have provided.

6) By submitting this application I, the applicant, voluntarily waive my privacy rights only to the extent necessary for the youth organization to verify the foregoing information through any reasonable means, including, but not limited to local, state, national and international criminal background check(s).

Printed Name: _____

Signature: _____

Date: _____

Release

I, _____ (name) hereby authorize *ORGANIZATION* to obtain any and all pertinent information pertaining to any charges, allegations and/or convictions of any kind I may have had or are currently pending relating to any state, federal or international criminal law violations. Such information can include, but is not limited to, any allegations, charges or convictions for crimes committed against children, people and crimes involving moral turpitude. Such information can be obtained from such sources as any and all law enforcement agencies of this state, other states, federal agencies and international law enforcement agencies to the full extent permitted by law.

Social Security Number _____
Driver's License Number _____ State _____
All states and counties which you have lived in over the past ten years _____
_____
Have you ever been convicted of any felony? _____
If yes, please describe the conviction and when you were convicted _____
_____

I affirm, under the penalty of perjury, that the following is true and correct information and I would testify accordingly if called to testify in any court of law.

Signature _____
Date _____

Interview Guidelines

The following interview rules, suggestions or cues for further investigation represent a partial list of issues that all interviewers should follow.

1) Interviewing is only effective when everyone is thoroughly screened.
2) If at all possible, try to have at least two people at each interview so if a discrimination claim is raised, you could possibly have two witnesses who can testify as to what happened. Furthermore, you can base decisions to hire or utilize someone based on the opinions of two people rather than one individual.
3) All interviewers should be intimately familiar with the organization's sexual abuse policy.
4) If possible, receive permission from the interviewee to videotape the interview.
5) Utilize all available resources such as police for investigation or fingerprinting, school districts for employee records and any other potential source of information concerning position applicants.
6) Prior to starting the interview, check at least two pieces of identification-at least one with a picture, to make sure the person interviewed is in fact the person that is applying for the job.
7) Ask more intense questions regarding an applicants background when there exists frequent, unexplained moves.
8) Ask more intense questions regarding an applicants background when there exists gaps in employment or education dates.
9) Ask more intense questions regarding an applicants background when there exists any criminal convictions or serious motor vehicle violations. Determine the specifics concerning the convictions or violations including specific dates, jurisdictions, exact charges, exact adjudication and the exact resolution of the conviction.
10) Follow-up with what hobbies are listed and if they are appropriate for someone of similar age and background.
11) Follow-up with what the applicant's attitudes are toward children.
12) Be cognizant of appropriate and inappropriate nonverbal queues.
13) Be cognizant of potential problems if the applicant is single with no "age- appropriate" romantic relationships.
14) Be cognizant of potential problems if all activities and interests center around children.

15) Be sensitive, but also cautious, when an applicant was sexually abused as a child.
16) Be cognizant of potential problems if the applicant is fearful of the adult world.
17) Be cognizant of potential problems if the applicant sees children as "pure." "innocent" and/or "clean."
18) Be wary if the applicant is overanxious to get the position.
19) Deny any applicant who is willing to bend the rules to allow overnights or other prohibited actions.
20) Deny any applicant who abuses alcohol or drugs.

Interview Questions

Besides developing some general guidelines for interviews, all interviewers should understand what questions they can ask and what questions will solicit the requisite information sought from the applicant. The following represent some acceptable questions that will provide useful information in analyzing the qualification of any candidate. It should be remembered that you should not ask leading questions, yes or no questions, nor questions that are too general. Provide the applicant with questions that allows them to elaborate on responses and provide information voluntarily that could not have been requested through traditional questioning. Additionally. all questions should be relevant and further the informational needs required to make a final decision concerning the applicant.

1) Why are you interested in the position?
2) How would you describe yourself?
3) Have you ever had to discipline a child, and how did you do it?
4) Why do you like to work with children?
5) What traits do you think you have that qualifies you to supervise children?
6) What about the position/job appeals to you the most/least?
7) Are you familiar with the issues associated with child sexual abuse?
8) Have you read XYZ's Organizational policy statement concerning sexual abuse?
9) What do you think about the policy?
10) Have you ever been convicted of a criminal offense including criminal driving violations?
11) Have you ever worked in a position for which you were bonded?
12) How do you interact with children?
13) Are you aware of any problems or conditions that could interfere with your ability to care for children or in any way endanger any child under your care?

All responses should be recorded in a response form to provide evidence concerning what questions were asked and relevant responses.

Interview Response Form

Name of Applicant _____

Interviewer(s) _____

Date _____

Position Title _____

Was the applicant given a copy of the job description? _____

Did the applicant read and sign the organizational sexual abuse policy statement and
complete job application including authorization to release records? _____

Did the applicant indicate if they needed any accommodation to perform the job's essential functions? _____

Personal Questions

Education _____

Past work experience _____

_____

Last salary (if appropriate) _____

Discipline actions at work _____

school _____

military _____

Military experience _____

Social security number _____

Can they provide proof of residence if they are hired _____

DO NOT ASK-age, race, nationality, religion, sexual orientation, marital status and related questions if the applicant is applying for an employment position.

How did you learn about this position? _____

Why are you interested in the position? _____

What things have you done that have given you the greatest satisfaction? _____

_____

What have been the biggest disappointment in your life? _____

_____

Where do you see yourself in 1 year, 5 years and 10 years down the road? _____

_____

Describe your temperament? _____

Have you know anyone that has been abused? _____

Tell me about that person and your relationship to him or her? _____

_____

How would you describe yourself? _____

Have you ever had to discipline a child, and how did you do it? _____

_____

Why do you like to work with children? _____

What traits do you think you have that qualifies you to supervise children?

_____

Are you familiar with the issues associated with child sexual abuse? _____

_____

Have you read XYZ's Organizational policy statement concerning sexual abuse? ____

What do you think about the policy? _____

Have you ever been convicted of a criminal offense including criminal driving violations?

Have you ever worked in a position for which you were bonded? _____
How do you relate with children? _____
Are you aware of any problems or conditions that could interfere with your ability to
care for children or in any way endanger any child under your care? _____

Why do you like working with children? _____
Have you ever had any unsupervised supervisorial obligation with children in any past
employment of volunteer position? _____
Is there any information you would like to share about yourself? _____

General observations as they apply strictly to candidate's qualifications _____

Areas possibly necessitating further investigation _____

Notes _____
_____
_____
_____

Have all references been contacted? _____
Any necessary follow-up? _____

Reference Interview Form

Applicant's Name _____ Position Applied for _____
Interviewer _____ Date _____
Reference Being Interviewed _____ Position _____
Company/Organization Name _____
Company Phone Number (_____) _____
How long have you known the Applicant? _____
In what capacity did you know the Applicant? _____
Please describe your relationship with the Applicant. _____

Please describe the Applicant's relationship with people in general. _____

Please describe the Applicant's relationship with children. _____

To the best of your knowledge, has the Applicant ever been convicted of a crime? _____
Would your company/org. ever rehire the Applicant? _____
Was the Applicant ever disciplined by your company/org. and why was he/she _____
Do you know of any traits, conditions, tendencies or problems which would be detrimental to his/her working with children? _____

Comments _____
_____

Interviewer's Signature _____

Appendix H

Sexual Harassment Policy

ACME Co. is committed to providing a work place free of any and all sexual harassment. It is both against the law and ACME Co. policy for any employee or non-employee to sexually harass any co-workers, employees, or customers. ACME Co. will strictly enforce this policy to the full extent of the law and adherence to this policy is a mandatory condition of continued employment with ACME Co.

Sexual Harassment Defined

Sexual harassment is defined as any unwelcomed sexual advances, or visual, verbal or physical conduct of a sexual nature. Any conduct which creates an offensive and hostile work environment is sexual harassment. Furthermore, any sexual conduct which is coerced by a person in a position of apparent or actual power or authority is sexual harassment. Sexual harassment involves a wide variety of behaviors between members of the opposite sex as well as members of the same sex. It should be clear that some conduct which might be appropriate in a social setting, between friends, or even between individuals involved in a consensual relationship may not be appropriate in the workplace. Some prohibited conduct examples are described below. These represent only samples and is not an exhaustive list of conduct which is defined by ACME Co. and the courts as sexual harassment.

Physical Harassment

Unwanted physical contact involving a sexual nature including but not limited to fondling, groping, suggestive touching, impeding or blocking movement, brushing-up against a body, and/or any other activity which causes contact or threat of contact which is unwanted.

Verbal Harassment

Sexual jokes, innuendo, suggestive comments, persistent and unwanted sexual advances, propositions or requests for companionship, any verbal offer of employment, advancement, or increased salary, or other benefits in exchange for sexual activity, threatened or actual employment reprisals, threats, demotions, or terminations after refusing any sexual advances, and/or any graphic lude or offensive comments about an individual's body or body parts.

Non-Verbal Harassment

Staring, leering, obscene gestures, displaying or distributing offensive or sexually suggestive objects, pictures, cartoons, drawings or posters, making or airing suggestive or insulting sounds/noises, and/or writing and/or distributing offensive, suggestive, or obscene notes or letters.

This is not an exhaustive list of prohibited conduct. The term offensive or obscene refers to any conduct, activity, words or sounds which an average person of normal sensitivity would find offensive or obscene.

Sexual Harassment Reporting Procedures

If you believe that you have been the subject of sexual harassment, immediately report the harassment to your supervisor, the Human Resources Department, or ACME's sexual harassment coordinator (Ms. Jane Doe). Do not report the conduct to the person who you allege harassed you, but to anyone who is independent or superior to the alleged harasser. Do not wait a significant period after the alleged harassment has occurred to report the incident. Such actions could jeopardize the ability to fully investigate a complaint or to find necessary witnesses. All complaints will be promptly investigated in a discreet manner. Information will be given to the complaining party only after a thorough investigation has been completed. Investigation will normally entail conferring with the parties involved and any potential witnesses disclosed by the complainant. ACME Co. will take any and all necessary steps, including all forms of discipline to stop the offensive or inappropriate conduct. The complainant will be informed of all findings uncovered through the investigation process and all actions taken as a result thereof. ACME Co. takes every sexual harassment claim seriously and will resolve any and all complaints. No punitive action will ever be taken against a complainant who files a valid compliant. ACME Co. will not tolerate any retaliation or conduct of a retaliatory nature against any individual who has filed a complaint or who is a witness in any sexual harassment investigation.

If ACME Co. is unable to successfully resolve a complaint through the use of internal procedures, or if any employee who suffers sexual harassment is reluctant to utilize the internal procedures, such employee can file a complaint with any appropriate state or federal agency. The employee information area contains a poster reiterating ACME Co.'s sexual harassment policy and describing appropriate contact agency for filing claims. State or federal agencies will normally conduct an investigation and attempt to resolve the matter. If evidence is found of sexual harassment, the matter can be brought to a public hearing. Possible remedies include backpay, promotion, reinstatement, hiring, changes in ACME Co.'s policy and procedures, emotional distress damages, and possible fines.

ACME Co. has never and will never tolerate, and the law specially prohibits, any retaliation against any employee for filing or otherwise participating in any hearing, proceeding or investigation associated with a sexual harassment claim filed with any government agency or commission.

If you have any comments, questions or concerns about sexual harassment, please contact ACME Co.'s Human Resource Director.

I, _____ have read and understand all the above statements. I have had an opportunity to ask any questions I have concerning ACME Co.'s sexual harassment policy. In consideration for being hired or continuing my employment with ACME Co., I hereby agree to follow ACME Co.'s sexual harassment policy and will indemnify and hold ACME Co. harmless for any and all liability and attorney fees if engage in inappropriate conduct including, but not limited to sexual harassment or retaliating against any individual involved in a sexual harassment claim.

_____   _____
Signature   Date

Adopted in part from Schachter, Kristoff, Orenstein, and Berkowitz, *Sexual Harrassment: Innovative Approaches for Minimizing Liability.* San Francisco, California (November 1, 1994).

Appendix I

Waivers

Agreement to Waive Liability Rights

BY SIGNING THIS AGREEMENT YOU MAY
BE RELINQUISHING VALUABLE RIGHTS

Voluntary Participation

1. I, ___(Name)___ acknowledge that I have voluntarily undertaken to participate in ___(Sport/Event)___ at the premises or event site of ___(event administrator)___, located at _____(Address)_____. I affirm and certify that I have recently seen a physician and I have been cleared to participate in this specific event. If I have any actual or potential health problems I have informed the event director of such health problems. Both parties exchange mutual consideration with me being allowed to participate and the event director agreeing to produce the event for which I wish to enter.

Assumption of Risk

2. I AM AWARE THAT ___(Sport/Event)___ IS A HAZARDOUS ACTIVITY. I AM VOLUNTARILY PARTICIPATING IN THIS ACTIVITY WITH SPECIFIC KNOWLEDGE OF THE NUMEROUS DANGERS INVOLVED, INCLUDING MINOR INJURIES, BROKEN BONES, BRAIN DAMAGE, INJURY TO ALL INTERNAL ORGANS AND/OR PARTS OF THE BODY, SERIOUS SPINAL INJURIES, PARAPLEGIA, PERMANENT INJURIES AND DEATH. SUCH DANGERS CAN RESULT IN SERIOUS INJURY, SERIOUS IMPAIRMENT OF MY ABILITY TO EARN A LIVING, ENGAGE IN OTHER BUSINESS, SOCIAL, RECREATIONAL ACTIVITIES AND TO GENERALLY ENJOY LIFE. I HEREBY AGREE TO ACCEPT ALL RISK OF INJURY OR DEATH, AND VERIFY THIS STATEMENT BY PLACING MY INITIALS HERE: _____.

Waiver

3. As consideration for being permitted by ___(EA)___ or one of its affiliated organizations to participate in the above activities and use their facilities, I hereby agree that I, my assignees, heirs, distributees, guardians,and legal representative will not make a claim against, sue or attach the property of ___(EA)___ or any of its affiliated organizations, officers, agents, employees, successors, assigns, assureds, sponsors, co-promoters (etc.) and all other persons, firms, corporations, associations or partnerships affiliated with the ___(Sport/ Event)___ for injury or damage resulting from the negligence or other acts, howsoever caused, by an employee, agent, volunteer, contractor (etc.) or any of its affiliated organizations as a result of my participation in ___(Sport/Event)___. I hereby release ___(EA)___ and any of its affiliated organizations from all actions, claims or demands that I, my assignees, heirs, distributees, guardians and legal representatives now have or may hereafter have for injury or damage resulting from my participation in ___(Sport/Event)___.

Knowing and Voluntary Execution

4. I HAVE CAREFULLY READ THIS AGREEMENT AND FULLY UNDERSTAND ITS CONTENT. I AM AWARE THAT THIS IS A LIABILITY WAIVER AND A CONTRACT BETWEEN MYSELF AND ___(EA)___ AND/OR ITS AFFILIATED ORGANIZATIONS AND SIGN THIS CONTRACT ON MY OWN FREE WILL.

Executed at ___(City)___ , (State) , on ___(Month)___ , (Year)

_____

Signature

_____

Print Name

Medical Waiver

1. I have been informed by ___(Physician/M.D.)___ that I have the following condition(s): _____

2. The physical condition(s) mentioned above existed prior to the date of my physical examination for the current season/event.

3. I have received a complete explanation from ___(Physician/M.D.)___ that to continue to participate in ___(Sport/ Event)___ may result in deterioration or aggravation of my pre-existing physical condition(s).

4. I fully understand the possible consequences of participating in ___(Sport/ Event)___ with the psychical condition(s) mentioned in Paragraph 1 above. Nevertheless, I desire to continue to participate in ___(Sport/ Event)___ and hereby assume all the risk of the matters explained in Paragraph 3 above.

5. As consideration for being permitted by ___(EA)___ or one of its affiliated organizations to participate in the above activities and use their facilities, I hereby agree that I, my assignees, heirs, distributees, guardians,and legal representative will not make a claim against, sue or attach the property of ___(EA)___ or any of its affiliated organizations, officers, agents, employees, successors, assigns, assureds, sponsors, co-promoters (etc.) and all other persons, firms, corporations, associations or partnerships affiliated with the ___(Sport/ Event)___ for injury or damage resulting from the negligence or other acts, howsoever caused, by an employee, agent, volunteer, contractor (etc.) or any of its affiliated organizations as a result of my participation in ___(Sport/ Event)___. I hereby release ___(EA)___ and any of its affiliated organizations from all actions, claims or demands that I, my assignees, heirs, distributees, guardians and legal representatives now have or may hereafter have for injury or damage resulting from my participation in ___(Sport/ Event)___.

_____
Signature

_____
Date

Parental Consent Form

Parent's and/or Guardian's Risk Acknowledgment and Consent to Participate Form

Participant's Name_____ Birth Date _____

Height _____ Weight _____

Name(s) and Address (s) for Parent/Guardian

_____

_____

My/our child wishes to participate in the sport of _____ in the ___(organization, EA, etc.)___ sports program/event during ___(Year/ Date)___. I/we realize that there are numerous risks involved in participating in the sport of _____. These risks could include: sprains, contusions, broken bones, brain damage, lacerations, concussions, permanent disability, injury to all internal organs or parts of the body, serious spinal injury, paralysis and possibly death. These risks could result in serious injuries along with serious impairment of my child's future ability to earn a living, engage in other business, social, and recreational activities and to generally enjoy life. We have been informed about the various risks associated with our child's participation in ___(Sport/ Event)___, and I/we and our child fully understand both the risks and the potential injuries that can be associated with ___(Sport/ Event)___.

I/we assume all responsibility and certify that my/our child is in good physical health and capable of participating in ___(Sport/ Event)___.

As a condition of our child's voluntary participation in ___(Sport/ Event)___, I/we agree to accept all the previously mentioned risks as a condition of my/our child's participation. Where applicable by law, my/our acceptance of the risks inherent in ___(Sport/ Event)___, for my/our child's benefit, discharges any and all claims my/our child might have for negligence or any claim derived from any party failing to comply with their required duty of care. I/We also waive any rights we might have as parent(s)/guardian(s) and will forever discharge and hold harmless all parties and individuals associated with running the event/sport program.

Date: _____

_____
Signature/Relationship

_____
Signature/Relationship

Appendix J

Football Equipment Logs

Purchase/Repair/Disposal Log

Team _____   City, State _____
Coach _____   Equipment Attendant _____

Type of Equipment	Purch Date	Supplier	Recondition Date/Co.	Disposal	Entered By
_____	_____	_____	_____	_____	_____
_____	_____	_____	_____	_____	_____
_____	_____	_____	_____	_____	_____
_____	_____	_____	_____	_____	_____
_____	_____	_____	_____	_____	_____
_____	_____	_____	_____	_____	_____
_____	_____	_____	_____	_____	_____
_____	_____	_____	_____	_____	_____
_____	_____	_____	_____	_____	_____
_____	_____	_____	_____	_____	_____
_____	_____	_____	_____	_____	_____
_____	_____	_____	_____	_____	_____

Instructions: enter in the type of equipment purchased (including serial numbers), when it was purchased, and from whom it was purchased. If the equipment is reconditioned, the reconditioning date and company that performed the work should be listed. If the equipment needs to be disposed, list the date the item was disposed. The person disposing the equipment should enter their name in the last column.

**WARNING: DO NOT DISCARD ANY EQUIPMENT
INVOLVED IN A SERIOUS ACCIDENT
WITHOUT CONSULTING AN ATTORNEY!**

Equipment Issue Log

Participant's Name _____
Participant's Address _____

Type of Equipment	Serial Number	Date Issued	Condition	Date Returned	Condition
_____	_____	____	_____	____	____
_____	_____	____	_____	____	____
_____	_____	____	_____	____	____
_____	_____	____	_____	____	____
_____	_____	____	_____	____	____
_____	_____	____	_____	____	____
_____	_____	____	_____	____	____
_____	_____	____	_____	____	____
_____	_____	____	_____	____	____
_____	_____	____	_____	____	____
_____	_____	____	_____	____	____
_____	_____	____	_____	____	____

Comments: _____
_____
_____

I verify that the follow equipment was issued to me during the _____ football season. I personally inspected each piece of equipment and the condition of the equipment described above is completely accurate.

_____
Participant's Signature

Instructions: indicate the type of equipment issued, its serial number, the date issued and fit to participant's body and it's condition upon being issued. After the piece is returned or exchanged list the date returned and it's condition upon being returned.

Appendix K

Concession Check List

Kitchen/Cooking

Item	Condition	Priority	Date	Inspector

Sales Counter

Item	Condition	Priority	Date	Inspector

Adjacent Areas (isles, floors, bathrooms, dispensing counters, etc.)

Item	Condition	Priority	Date	Inspector

Personnel Issues

Person's name	Describe situation	Priority	Date	Reporter

Appendix L

Risk Management Audit for a Martial Art Studio

The following risk management review of the above named facility was conducted by an attorney and/or attorneys from XYZ Law Firm in New Haven, CT under the express assumption that this report will be an official communication from an attorney to a client and as such is covered by the attorney client work product privilege.

General Overview

The Martial Art Studio (hereafter "facility") is located at a major intersection in a strip mall with two major anchor tenants. The Mall has several stores ranging from a an electrical store to a fish store and a bakery. The mall is designed with a glass enclosed and air conditioned corridor between the actual storefront and the mall entrance. This enclosed area serves as a walking area for local seniors who want a workout, but do not want to walk in the hot and humid New Haven weather. While these walkers do not necessarily pose a risk, there are risks that can be associated with their activities and the facility in question.

The facility is a martial arts studio specialized in karate. The owners are the chief instructors and no other employees currently work at the facility. The business has been in operation since May 1, 1995. In 1998-99 the Martial Art Studio was officially incorporated as a LLC.

The following more specific details are based on a site visit on Monday, January 25, 1999 and Thursday, January 28, 1999 and a review of additional documentation provided by the owners.

Exterior

Parking appeared adequate with well over 150 + parking spaces for all mall visitors. The facility is just east of an anchor tenant (grocery store) with significant parking available. The parking lot has six (6) light poles within the parking area with each having four lights posted on poles between 25-30 feet above ground. Most light appeared to produce sufficient foot-candles, with three to four lights needing to be replaced due to low foot-candle dissemination. The parking lot also had three poles with two halogen bulbs on them, but the lights on the far north-end of the parking lot were not turned on when I made my night inspection.

There was no indication of a security phone and/or security cameras around the parking lot or attached to the building if anyone needed assistance. While I was unable to determine the potential for criminal activity (the neighborhood is a typical middle class neighborhood with single family residences), the Owner (hereafter "owner") informed me that his truck was broken into and someone tried to break into the facility's rear door. A sticker on one of the front doors to the mall indicated that the area was patrolled by Acme Patrol.

The sidewalk outside the mall entrance is a narrow walkway. There exists several wheelchair cutouts, which are fairly steep and possibly difficult for some mall users. Doors leading into the facility are glass doors with pull/push handles in the horizontal mid-plain of the glass doors. While several doors have handicap decals on the doors, they do not appear any wider than other doors nor are they electrical or push button activated.

Suggestions for External Safety

1.   Remind landlord whenever lights are not turned on and ask for a phone number to call at night if the lights are not on.
2.   Suggest to the landlord adding a safety phone or security cameras to increase safety related feelings of current and potential clients.
3.   Post warning signs by the facility front door whenever any criminal activity has occurred, and which you are informed about.
4.   Mention safety issues to classes, especially night classes and ask men in the class to act as escorts for women wishing to go to their cars. You can also inform students that if they have any fears or concerns that a facility agent will gladly walk anyone to their car.
5.   Remind students about risk reduction techniques such as walking with your auto key ready to insert into the key hole, check for suspicious individuals, check under your car and in rear seats, etc.
6.   If criminal activity starts to increase, talk to the landlord about possibly installing a security cart or increasing constable/police patrols.
7.   Be cautious concerning disabled patrons. If they have a hard time entering the facility, you should talk with the landlord about accommodation strategies. Both landlord and tenants are liable for any potential Americans with Disabilities Act (ADA) violations.

8.   Find out how often Acme Patrol actually patrols and if they in fact are the landlord's official security company. Obtain a contact phone number and meet with them on a periodic basis to inform them of class times and any security related concerns.

Entryway

The facility is entered into by someone passing through the mall's glass entry doors, walking across a brick walkway and entering the facility's sole entrance, a glass door. The glass doors appeared to be in good condition and fairly visible to prevent someone from walking into them. However, at least one metal plating for the threshold to a door in front of the facility had some pitting which could cause a heel to get stuck. There were no non-slip mats to remove any rain water from the outside. The bricks can become slick when wet. The bricks are red-brown or maroon color and water is hard to see on the bricks from certain angles. The bricks have mortar between each other which are fairly uniform. However, some bricks have a height difference from other bricks which can be negligible through ¼ of an inch. Such a height discrepancy is not significant. However, if the bricks every shift or chip and a height discrepancy of ½ inch or more is created, then the tripping hazard could lead to liability. While the landlord would be the primary defendant, if the accident occurred in front of the facility, the facility owner could also be sued. There were no significant warning signs posted in front of the facility's main entrance.

Suggestions for Entryway Safety

1.   The landlord should be contacted to determine where non slip mats are located and when they are placed by entry ways. You should also have access to post "slippery when wet" or similar signs by the mall entrance and facility entrance whenever it rains and people track-in water.
2.   Make a point to tell people to walk carefully on rainy days.
3.   Keep a mop handy in case some water accumulates during "off" hours and janitors are not around.
4.   Monitor the brick to determine if any deterioration occurs and immediately notify management in writing (retain a copy for your records) when a problem occurs.
5.   If someone complains about slipping in the corridor, fill out an incident report (see attachment) and take the time to examine the spot they claimed to slip at and what type of shoes they were wearing.

6.   Post appropriate signs on your outer glass walls concerning specific facility rules such as no eating or drinking through signs asking individuals not to warm-up while waiting for their class in the corridor.

Facility Front Section

The facility front section includes several waiting benches, a mini retail section a single office and some cubicles to store personal gear. While a mini-poster sets forth facility rules, the type is so small that it makes the poster less valuable as a warning mechanism. It should be stated that many of the policies are contained in additional materials and reinforced through the learning process which leads to significant rule retention by students, but not necessarily by visitors/spectators.

Foyer—The tile floor appeared to be in good condition and did not seem slippery. However, there was only a small non-slip mat if someone came from outside with wet shoes. Three wood benches appeared to be in good shape with no splinters or buckling. The screws/bolts were not tested for tightness.

Office—On the first visit there appeared to be some baby supplies around. While it appeared that such items were for the owner's own child, there could be a workplace safety issue associated with a child being injured or if inadequate supervision is provide for the child. There also could be ramifications if the child is injured and an insurance claim is raised against the carrier.

The office has two window areas that are made with plexi-glass to reduce potential injuries.

A first aid kit was in the office which had several types of bandages and gauges. The kit also had some medicine and antiseptic solutions. Lastly, some unmarked lotion for "healing" purposes was also in the cabinet

The office had multiples wires running along the floor which presented a tripping hazard. The office should be cleaned to prevent tripping hazards on boxes or dust bunnies.

Sales area-Several types of products are made available from protective equipment to uniforms and weapons.

Suggestions for Facility Front Section

1.   Keep an open and empty cash box on the sales counter after closing time to imply that no money is kept on the premises.
2.   Check benches on a regular basis for any potential splintering, warping or loosening of screws/bolts.

3. Purchase a larger non-slip entry mat and sign to put out whenever weather conditions warranted such warning.
4. Equipment sales should be reinforced with a sign indicated "sold as is," especially with used equipment.
5. Make sure you have a sufficient first aid kit with necessary equipment such as splints, wrapping tape, etc..
6. Do not keep any drugs/unmarked lotions in the first aid kit, even aspirin or antacid tablets. Develop a policy not to provide any students with any drugs, even if they are very close friends.
7. Purchase and keep in an accessible location a blood clean-up kit with all the necessary disposal bags and cleaning solutions (see provided safety catalog for several available kits).
8. Clean the facility on a regular bases and keep boxes and supplies in the back closet if they are not used on a regular basis. All floor obstructions such as wires should be moved, put through walls, covered by a walking tunnel or other protective device/technique.

Facility Workout Section

The facility workout area is comprised of red carpeting throughout the floor area. Between the foyer area and the carpeting is a plastic strip approximately 2-3 feet wide running the length of the entry way used as a transition strip. This strip was not secured and was crumpled in certain areas which could lead to a tripping hazard. The carpet is cleaned on a regular basis with baking soda and related products to keep the carpet smelling fresh and clean.

Two support poles were located in the middle of the workout area. These poles had sparing apparatus secured at a safe height above where any participant might come in contact with the poles. The poles were covered with black matting wrapped entirely around the pole. The ropes securing the matting appeared fairly tight with little give.

Rules were posted in both the foyer area and by a weapon rack area. The rules should be carefully scrutinized for accuracy on a regular basis.

A crash pad was leaning against one wall. Care should be exercised in moving and storing the crash pad so it does not interfere with workouts.

A phone was located on the offices rear wall in the workout area. There were no numbers posted by the phone.

One wall had several mirror sections which were approximately five feet tall and made out of what appeared to be glass. The owners indicated that the mirrors were specifically installed with thermal glue to prevent them from falling over if someone contacted them. However, the glass was not shatterproof.

Two fans were on to help circulate the air. It is unknown how frequently the mall air conditioning system helps to circulate the air. The air should be circulated 8 to 12 times per hour according to the ACSM's facility standard guide.

Suggestions for

1. The rules should be carefully scrutinized for accuracy and additional rules added as necessary such as "no touching weapons on the rack" or "all weapons brought into the facility need to be presented first to the instructor." The rules should also be uniformly enforced for both men and women.
2. A list of important safety numbers should be made and taped near and on the phone. A sign should also be posted on the phone indicated that the phone is for official use.
3. A sign should be posted on the office's external wall facing the workout area indicating that a first-aid kit is located in the office.
4. The carpeting should be cleaned with an anti-fungal cleaning agent on a monthly basis.
5. The carpeting should be checked on a regular basis for rips, exposed seams, and ripples. The carpet should be pulled up whenever ripples occur and should be stretched to eliminate ripples.
6. Ropes securing pole padding should be checked on a monthly basis and tightened whenever necessary.
7. Every other month handles on blocking mats should be checked to make sure they are not falling apart.
8. The carpet in front of the glass mirrors should be colored a different color or a demarcation line should be added to help remind individuals to stay away from the glass.
9. The owner made an announcement that any equipment left on the floor can be taken by anyone else. This policy should also be in writing.
10. A photograph or video recording of the facility should be taken ever month to help demonstrate the facility's general condition. These photos should be kept for several years.

Facility Restrooms

The restrooms were fairly clean at the end of the day. While the trash cans appeared to be filling-up, that would appear to be normal for a busy changing room. The restroom is located in the men's changing room. The women's changing room did not have a bathroom. The restroom was not ADA accessible. If any renovations are made to the existing facility, all renovations need to comply with the ADA. If the current set-up for the restrooms was in place prior to 1994 then no ADA issues currently exists. If however, the restrooms have been modified in anyway since then, ADA related liability could arise.

Piping under the sink was exposed. It is not known whether or not the piping becomes hot if hot water is run through the system.

Outside the men's changing room is a water cooler, it did not appear that the unit was to old or dirty. The water release mechanism should be regularly cleaned to prevent any diseases or contamination.

Suggestion for Facility Restrooms

1.   Policies should be posted concerning individuals using the bathroom one at a time while others might be changing.

Administrative Issues

Various flyers were posted around the facility covering issues such as testing and class registration. Such fliers were not reviewed for accuracy.

Registration cards were not completed. They lacked emergency contact and phone numbers.

There currently are no employees.

The insurance policy the facility currently has is from Acme States Ins. Co., Ltd. based in Iraq. An insurance industry acquaintance checked the company in the Best rating guides and could not find them listed which is a concern. The policy has a $1 million limit, $2 million aggregate and $5,000 medical. The insurance policy covers attorney fees and costs, but there is no indication as to who chooses the attorney. The policy does not cover competitions, but only injuries to students enrolled in classes. Property damage is not covered. The policy appeared to indicate that no coverage would be provided for selling item used by students at home or at another facility. The waiver required by the insurance company applies to only those enrolled in courses.

The policy specifically **does not** cover any: advice given on dieting or injury care, ADA compliance, assaults and battery, communicable diseases, sexual abuse and discrimination. Martial arts weapons are covered as long as they are used by an insured. An independent contractor teaching a course would not be covered unless they had a separate policy. There is a point of contact exclusion for free sparing. The owners are required to report any change in enrollment which affects enrollment, either positive or negative, more than the (10) percent.

Suggestions for Administrative Issues

1. Brochures should contain a standard phrase such as "subject to final approval by management" to indicate that the owners have final say over testing, class schedule, registration, etc..
2. Have students complete all emergency information on their registration cards and have a master list for all students containing all pertinent contact information and any medical issues that might need to be relayed to EMT professionals.
3. The owners might want to offer volunteer workers some stock in the company so there is no question that he/she is not an employee, but rather he/she could be volunteering his time as a part-owner. Even volunteers are owed duties similar to employees. However, if he was an owner then he could not sue the facility, nor might some of the workplace safety laws apply.
4. The baby-sitter should be paid from personal funds such as a personal checking account rather than a business account. Otherwise she could be considered an employee and you would need to purchase workers' compensation insurance, etc...
5. There did not appear to be a sophisticated cash management system, however polices should be in place to help prevent petty theft.
6. The Application for Testing should contain specific questions about an applicant's medical risk and an assurance from the test taker that they have their doctor's approval to compete. The form should also specify that a test taker has to be both mentally and physically ready to take the test and increase in belt level or can risk serious injury if they do not have both their mind and their body dedicated to advancement.
7. The Student Enrollment Agreement has several problems as listed below:
    A. The term competent and qualified instructors are vague and can mean different thing to different people.
    B. The term "successful" should be inserted before the word examination to imply that a test taker will only be promoted after successfully taking the exam, not just taking the exam.
    C. Specify that the student had been cleared to participate by their doctor and they have no outstanding medical conditions that were not reported to the owners.

D.   No guarantee on the equipment used or purchased.

E.   There is a significant inconsistency as sometimes the word "student" and sometimes the word "member" are used throughout the form.

F.   Make sure to use neutral gender language so whenever a he is used, it should be followed with a back slash and then she (i.e. he/she).

G.   The provision concerning civil codes not applying is illegal as a contract cannot affect a legal duty imposed by the state.

H.   There is a duplication of consumer rights provisions as they relate to cancellation.

I.   You should add a mediation/arbitration clause and a clause that any dispute would have to be brought in Connecticut, pursuant to Connecticut law. You should also include a provision that anyone who brings a claim about their enrollment and losses will have to pay the prevailing party's attorneys' fees and costs.

You should examine similar contracts from local Connecticut businesses such as Bally's or 24 Hour Fitness to get a good idea of what elements they have covered.

Teaching Issues

The teachers appear to have received significant training through obtaining at least 8th degree black belts. Instruction by the owner appeared to be lively with a good student rapport. Safety instructions were reiterated on several occasions and individuals without the proper equipment were prohibited from participating in sparring activities.

Weapons—Some weapons, such as a bamboo stick, are fraying and taped together. While fraying equipment utilized just for movement practice should not be a significant risk, such weapons should not be utilized for sparring if they will come in contact with other weapons or people.

The owner is taking a proactive approach to risk reduction and education through developing an Instructor Training Manual which is more thoroughly discussed in the suggestions below.

Suggestions for Teaching Issues

1.   Provide specific rules for individuals such as whether or not glasses are allowed and if used, should thongs be utilized to secure the glasses from falling off.

2.   A sign should be posted specifically indicating the maximum class size allowed.

3.   The chains on all weapons should be checked to make sure no links are broken or rusted.

4.   All weapons should be tested before use such as taping poles against the ground to determine if they are broken or splintering.

5.   Post a sign and make an announcement after each class asking anyone to immediately report any injuries they might have sustained.

6.   The following suggestions apply to the Instructor Training Manual:

    A.   It should be clearly communicated that the manual does not specify or establish standards and each school is different.

    B.   It should be clearly established that the teaching program is just an opportunity and that successfully completing the course does not guarantee employment or the opportunity to teach at Martial Art Studio.

    C.   The program being established might be considered a trade school type program which could raise some licensing issues. The educational program should be labeled an internship or apprentice program. The fee should be characterized as the cost for utilizing the facility during the internship/apprenticeship and for taking part in the lessons.

    D.   Carefully define terms such as "qualified instructor."

    E.   By developing an internship/apprentice program, the owners will open themselves up to significant employment law concerns such as affirmative action, equal employment opportunities, ADA, etc.

Conclusion

The Martial Art Studio was in overall excellent condition on the dates of my visits. While there are some changes, highlighted above, that need to be made, the owner is very cooperative and enthusiastic about implementing risk management techniques and strategies. In fact, prior to completing this report, some of the suggestions orally conveyed to the owners were already fixed. The key areas for improvement would include proper signage, keeping the facility clean, ensuring proper first aid supplies and policies, and purchasing reliable insurance coverage.

References

$757,710 awarded to little league coach for assault at athletic field. (1998). *From the Gym to the Jury* 9 (5), 1.

Academe today's daily report. (1998, January 16). *The Chronicle of Higher Education.*

Action outside the ring must have been better. (1990, March 27). *The Columbus Dispatch*, 6C.

Assistive Listening Systems, United States Architectural and Transportation Barriers Compliance Board. (1991). Washington, DC.

Balousek, M. (1996, June 22). UW officials can't be sued over badger crush. *Wisconsin State Journal*, 1A.

Barnes, R. (1989, February 6). Product liability tackles manufacturers. *National Underwriter*, No. 6.

Batsell, J. (1997, August 2). 3 sue former Snohomish school official, allege harassment. *The Seattle Times*, B8.

Beaton, R. (1996, October 4). Pallone Knows spit-upon feeling. *USA Today*, 6C.

Behrens, T. (1998, February 28). Boater education programs now mandatory for Texas teens. *Houston Chronicle*, 8.

BNA's Americans With Disability Act Manual. (1994, December). 3 (24), 91.

BNA's Americans With Disability Act Manual. (1995, February). 4 (3), 18.

Boxed in. (1996, September 26). *USA Today*, 1C.

Bryant, P. (1998, December 22). Deltona mom sues league, coach over son's injury. *Orlando Sentinel*, D1.

Bulldozer strikes golfer. (1998, March). *California Bar Journal*, 4.

Burling, J. (1992). Managing athletic liability: An assessment guide. *Education Law Reporter* 72 (503), 6–7.

Byron, K. (1996, December 16). Judge Scolds Plainville $1,000 to be paid in Ex Coach's case. *The Hartford Courant*, B1.

Chen, S. (1996, December 12). David Douglas, basketball player settle suit. *Portland Oregonian*, B04.

Christensen, J. (1996, November 29). Athletes ask blessings: Most county public high school teams pray before games, but critics say the practice violates the law. *The Press-Enterprise*, Riverside, CA, A01.

Coleman, D. (1996, September 26). Suit spurred by racial slurs advances: Ex-coach at Clovis High doesn't deny using inflammatory words. *The Fresno Bee*, B1.

Cohen, A. (1998, July). All fall down. *Athletic Business*, 17.

Cohen, A. (1998, July). Waiting to exhale. *Athletic Business*, 50–57.

Cohen, N. (1997, August, 31). Perdue wins legal battle vs. CUNY. *Newsday*, B23.

Conklin, A. (1998, July). Saved? *Athletic Business*, 65.

Conklin, A. (1998, July). Down the drain. *Athletic Business*, 14.

Corcoran, K. (1993, May 30). Society's violence mirrored on ball field. *Houston Chronicle*, 1A.

Cotten, D. and Cotten, M. (1997). *Legal aspects of waivers in sport, recreation and fitness activities*. Canton, OH: PRC Publishing, Inc.

Court revives lawsuit by ex-St. Joe's hoop player. (1997, June 7). *Bangor Daily News*, Bangor, ME, PDA.

Court says $40,000 injury award was par for the course. (1995, July 20). *San Jose Mercury News*, 1C.

Court upholds ruling barring NCAA from limiting salaries. (1998, January 24). *The Star-Ledger*, Newark, N.J., 031.

Cronin, E. (1998, June). Torts: Primary assumption of the risk in sports. *California Lawyer*, 29.

Danger at the plate. (1998, January 12). *Sports Illustrated*, 27.

Danish asks $650,000 over hazing incident. (1998, October 22). *The Columbian*, C2.

Dedman, B. (1998, July 29). Umpire say sports for kids becoming adult brawl game. *Houston Chronicle*, 2A.

Disney to aid deaf park patrons under justice dept. agreement. (1997, January 18). *Houston Chronicle*, 2D.

Dodge, S. (1991, June 12). Use of kegs banned by some colleges and national fraternities. *The Chronicle of Higher Education*, A27.

Donnelly, K. (1998, March 12). Coaching for coaches. *Houston Chronicle*, D1.

Dorsey, V. L. (1992, May 10) Violence grabs growing share of spotlight away from events. *USA Today*, 4C.

Drunken golfer wins $41,540 after fall. (1996, October 30). *San Jose Mercury News*, 6A.

Edwards, K. (1993, August). Risk-management program. *Scholastic Coach*, 5–6.

Eldorado wrestling coach faces lawsuit by student. (1996, March 17). *The Las Vegas Review-Journal*, 4B.

Extreme measures. (1996, Febraury 22). *USA Today*, 3C.

Eye injury fact sheet. (1997, July 7). Boston, MA: National Youth Sports Safety Foundation, Inc. (NYSSF).

Fachet, R. (1996, March 16). Fanfare. *The Washington Post*, B02.

Fair play for volunteers. (1996, February 26). *The Hartford Courant*, A8.

Fan's suit over mascot revived. (1997, July 2). *The Orange County Register*, D3.

Farmer, N. (1999, January 26). A swing toward safety. *Houston Chronicle*, 7B.

Father sues after son cut from team. (1997, June 4). *The Boston Globe*, B5.

Flynn, G. (1995, September 15). Tennis club liable in death of boy, 3. *Houston Chronicle*, 37A.

Flynn, G. (1997, June 7). Jury fines man $1.1 million in sex assault case. *Houston Chronicle*, 33A.

Four arrests after football game brawl. (1992, November 8). *San Jose Mercury News*.

Fried, G. (1999) Punitive damages and corporate liability analysis in sports litigation. *Marquette Sports Law Journal*.

Fried, G. (1998). ADA and sports facilities. In *Risk Management in Sport*, Herb Appenzeller (ed.). Durham, NC: Carolina Academic Press.

Fried, G. (1997). Freedom of the press at sports facilities. *Sports Facility Law Reporter* (II) 6.

Fried, G. and Bradley, L. (1994). Applying the first amendment to prayer in a public university locker room. Marquette Sports Law Journal 4 (2), 301–321.

Fried, G., Miller, L. and Appenzeller, H (1998). *Employment law: A guide for sport, recreation, and fitness industries*. Durham, NC: Carolina Academic Press.

Gatehouse, J. (1997, March 17). Ex-coach files lawsuit: Seeks $40,000. *Montreal Gazette*, A3.

Gifis, S. (1984). *Barron's legal guide, law dictionary*. New York: Barron's Educational Services, Inc.

Girls cross-country has highest rate of injury, study say. (1994, August 16). *San Jose Mercury News*, 2c.

Go figure. (1998, July 6). *Sports Illustrated*, 18.

Good sports. (1992). Washington, DC: Association of Trial Lawyers of America.

Gobrecht, Florida State settle. (1997, September 4). *Seattle Post-Intelligencer*, D3.

Greenwald, A. (1980, August). Gymnastics litigation: The standard of care. *Trial*, 24–36.

Gross, S. and Syverud, K. (1996). Don't try civil jury verdicts in a system geared to settlement. *UCLA Law Review* (44), 1.

Hazel, K. (1993, July). Industry growth brings added exposure. *Agent & Manager*, 63–65.

Hazings force suspensions. (1998, January 14). *Houston Chronicle*, 12A.

Henderson, M. (1996, August 24). Softball player sues school for injury suffered in practice. *Los Angeles Times*, C12.

Herbert, D. (1991, March). Standards setting organizations may be liable to consumers. *The Sports, Parks & Recreation Law Reporter* 4 (4), 61.

Herbert, D. (1998, January). Concerns related to California Senate Bill 891 and exercise/fitness professionals. *The Exercise Standards and Malpractice Reporter* 12 (1), 1.

High court refuses to hear appeal. (1997, June 17). *Houston Chronicle*, 6B.

History of disputes. (1996, October 4). *USA Today*, 6C.

Hockey arrest. (1998, January 26). *USA Today*, 3C.

Hockey isn't even immune from lawsuits. (1996, March 16). *The Patriot Ledger*, Quincy, MA, 07.

Horman, W. (1993, January). A turf timetable. *Athletic Business*, 51–54.

Horswell, C. (1995, November 11). Dayton high school coach agrees to resignation. *Houston Chronicle*, 35A.

Hoskinson, C. (1996, August 17). College sued by ex-player. *St. Petersburg Times*, 3B.

Hummel, R. (1998, August 30). McGwire is ejected; fans erupt, umpire tosses slugger in 1st inning after disputed strikeout, angry crowd throws debris. *St. Louis Post-Dispatch*, A1.

Illegal tackling suspected in head injuries. (1997). *From the Gym to the Jury* 9 (2), 4.

In-line skating injuries projected to soar. (1995, June 22). *San Jose Mercury News*, 3C.

Johnson, G. (1998, May 5). Kids' accidental injuries cut by 26 percent in past decade. *Houston Chronicle*, 4A.

Jurisprudence. (1997, May 22). *USA Today*, 13C.

Kelly, M. (1998, March 5). The football hazing ritual that refuses to go away. *The Record*, Northern New Jersey, A03.

Kepple, D. (1998, May 7). Courts-Father sues Trotwood-Madison in son's death. *Dayton Daily News*, 3B.

Kilby, B. (1996, April 17). Family files lawsuit over student's death. *Tulsa World*, A11.

Law and order: Umpire arrested in molestation. (1997, May 28). *The Atlanta Constitution*, C05.

League settles lawsuit: Coach in wheelchair called no hazard. (1997, November 27). *The Cincinnati Enquirer*, C04.

Lee, L. (1997, April 27). Parking lots open to crime. *Houston Chronicle*, 1E.

Levy, D. (1997, March 14). 2nd blow to head in short span can kill. *USA Today*, 1D.

Loggins, K. (1996, August 6). Mother's suit names VU. *The Tennessean*, 1B.

Long, D. (1997, April 12). Prep athlete sues district. *Dayton Daily News*, 1A.

Louey, S. (1996, December 10). Sophomore who sued to play varsity moves: Family leaves Plano for "fresh start" in Allen. *The Dallas Morning News*, 2Z.

Man granted right to play on school's football team. (1996, September 28). *The News Tribune*, Tacoma, WA, A3.

Marchetti, D. (1998, April, 9). Court finds boy scouts exempt from Cal. civil rights law. *The Chronicle of Philanthropy*, 40.

Marcus, N. (1997, May 22). Board wins coach case on appeal. *Sun-Sentinel*, Ft. Lauderdale, 1B.

McClurg, A. (1997, June). Rungful suits. *ABA Journal*, 98.

McCullough, J. (1995, September). Handling catastrophic incident requires cool head, warm heart. *University Risk Management and Insurance Association Journal* 2 (1), 16–19, 32.

McDonough, E. (1996, October 13). School board in control. *The Salt Lake Tribune*, AA3.

Minzesheimer, B. (1997, Febraury 6). N.Y. deals blow to Extreme Fighting. *USA Today*, 3A.

Monahan, D. (1997, November). *Parking Today*, 18–19.

Mumma, C. (1997, May 14). Injured pole vaulter sues school, coach says that landing mat was too small. *The Record*, Northern New Jersey, L03.

Murphy, K. (1997, June 19). $175,000 settlement reached in school sex case. *The Milwaukee Journal Sentinel*, 4.

Murphy, K. (1998, February 5). UW officials not liable for injuries in '93 stampede. *The Wisconsin State Journal*, 5A.

Murray, B. (1997, March 20). Little League coach makes pitch in court: Banquet ban gets official suspended. *The Star-Ledger*, Newark, NJ, 021.

Nelson, J. (1991, January 10). Look out! Lawyers are on the ski slope. *San Jose Mercury News*, 5D.

Novice skier injures knee. (1997, January). *California Bar Journal*, 5.

Nygaard, G. (1989). *Law for physical educators and coaches*. Worthington, OH: Publishing Horizons, Inc.

Outside the arena, parking is the name of the game. (1997, October). *Parking Today*, 16–17.

Owens, S. (1996, March 15). Female Little League coach sues over parents' insult: The suit claims she is no longer allowed to or umpire in the Windermere League. *Orlando Sentinel*, A1.

Pai, D. (1996, April 22). Study of sudden death in young athletes. *USA Today*, 12C.

Parental guidance? (1998, October 21). *USA Today*, 3C.

Parents of heatstroke victim sound warning. (1996, June 7). *The Commercial Appeal*, Memphis, TN, A16.

Parents sue Auburn coach. (1997, March 22). *The Seattle Times*, A5.

Parrott, S. (1997, April 11). Edmonds all sports alleges conspiracy. *The Daily Oklahoman*, 27.

Peters, G. (1980, March). Unsafe swimming pools and spas claims unsuspecting victims. *Trial*, 42–43.

Pitorri, P. (1998, September). Security workshop. *Parking Today*, 32–33.

Player sues OU, coach for heat stroke. (1997, August 15). *Austin American-Statesman*, C2.

Players sue school board. (1996, December 10). *Sun-Sentinel*, Ft. Lauderdale, FL, 1B.

Pregnant swimmer sues over coach's treatment. (1997, August 31). *Pittsburgh Post-Gazette*, B7.

Rafinski, K. (1996, November 28). Study on in-line skating urges: Actually wear the protective gear. *Houston Chronicle*, 4A.

Reis, J. (1998, May 7). Easton sprinter seeks reversal. *The New Orleans Times-Picayune*, D1.

Rosenberg, I.J. (1996, April 13). Injured fan sues Braves, Pendleton. *Atlanta Journal and Constitution*, H03.

Rytina, N. (1994, August 5). *Update in-line skates deaths and injury estimates*. Washington, DC: U.S. Consumer Product Safety Commission.

Rytina, N. (1994, August 12). *Hazard sketch: Soccer-related deaths and injury estimates*. Washington, DC: U.S. Consumer Product Safety Commission.

Salmon, J. (1996, November 9). Coach goes to bench; Boys may lose out: Suit over soccer rule could sideline 10. *The Washington Post*, B01.

Savage, D. (1999, April). Differently disabled. *ABA Journal*, 34.

Schneid, T. (1992). *The Americans with Disabilities Act, A practical guide for managers*. New York: Van Nostrand Reinhold.

School board to pay for football injuries. (1996, November 10). *The New Orleans Times-Picayune*, B2.

School fails to care for injured student. (1998, April). *California Bar Journal*, 4.

Schools rule rowdy crowds off-limits at sporting events. (1991, February 11). *San Jose Mercury News*, 6A.

Scorecard (1997, October 6). *Sports Illustrated*, 10.

Scuba diver suffers 'bends'. (1997, March). *California Bar Journal*, 4.

Shackelford, A. (1997, March 15). Old Kent Park owners sue architects over flaws: The stadium still does not comply with federal requirements for he physically handicapped. *The Grand Rapids Press*, A3.

Shipley, S. (1997, September 30). Suit: Boy suffers brain damage at school: Supervision was lax mother says. *The New Orleans Times-Picayune*, B1.

Shurmaitis, D. (1996, April 10). Woman who fell at ballpark sues Rangers. *The Fort Worth Star-Telegram*, 19.

Smith, G. (1998, March). Injuries to children in the United States related to trampolines, 1990–1995: A national epidemic. *Pediatrics* 1 (3).

Smith, S. (1998, March 7). Ban backyard trampolines, doctors say. *Houston Chronicle*, 19A.

Snow-fed rapids take grim toll in California. (1998, June 25). *Houston Chronicle*, 14A.

Soccer match deaths bring inquiry. (1991, January 15). *San Jose Mercury News*, 3A.

Sol, N. and Foster, C. (1992). *ACSM's health/fitness facility standards and guidelines*. Champaign, IL: Human Kinetics.

Sports Illustrated Sports Desktop Calendar (1998, June 20/21).

Sports injury risk management and the keys to safety. (1991). North Palm Beach, FL: Coalition of Americans to Protect Sports.

Sports lighting: answers to 7 common questions. (1997). *Musco Lighting*, Oskaloosa, IA.

Sports-related ER visits. (1995, February). *Taking Care*, 2.

Study cites high school football death. (1998, July 8). *Houston Chronicle*, 6B.

Sunderland, B. (1993, January 7). Deep powder dangerous for novices on the slopes. *San Jose Mercury News*, 9D.

Sunderland, B. (1994, Oct. 13). Manufacturers, dealers divided on bike check list. *San Jose Mercury News*, 12E.

Survey shows customers have dim view of parking. (1998, November). *Parking Today*, 12–14.

Sward, S. and Doyle, J. (1997, December 30). Rising tide against jet skis. *San Francisco Chronicle*, 1A.

Tedford, D. (1998, February 26). Former high school athlete strikes out in court challenge. *Houston Chronicle*, 28A.

Tedford, D. (1996, November 16). Parents sue PISD over son's death. *Houston Chronicle*, 30A.

Teen killed at truck show. (1997, June 8). *Houston Chronicle*, 23A.

The razor's edge. (1996, November 4). *Sports Illustrated*, 22.

The torts of summer. (1998, July). *ABA Journal*, 12.

This week's sign that the apocalypse is upon us. (1998, June 22). *Sports Illustrated*, 33.

Track heightens fence in wake of fatal crash. (1998, August 4). *Houston Chronicle*, 5B.

Watson, T. and Ruibal, S. (1999, January 18). Collision kills skier, snowboarder. *USA Today*, 10A.

Weaver, J. (1997, July 4). Paralyzed teen wins benefits. *Sun-Sentinel*, Ft. Lauderdale, FL, 3B.

Wiley, L. (1996, October 29). School wants power to screen undesirable ads. *The Patriot Ledger*, 15C.

With suit dismissed, Nord teams play. (1997, November 27). *The New Orleans Times-Picayune*, B6.

Yarborough, J. (1998, October 15). Let it Snow. *American Way*, 78.

Young, D. (1989, Nov./Dec.). Snowmobiling. *Home & Away*, 6–7.

Zambito, T. (1996, April 4). Parents of boy who broke foot on stadiumescalator file suit. *The Record*, Northern New Jersey, NO3.

About the Authors

Gil Fried, Esq. Mr. Fried is an Associate Professor in the Management of Sports Industries Program in the Business School at the University of New Haven. He teaches and writes on various topics including sports law, finance, risk management, facility administration and human resource administration. Mr. Fried is an active attorney, expert witness and financial analyst with a specialization in issues affecting smaller sport facilities and the buying, selling and/or financing of sport businesses. The author can be reached at gfried@charger.newhaven.edu or (203) 932-7081.

Dr. Herb Appenzeller Dr. Appenzeller is the Jefferson-Pilot Professor of Sport Management (Emeritus) and former Athletic Director at Guilford College. He is a member of four Halls of Fame (NACDA, NAIA, Chowan College and Guilford College). He is co-editor of *From the Gym to the Jury,* and special consultant to the Center for Sports Law and Risk Management. Dr. Appenzeller is the author of twelve books, ten of which are on sports law and risk management. He received the Leadership Award in 1999 from the Society for the Study of the Legal Aspects of Sport (SSLASPA).

Index

acknowledgment, 43, 344, 391, 493
airplane(s), 295, 300
alcohol, 19, 75, 77, 118, 130, 132, 166, 210-211, 255, 271-272, 275, 324-325, 329, 331-334, 339, 402, 417, 482
Americans with Disabilities Act (ADA), 11, 101-105, 107-109, 113-114, 282, 498, 503, 506
application, 30, 71, 77, 90, 95, 104, 262, 344, 356, 358, 363, 369, 387-390, 395-398, 400, 403, 429, 446, 476-479, 484, 504
artificial turf, 189-190
assistive listening services, 113
assumption of risk, 10, 25, 42-44, 69, 84, 94-95, 121, 164, 186-187, 193, 220, 260, 262, 268, 281, 313, 339, 490
attractive nuisance, 29, 157, 213, 253
automobiles, 259, 295-296
auto racing, 230

backstop, 29, 147, 153-154, 160, 167, 315
baseball, 8, 13, 20, 35, 62, 69, 79, 93, 102, 104, 114-115, 126, 131, 147, 149-157, 159-167, 181, 189, 191, 195, 227, 277, 285, 308-315, 317, 320, 322, 335-336, 350, 360
bases, 100, 147, 151-153, 167, 174, 242, 355, 501
basketball, 7-9, 13, 50, 56, 65, 67, 76-77, 79, 116, 144, 157, 169-177, 179-181, 195, 225, 280, 285, 287, 299, 307, 310, 318, 324, 435, 444-445, 460
bat(s), 148, 159-161, 164, 166-167, 312

batting cages, 156
bicycle(s), 8-9, 251, 259, 263-264
bleachers, 61-62, 147, 169, 176-177, 181, 187, 260, 309-310, 318
boating, 13, 102, 253-254
boxing, 7, 119, 183-184, 187, 279

civil rights, 10, 73, 101
comparative negligence, 43-45, 97, 186, 224
concessions, 327, 329, 339, 466
constitution, 78
constitutional, 73, 77-78, 351, 392, 400, 412
consumer product safety commission, 9
contract(s), 10-11, 13-14, 19, 21, 37-38, 47, 55, 64-65, 72-75, 81-82, 84-87, 89, 91, 93-94, 98, 133, 136-137, 140, 186, 278, 299-300, 308, 328, 334, 360, 388, 407, 412, 463, 465-466, 469-472, 491, 505
contributory negligence, 41, 44, 46, 84, 214, 254, 307
crowd management, 19, 131, 136, 277, 280, 307, 322

damages, 3, 10-11, 22, 26, 38-41, 44-45, 51, 53, 61, 63, 85, 89-90, 92-93, 99, 109, 116, 120, 133, 177, 195, 208, 223, 225, 227, 346, 351, 362, 463, 466-467, 470-471, 489
death, 8, 12, 15-16, 57, 85, 88, 92, 162, 176, 197-198, 250, 309, 321, 463, 490
defect, 23, 25, 31, 162, 232, 261, 308, 315

discrimination, 10-11, 14, 73, 75, 78-80, 101, 105, 392, 400, 408, 481

diving, 12, 14, 56, 245-247, 249, 251-255, 258

documentation, 57, 71-72, 109, 292, 308, 384, 431-432, 462, 497

dram shop, 332-333

duty, 11, 21-23, 25-46, 50, 53-54, 65, 67, 69, 85, 94, 98, 116-117, 119-123, 129-132, 149, 160, 162, 164, 171, 173, 178, 185, 187, 189, 193, 196-197, 199-200, 204-205, 207, 215, 219-220, 233-234, 247, 250, 252, 255-258, 261, 265, 267-269, 274-275, 281, 285, 293, 297, 300-302, 308-309, 312, 314, 318, 328, 332-333, 335, 337, 339, 350, 352, 440, 471, 493, 505

ECT, 55, 148, 167

education, 35-36, 48-49, 62, 80, 103-104, 109, 114-115, 117, 126-127, 130, 158, 160, 176, 187, 209, 215, 218, 220, 224, 254, 258, 290, 298, 345, 352, 354, 360-361, 366, 368, 373-374, 379, 387-388, 396, 401, 403, 414-415, 419, 424, 427-428, 430-431, 481, 484, 505

employment, 10-11, 19, 37-38, 47, 73-75, 104, 107, 223, 277-278, 283, 351-352, 355, 362, 374-375, 391-393, 395-397, 401, 403-405, 407, 412-413, 467, 476-478, 481, 484-485, 487-489, 506

equipment, 3-4, 9, 14, 23, 25-27, 39, 41-44, 56-57, 66, 69, 73, 88-89, 91, 95, 98, 100, 107, 119, 122, 125-128, 147, 149, 154, 158-160, 162, 166-167, 189-197, 201, 203, 208-210, 213-214, 217-219, 221-225, 227-228, 231, 235, 238, 240, 242-243, 248, 251, 255, 259, 262, 265, 269, 272-273, 275, 286, 288-289, 292-294, 297, 302, 327-328, 335, 359, 410, 432-434, 444-446, 463, 475, 494-495, 500-502, 505

event administrator, 3, 5, 36, 59, 83, 90, 143, 187, 230, 295-296, 490

event director, 59-61, 63-65, 67-71, 490

face guard(s), 160-161, 194, 228

fences, 100, 147, 154-156, 167, 170, 185, 204, 235, 241, 322

field, 3, 9, 11, 35, 39-40, 70, 100, 109, 114-115, 147-157, 160, 162, 166-167, 169-170, 181, 189-191, 198, 201, 227, 237, 239-241, 243, 274-275, 281-282, 286, 291, 310-312, 315, 318, 323, 360, 432, 448, 463-465

first aid, 19, 30, 33, 39-40, 71, 123, 200, 249, 274, 285-294, 445-446, 453, 500-501, 506

football, 7-9, 12-13, 20, 40, 43-44, 49, 56, 61, 70, 74, 83, 99, 118, 126, 128-129, 134, 144, 157, 161, 189-201, 237-238, 240, 242, 279-280, 285-286, 291, 307-308, 314, 318-319, 321, 323-324, 333, 335, 351, 358-359, 494-495

goals, 9, 225, 239, 322, 344, 362, 368-370, 414, 420, 427

golf, 8-9, 13, 102-103, 190, 203-211, 272, 289, 321-322, 336

golf cart, 13, 207, 209-210, 289, 322, 336

government, 10-11, 17, 19, 49, 55, 59-61, 63, 73, 75, 101, 103, 115-118, 125, 130, 132-133, 179, 183, 187, 295-296, 298, 307, 366, 393, 489

gymnasium, 67, 100, 103, 118, 144, 169-171, 175, 198, 216, 444, 448

gymnastics, 13, 28, 36, 39, 41-42, 49, 79, 213, 215-217, 219, 221-224, 353, 359

helmet(s), 8-9, 126-127, 129, 160-161, 166, 189, 193-196, 200-201, 228-230, 237, 261, 265, 273-275, 279, 286, 292

hockey, 7, 13, 27, 126-127, 225-230, 312, 314, 316-317, 320

ice, 121-122, 127, 154, 225-230, 265, 267, 272, 274, 287-288, 316-317, 319

immunity, 11, 30, 41, 46-49, 52, 59-63, 97-98, 100, 115-117, 149, 160, 175, 179, 191, 199, 216, 223, 277, 290, 365, 373

impairment, 104-105, 490, 493

in-line skating, 9-10, 225, 229, 259, 264

in loco parentis, 29, 164

incident reporting, 57, 431-432, 435, 438-440, 462

indemnify, 81, 88, 90-92, 94, 137-138, 356, 397-398, 407, 463, 466, 477, 479, 489

indemnity, 55, 85, 91, 93, 133, 328, 463, 466

independent contractor, 37-38, 277-278, 299, 301, 503

inspect, 23, 25-26, 32, 35, 52, 55, 169, 181, 184-185, 189-190, 201, 207, 217, 219, 221, 231, 234, 236, 259-260, 262-263, 268, 271, 273-274, 308, 328, 334, 471, 474

inspection, 31, 42, 55-57, 64, 69, 71, 89, 128, 143, 148, 176-177, 185, 189, 209, 217, 219, 232, 246, 251-252, 261, 269, 275, 277, 280, 292, 298, 309, 369, 424, 473-474

insurance, 10, 19, 38, 55-56, 62, 66-67, 90, 97, 114-115, 130, 132-141, 143, 183, 193, 199, 269, 295-296, 299-303, 320, 351, 355, 365, 436, 449, 463-464, 466, 471, 500, 503-504, 506

interview, 50, 71, 344, 385, 387, 400-403, 405-409, 481, 483-484, 486

interviewing, 71, 385, 387, 392, 396, 400, 481

invitee, 10, 31-32, 34, 61, 173

jet ski, 254

job description, 70-71, 344, 358, 387, 393-395, 403, 476, 484

karate, 183-184, 350

last clear chance, 35-36, 223

licensee, 10, 31-34, 465

lifeguard, 24, 71, 98, 119, 122-123, 245, 248, 251, 254-257

lights, 33, 81, 114, 147, 156-157, 167, 172, 178, 232, 234, 236, 246, 249, 269, 281, 298, 325, 497-498

lime, 151, 191, 201

locker room, 91, 101, 162, 177-179, 181, 195, 349, 473

matting, 214-216, 218, 224, 501

medical releases, 81, 83, 85, 87, 89, 91, 93-95

minor, 8, 14-17, 32, 83-84, 91, 155, 285, 309, 348, 351, 372-373, 393, 411, 434, 436-437, 447, 490

motorcycles, 261-262

motor sports, 9, 320

negligence, 9-10, 19, 21-22, 26, 34-36, 39-47, 50-51, 60, 71, 84-85, 87-89, 94, 97, 99, 119, 123, 127, 129, 131, 138, 158, 160, 165, 167, 186, 191, 210, 214, 216, 224, 248, 254, 264, 281, 286, 288, 291, 307-308, 314, 327, 351-352, 491-493

gross, 26, 40-41, 87-88, 149, 355, 463

ordinary, 25, 31, 33, 35, 40-41, 60, 85, 87, 106, 119, 121, 171-172, 232, 250-251, 311, 331

per se, 34, 40-41, 119, 288

simple, 3-4, 24, 40, 47-48, 55, 69, 82, 87-88, 92-94, 149, 180, 209, 236, 243, 264, 277, 288, 407, 409

notice, 24-25, 27, 32, 41-42, 51, 53, 152, 155, 163, 172-173, 178, 186-187, 190, 200, 205, 227, 241, 255, 277, 308, 312, 439, 466, 468, 470-471

non-profit, 47, 59, 61-62, 74-75, 97, 103, 116, 343, 348, 351-352, 354-355, 364, 393

official(s), 10, 47-48, 50-51, 54, 56, 70, 74-75, 88, 92, 116, 118-119, 125, 153,

180, 184-185, 195, 235, 241, 243, 260, 277-279, 281-283, 296, 359, 377, 379, 395, 420, 427, 442, 445-446, 476, 497, 499, 502

padding, 169-170, 174-175, 181, 192, 201, 221, 224, 228, 237, 242, 502

paralysis, 12, 14-16, 91, 105, 221, 252, 262, 279, 493

parental, 7, 82, 348, 361, 378, 386, 415, 493

parents, 7, 18, 29, 56, 64, 68, 73-74, 78-80, 82-85, 94, 107, 126, 163, 166, 180, 187, 193, 197-198, 201, 255, 262, 285, 290, 296, 301-302, 307, 309, 344-345, 349-350, 352, 359-362, 362, 364, 366, 368, 370, 372, 375-379, 382, 384-387, 395, 411, 414-415, 417, 419-420, 423-430, 433-434, 436-437, 446, 448, 476, 493

parking, 57, 66-67, 91, 101, 106, 110, 131, 134, 165, 272, 325, 329, 334-337, 339, 361, 432-433, 444, 448, 465, 472, 474, 497-498

playground, 9, 13, 154, 285, 290, 432, 444, 448

pre-test/post-test, 345, 387, 395, 414, 418-419, 476

product liability, 19, 89, 258, 464

proprietary function, 60

proximate cause, 22, 39, 42, 44-45, 50, 74, 165, 174, 193, 223, 255, 291, 314

prudent person, 3-4, 28, 35, 41, 290

public policy, 38, 82, 84-87, 104, 118, 489

racing, 60, 87-88, 230, 253, 259-262, 264, 320-321, 331

reasonable, 22-31, 33, 35, 40-44, 55, 67, 74, 77, 83, 85, 89, 104-109, 114, 119, 121-122, 128, 148, 157, 160, 164-166, 173, 175, 178, 186-187, 196-197, 201, 206, 210, 214-215, 218, 225, 228, 230, 235, 241, 247, 250-251, 256, 268, 275, 281, 287, 291, 294, 309, 312, 316, 319, 323, 327, 334, 352, 389, 397-398, 415, 440, 464, 466-467, 471, 478-479

recreational user statute, 98-100

referees, 7, 91, 116, 175, 179, 195, 229, 277-283, 372, 409, 445

release(s), 19, 55, 81, 83, 85-91, 92-95, 152, 187, 248, 263-264, 344, 355, 364-366, 369, 374, 387, 389-390, 395-396, 399, 403, 405, 408, 472, 476, 480, 484, 491-492, 503

repair log, 459, 475, 494

religion, 75, 78-79, 101, 403, 420, 424, 426, 484

rink, 154, 225-227, 230, 265, 316-317

risk management, 3-4, 7, 9-11, 13, 15, 17-21, 55-57, 62, 67-68, 81, 97, 135-136, 139, 143, 156, 165, 167, 194, 225, 240, 243, 253, 258-259, 265, 301, 308, 314, 339-340, 343, 346-349, 352-353, 357-358, 362, 367, 372, 396, 411, 428-429, 435, 441, 462, 497, 506

safety committee, 18, 68-69, 72, 94, 97, 126-127, 138-139, 141, 143, 148, 280, 286, 295, 308, 323-324, 339

save harmless, 81, 88, 90, 116-117, 137

screen, 153, 156, 171, 295, 315-318, 352, 364, 369, 393, 396

sexual abuse, 37, 79-80, 343-344, 346-351, 353-354, 356-362, 365-369, 372, 374-376, 378, 381, 384-389, 391, 393-395, 401-404, 407, 409-410, 413-430, 476, 481, 483-484, 503

sexual harassment, 11, 46, 74, 80, 347-348, 362, 389, 392, 487-489

skating, 9-10, 13, 154, 225-226, 228-229, 259, 264-265

skiing, 13, 24, 83, 88-89, 119-121, 230, 267-273, 321

ski lifts, 270

snowmobiling, 273

softball, 8, 13, 37, 100, 151-152, 154, 156-159, 164, 166, 277, 281, 315, 352

standards, 3-5, 27-28, 35, 55, 86, 97, 117-119, 121, 125-133, 143, 158, 172, 174, 187, 193, 206, 209, 217-219, 225,

228, 232, 242-243, 245, 250, 256, 265, 286-287, 295, 339, 349, 388, 506
strict liability, 38, 40, 88-89, 301
supervise, 23, 26-30, 32, 40, 44, 49, 60, 95, 179, 181, 185, 196, 201, 214-216, 222-223, 236, 240-241, 245, 255-256, 258, 270, 282, 286, 332, 334, 352, 395, 402-404, 409-411, 476, 483-484
supervision, 3, 10, 19, 23, 27-28, 35, 37, 48, 64-66, 68, 128, 141, 161-167, 178, 180-181, 185-189, 195-198, 200, 209-210, 213, 219-226, 229, 231, 235, 237-243, 253-254, 257-259, 264, 270, 281, 286, 294, 300, 331, 335, 339-340, 345, 372, 392, 410-411, 500
swimming, 8, 12-13, 29, 40-41, 56, 121-122, 206, 245-246, 248-251, 254-258, 285, 393, 417, 458, 473

tax, 19, 60, 108, 113
tennis, 9, 27, 60, 108, 157, 231-235, 298
termination, 10-11, 74, 345, 411-413, 440
Title IX, 10-11, 13, 80, 101, 351
tort, 21-22, 41, 47, 49, 59, 61, 71, 74, 82, 84, 116
training, 20, 27-28, 49, 68, 70, 79, 92, 116, 119, 125, 138, 161, 190, 200, 215, 222-223, 229, 279, 286, 288, 344, 353, 358, 361, 366, 369-370, 374, 379, 387-390, 392, 394, 409-410, 415, 425, 428, 430, 468, 505-506
trampolines, 213-214, 219-220, 222, 224
transportation, 19, 56, 66-67, 102-103, 143, 295-297, 299-303, 452

trespasser, 10, 31, 34

ventilation, 172, 216
vicarious liability, 36-38, 352
violence, 7, 9, 19, 147, 162-163, 169, 179, 184, 187, 195, 201, 225, 227, 239, 283, 349, 351, 353-354, 356, 390, 446
volleyball, 13, 50-51, 53, 172, 175, 350
volunteer(s), 19, 36-37, 66-68, 70, 72-74, 80, 90-92, 116, 139, 155, 186, 223, 282, 293, 302, 328, 344, 350, 352-356, 358-359, 361, 363, 366, 369-377, 384, 387-392, 394, 396, 398, 400, 404-405, 407-408, 410-413, 427, 429, 433-436, 438, 440, 446-447, 449, 453-455, 458, 479, 485, 491-492, 504

waiver(s), 19, 30, 38, 43, 47, 55, 57, 81-95, 115, 128, 132, 141, 143, 172, 187, 221, 225, 242, 260-264, 289, 321, 370, 467, 469, 472, 490-492, 503
warning(s), 23-25, 29-30, 32, 34, 42-44, 56, 68, 70, 81-82, 84, 86, 90-91, 93-95, 141, 143, 155-156, 161, 163, 175, 178, 190-191, 194, 197, 204-205, 207, 209, 213-214, 220-221, 226, 229, 231, 237, 239, 241, 247, 249, 252-255, 257, 259-260, 263, 268-270, 274-275, 309, 311-314, 316-317, 319-322, 359, 411-412, 443, 458, 472, 494, 498-500
wrestling, 74, 76, 86, 119, 138, 183-187, 223, 279-280, 308, 321-322
wrongful termination, 10-11, 74, 413